We Remember,
We Love,
We Grieve

We Remember,
We Love,
We Grieve

*Mortuary and Memorial Practice in
Contemporary Russia*

ELIZABETH WARNER AND
SVETLANA ADONYEVA

THE UNIVERSITY OF WISCONSIN PRESS

The University of Wisconsin Press
728 State Street, Suite 443
Madison, Wisconsin 53706
uwpress.wisc.edu

Gray's Inn House, 127 Clerkenwell Road
London EC1R 5DB, United Kingdom
eurospanbookstore.com

Printed in the United States of America
This book may be available in a digital edition.

Library of Congress Cataloging-in-Publication Data
Names: Warner, Elizabeth, 1940– author. | Adon'eva, S. B., author.
Title: We remember, we love, we grieve : mortuary and memorial practice in
contemporary Russia / Elizabeth Warner, Svetlana Adonyeva.
Description: Madison, Wisconsin : The University of Wisconsin Press, [2021] |
Includes bibliographical references and index.
Identifiers: LCCN 2020017013 | ISBN 9780299330705 (cloth)
Subjects: LCSH: Funeral rites and ceremonies—Russia (Federation) |
Memorial rites and ceremonies—Russia (Federation) | Mourning customs—Russia
(Federation) | Death—Social aspects—Russia (Federation)
Classification: LCC GT3256.2.A2 W37 2021 | DDC 393/.90947—dc23
LC record available at https://lccn.loc.gov/2020017013

Contents

Illustrations

Preface

This book is the by-product of collaboration between Svetlana Adonyeva and Elizabeth Warner, whose first experiences of fieldwork, before they met in St. Petersburg in the mid-1990s, had already drawn them independently to the study of funeral and memorial ritual. This became one of the topics of mutual interest they explored together during the annual folklore expeditions of St. Petersburg State University between 1997 and 2013. It was not until 2014, however, that they decided to work together on this book, a project pursued intermittently over the next five years during working holidays in Russia, Scotland, and Finland. Although each chapter has a single author, whose particular research interests it reflects, both coauthors contributed ideas and comments to each chapter throughout the many discussions and exchanges that occurred in the course of working on the book.

The authors' fieldwork took place mainly in north Russia, in Vologda and Arkhangel'sk provinces (*oblasti*), concentrating first on the Kirillov, Belozersk, Vashka, and Syamzha regions of Vologda province and later on the Mezen' and Leshukon'e regions of Arkhangel'sk province. Transcripts of interviews and conversations on funeral and memorial practices and, indeed, on other relevant aspects of Russian folklore (such as calendar customs and dreams), recorded by the authors and other members of the research group—staff and students of St. Petersburg State University as well as scholars from other institutions in Russia and abroad—provided the base material for the book and are held in the Folklore Archive of the university and in the electronic archive "Russian Everyday Life" (*Russkaya povsednevnost'*) of the Propp Centre in St. Petersburg. Elizabeth has also used material from her own fieldwork in Pskov, Tver', and Novgorod provinces (2014–16). It should be noted that if the authors refer to "we" in the various chapters of the book, this is a recognition of the constant mutual support and cooperation between members of the research group, whose composition varied from year to year.

Personal details of the people interviewed for the book are kept in the relevant archives. In order to preserve their privacy, however, details are kept to a minimum in the book.

The number of places involved in our research, ranging from tiny hamlets to larger villages serving as regional provincial centers and small provincial towns, is very large, and we have only been able to show a few of them on the maps. Nevertheless, we hope the maps will help readers to orientate themselves throughout the book.

This work is mainly, though not exclusively, concerned with events in rural Russian settings. This choice reflects our extended experience of, and hopefully insights into, village life in remote areas of the Russian hinterland.

Acknowledgments

First we must thank the many people in Russian villages and towns who, over the course of many years, selflessly offered their time to talk with us. They shared not only their knowledge and experience of funeral and memorial practice but also their deeply felt personal sorrows as well as their beliefs and convictions about life and death. Without their remarkable openness, generosity of spirit, and trust this book could not have been written. We have reason to be grateful for their generosity on a more practical level, too—particularly for their hospitality. So many of our conversations took place around kitchen tables with tea and homemade pastries, adding a welcome taste of home comforts to our otherwise austere expeditionary existence.

Many people—teachers, librarians, local historians, museum workers, priests, and representatives of regional and village authorities—eased our passage into new territories, helping us with introductions, transportation, accommodations, and other practical issues. Our thanks go out to them.

Our folklorist and ethnographer colleagues from St. Petersburg—Inna Veselova, Lyubov' Golubeva, Yuliya Marinecheva, Antonina Semenova, Anastasiya Gavrilenko, Ekaterina Mamaeva, Andrei Stepanov, and many others—were a constant source of support and assistance. Elizabeth is particularly grateful to Anastasiya for her help and companionship during her expeditions to Tver' province in 2015 and 2016.

Our thanks to St. Petersburg State University, which facilitated Elizabeth's regular visits to the city and her participation in the folklore expeditions. Elizabeth is also indebted to the Chistov family in St. Petersburg—Kirill Vasil'evich and Bella Efimovna (both now alas deceased), Yurii Kirillovich and Elena Borisovna—who for more than three decades made their home her home-away-from-home.

We are also grateful to the Universities of Durham and Edinburgh, whose invitations to Svetlana allowed her to visit the United Kingdom to continue collaboration on our research project. We thank the readers for the University of Wisconsin Press for their specialized and helpful comments, and we also thank the press's editors and other staff, especially Gwen Walker, who welcomed our manuscript in its early stages, Amber Cederström, who patiently shepherded it toward publication, managing editor Adam Mehring and copyeditor Judith Robey for their attention to detail and their patience, and art director Jennifer Conn for the cover design.

Archive References and Abbreviations

A reference beginning with FA indicates the Folklore Archive of St. Petersburg State University. The Folklore Archive contains interviews recorded between the late 1970s and 2018. FA is followed by an abbreviated reference to the region (*raion*) where the interview was recorded. "Province" is used for the larger geographical unit *oblast'*.

FA Bel	Vologda province, Belozersk region
FA Kir	Vologda province, Kirillov region
FA Lesh	Arkhangel'sk province, Leshukon'e region
FA Mez	Arkhangel'sk province, Mezen' region
FA Onezh	Arkhangel'sk province, Onega region
FA Syam	Vologda province, Syamzha region
FA Vash	Vologda province, Vashka region
FA VUst	Vologda province, Velikii Ustyug region

Material is organized thematically within the territorial collections, each theme being indicated by a number. In each thematic category, individual files are listed numerically. For example, the reference "FA Lesh 17-6" would indicate file 6 in category 17. The following thematic categories are referred to in the book: 15. Occasional rituals for exceptional circumstances; 17. Funeral rituals; 17a. Laments; 18. Calendar ritual and folklore; 22. Signs and omens, prophetic dreams and fortune-telling.

A reference beginning with EW indicates the personal archives of Elizabeth Warner. EW is followed by -A (audio), -V (video), or field notes as well as an abbreviated reference to the province and region where interviews were recorded.

EW-A Arkh-Lesh	Arkhangel'sk province, Leshukon'e region
EW-A Pskov-Dno	Pskov province, Dno region

EW-A Tver'-Bol	Tver' province, Bologoe region
EW field notes, Arkh-Lesh	Arkhangel'sk province, Leshukon'e region
EW field notes, Arkh-Mez	Arkhangel'sk province, Mezen' region
EW field notes, Nov-Bor	Novgorod province, Borovichi region
EW field notes, Pskov-Nov	Pskov province, Novosokol'niki region
EW field notes, Vol-Kir	Vologda province, Kirillov region
EW-V Vol-Bel	Vologda province, Belozersk region
EW-V Vol-Vash	Vologda province, Vashka region

A reference beginning with SA indicates the personal archives of Svetlana Adonyeva. SA is followed by a reference to the region and province or the city where interviews were recorded.

SA field notes, Vol-VUst	Vologda province, Velikii Ustyug region
SA field notes, Vol-Bel	Vologda province, Belozersk region
SA field notes, St. Petersburg	

References beginning with DAu and DV indicate audio files and digital video files, respectively, from the electronic database "Russian Everyday Life" (*Russkaya povsednevnost'*) of the nonprofit organization the Propp Centre for Humanities-based Research in the Sphere of Traditional Culture, St. Petersburg. The reference in the captions beginning with DPh refers to the Yu. A. Galev Photo Archive in the electronic database "Russian Everyday Life."

Note on Transliteration and Translation

For Russian words and names, the British Standard 2979:1958 has been used, with some modifications. To simplify reading, diacritical marks and the hard sign (ъ) have been omitted, and *e* has been used for both Russian *ё* and *e*.

Unless otherwise stated, translations from the Russian are by Elizabeth Warner.

We Remember,
We Love,
We Grieve

Map of Russia. (A. Nekrasov and I. Ereshko)

Introduction

People, Places, and Approaches

ELIZABETH WARNER AND SVETLANA ADONYEVA

This is a book about death and the stratagems for coping with loss and grieving on individual and community levels. Over the many years spent researching this subject in the Russian North, posing questions of the most intimate nature in lengthy conversations with people we have come to know well, we have both been faced with emotionally powerful situations. These experiences have drawn us into an appreciation of the world of our interlocutors in a way that textual information and descriptions alone could not have done.

The title of our book—*We Remember, We Love, We Grieve*—forms one of the most popular epitaphs on Russian grave markers today.

In 2007, I was in Kimzha in the Mezen' region of Arkhangel'sk province. I frequently visited Galina, who was lively, amusing, and informative. She loved bright colors and would sit in her purple dress crocheting as we talked and drank tea. One day, the simple domesticity of our encounters was broken by a startling glimpse of what lay at the heart of things for Galina. We went into her bedroom and she lifted down a small suitcase, gaily checkered in red and black, from the top of her wardrobe. She opened it and began to lay out its contents. "These are my death clothes," she said. As I watched, silenced by a moment of culture shock, she laid out the garments and other objects one by one without any sign of distress or embarrassment. There was a white sheet and a pink and gray coverlet, underwear, a small cross, and a roll of cloth bearing holy pictures and the words of the Trisagion prayer: "Holy God, Holy Mighty, Holy Immortal." The most striking garment was an elaborately worked long, pink and gray crocheted dress with a fringe, clearly Galina's own work. I understood then that Galina had a vivid mental image of herself after death not as an abstract "body" but as a real person (EW field notes, Arkh-Mez, 2007).

In 1994, I met Taisiya Toporkova, who lived in Belozersk in Vologda province. It was a meeting that shaped my interest in the "cult of the dead" as a theme in Russian contemporary culture. She was sixty-two years old at the time. After much pleading, she agreed to demonstrate her skill as a lamenter. She chose the place to do this herself—a bench beside the bathhouse on the shore of the lake. We spoke for more than two hours. What particularly struck me from our conversation was that care for the dead—for her parents, her first husband, and the parents of her first and second husbands—was a permanent and intensely private ritual she performed without witnesses. Every year on the remembrance days for each of them, she would heat the bathhouse and carry in buckets of water for washing along with soap, a wash cloth, a towel, and clean underwear, kept specially for each individual. After that she would lament in the bathhouse, inviting the deceased to come and wash. For Taisiya, remembering her dead meant caring for them, allowing them to bathe, washing their clothes, and conversing with them. She didn't just remember her dead, she spoke to them and maintained a relationship. Her dead were alive for her. They were just far away but came back home every year, unseen, in order to wash in their bathhouse (SA field notes, Vol-Bel, July 16, 1994).

July 1997, somewhere near Kirillov, Vologda province. I am standing at the side of an unpaved road. It is hot and dusty and completely still. A pony-drawn wooden cart comes into view, driven by an old man wearing a padded work jacket. His hair and beard are as shaggy as the pony's mane. On the back of the cart is a single object, a simple, handmade wooden coffin. As the cart slowly passes, we observe each other, the woman in blue jeans and a smart blouse holding a video camera and clearly not from these parts, and the man with the imprint of his laboring life easy to read on face and hands. We do not speak. We are worlds apart but joined in that almost biblical moment by the reminder of our common mortality (EW field notes, Vol-Kir, July 1997).

PLACES AND PEOPLE

The Russian North, where most of the fieldwork for this book has been carried out, is an area encompassing the huge landmass of Vologda and Arkhangel'sk provinces. Relative to their size, both provinces have tiny populations of a little over one million each, with more than 70 percent of residents living in urban centers such as Vologda, Cherepovets, and Arkhangel'sk. During the course of the twentieth and twenty-first centuries the population has been steadily declining. In Vologda province, according to statistics, the population density was only 8.5 people per square kilometer at the beginning of the twenty-first century while in Arkhangel'sk province it was as low as 2.2 at the beginning of 2020.[1] Even today, reaching the thinly scattered villages in the region's remotest areas is difficult and not without its dangers. Once you have left the comfort of the few paved roads near the towns, travel in both provinces is problematic, with poorly maintained dirt tracks that throw up suffocating dust in the summer and become impassible when the snow melts in the spring.

For centuries, historical circumstances have helped the North to preserve the integrity of its own culture, its way of life, its traditions, and the spirit of its people. Arkhangel'sk province avoided the deadening burden of the serf system. It was also spared the destruction caused in other parts of Russia by the thirteenth-century Mongol invasions, and Vologda province, too, remained relatively unscathed. The very remoteness and inaccessibility of the region's settlements provided protection. But that changed in the twentieth and twenty-first centuries as the rural population suffered one catastrophe after another. During Soviet agricultural collectivization in the 1930s, the peasants were deprived of their land, their cattle, their rights, and independence. Some faced deportation or execution during Stalin's program of dekulakization.[2] Everywhere we went we heard harsh words and expressions of resentment over the treatment of workers on the collective farms. As one woman put it, "We lived in penal servitude [*zhili my v katorge*]." Food was also scarce. From the 1930s until the early 1970s, workers on collective farms (*kolkhozy*) had no passport; in other words, they were more or less tied to their native villages and received payment mostly in kind for their labor. Conditions only improved marginally from the late 1960s, when state farms (*sovkhozy*), which paid wages, began to outnumber the kolkhozy. In the war against religion that began shortly after the revolution, the core set of beliefs and practices that had framed the moral and spiritual bedrock of peasant society also began to crumble. These disasters destroyed the social and economic framework of village life.

The heavy losses inflicted on villages throughout Russia by the Great Patriotic War of 1941–45 and the terrible famine that followed it decimated the rural population. Of the Syamzha region of Vologda province, which we visited in the first decade of the 2000s, Anatolii Zagoskin has written, "History knows no war more cruel, or more bloody, than the Great Patriotic. Out of 6,146 from Syamzha region called up to serve in the Red Army and the Navy . . . 2,841 returned" (Zagoskin 1999, 89). For the defense of Vologda, the civilian population, including many women from the villages of the Syamzha and Vashka regions, was conscripted to dig trenches and earthworks. As one of them, Lidiya Kirillovna, recollected, "We slept in huts. There was no water. We didn't wash.

Memorial dedicated to the sacrifices and courage of village women during the war, Azopol'e, Arkhangel'sk province, 2008. (Photo by Elizabeth Warner)

We suffered such hardship during the war. We built a rampart out of snow, just with our hands." In both Vologda and Arkhangel'sk provinces we heard terrible stories of the women who remained in the villages in order to provision the army. If they had no horses left, they pulled the plows themselves. Some were reduced to eating bark and acorns. Lidiya Stepanovna was just a child during the war. From her village on the Mezen' River in Arkhangel'sk province all the food was sent away for the soldiers at the front: "We used to gather dried horse manure," she said, "rinse it in the river and take any undigested seeds home to be cooked."[3] The heavy toll of the war caused incalculable damage to the rural economy and left many villages with a population of widows and fatherless children.

The benefits of the state farms, ironically, were wiped out by the market reforms of the 1990s and the accompanying wholesale closure of farms and industries across the region. Things were particularly bad in the early 1990s. Some villagers in Arkhangel'sk province told us they had no electricity, even in winter. The migration of the working-age population to the cities, which had continued throughout the twentieth century, became a flood, unstoppable and irreversible.

The words "we remember, we love, we grieve" reflect more than individual loss. They also encapsulate a sense of dispossession and bereavement on a much wider scale, alongside the determination of villagers to remember, preserve, and repossess what others have been determined to destroy.

In geographical terms Vologda and Arkhangel'sk provinces are both situated in the northern part of the East European plain. Vologda, the more southerly of the two, has a border with Arkhangel'sk province and the Republic of Karelia to the north and Leningrad province, where St. Petersburg (formerly Leningrad) is situated, to the west. Arkhangel'sk province stretches northward toward the Barents Sea, eastward into the Nenets autonomous region, and southward into the Komi Republic.

One's first impression from the road or railway, and especially from the air, is that the whole of this huge territory (the landmass of Arkhangel'sk province alone is greater than that of France) is completely covered in trees. Forests of fir, pine, and larch stretch as far as the eye can see, interspersed with the birch groves that provide a perfect environment for the mushrooms and berries so enjoyed by Russians and that are a useful supplement to villagers' diets. To some extent, however, the impression that the region is covered in forest is deceptive. Vast areas of impenetrable swamp and flowing water are also prevalent. Vologda province, where our journeys together began, is a land of waterways, great rivers like the Sukhona and the Sheksna, lakes, canal systems dating back to the eighteenth century, and reservoirs, the largest of which, the Rybinsk reservoir near the capital city Vologda, is like an inland sea.

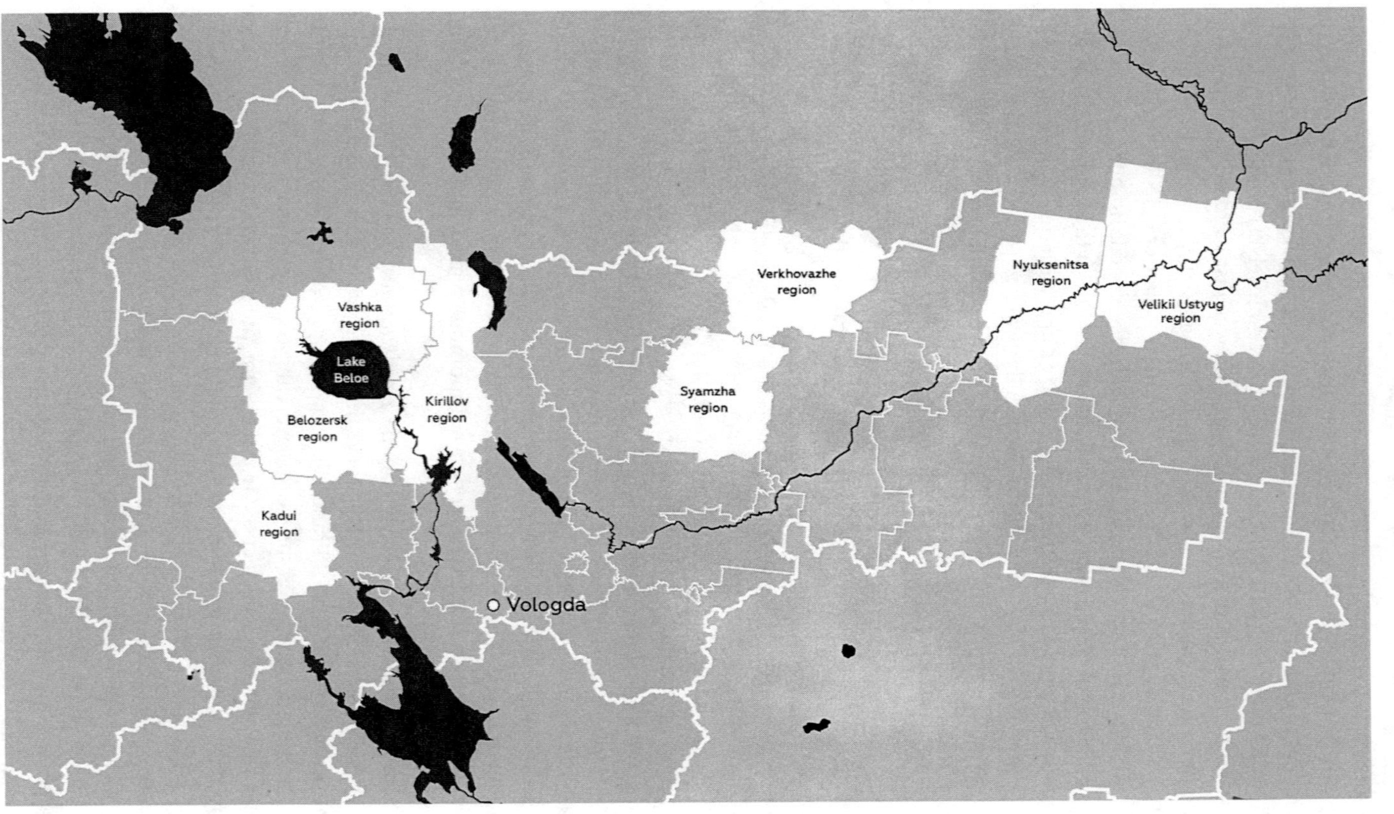

Map of Vologda province. (A. Nekrasov and I. Ereshko)

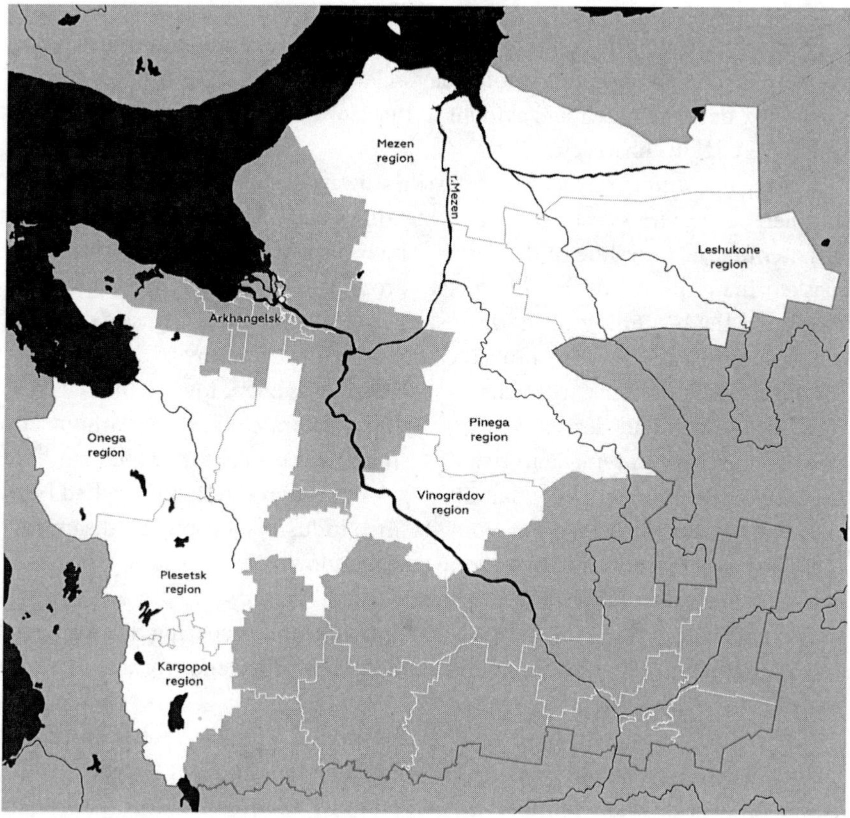

Map of Arkhangel'sk province. (A. Nekrasov and I. Ereshko)

SOME IMPRESSIONS FROM FIELD NOTES

Between 1997 and 2006 we carried out research in villages of the Belozersk, Kirillov, and Vashka regions on either side of the great Lake Beloe, which forms a major part of the Volga-Baltic waterway. We also visited the Syamzha region, farther to the northeast.

Belozersk and Kirillov are two small towns with great cultural significance. Kirillov is famed for the Kirillo-Belozersk monastery complex, founded in the fourteenth century; the nearby Goritsy nunnery; and the Ferapontov monastery, a world heritage site since 2000 with frescoes by the monk Dionisius. By the time of our first visit in 1997, both Kirillov and Goritsy once again had small, functioning monastic communities. This whole area played a significant part in the development of Russia's Orthodox landscape. Between the thirteenth and seventeenth centuries hundreds of monasteries and monastic communities were founded, both in small towns and in the uninhabited wilderness, as monks sought solitude and the contemplative life. In spite of the religious persecution of the past and the skepticism of today's clergy, we felt an awareness here of Orthodox heritage much less evident in the more northerly regions with quite different religious histories.

During our summer expeditions the skies always seemed to be a brilliant blue, and here and there swaths of rolling meadows were ablaze with wildflowers, brightening the dark line of the forest. The beauty of this landscape, however, masked many problems. In the villages around Lake Beloe at the end of the 1990s and the beginning of the 2000s, the negative impact of Russia's sudden and uncoordinated switch from state control of the economy to a free market economy was visible and freely discussed. There was anger toward the "fat cats" in Moscow who had destroyed the existing economic structure without any clear idea of how to replace it. Arable farming was never very important here because of the poor soil, but what little agricultural production there had been (particularly flax for the famous Vologda linen industry) was rapidly disappearing. The beautiful profusion of meadowland wildflowers was caused by the reversion of farmland to wilderness as collective farms closed. "We did everything," said Zinaida, describing the hard work of growing and preparing flax for linen. "It was tough but somehow we got through it. We worked and worked. But now we have lost everything."

The reduction of large herds and the closure of some beef cattle and dairy farms was an even greater loss, given Vologda's reputation for excellent milk, butter, and meat. Many families we met still owned one or two cows of their own. Over the centuries the milk cow had often been the only thing standing between the peasant and starvation, and as such it was a treasured member of the family: "You have to love your animals," said Vera, stroking the air to show how she petted her cows. Each one had a name and they all knew her voice. We found that giving up the family cow often became a sad necessity for elderly women living alone and unable to cope with the unrelenting work of milking and caring for the animal. Here and there, apart from cows, there would be someone with a pig in a sty or a few goats, chickens, or rabbits. In some villages there were small flocks of friendly sheep. Like the village cows, they returned home from their pastures in the evening on their own, trotting down the village street, each turning obediently into its own gate.

Lake Beloe was famed for centuries for the rich variety and quality of its fish. There were many villages close to its shores where fishing had been the main source of livelihood. By the late twentieth century, fishing, like agriculture, was seriously on the wane. Pollution, overfishing, and poaching had all contributed to the decline of the lake's fortunes; the closure of the state-run fishery was the last straw. The only fish normally seen were the tiny smelt (*snetok*), which, when dried and salted, were an excellent accompaniment to beer.

It was against this backdrop of decline and poverty that our group began collaborating with the villagers on the recording and preservation of their memories and accounts of their past and current ways of life. They described their family rituals of birth, marriage, and death, but the last of these in particular continues to have the greatest relevance as people speak volubly about death and the dead in the present tense, both literally and metaphorically. Such was the case, for example, with Tamara, who lived near the incongruously named village of Karl Liebknecht in the Belozersk region.[4]

We sat for hours in her comfortable living room while Tamara spoke at length about funerals and memorial occasions, always maintaining her good-natured grin and eagerness to be of help to us as she sipped her sweet tea with audible relish from a saucer in the old-fashioned way. Tamara's narrative showed that tangled mix of sources and influences that have shaped and continue to shape funerary and memorial customs in Russia. She was born into an officially and antagonistically atheistic environment and educated in its ideology. All across the North the destructive effects of the anti-religious campaigns are still visible. The landscapes of Vologda and Arkhangel'sk provinces are pocked with ruined chapels and churches, their insides desecrated with cow dung and polluted with the chemical fertilizer stored there. Trees grow through the floors. Lit by windows without glass, the impassive eyes of Christ with his saints and prophets gaze down from the remnants of frescoes on walls blackened with mold and moss.

As a member of the communist youth movement, the Komsomol, Tamara had set off to the "virgin lands" in the southeast of the Soviet Union to help build communism. Now baptized as an Orthodox Christian, she described the accepted church practice for a Christian burial, as she understood it. When she turned to the deeply held, long-established local traditions of commemoration, such as the meal on the fortieth day after a death, her account became both deeply personal and tied to the norm in her own home, village, and region. The table would be set for a meal "just like we are sitting now," a drink would be provided for the deceased and some food on a saucer "just like this one" (see chapter 2 for information on the fortieth-day meal).

Our first destination in Syamzha region was the tiny village of Goluzino, population around seventy-five, situated some fifty-five kilometers from the large village of Syamzha, which gives its name to the region. Our first glimpse of Goluzino offered a rather depressing picture—a field of rusting farm machinery; the foundations of an abandoned school; and a huddle of ramshackle wooden houses set along a dirt track that was overgrown, as in so many other villages, with weeds and tangled grass. At the single village shop, where an abacus was still in use, a queue of men in camouflage jackets and sturdy women in head-scarves and rubber boots would form outside whenever a delivery was made. Here, and across the North, the heavy, two-story wooden houses with their small windows serve as both living quarters and room for animals and storage. At the heart of every homestead is the huge wood-burning stove built of bricks. There is no running water; instead, as in other villages, residents must fetch water daily from the nearest river, lake, or spring. Beyond the village, the dirt track wound on. Road signs indicated other villages along the way, but the few houses there were empty and rotted, their windows obscured by new growth from the encroaching forest. On one crumbling house facade a sign with the original owner's name, written using the prerevolutionary alphabet that was simplified in 1917, served as a stark reminder of past history and lost generations.

Between 2007 and 2013 our expeditions took us to small villages along the banks of the river Mezen' in Arkhangel'sk province. Arkhangel'sk describes itself as "the capital of the North." The train from St. Petersburg trundles along slowly for almost twenty-four hours, through Leningrad province past Tikhvin, home of the miracle-working icon of the Mother of God, an object of veneration and pilgrimage. Traveling to our farthest destinations in the province is a slow and laborious process involving interminable hours in minibuses on rough, pot-holed tracks. The most isolated villages are often reached by tractor or horse-drawn cart. Many are accessible only by boat.

Typical north Russian homesteads, with living quarters for farm animals, in Kimzha, Arkhangel'sk province, 2007. (Photo by Elizabeth Warner)

The first village we visited in 2007, Kimzha, is known for its many houses preserving the traditional style of the Mezen' homestead, dating from the nineteenth and early twentieth centuries. These huge structures of heavy timber face the Kimzha river, a tributary of the Mezen', their ridgepoles decorated with crude horsehead sculptures. The stocky, red-brown ponies, known as Mezenki and bred for harsh weather, are a familiar sight in the villages in the region. Kimzha is also famed for its eighteenth-century wooden church dedicated to the Hodegetria Mother of God, in disrepair at the time of our visit, but miraculously still standing. Like many other villages in the region, Kimzha once had a large population of Old Believers. These opponents of the seventeenth-century church reforms promulgated by Patriarch Nikon were either sent into exile in these harsh and inhospitable lands or escaped persecution in their very remoteness. Unbending defenders of their right to worship as they chose, they undoubtedly played their part in forming the tough, independent character of the local people and the religious profile of the region.

Economically, Arkhangel'sk province, like Vologda province, has many problems. Poor land, a short growing season, and the severe climate have meant that agriculture has always been a limited means of livelihood. For a province whose territory is over 70 percent forested, the timber trade has been a major industry for centuries. In Soviet times it provided work for men in far-flung villages in logging and log-driving. Now, however, small-scale village enterprises are no longer viable. Few roads connect the region to the outside world, and with each year of our visits we witnessed the Mezen' river slowly silting up and ferries being replaced by rickety pontoon bridges. Also, fish are disappearing. From the more northerly villages on the Mezen', boats setting out to fish for flounder and hunt seals in the Barents Sea were once a common sight. Today, fishing no longer offers full-time employment, and few fishermen venture out to sea. One day in Kimzha, however, we were surprised to see a large barrel set on a platform beside a few stalls selling fishing nets and cheap clothing. The barrel contained a great local delicacy, a type of cured flounder (*ersh-kamballa*) salted at sea, for which the villagers were queuing enthusiastically. For the next week, there was no escape from the all-pervading smell of salty and fermenting fish. Even the teacups tasted of it. In addition to fishing, the men of Arkhangel'sk province, particularly in its wilder reaches, provide for their families as hunters, trappers, and wildfowlers. Bears, wild boars, elk, beavers, and deer are harvested for their meat, fur, or hides. In Vozhgora, a large village on the right bank of the Mezen' near the Komi Republic, the men described their complex and jealously guarded system of hereditary, family trapping territories (*putiki*) in the forest.

In spite of their problems, larger villages like Kimzha, which has received government support for the restoration of its church and whose architectural uniqueness is an attraction for visitors, may still have a future. But an inescapable sense of decline prevails in the smaller villages. In Selishche in Leshukon'e region, for example, which we visited in 2009, almost half the housing stock was empty and abandoned, and the remaining population consisted, as one resident put it, of widows, drunks, and unmarried men who did not look for work but lived off their mothers' pensions. In winter many villages are completely empty, when the elderly move in with their town-based children.

Our expeditions take place in summer. At this time of year, the villages along the Mezen' seem very picturesque when viewed from the river, as you approach by ferry. Against a bright-blue sky you see ridges of dark-gray timber houses, interspersed with patches of emerald grass not yet burnt yellow by the sun, perched above the steep, red-brown sandstone of the riverbank. Despite the benign appearance of the slow-moving river, sudden storms, currents, and quicksand can make it unpredictably treacherous. In every village we hear tales of drowned children, husbands, and grown sons. As soon as it rains the village tracks turn to mud, and even the inhabited houses seem quite dilapidated, sagging tiredly into the earth, with cracked windowpanes. Interiors are unpretentious, pared down to essentials with their simple furniture—a bench and table by the window, a couple of chairs, a cupboard for a few dishes, a metal bedstead piled high with puffy pillows. On the wall hang photographs of deceased parents, a religious calendar, a towel beside a metal water container for handwashing, a pair of scissors, and other useful objects. Although interiors are simple, they are not usually drab and typically feature striped runners, round crocheted rugs and rag rugs to brighten the brown paint of the floors, and wall hangings in gaudy colors over the beds. Most houses have an icon corner, although the icons displayed there are sometimes only cheap reproductions printed on cardboard.

Leaving aside the region's long acquaintance with sorrow as a consequence of historical circumstances, it should be said that tragic, early, and violent death remains an ever-present phenomenon of village life, especially in Arkhangel'sk province, with its harsh climate and living conditions. One elderly widow interviewed in 2009 in Edoma in the Leshukon'e region was grieving not only for her dead husband but also for her daughter, burnt to death in a house fire; for her son, killed by a hammer blow in a brawl; and for her grandson, drowned in the river.

Over many years, people have shared with us their life histories, answering our questions about their way of life, customs, and traditions. Some aspects have been subject to change and are slipping, or have already slipped, into the past. The oldest women, born at the beginning of the twentieth century (1900–1918), could barely remember the old-style, crowded weddings, with their matchmaking, bridal laments, and songs ringing out as the weeks-long wedding event

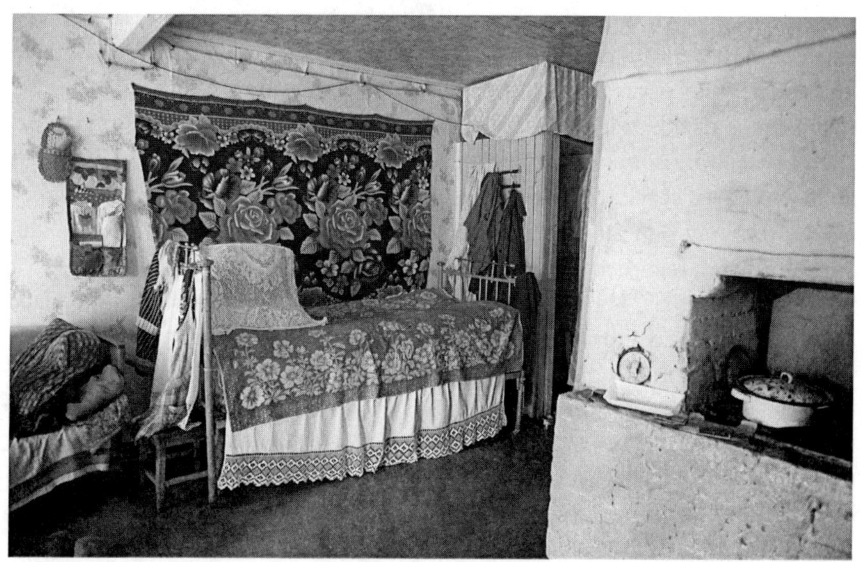

The living room of a house in Azopol'e, Arkhangel'sk province, 2008. A corner of the large, traditional stove used for cooking and heating can be seen. (Photo by Elizabeth Warner)

The icon corner in a house in Kimzha. (Photo by Elizabeth Warner)

progressed. Everything connected with the dead, on the other hand, was very much a matter of the present, described with careful attention to detail. "The Russian people," wrote the ethnographer G. S. Vinogradov in 1923, "attach huge significance to the process of death itself. For them, it must be accomplished with a solemnity commensurate to the importance of the moment. They need to have a burial service, a proper send-off [*provody*] and farewells said to them before the grave" (Vinogradov 1923, 271). The words of Evgeniya Markovna (born in 1927), recorded in Pskov province in 1995, echo these sentiments to a remarkable degree: "The priest says prayers and hands over some earth to place on the grave, then they give the deceased a paper crown with holy pictures drawn on it and the required prayer. So everyone can see that he has been 'seen off' [*provedennyi*]. Burying someone who has not been 'seen off' is just like discarding a piece of meat" (EW field notes, Pskov-Nov, July 1995). The closure of churches and the absence of priests after the revolution did not stop people from caring for and remembering their dead, but the lost bodies of so many soldiers during the war and the hidden casualties of the Stalinist terror who did not come home for burial and were not "seen off" deprived a whole population of its right to mourn in its own way and to ensure the proper passage of their dead into the next world.

"DEATH STUDIES": THE RUSSIAN PERSPECTIVE

The overall theme of our work, funeral and memorial practices and beliefs, is a subject that has been and remains central to the research of anthropologists, irrespective of the particular culture they are studying. Russian scholarship has certainly devoted its share of attention to this topic, but for several unavoidable reasons has lagged behind the field in terms of theoretical advances and methodologies.

Serious scholarly research into the culture of the Russian peasantry dates roughly to the middle of the nineteenth century, with increased interest from the 1870s in the study of material and spiritual culture as well as the artifacts and rituals of daily life, including weddings and funerals. Nevertheless, in the period before the revolution, few large-scale works dealing with the traumas and rituals of death, and even fewer dealing specifically with the contemporary Russian village, had appeared. Two works deserve mention: E. V. Barsov's major collection of north Russian funeral laments (Barsov 1872) and D. K. Zelenin's work on the phenomenon of "unnatural" or "untimely" death (Zelenin 1916). From our own perspective, Barsov's and Zelenin's works, especially the former, are unusual and noteworthy for their reliance on fieldwork and contemporary material. Barsov was very sensitive to the common humanity of those whose laments he recorded in northern Russia: "There is hardly a soul who would remain indifferent to what the people relate in their moments of grief both to themselves and for themselves, to what they say of their own lives as they address their dear deceased, the hewn coffin of light oak and mother-moist-earth" (Barsov 1997, 1:5). Such concern for the viewpoint of the individual mourners remained rare in Russian scholarly studies of funeral ritual until almost the twenty-first century.

Throughout the nineteenth century, scholarship in Russia, as elsewhere, was dominated by the "comparative-historical" method, the notion that societies in different countries passed through identifiable, and therefore comparable, evolutionary stages, from primitive to advanced, and that more advanced civilizations might trace their own past by studying the culture of so-called "primitive" peoples. Peasant culture was studied with a sense of its place on an earlier rung of the cultural-evolutionary ladder and of its separateness and marked differences from the cultural (i.e., urban and "civilized") norm. The people whose lives were defined by this "other" culture were thought of as tradition-bearers—guardians of ancient customs, institutions, and beliefs—while their customs and practices were regarded as mere relics of some earlier, complete worldview that scholarship could reconstruct.

By the beginning of the twentieth century, in Europe and the United States, evolutionism had lost its dominant position in cultural anthropology. In Russia, by contrast, folklore and ethnographical studies, bolstered by the theory of social-economic development advanced by Karl Marx and Friedrich Engels, were unable to move on and continued to be governed by a single analytical approach to the study of cultural traditions in the rural population of the USSR, the historical-comparative or, in Soviet parlance, the "stadial" method. From the late 1920s and for most of the Soviet period, scholars had few prospects of publishing anything in Russia that refuted the Soviet ideal of rural progress or that reflected the true state of contemporary village life. This was especially true, given the war against religion, of anything focusing on the spiritual side of village life, both its Orthodox religious beliefs and practices and its wider relationship with the metaphysical world. Recording and writing about the existence of beliefs having to do with the irrational, the supernatural, the powers of sorcerers and demons (e.g., the forest demon, or *leshii*), and the souls of dead ancestors—all disappeared from the main agenda of folklorists and ethnographers for almost half a century. Very few works dealing in any way with funeral or memorial ritual were published during this time. V. Ya. Propp's monograph on Russian agrarian festivals (1963) is regarded as essential reading for anyone studying the rituals of the Russian calendar cycle and as a classic of twentieth-century scholarship. It may serve as an example of then-current attitudes. His analysis of calendar customs concerned with commemorations of and food offerings for the dead, especially in connection with the festival of Radunitsa during St. Thomas's week (Fomina nedelya) and with Troitsa Saturday, is entirely reliant on nineteenth-century and earlier material. Propp, who was notoriously unwilling to take part in fieldwork, gives no hint that for his contemporaries in the villages these practices were not merely "decayed and faded forms of a once highly developed ancestor cult" (Propp 1963, 29), but instead were part of a still extant tradition (the contemporary practice of offering food to the dead at Troitsa is addressed in chapter 5).

The 1960s witnessed the emergence of alternative evolutionary theories in descriptions of Russian village culture, the structural-typological and comparative-typological approaches. By analogy with linguistic research, whose aim was revealing a "proto-language," research into traditional culture was posited on the notion of an invariant model, which could also be revealed and eventually reconstructed by utilizing the semiotic codes of texts of all kinds, in all their variants. Folk narratives, laments, and descriptions of funeral and memorial acts were all subjected to the same treatment. From the 1970s onward, reconstruction of the conjectured invariant was adopted as the most authoritative methodological approach to the study of folklore and ethnography, and it served as the basis for ethnolinguistic and structural-typological research into both historical material and extant rituals and beliefs. The structural-typological approach was applied in numerous new works on funeral and memorial ritual in the 1980s and 1990s (see, e.g., Nevskaya 1980a, 1980b, 1982, 1990; Sedakova 1983; Ivanov and Nevskaya 1990). The structural-typological method is also applied by B. B. Efimenkova in *Severnorusskaya prichet'* (1980), her collection and study of funeral, memorial, and wedding laments from Vologda province. In addition, it is worth noting that the 1970s and 1980s saw the publication of materials based on the fieldwork of universities and institutions, some of which included commentary on funeral ritual and lamenting (see, e.g., Savushkina 1980, 129–58).

The beginning of the twenty-first century saw the publication of two important works, S. M. Tolstaya's examination of Slavonic concepts of the soul (2000) and O. A. Sedakova's semantic dissection of the funeral ritual of East and South Slavs (2004). Nevertheless, there was still little overt interest in funeral ritual as an existential factor of contemporary village life. In Russian scholarship, the domination of both comparative- and structural-typological methodologies has meant that, until the beginning of the twenty-first century, funeral and memorial ritual practices were by and large "read" and interpreted externally as text—as elements serving the construction of a coherent "worldview." Russian scholarship was not equipped to "hear" and understand these practices as communication from within the "life-world," to use Edmund Husserl's expression, of individuals and communities.

In 1992, Marjorie Balzer drew attention to the "spotty" and "uneven" nature of anthropology fieldwork in rural Russia at that time, a situation that was particularly regrettable given the significant changes taking place there (Balzer 1992, xvi). The impulse behind our own fieldwork and study of funeral ritual was created by similar concerns over the continuing lack of extended, on-site observation of funeral and memorial practices in rural areas.

For European and US scholars, the post-Soviet lifting of taboos on what might legitimately be studied and the increasing freedom to travel and engage in fieldwork in Russia from the mid-1990s have facilitated research in subjects and places hitherto inaccessible. Our own joint work on funeral and memorial practice in contemporary Russia, the largely private nature of which seems to cry out for contact and interaction between the researchers and those whose beliefs and practices they describe, has clearly been made possible by such changes. We are not alone in making use of such opportunities. The appearance of a number of major studies and shorter works referencing the lives of ordinary Russian people in the twentieth and twenty-first centuries—their beliefs, customs, family and community interactions, and rituals, including those associated with death—have made extensive use of interviews, informal conversations, and testimonies recorded in many different locations far beyond the limits imposed on foreign researchers during the Soviet period. Of particular relevance to our work are those concerned, at least in part, with death, funerals, memorialization, and the interrelationship between the living and the dead (see, e.g., Warner 2000a and 2000b; Merridale 2002; Bouchard 2004; Paxson 2005; Rouhier-Willoughby 2007 and 2008; Olson and Adonyeva 2012). Based on fieldwork in village settings both Margaret Paxson's *Solovyovo: The Story of Memory in a Russian Village* and Olson and Adonyeva's *The Worlds of Russian Village Women: Tradition, Transgression, Compromise* share common elements with *We Remember, We Love, We Grieve*. Neither, however, is a work primarily about funeral and memorial ritual; rather, both address this topic as an aspect of "the stuff of social memory," in the case of Paxson's book (2005, 9), and in connection with identity, in the case of the other.

In Russia, in recent years, numerous works relating to death and memorialization have appeared. Generally speaking, there has been a shift toward studying contemporary phenomena in a mainly urban environment, such as memorialization of the site of a violent death or a terrorist atrocity, as well as considerable interest in changes to traditional practice, both urban and rural, in the new social environment of post-Soviet Russia. This new environment is attributed to increasing commercialization, the growing involvement of professional morticians in the organization of funerals, the influence of mass-media, and so on (see, e.g., Sokolova 2011; Elyutina and Filippova 2012; Sokolova and Yudkina 2012; Sokolova 2014; Sokolova and Yudkina 2015).

QUESTIONS OF RELIGION

Since the end of the Soviet period, interest in both institutional religion, in the form of the Orthodox Church, and what is often referred to as Russian "popular," "village," or "folk" religion, as well as "folk Orthodoxy," has become an increasing focus of scholarly attention, both inside Russia and beyond (see Badone 1990; Balzer 1992; Batalden 1993; Chulos 2000; Kivelson and Greene 2003; Himka and Zayarnyuk 2006; Korogodina 2006; Rock 2007; Rouhier-Willoughby and Filosofova 2015). Within Russia, this may be seen as the natural corollary to developments since the early 1990s: the collapse of an atheistic and materialistic ideology, the resurgence of the Orthodox Church, and a growing absorption with questions of national identity. Scholars have moved away from notions of cultural hierarchies toward the study of new forms of Orthodox spirituality (see, e.g., Kormina 2008, 2012, 2013, 2018; Kormina and Shtyrkov 2015 and 2017; Kormina and Luehrmann 2018) and contemporary examples of vernacular religious customs (see, e.g., Panchenko 1998 and 2014 on rural shrines and holy places).

According to Tat'yana Bernshtam, "Traditional peasant culture was formed, as is well known, on the basis of religious awareness, which was not only the spiritual kernel of life but also the spiritual nature of what filled life, conditioning how the world was seen and understood, ways of assimilating the sensual and the supersensual, the emotional order and the code of moral criteria" (Bernshtam 1989, 91. A translation of Bernshtam's article may be found in Balzer 1992, 34–47). This raises questions: What was the nature of this religious awareness? Does it still exist today among the villagers, and does it have any relevance for the beliefs of those we spoke to regarding death, funerals, and memorializing? Clearly, the history of Orthodoxy in Russia, its evolution from inception until the end of the nineteenth century and its suppression in the twentieth century, has played a part in the equation. Until the revolution, the conduct of funerals would normally have been overseen by Orthodox clergy, but this convention was broken after 1917 and ceased to be an integral part of village spiritual culture.

"As far as we can tell," writes Sheila Fitzpatrick, "the great majority of Russian peasants regarded themselves as believers (*veruiushchie*) in the 1930s, and more than half took the risk of publicly identifying themselves as such in response to a question in the 1937 population census" (Fitzpatrick 1994, 7). It is interesting to compare the figures given by Fitzpatrick with the situation at the present time, bearing in mind the changes wrought by a prolonged period of atheist propaganda. Father Nikolai Emel'yanov addresses the problem of quantifying the number of Orthodox believers in the population of Russia today. According to statistical information from the Levada Centre and the Public Opinion Foundation (1991–2014), as he points out, there has been a steady growth in the numbers of those who consider themselves Orthodox from 31 percent in 1991 to 68 percent in 2014, while the number of those committed to regular observance of Orthodox obligations (e.g., receiving Holy communion and going to confession) has remained stable at 2–3 percent. One of the commonest explanations for this discrepancy is that for many people adherence to Orthodoxy has become more a question of national identity than religion (Emel'yanov 2019).

By the eve of the revolution, religious awareness among the peasantry had been formed by many different and often conflicting factors. These included beliefs inherited from a time before Christianization, beliefs reflecting Orthodoxy both "from below"—in its multifarious local versions, in the influence of various cults and especially of Old Believer religious culture—and beliefs reflecting Orthodoxy "from above," as the Church attempted at different times, and largely unsuccessfully, to impose some uniformity and order on what people believed and how they practiced their religion on a daily basis. There was little learned understanding of the basic tenets of Orthodox rite and teachings among ordinary people, something that is as true today as it was then. Both Tat'yana Bernshtam (1989 and 2007) and Gregory Freeze (see Belliustin 1985; Freeze 1996, 1998, 2004) have described the great complexities and anomalies of the Christianization of Russia, a process that was neither monolithic nor straightforward. In the beginning there was no clear-cut division between the faith of ordinary people and that of more educated layers of society. Over much of its history, the priest class, particularly in its lower orders, was little different in education or social standing from its peasant parishioners.

During our research we did not, in fact, ask people about their religious affiliation. Their experience of Orthodoxy, the "traditional or majority religion in the territories of the East Slavs," as Himka and Zayarnyuk define it (2006, 8), is diverse and patchy and in many cases nonexistent. Some told us that they were Orthodox, had been baptized, and wore a cross (often alongside a safety pin to ward off the evil eye). Some claimed they were not believers or knew nothing about religion. Most of the villagers we spoke with talked about their experiences and actions rather than their belief systems, and when asked to explain their beliefs they often provided confusing or incoherent answers.

In our study of funeral ritual in contemporary Russia we try to avoid terms like "folk" or "popular" to categorize people's opinions and behavior since such terms, according to Leonard Primiano, suggest a two-tiered religious model that on the one hand "residualizes the religious lives of believers" and on the other "reifies the authenticity of religious institutions" (Primiano 1995, 38). We use Leonard Primiano's own terms—"vernacular religion" or "religion as it is lived"—with some caution too, since surely all religion is lived, as Primiano himself acknowledges: "Since religion inherently involves interpretation it is impossible for the religion of an individual not to be vernacular" (Primiano 1995, 44).[5] It is important not to become bogged down in terminology. We have already seen that belief systems in Russia have been influenced not by two, as in the concept of dual faith (*dvoeverie*), but by a multitude of different factors. We may also say that representatives of so-called institutional Orthodoxy, the many rural priests with whom we have spoken and who have been unstinting in their advice and assistance, also live their religion and have a point of view. What is important is not whether a belief is right or wrong on some sort of academic scale but how it is used and what it tells us about the people who apply it in their daily lives.

Questions concerning religious awareness or faith have rarely arisen in our research. In matters of belief our interlocutors are capable of simultaneously embracing things that appear to be contradictory, such as the different dwelling places of the dead or the nature of the soul. We have often encountered two principles, however, that play an important part in governing transactions with the transcendental, whether in relationship to a deity, spirit beings, or the dead. These are "obeying the rules" or "doing the right thing," on the one hand, and "negotiating," entering a pact in which obligations are fulfilled in return for privileges, on the other. In Smolenets (Arkhangel'sk province, Leshukon'e region) Galina took us to see a votive cross deep in the forest. She told us how she had gone there years before, with her husband and daughter, who were both ill, and how they drank tea and prayed together. She showed us the special cloth she had made as a gift-offering, with a cross on it. The cloth was still there although faded and rotting with age: "You can't approach God with a stick in your hand," explained Galina. A priest we interviewed in the Kirillov region in 2003 commented on the strange attitude of members of his congregation when praying to God: "It's like an 'on-off' switch. 'If something happens I'll go and pray . . . If you help me' [they say], 'I'll believe in you. If you don't help, then you don't exist. If you help me, then so be it, I'll believe.'" Gifts, offerings and prayers may also be used as bargaining tools in interactions with the dead.

THE PRESENT WORK

"Life becomes transparent against the background of death and fundamental social and cultural issues are revealed" (Metcalf and Huntington 1995, 25).

Huntington's observation has universal application, as he himself points out, and appears to be particularly relevant in the communities we have been researching.

It is difficult to exaggerate the importance of funeral and memorial ritual in Russia today. The contemporary social order is firmly based on the values associated with honoring ancestors and caring for one's own dead. Performing funeral rituals and, even more importantly, "remembering" the dead in a variety of different ways, are acts of healing that help to bind what has been fractured, restore what has been disrupted or forbidden, and compensate for what has been lost or taken away. These acts support and bind together families, communities, and today's society, uniting them with the generations of ancestors who preceded them. These are the premises upon which our book is based.

Although much of our research has been carried out in a rural environment, concern for the dead and understanding the relationship between the living and the dead is by no means an exclusively rural phenomenon in Russia. At the beginning of the twentieth century, most of Russia's population consisted of peasants. According to statistics, in 1926 only 17 percent of Russia's population was urban. By 1939 it was still only 34 percent; in 1959 it reached 52 percent, rising to 73 percent in 2002 (Becker, Mendelsohn, and Benderskaya 2012). Urbanization came relatively late and at a slow pace. Furthermore, the villagers who migrated to the towns took their values with them. The collective practice of care for the dead is woven into the fabric of everyday life and is equally important to bereaved villagers and city-dwellers. Russians understand this from an early age. Any small child visiting a cemetery for the first time quickly learns not to pick the wild strawberries on the graves because, as some elderly relative will surely point out, they belong to the *pokoinichki*, the dear dead people. Whether they live in the town or the country, parents take their children to the cemetery to visit the graves of their "own people" (*svoikh*) as a matter of course. For them it is the correct thing to do and, more often than not, it is done without giving any logical reasons or religious explanations. The mere fact that they have come to the cemetery together on an ancestor day to put flowers on the grave, to paint the fence around the grave, to eat there, suggests something of value they share—namely, that the world of the children, the parents, and the wider family—alive and dead alike (in short, their circle) —is a life-world they hold in common, one whose meanings and merits are not agreed upon in words but confirmed by these actions.

Robert Herz has suggested that beliefs and rituals associated with death could be classified under three headings—the body of the deceased, the deceased's soul, and the survivors (Herz 2004, 3). This division can also be applied to *We*

Remember, We Love, We Grieve, where all three elements are discussed with differing emphasis and from different points of view from one section to the next.

The first chapter deals with the relationship between all three as the attention of the bereaved moves from preparation of the body for burial to the well-being of the soul, the enigmatic nature of which emerges through presentation of the principal elements of funerary and memorial practice. The primary acts of the bereaved are concerned with provisioning and comforting a "living" and tangible presence and maintaining the link between their own world and the other world of the dead (*tot svet*). Giving nourishment to and upholding communication with the dead are two of the recurring themes of the book that are addressed specifically in the following two chapters.

In Russia through the ages, during the atheistic years of the Soviet Union and today, in town and country alike the rituals of sharing food and gathering together at the table on special occasions (*zastol'e*) have always affirmed the unity of particular groups. In chapter 2 we show that supplying the dead with food and drink and joining with them in the act of eating is a reminder of the enduring bond between living and dead generations.

Offering food is one way of communicating, but the lament, discussed in chapter 3, is par excellence the language for addressing the dead. In this chapter there are two main protagonists, the deceased and the bereaved, the widows and "orphaned" mothers whose change of social status is as marked as that of the deceased when they pass into the other world of the dead.

In chapter 4 we deal with the changing face of cemeteries, from Soviet times to the present day. These are the homes of the dead, whether envisaged as bodies or souls or some combination of the two. At the same time, they are also spaces for legitimate intercourse between the dead and the living. The visual profile of the cemetery suggests an interplay between the living and the dead in which the demands of survivors are balanced with the requirements of the departed. The aesthetic and practical criteria that shaped the appearance of cemeteries, from decorative symbols on grave markers to graveside picnic tables, may have been established by the living but also take into account the pleasure and well-being of the dead. Some aspects of graveyard aesthetics go beyond the purely decorative. The birch tree symbol visible on many gravestones, for example, is multifaceted, evoking associations with femininity and traditional spring-time courtship rites, love of nature, and love of Russia, themes that are explored in the next chapter.

In chapter 5, through analysis of the calendric festival of Troitsa, we consider the theme of death and memorialization in a wider historical and cultural context. In its creation of the Troitsa festival, the Orthodox Church united the doctrine of the Holy Trinity with the beliefs and rituals of its rural population.

The festival, with its pervasive symbol of the birch tree, celebrates life and overcoming death. It therefore provides an occasion for analyzing many of the themes addressed in the book, both secular and religious (in a narrow and also wider sense). Here we argue that graveside remembrance rituals, discussed in earlier chapters of the book as largely private events, may have wider implications on a national level.

The memorial practices of the general population demand stability and continuity, but the facts of war and other brutal events of the twentieth century, with their inevitable dispersal of burial sites and bodies, have diminished them. The final chapter, about the ritual memorial structures of the Soviet era, is the only one to address memorialization in an urban context. Here we show how sepulchral monuments and cenotaphs dedicated to the "unknown" soldiers and heroes of revolution and war were used as a substitute for personal memorial practices at the graveside and as a form of initiation into Soviet ideology.

Our book as a whole is grounded on our extensive fieldwork and personal observation. It was inspired by long conversations with women (and on more rare occasions with men) with whom we met regularly, often returning to visit year after year, sometimes sharing their homes. We have tried to enter into the lives of our interlocutors as much as possible, watching and learning the skills required in their daily existence, from baking bread in a Russian stove to setting traps for wildfowl in the forest. We have taken part with our village companions

A recording session with members of the local choir in Azopol'e, Arkhangel'sk province, 2008. (Photo by Elizabeth Warner)

in the backbreaking summertime process of haymaking. We have attended christenings and funerals, joined in personal and village celebrations, and shared umpteen pots of tea (and, occasionally, something stronger).

Judicious use has also been made in our book of the many factors—theological, folkloric, literary, cultural, and historical—that have played their part in shaping and elucidating the customs and beliefs we describe here. In the absence of documented ethnographical material, we have occasionally referred to the observations on funeral and memorial customs made by early travelers to Russia, such as Samuel Collins, Giles Fletcher, Johann Korb, and Adam Olearius (see, e.g., chapter 5). Although the historical accuracy of all such memoirs should be treated with due caution, they do open a window onto practices relevant to the present work from perspectives of earlier times that are otherwise inaccessible. It is noteworthy that Anthony Cross, an authority on foreign writings about Russia, has commented on the "generally trustworthy account" of these diplomats and on Collins's firsthand experience of Russian life during his nine years (1660–69) as physician to Tsar Aleksei Mikhailovich (Cross 1971, 24 and 27).

In a village in the Mezen' region of Arkhangel'sk province, an elderly woman was asked why she bothered to carry out remembrance rituals at the cemetery. After all, the dead could not hear her. Zoya Fedorovna's family had been repressed as kulaks. Her father had died in a camp, and her mother also died shortly after his arrest. "We have to do it," she kept saying. "Our whole life is grounded on it. . . . We must always remember. . . . I don't know anything. They say we all walk under God. They say they [the dead] see and hear everything. I don't know. . . . I'm not religious. We weren't taught anything about that." She had learned the rules of remembrance from her mother-in-law, "who followed what was right."

Beliefs about the Soul, the Living Dead, and the Afterlife in Contemporary Rural North Russia

ELIZABETH WARNER

In 2008 I attended a funeral in a village in the Mezen' region of Arkhangel'sk province. The deceased was unknown to me in life but in death became a compelling material presence. With several other women I sat on a bench on the open back of the truck carrying the coffin as it jolted down the long, rutted track to the cemetery. The dead man lay in front of us, his face pale and sharp, his cap placed beside his hands. If I had leaned forward, I could have touched him, as the women did later in their final farewells before the coffin was lowered. A young man in camouflage trousers and a denim jacket smoked a cigarette as he led the small procession of mourners trudging down the track through the village behind the truck. As we stood beneath the fir trees, tormented by clouds of mosquitoes, the men dug a grave with their long spades, surrounding us with piles of red soil. No priest was present. There were no prayers, no eulogy, and no music. None of the mourners wore black suits and ties, although a few women wore black headscarves. Instead, the setting demanded rubber boots and workaday clothing. The ritual was carried out with a quiet sense of purpose, while the dead man in his open coffin seemed like a silent observer of his own obsequies. The proceedings appeared to be entirely devoid of a spiritual dimension and served only to stress the physical nature of death.

Across north Russia many different types of grave markers can be seen in rural cemeteries. Today, grand marble slabs in contemporary designs are often used to convey the feelings of the bereaved: "We remember, we love, we grieve" (pomnim, lyubim, skorbim). There are many of the large wooden crosses for which Arkhangel'sk province is famed, with their carved quotations from Scripture about future resurrection, and there are unadorned wooden posts bearing the simple statement "Here lies buried the body of such and such a person," followed

Crosses with scriptural messages in Smolenets, Arkhangel'sk province, 2010. (Photo by Elizabeth Warner)

only by the dates of birth and death. The latter caught my attention because of their focus on the whereabouts of the deceased person's mortal, bodily remains. I began to wonder about spiritual remains. Do the inhabitants of these remote communities believe in the notion of a soul? If so, what is its nature, and what do they think happens to it after the death of the body?

Following the post-Soviet revival of the Orthodox Church, a number of works concerning folk beliefs about the soul appeared in Russia in the 1990s and early 2000s (see, e.g., Mikheev 1999, 145–58; Tolstaya 1999a, 162–67; Uryson 1999, 11–25; Vinogradova 1999, 141–60; Tolstaya 2000, 52–95).

Differentiating between the soul of the living individual and the fate of the soul after death, Svetlana Tolstaya, in her wide-ranging article of 2000 "Slavonic Mythological Concepts of the Soul" ("Slavyanskie mifologicheskie predstavleniya o dushe"), discusses many aspects of beliefs about the soul common to the Slavonic peoples, such as where the soul originates, its relationship with the body, how it departs the body after death, what material and immaterial forms it can adopt, and where it dwells.

This and other cited works combine a common interest in semantics and in systematizing the huge body of available ethnographical material, mainly historical but also contemporary, with the underlying premise of reconstructing from this material an archaic mythopoetic model of the world, Russian and/or common Slavonic: "As in many other instances, language preserves over many centuries the most essential parameters of the cultural concept associated with the words 'soul' and 'spirit' and other close or related linguistic units (words and expressions). However, the signs preserved by language can only serve as an indirect source, allowing only the fragmentary restoration of ancient (Praslavic, medieval and earlier) 'naïve' anthropology. The evidence of oral tradition, its verbal and non-verbal forms—beliefs, rituals, interdictions, prescriptions, folklore texts and so on can provide an incomparably fuller picture" (Tolstaya 2000, 57). For Tolstaya, the basis for elucidating meaning is the combined study of text and language. The purpose of our book, however, is to present the funeral and memorial strategies of contemporary Russians as communication rather than text. In the "life-world" of the people we have met, death is not an abstract component of mythological text but a personal event, and dealing with it through ritual is one of the most fundamental conventions by means of which people create and support that commonly experienced life-world. In contrast to the relative certainties provided by linguistic and textual analysis, when I have asked villagers what they know about the nature of the soul (*dusha*), its fate and destination at the death of the body, in most cases they have struggled to provide precise or unequivocal answers, limiting themselves to vague and often contradictory comments about souls that "fly away" or are transported to heaven or some other, ill-defined destination. I have often heard accounts in which souls are transformed into birds or reveal themselves as mice or butterflies. All of these metaphors for the soul have been recorded many times in different Slavonic countries over the centuries. Now and then, and usually in the context of relating a dream, reference may be made to the life of the soul in paradise. The word *dusha* carries with it an inevitable baggage of religious-philosophical-historical meanings that may be understood differently by the interviewer and the interviewed. Asking villagers to provide a definition of "soul," as they understood it, was rarely productive as they would usually evade the question and refer us to a priest or someone more devout than they were.

Posing questions about how they treat their dead and relate to them during key stages of funerary ritual, both before and after burial, on the other hand, was much more fruitful. What emerged from discussions of these rituals and attitudes was something approaching a detailed and coherent pattern of beliefs about what is left of the individual beyond the corruption of the body. It is this notion of soul, closely bound up with how the villagers live their world, that I examine here.

THE RITUALS OF DEATH

The smaller details of traditional funerary practice in north Russia are by no means uniform. They can vary from region to region, village to village, family to family, and generation to generation. However, the main structure of the ritual remains largely similar, and this is true across Russia. Leaving aside the question of pre-death signs and omens, contemporary funerary ritual may be said to concentrate on the following areas: the day of the death, when the body is washed and dressed; the following day, during which the corpse is normally at home in an open coffin, so that relatives and friends may pay their respects; and the day of the funeral, which includes preparation of the grave site (if that has not been done earlier), final farewells, carrying out the body, the funeral procession to the cemetery, interment, and the post-funeral meal. After the burial, the period until the end of the fortieth day, during which the soul is, as many believe, at liberty to return home, is of particular significance. Last, but by no means least, are the many post-funeral acts of commemoration. All of these stages of traditional funerary practice throw light, in one way or another, on how people assess the status of both body and soul after death.

Preparation of the Deceased for Burial

One dominant characteristic of north Russian mortuary beliefs that is apparent from the outset is ambiguity about what, apart from the cadaver, remains of an individual after death. The belief that the newly deceased retained some aspects of sensation was once widespread. In parts of Vologda province in the second half of the twentieth century, keening over the body was still usually postponed until the deceased had been given time to calm down after the trauma of death (Efimenkova 1980, 16), and today several hours are allowed to pass before washing and dressing the corpse. Vestiges of belief in a sentient corpse may also take a more overt form. For example, in one case a daughter dreamed of her father while his body still lay at home. He complained that one of his shoes was pinching. In the morning she removed his shoes, concerned that perhaps one of his socks was twisted, and discovered a cuff-link mislaid by the old women who had dressed him and inadvertently dropped it into his shoe (FA Lesh 22-138, July 5, 2011).

Many elderly people appear unusually aware of a postmortem self, envisaging their own death as an event in which they will play an active and central role. This is particularly apparent in the preparation of burial clothes, usually referred to as "death clothes" (*smertnaya odezhda*). Although it is not obligatory, many elderly women, in both Vologda and Arkhangel'sk provinces (as in other regions), begin to choose their own burial attire when they feel the onset of old age, or after a serious illness, while men, on the whole, delegate this task to their womenfolk. Garments and footwear are chosen with great care and attention to both quality and appearance: "I bought a dress for 500 rubles—It's gray, with embroidery—also some cloth, a vest, slippers, stockings, all good quality, all new" (FA Lesh 17-12, July 10, 2009).

Typically, men are dressed in clean and respectable (or even, if the relatives can afford them, new) garments: a suit, shirt, socks, and underwear. Men are buried bare-headed but usually with a hat or cap laid on the pillow next to the head. A headscarf, on the other hand, is obligatory for women. These scarves are noticeably decorative, often white with a floral pattern, in contrast to the darker and plainer ones worn by the bereaved. "Yes" commented Ulyana, "we have a nice scarf ready. The road ahead is long. There's no way back. Why would we give her an inferior one?" (EW-A Arkh-Lesh, July 15, 2009). Even underwear must be up to standard. When a neighbor died without having put together her death bundle (*uzelok*) in advance, Tamara was asked to find suitable clothing among the deceased woman's possessions. This she did, with the exception of the underpants. Unable to find "good ones," Tamara fretted over this deficiency, but after she and a friend ransacked the neighbor's house from top to bottom, they at last found some decent underwear at the bottom of an old cupboard in the loft (EW-V Vol-Vash, tape 6, July 18, 2001). The unexpectedly festive appearance of the deceased is a matter for comment in funeral laments: "I shall ask where you are going so smartly dressed, dear sister. / You have put on your bright-colored dress / and washed with scented soap. / There is no festival in the neighborhood, no merry gathering near at hand. / Now we have guessed the answer. / You are leaving us to set out on a long journey, / A journey from which there is no return" (Razova 1994, 174–75).

Naturally, this attentiveness to detail and presentation may be motivated by a variety of different concerns, including straightforward practical and social considerations. The isolated nature of many villages and the difficulties of travel at certain times of year mean that objects required for a funeral may be difficult to obtain on short notice. By making choices early, elderly people are able to put their affairs in order before it is too late and to remove a cause of anxiety and expense for relatives left behind. The elderly's sense of self-respect and family standing within the community also dictate the need to ensure both a well-turned-out corpse for public view and fully observed funerary etiquette.

The clothing of the dead may also be regarded as one example of the importance attached to the material body throughout the funeral ritual. In some regions it is quite common, for example, to dress the dead not merely attractively but also appropriately for the season in which they died, with a special emphasis on warm clothing, including footwear, for those who died in winter. This is true of both Vologda and Arkhangel'sk provinces although it is perhaps more strictly adhered to in the latter location, where the climate is more severe. Going through an album of old funeral photographs in the village of Selishche in 2009, I remarked on the white slippers the deceased in one image appeared to be wearing, thinking this was a remnant of the old custom, now largely abandoned, of sewing lightweight cloth footwear for the dead (see, e.g., Warner 2000b, 259). According to Roza, however, these were not slippers but boots—and warm winter boots at that—because the death had occurred in April, when the weather was still chilly and the roads virtually impassable because of melting snow (EW-A Arkh-Lesh, July 15, 2009). Two elderly sisters in Smolenets (Arkhangel'sk province) describing their mother's funeral, which took place around 1986, commented that they had dressed her in two pairs of underpants, a warm pair and a thinner pair. Since their mother was very old, they feared she would suffer from the cold: "She would freeze so we dressed her warmly." They added a long-sleeved vest of jersey fabric, a blue, woolen dress, and a new, white, woolen headscarf with a flower pattern. They also refused to bury her wearing the rubber boots she had asked for but instead bought some winter ones to replace them (FA Lesh 17-35, July 15, 2010). Commenting on suitable clothing for elderly female corpses, another individual criticized the recently introduced fashion of burying women in a dress or dressing-gown. In spring, autumn, and winter, they should have a knitted cardigan as well because "Just a little frock is not sufficient" (FA Vash 17-3, July 8, 2000). Such examples abound.

Sometimes provision is even made for a change of clothes. K. K. Loginov comments regarding the Russian inhabitants of the Transonega region of northwest Russia (Republic of Karelia) that, while they did not dress their dead in warm clothing, they would pack a warm change of clothes in the coffin with the deceased to allow for a change of clothing when needed. At the time of Loginov's study, he reports, the preferred warm garment was a fur or padded sleeveless jacket (1993, 152). In some cases the reasons for supplying a change of clothing appear to have been aesthetic or personal rather than utilitarian, as the following example shows. A woman's son had committed suicide. Before the act, he dressed himself carefully in his jeans, a good sweater, and boots. He left a note on the table asking to be buried as he was. His mother thought this was unsuitable attire for a funeral and redressed him in a suit and shirt. However, she did put his chosen garments in the coffin (EW-V Vol-Bel, tape 4, July 11, 1999).

Provisioning the Coffin

Not only clothing for the dead but also the objects required to wash the corpse and provision the coffin are usually collected ahead of time. The soft items used to furnish and dress the coffin might include a sheet, a pretty coverlet, and material to line the inside and cover the outside.[1] In the past, this desire to be well-prepared even extended to making the coffin while the prospective tenant was still alive. Today, this is rare, although in 2009 in the village of Yuroma, Arkhangel'sk province, I did meet a handyman who showed me the coffin he had made for himself in his own workshop.

In addition to considering her own appearance as a corpse, an elderly woman contemplating death might also take an interest in whether or not the coffin will be comfortable. When asked whether it was better to have a pillow stuffed with the traditional dried birch leaves or with cotton wool, Zinaida replied: "Cotton wool of course. It's much better, it's softer" (FA Mez 17-34, July 8, 2007). Another woman explained that she had been hoarding her hair clippings with the intention of stuffing a pillow with them for her coffin (FA Mez 17-65, July 20, 2008). The custom of cutting the hair of a deceased woman and placing it with her in the coffin was recorded among Russians and other East Slavs in the nineteenth century (see, e.g., Barsov 1997, 1:247). As is well-known, hair was regarded as having many magical properties. It could be used in witchcraft and folk medicine both for harming and curing a victim and was often, therefore, collected and kept safe (see, e.g., Tolstoi and Usacheva 1995, 420–24). However, the person mentioned above was more concerned with the fact that hair, as she believed, would not rot, so she would always have a nice soft pillow to lie on. Where alternatives existed, informants also tended to express preferences about where they wished to be buried. One cemetery might have been preferred for its more pleasant location: "I'd prefer to be buried here. The cemetery is dry. It's nice. They say the one in Leshukon'e gets muddy in the autumn when it rains. It's muddy, not nice" (FA Lesh 17-17, July 7, 2009). More important, however, was the presence or absence of close family within reasonable traveling distance of the cemetery. In particular, the traditional attitude to burial in Arkhangel'sk province, where there are very strong kinship bonds, envisages a place surrounded by the graves of kith and kin and the existence nearby of living family members who will regularly visit the graves and their occupants during the many acts of remembrance that take place throughout the year. Those contemplating death expect company and attention in their final resting-place. Indeed, dissatisfaction at a lack of visitors can be one cause of the dead returning to haunt the living. Asked whether she had ever dreamed of the dead, Nona recollected once seeing her mother, who was in tears because, as she moaned, "Nobody loves me." It turned out that her daughter was the only one left in the village to visit the mother's grave. Everyone else had gone away (FA Mez 17-23, July 13, 2007).

Concern for the material well-being of the deceased has traditionally extended beyond procuring warm garments and a comfortable bed. Nineteenth-century descriptions of north Russian funerary practice suggest that a variety of objects with a purely secular function were also provided as a matter of course. Among these, according to Barsov, one might find bread, pies, an Easter egg for a person who died at Easter, a needle for a woman, in case she had to mend her clothes in the "other" world, and so on. One of Barsov's oddest observations concerns a flask of vodka discovered by workmen in a coffin dug up during renovation work at the Aleksandr-Svirskii monastery in northwest Russia: "They immediately drank it," he writes. "The vodka turned out to be so strong that they immediately collapsed and only woke up the following day!" (Barsov 1997, 1:248). Today, in the twenty-first century, it is rare to hear of someone placing food or drink, such as a bottle of vodka, in a coffin. While villagers may now even express distaste at the very idea of this practice, it was well-known until comparatively recently in some places.

The tradition of placing other grave goods in coffins has continued to the present time in both Arkhangel'sk and Vologda provinces, although it is less widespread than in the past. Among the most common items are false teeth, spectacles, wristwatches, and combs, which are arranged beside the corpse, while a smoker may be given a packet of cigarettes and a cigarette lighter. Items of particular significance to the deceased are sometimes mentioned. One person remembered an occasion when a guitar, for example, was laid in the coffin of a youth who had committed suicide (FA Mez 17-16, July 27, 2007), and another spoke of an accordion being put in a man's coffin, although it is difficult to imagine how room could possibly be found for such large objects (FA Bel 17-53, July 24, 1994). Toys may find their way into a child's coffin and may also be seen on the graves of children (this is a point to which I shall return). In Tver' province in 2015, a woman told me how, after her husband died, she was warned by a relative, who had seen him in a dream, that the poor man had no gloves: "You have to give him some, put them somewhere." "I thought and thought," said the widow, "and other people said I should buy some new gloves, ordinary gloves. . . . I had put everything in his coffin. He had clothes and everything was put in there, even his glasses. Everything was there, his shaving things went under the pillow. Sometimes people put the shaving things in the grave, but I just put them [in the coffin]. I stuck his glasses in that he wore and then a little cross. I put a little cross on him but I didn't put in any gloves." She solved the problem by buying gloves and taking them to the funeral of her cousin. The gloves were placed in the coffin near the deceased's hands with the request that he pass them on (EW-A Tver'-Bol, June 16, 2015).

On rare occasions money may be secreted in the corners of the coffin by way of payment for occupancy. More common is the custom of tossing small change into the grave itself in order to buy the deceased's place in the cemetery. An additional item frequently seen in coffins is a white handkerchief. It may be tucked into the pocket of a suit jacket or held in the deceased's hand for the purpose of (according to one explanation) being able to wipe away tears until the final Day of Judgment (EW-A Arkh-Lesh, July 17, 2011).

In the past, the deceased were often buried with items associated with their previous jobs, in the expectation that some form of occupation would be expected in the afterlife. Hints of this practice still linger. Tamara, for example, remembered being told about a dream in which a neighbor was visited by her dead husband. Apparently, he told his widow not only that he had a good life in the other world but also that he was employed in some way, that he was kept busy (EW-V Vol-Vash, July 18, 2001). More recently, I was told that a father's memorandum book had been placed with him in his coffin. It was something he never parted with during his working life, and his family "kind of felt his work was not yet done" (EW-A Arkh-Lesh, July 9, 2010).

Some of these objects clearly have purely sentimental or symbolic connotations. Nevertheless, the dead do seem to retain a jealous hold on their material possessions. One widow said she would never touch any of her dead husband's things again after the trouble he caused when she moved his ladder. He even managed to break some of the rungs! After that she shut the ladder in the woodshed, where it remained, thirteen years later, at the time of the interview (FA Mez 17-53, July 8, 2008).

The function of objects placed in coffins may be different from those described above, which are clearly intended for the comfort or use of the dead individual. Wood shavings left over from making the coffin and items used for washing the corpse, such as soap, a wash cloth and towel, are also usually secreted in the coffin since they are believed to pose a threat to the living through their polluting association with death (see Douglas 2002 for discussion of the physical and symbolic notions of defilement).

Not all objects placed in coffins remain there. A cushion displaying the deceased's war or service medals is often laid beside the head, but it will be removed before the lid is fastened down. These symbols of status and attainment will become heirlooms in the deceased's family. Fresh flowers are also taken away before the coffin is sealed and used to decorate the grave. This particular practice considerably vexed one lady who went on at some length about the need to leave at least one flower for the deceased to enjoy (FA Mez 17-77, July 16, 2008).

In more recent years it became common to see two other items in coffins. These are monetary contributions toward the funeral expenses, usually arranged close to the feet of the corpse, and telegrams or letters of condolence, also often placed in contact with the body. Like the medals, they are eventually removed. The display of these items inside the coffin, in close proximity to the deceased, suggests an attempt to show the dead person, as well as others, how much he or she is missed and valued.

In the introduction to this book we have remarked on the complexity of the relationship between belief as practiced among ordinary folk and representatives of institutional religion in Russia. Where disparities arise, the interesting point is not that there is a conflict between "elite" or "official" practices on one hand and folk or "popular" practices on the other. Instead our focus is on what these disparities reveal about the people we are researching. With regard to dressing the corpse, for example, the requirement for new or clean clothing can be seen both in popular practice and in the symbolism of church literature. Since the Orthodox Church regards the body as the "temple" of the soul, it must be treated with reverence after death. It is washed to symbolize the clean life supposedly led by good Christians and the state of spiritual cleanliness in which they should appear before God. Next the body is dressed in clean clothes (if possible, new ones), denoting the "new garments of incorruption" (Hapgood 1965, 609). In reality, the purely spiritual imagery of Orthodoxy is replaced with the individual and social imperative to appear well-dressed and appropriately dressed. The mental and physical well-being of the deceased is paramount. Differences of opinion and some dismay may arise, in cases where there has been contact with a priest, about what objects may be placed in the coffin. Strictly speaking, the only objects permitted by the Church in a coffin are closely linked with the religious nature of preparation for burial, the belief in an immortal soul, and the resurrection of the dead at the Day of Judgment. The body, therefore, may be covered with a white coverlet that is embellished with an image of the crucifixion and relevant quotations from the Scriptures. A paper wreath, depicting Christ the Savior, Mary the Mother of God, and John the Baptist may garland the deceased's forehead, while an icon or a crucifix is placed in his or her right hand. At the end of the burial service (*otpevanie*) the priest should also place in the deceased's hands a copy of the prayer for absolution. It is by no means always the case, however, that a priest conducts the funeral, whether or not the mourners prefer it.

In village practice the presence in coffins of Christian symbols does not preclude the presence of other artifacts. Generally speaking, however, the provisioning of coffins highlights the importance of material objects and physical comfort in the afterlife. While the message of spiritual comfort conveyed by Christian articles may be difficult to comprehend, the benefits of warm gloves and a set of false teeth are fully understood.

The Last Look

Traditionally, the corpse lies at home for three days, or at least until the morning of the third day, when the funeral usually takes place. Before the coffin is finally removed from the house to the cemetery for burial—or in some cases, at the graveside before the coffin is lowered—it is still customary for many families to have a photograph taken. This practice was especially widespread during the Soviet period. These photographs are formally composed and follow a distinct pattern. The mourners are arranged very close to the coffin, in many cases touching it and/or the deceased person. Members of the immediate family are grouped at the front, with more distant relatives, friends, and neighbors standing in the background. The gaze of the mourners is intense and directed only toward the deceased. Naturally, there is an element of social commentary in these photographs. They demonstrate "how we are all mourning," united as family and community, in our grief and respect for this person. They may be compared with similar photographs popular in Victorian England and in America in the late nineteenth and first half of the twentieth century (see, e.g., Ruby 1995, 94–103). In formal photographs of other social occasions, such as weddings or birthdays, however, the gaze of the participants is directed outward toward the viewers, affirming their connection with the world of the living. In

Relatives of the deceased gather round the coffin before setting off for the cemetery, Vozhgora, Arkhangel'sk province, early 1970s. (DPh 4_302_0065 from the Yurii A. Galev Photo-Archive)

the funeral photographs, on the other hand, the mourners have eyes only for the face of the dead, as if they were fixing the physical remains of the deceased in their minds before those remains are committed to the earth. In the intensity of this moment there is a sense of communion between the living and the dead. The dead are looking at the living for the last time too. This notion may also be found in funeral laments, where a woman might, for example, exhort her dead husband to take a final look at his "dear little children" (Razova 1994, 170) or the corpse of a young woman might be told, "open your bright eyes" for a glimpse of husband, children, and friends soon to be left behind (Efimenkova 1980, 95). The photograph fixes one of those turning points, both physical and metaphorical, that affect the deceased's journey from life to afterlife in the course of the ritual. In north Russia such photographs are kept in special albums or displayed in collages with other family snapshots, and there is no reluctance to show them to others, whereas in America they are rarely seen nowadays outside the family circle.

The Coffin-Home, the Cemetery, and the Gravesite

"Transitions from group to group and from one social situation to the next are looked on as implicit in the very fact of existence, so that a man's life comes to be made up of a succession of stages with similar ends and beginnings" (van Gennep 1977, 3). Death itself, as the final "rite of passage," to use van Gennep's terminology, also takes place in stages.[2] One of the most significant moments in the progress of that passage and the change in status it brings with it is the transference of the cadaver from its former dwelling in the village to the cemetery. After death the deceased, as altered beings, simply take up house in a new location and can only return to their old homes as visitors, welcome or unwelcome, and only under certain circumstances. In their new abodes, on the other hand, they act as hosts to the living and may, in turn, impose certain conditions upon them.

This idea is emphasized by a number of different metaphors used in relationship to the gravesite. First, there is the coffin. With its mattress, pillow, and coverlet, the coffin obviously simulates a comfortable bed in which the deceased lies "asleep." This metaphor is by no means restricted to Russia. More interestingly, there is an etymological link between the coffin, often referred to in the North as *domovishche* or *domovina*, and a house (*dom*). The transfer of residence experienced by the newly dead is made explicit in the saying "*doma* net, a *domo*vishche budet" ("You no longer have a house but you will have a coffin-home"; Dal' 1957, 284). In north Russian funeral laments the coffin is sometimes also referred to as the "new living room" (*novaya gorenka*), specially made for the deceased. This domicile, however, is strictly differentiated from the old. As described in laments, it is dark, "without doors, without windows," and also cold without its "brick-built stove" (Efimenkova 1980, 135). This lack of light and warmth, which seems to characterize that "other" world in which their dead now reside, appears to worry the bereaved. Indeed, in many parts of Arkhangel'sk province, light is deliberately restored to the inside of the coffin by the provision of windows, situated by the head of the deceased. Nowadays, these windows are mostly symbolic, drawn with chalk or pencil, but in the past proper windows with glass were made: "In some parishes," wrote Barsov, "such as those of Syamozero and Badogi, openings into which glass is placed are made in the sides of the box. This is done in such a way that the little windows are situated on either side of the deceased's shoulders. In other places, glass is placed in the coffin without making openings" (Barsov 1997, 1:247). If the coffin is left without windows, it is thought, the deceased may become distressed. Elba described a dream someone had told her about in which the deceased had complained of the "house" they had built for him and asked to be released from it. This house had no windows, so he was unable see anyone or, indeed, anything at all from it. Upset by this information, Elba decided that at the next funeral she attended she would draw windows on the coffin herself. However, as is frequently the case with folk beliefs, her "positive" became someone else's "negative," for, as she was warned, if the deceased could see out, he might well seek a companion to join him (FA Mez 17-104, July 16, 2008). As we shall see later, this attempt to counteract the harshness of death by reinstating a lost benefit is typical of other aspects of north Russian mortuary ritual, in particular with relation to food (see, e.g., chapter 2).

The next metaphoric reference in relation to the grave site focuses on the grave pit. When digging a grave in the North, it is still usual in many areas to erect within the pit itself a box-like housing made of planking, into which the coffin is lowered. A wooden ceiling is then laid over it. At the present time, this construction is usually simply called the "box" (*yashchik*). It has a practical purpose. In the climate of north Russia, the cemetery ground can be problematic for burials because the earth remains frozen for long periods, and melting snow may cause flooding. Alternatively, the soil may be too sandy. As a result, graves may collapse. If this happens, the wooden ceiling provides some protection for the flimsy coffins. Although the terms *domovina* and *domovishche* were and still are in common usage across north Russia to describe a coffin, the box of the burial chamber is sometimes also referred to as domovina in Arkhangel'sk province. In any case, the home-like nature of the structure is fully recognized: "We don't put the coffin in the ground straight away. A box is made out of planks, an ordinary box, a big square box. The coffin is put in the box and the box is closed. It's as if the coffin inside is in a little house, a little house" (FA Mez 17-96, July 9, 2008). Partly in connection with the high cost of materials, there

A place to sit and remember the ancestors buried in this cemetery in Azopol'e, Arkhangel'sk province, 2008. (Photo by Elizabeth Warner)

is a tendency nowadays to simplify these box-houses, providing only a rough, trestle-like framework with a "roof" to protect the coffin.

Finally, the appearance and positioning of the grave within the cemetery have their own metaphoric significance as domiciles of the dead. Funeral ritual in the researched areas often reflects the importance of family relationships characteristic of north Russian rural communities, especially in Arkhangel'sk province. In the pre-Soviet past most chapels in north Russia did not have their own cemeteries. It was therefore possible, and not unusual, for burials to take place on, or near, family land, at the edge of a vegetable plot, for example, or next to a barn, so that there was a constant visible reminder of the presence of dead kin. Closeness to other members of the immediate family remains a prerequisite for burial sites. Cemeteries, therefore, often contain enclosures with multiple graves where several generations of one family are buried close together. Today, these family plots are most often surrounded with a metal railing or palisade fencing. Inside the enclosure one will expect to find a table and a bench, adding an element of domesticity to the area. It is within this space that the dead are remembered and treated to meals shared with the living. I asked the reason for fencing in gravesites and received the answer, "That is our way. After all, without a fence he's just like an orphan. But if it's fenced then it's his house. The grave looks nicer when it's fenced. It looks cared for and sort of pretty" (EW-A Arkh-Lesh, July 15, 2009). It is now usual to attach a likeness of the deceased—a photograph, ceramic plaque, or engraving—to the cross or other grave marker. This serves to emphasize the physical identity of the once-living person now rehoused under the earth. Remembering the loved one is clearly a question of tangible as well as emotional needs. In 2010, at the cemetery in Leshukon'e, Arkhangel'sk province, I came across a middle-aged woman crouched beside the graves of her parents. Her mother had died the previous year. In tears, she was whispering words of endearment and stroking the cold granite of the grave markers with their ceramic faces. The inference that the dead can hear and see their visitors is reinforced by the custom of knocking upon the grave marker, as one might knock upon the door of a house to inform the householder of one's presence.

We have seen that objects of potential use to the deceased, such as dentures, spectacles, and watches, are sometimes placed in coffins. Other items that they may appreciate can occasionally be seen on graves. Apart from the ubiquitous sweets and scraps of food from memorial meals, of which more in the next chapter on feeding the dead, together with the deceased's plates, cups, and glasses, which are kept at the graveside, I have seen cigarettes, walking sticks, and toys. When a six-month-old twin girl died, her mother kept a comforter hanging for a long time on the grave marker (FA Mez 17-35, July 14, 2007).

Taken together, details such as those given above suggest belief in some sort of domestic continuity for the dead in their new abode, however altered and circumscribed that continued existence may be. Objects placed in or near the deceased's "new living room" are not mere tokens of affection but usually have a practical purpose. They are needed by the dead. Asked by an interviewer if she had left toys on the grave of her dead infant, a woman pointed out that this would have been a pointless gesture: "What use would they be to him? He wasn't a full-term baby. He was just little. He had never played with anything" (FA Mez 17-31, July 13, 2007).

The Funeral Meal and Food during Graveside Remembrance (Pominki)

It is important to understand that chief among the many concerns of the bereaved is the fear that the deceased may suffer from hunger, and to a lesser extent cold, in the world of the dead. Accordingly, offering food to the deceased, overtly or in symbolic ways, is a consistent element of all occasions involving remembrance of the dead, and it is one of the elements that most convincingly illustrates the "material" persona of the deceased. However, as these topics are dealt with in depth in the following chapter, I will restrict myself to some more limited comments here.

The first major opportunity to ensure the dead individual does not go hungry comes at the meal held after the return of the mourners from the cemetery. A place is always set for the deceased with the assumption that he or she is present and requires sustenance. The offering of food continues during the traditional visiting of graves on the ninth and fortieth days after a death. Remembrance on certain dates in the calendar also involves the sharing of food. On the Saturday of Troitsa week, one of the days set aside by the Church for remembering the souls of the faithful departed in general, as well as on the Sunday that follows, the cemeteries are full of large family picnics by the graves (see chapter 5 for discussion of remembrance as part of this country-wide celebration). For the rural population, however, commemorating is by no means limited to these times.

In fact, it is difficult to imagine any ritual act that has a greater hold on the heart and conscience of village people, whether or not they regard themselves as believers, than the remembrance of their deceased parents and forebears. Remembrance of family dead is carried out with great intensity and is one aspect of religious observance that not only survived the advent of communism but may have been intensified by its attempts to destroy family and kinship ties. Note the popular saying, "The living demand praise, the dead remembrance" (Zhivoi trebuet pokhval'by a mertvyi pominok). For ordinary people the importance of food at these times is so great that it might be said to define the notion of commemoration. Sharing food with the dead is the equivalent of "remembering" them. The question, "How do you commemorate the dead?" is almost invariably answered with some reference to eating: "Well, it's whatever you take to the cemetery and then you make a meal at home. . . . You take something for them [the dead]"; "The deceased expects remembrance . . . even if it's only with bread" (FA Lesh 17-50, July 17, 2010).

Here, as in the provision of grave goods, there may be some disagreement between what the villagers regard as necessary elements of their memorial practices and what they may be told by a priest or hear on an Orthodox TV channel. Giving the deceased his or her portion of the meal, for example, is usually frowned upon by village priests, as is the sheer abundance of food and drink, including meat and especially alcohol, at such meals. In the village, where, for those who embrace Orthodoxy, religion is mostly "lived" rather than learned, the abstract notion of comfort for the soul of the dead through prayerful remembrance is transformed into the more prosaic but comprehensible one of providing food.

Interestingly, the Church's present-day ascetic view of the funeral meal is somewhat at odds with common village practice in the nineteenth century, when funeral and memorial food had considerable significance for the local clergy: "The clergy were always invited to the memorial meals after a funeral and on the ninth and fortieth days, since it was considered that the presence of the priest helped the soul in its travels beyond the grave"; "In the Solvychegodsk region of Vologda province, after prayers and remembrance on the graves, a memorial meal was put together by all the parishioners at the priest's house. They brought fish pies, pastries, beer, wine, and other foods. The leftovers from the meal were for the benefit of the clergy"; "At a memorial meal with the clergy in Vladimir province, they made a real effort to provide seventeen different courses so as to have the right to say 'we remembered well and gave the popes good cheer' because here they maintained the belief that 'one pope is the equivalent of ten beggars or *startsy*'" (Bernshtam 2007, 221–22. For discussion of the role of beggars in memorial ritual, see chapter 2). This reference to Vladimir province is particularly interesting. In 2013 in Vozhgora, Arkhangel'sk province, I heard about a young missionary priest who had been in the village a few years previously. Advising abstinence at funerals, he quoted the example of his superior, who had refused to attend a funeral dinner, coincidentally in Vladimir province, because of the prolific gourmandizing of the villagers, who served ten or twelve different dishes as a matter of course. Clearly, in this case, popular custom had not changed, as people clung to what was important to them, while the behavior of the clergy had been reformed. In its practices, institutional religion is just as susceptible to change and variation as is the "lived" religion of ordinary people, and there is room for compromise and accommodation on both sides.

The following question obviously arises—with what, or with whom, do the living share the food they bring on memorial days? Some will say the soul, others the dead person (*pokoinik*). There are many examples of current practice suggesting that food is left for a specific "corporeal" presence, capable of eating, in or close to the grave. A woman interviewed during a visit to the side-by-side graves of her husband and son first knocked loudly on the cross over her husband's grave upon arriving and asked him how he was getting on. Then, turning to her son's grave, she placed some sweets and biscuits on the cross. After that, she brought out some fish and laid it on his grave with the words, "Now, I'm just putting down a little fish. There you are, Pavlik, some more for you." Finally, as she poured a glass of vodka for herself and the group of folklore students accompanying her, she said, "Now let us remember" (FA Lesh 17-59, July 7, 2010).

Censing the Grave

An important element of graveside remembrance is the common practice in the North of encircling the grave with the smoke of burning incense. This too may reinforce the idea of a presence in the grave that is still responsive to physical stimuli.

Censing plays a significant part in Orthodox funeral practice. The body is censed while it lies in the open coffin. Before and during funerals and at requiem *litii* the grave is censed. In strictly "institutional" terms this is an indispensable

Censing a grave in Edoma, Arkhangel'sk province, 20011. (Photo by Elizabeth Warner)

aspect of the Orthodox Church's care for the soul of the deceased. In general, the rising smoke of the incense supposedly reminds the Christian of the need for prayer ("Let my prayer be counted as incense before thee," Psalm 141) and of the presence of the Holy Spirit, while in the funeral context it may also be said to symbolize the path of the soul heavenward.

Censing at funerals and on memorial occasions is a custom long established and rigorously adhered to in many village communities across the North. In answer to questions about it, one person may say it is somehow beneficial to the soul and may accompany it with a prayer for the soul's repose. Another may say it is a tribute to the memory of the deceased or that it will chase demons away. For most people, however, the significance of this activity lies elsewhere: "Well, it's like warming them" (FA Mez 17-6, July 14, 2007).

We saw earlier that concern about the physical well-being of the deceased affected the manner in which they were dressed and that it was feared, above all, that they would suffer from cold. Dreams in which the dead return to complain may be caused by subconscious worries about this happening. On her frequent visits to the cemetery to visit her father's grave, one winter a woman was in the habit of brushing fallen snow from his grave and the gravestone. She soon began to experience a recurring dream in which her father asked her to stop doing this as he was cold: "Cover me up. I'm frozen. I'm cold," he would say. Then she began to dream of the cemetery and noticed that all the graves seemed to be covered with soft, cotton-wool eiderdowns of different colors—red, green, and blue. Only her father's grave was bare. After that she stopped removing the snow from his grave (FA Mez 17-104, July 16, 2008). In another dream a woman saw her dead brother reclining on the couch in his flat in Arkhangel'sk with his head bowed in dejection. In this case the deceased was dissatisfied because his grave had not been censed. His sister went to the cemetery to rectify this because, as she said, "It's as if you're laying a coverlet over the body" (FA Mez 17-75, July 16, 2008). Seemingly poetical references, such as this, to the layer of smoke enveloping the grave nevertheless derive from deeply ingrained beliefs about the suffering of the dead: "We need to warm the feet. His feet, or her feet are frozen. So let's cense the feet" (FA Mez 17-30, July 14, 2007). Typically, in Arkhangel'sk province the surface of the graves is built up with a mound of earth, and it is said that the purpose of this mound too is to keep the dead warm.

Censing the grave is one of those Orthodox traditions that have survived and flourished in their vernacular form. Long ago, the Church accepted that, in cases where no cleric could be present, censing the grave might be carried out by laypeople. The same kind of dispensation also allowed the readings from the Psalter, which took place for the three days in which the deceased lay at home, to be conducted by competent laypersons. Zelenin describes the northern custom in the late nineteenth to early twentieth century of taking a pot of burning coals to the gravesite. The coals, onto which incense had been sprinkled, were then piled on the spade that had been used to dig the grave, and this acted as a makeshift censer (Zelenin 1991, 351).

Today, censing is regularly practiced in many villages by respected, elderly female members of the community. In some villages, the role of the censer has become virtually hereditary, passing from mother to daughter. Although not specifically excluded, men are rarely involved in this activity. Censing begins at the foot of the grave and proceeds in a clockwise direction around it. Unlike the familiar vase-shaped thuribles suspended from four chains symbolizing the Holy Trinity and the Oneness of God, the censers used in village ceremonies are shaped like a small pan with a handle or sometimes like an old-fashioned iron. Many are simply formed from an old tin can pierced with holes in the side. They can be glimpsed in cemeteries and in the vicinity of votive crosses, hanging from a convenient tree or tucked behind a gravestone. Small censers with handles (*katseya*) were used in Russia before the introduction of the larger vessels we see in churches today and are still used by laypeople in communities of the "priestless" (*bespopovtsy*) branch of Old Believers. In the rural context, I think it is fair to say that the spiritual significance of censing is largely absent. It is carried out either because it is the "right" thing to do or because it comforts the dead in their new homes "without the brick-built stove."

THE SOUL: AN ELUSIVE AND CONTRADICTORY SUBSTANCE

So far, there has been little to suggest the existence among the villagers of any strong belief in an immaterial and immortal soul that leaves the body at death and is dispatched for divine judgment. Preparation for death and its aftermath appears to concentrate on the needs of the postmortem body or "body-soul" and its transference of abode from home to cemetery. However, this is not the whole story.

The following was written about the peasants of the Pinega region of Arkhangel'sk province in the second half of the nineteenth century: "The inhabitants believe in the immortality of the soul and have some notion, although not a clear one, of the life to come. But they also believe that the dead, both at home and in the grave, can hear the words that reach them" (Efimenko 1877, 137). This idea, that *both* body and soul may somehow survive death, typifies many aspects of funerary beliefs and practices in north Russian rural communities to the present day.

According to basic Orthodox teaching, after it has left the body, the soul remains in or close to its home for the first two days. On the third day it appears before God and is taken by an angel to see paradise. On the ninth day the soul is again summoned into God's presence and afterward is shown hell. Finally, on the fortieth day, God decides what is to be the individual fate of the soul until the day of the Last Judgment. According to his decision, the soul will enter into a state of bliss or suffering. To use more concrete terms, the soul will receive a place in either heaven or hell (Kuz'menko 1996, 49; *Zakon Bozhii* [*God's Law*] 1998, 674–75). Villagers will often give a much-simplified version of these teachings, suggesting that the soul does indeed leave the body when death occurs but remains in and around its home for the following two or three days. There is widespread belief that a person's soul, after the burial has taken place, can still visit places familiar to it until the fortieth day after death, when it finally abandons the earth and flies up to the heavens. However, the character, substance, and purpose of this soul—where it lives when it is not visiting its former home, how it moves about, where it goes after the fortieth day, and why—all remain obscure. Its relationship to the abandoned and corrupting cadaver also remains extremely ambiguous.

Given the complexity of the theological arguments about the soul, simple catechistic assertions, such as those from *God's Law*, given above, do little to clarify what it actually is: "The soul is a difficult thing to speak (or write) about. First, the word is used so commonly and widely that its true meaning becomes obscured. Second, the soul is largely unknown to each of us, despite its primary importance. So, I will begin by giving its simple meaning: the soul is our life. When we hear the story of Adam's creation, we learn that he is fashioned out of the earth. Then, God breathes into him, 'and he became a living soul'" (Freeman 2019). An understandable inability to define what exactly is meant by soul in the village context too may be detected in the inconsistency and vagueness of terms people use to describe it, even though, as we will see, the idea of a "living soul," however that may be interpreted, is at the heart of people's commonly held beliefs. Alongside *dusha*, one may hear references to *ten'* (shade or ghost) and *dukh* (spirit). A question about the significance of the fortieth day after death elicited this typically hesitant and unclear response: "The fortieth day? It's probably when the person . . . he . . . they arrive there. They are called to God" (FA Mez 17-56, July 21, 2008). The speaker admitted her ignorance and recommended that the questioner get in touch with someone who knew about Orthodoxy. Frequently, the terms "soul" and "deceased" (*pokoinik*) are used interchangeably, as in "The deceased flies down in the shape of a little bird" (FA Bel 17-1, July 22, 1988) or: "Until the fortieth day we're afraid, everyone is afraid. Everyone says the dead people [*pokoiniki*] walk." Later, Aleksei corrected himself and said that it was the soul that walked, that "it was probably an apparition. Devil knows! After all, the person was buried. But what kind of a soul is it? What soul?" (EW-V Vol-Bel, tape 8, July 20, 1997). Sometimes, there is simply a reference to a postmortem encounter with "my neighbor," "my father," "my uncle," and so on.

One common set of descriptive images of the soul presupposes a birdlike or other winged creature. In the shape of a bird it may peck at grain scattered on graves. Birds are frequently mentioned in folk beliefs as go-betweens, traversing the spaces between the worlds of the living and the dead and bringing news of a death by tapping on a window, for example. One woman told how, for a whole year after the death of her father, a black crow kept reappearing (FA Mez 17-53, July 8, 2008). Alternatively, after the fortieth day, the soul may be borne to a resting place in heaven in the arms of those other winged beings, the angels. The idea of a soul capable of flight reflects both the belief of some Christians that the soul must somehow traverse the vastness of celestial space, and the mythologies of the Slavonic peoples, in which the soul may take the form of a bird, butterfly, or moth. Barsov wrote of the peasants of Olonets province in the nineteenth century that when they saw a butterfly, they assumed it was someone's soul (Barsov 1997, 1:13). In funeral laments the deceased is frequently described as a bird—a "little gray dove," perhaps, a "little swan," or a "fork-tailed swallow." The deceased may "grow wings and sprout feathers," but nevertheless, its flight ends in the grave and the damp earth (Efimenkova 1980, 146).[3] The role of bird-souls as a means of transferring food to the dead is discussed in the following chapter on ritual feeding of the dead.

People we interviewed clearly found it difficult to explain what the soul is; however, they were often able to describe what it does and what they themselves do for it during the forty-day period after a death. Descriptions of how the soul behaves and of how the bereaved prepare for its visitations offer insights into the nature of the post-mortem individual. In both Vologda and Arkhangel'sk provinces, relatives of the deceased depicted the soul as sharing the needs and emotions of the living and as more likely to walk than fly. Gates were intentionally left unlocked or open so that the soul could come and go. "You shouldn't close your gates until the fortieth day because the soul walks. It walks until the fortieth day and then it rises up to heaven. Then you can close the gates" (FA Lesh 17-29, July 7, 2009). Leaving the gates open suggests a conception of the soul as a being that is somehow subject to the normal rules governing material bodies with feet. Most importantly, for the duration of the forty days, the soul must have access to food and drink. One woman interviewed would leave out a cup of tea, together with some pies or other food (FA Vash 17-109, July 14, 1998). Another explained that food and drink were always provided so that the returning soul would know that his family was pleased to see him (EW-V Vol-Bel, tape 2, July 10, 1999).

Back home after its post-death wanderings, the soul may also expect to wash. Heating the bathhouse for the weary traveler is a normal act of hospitality in

Russian villages, even today. After a death, therefore, it is usual to hang a towel beside the deceased's bed or in the corner where the icons hang. There it will remain for forty days, after which it will be taken to the cemetery and tied to the cross or the fence surrounding the gravesite. Alternatively, it may be buried near the grave (FA Mez 17-27, July 19, 2007). This curtailment of washing facilities for the soul (or its alter ego the pokoinik) is one of many reminders that after forty days its residence among the living is no longer expected and may be accompanied by an explicit message to the deceased at the cemetery: "[I would say] 'Here you are, Mama,' if it was for my mother. 'Have a wash and dry yourself. Don't come to me. I'll come and visit you'" (FA Mez 17-5, July 18, 2007).

In Vologda province, according to tradition, the bathhouse is heated so that the soul may wash. This can happen on the ninth day or the fortieth day after a death and also on other remembrance days such as the anniversary of the death. The soul, it is believed, will enter the bathhouse after midnight, when no other member of the family will be there. Clean clothes are left out in addition to hot water and items for personal use such as a washcloth and basin (EW-V Vol-Bel, tape 8, July 20, 1997).

In addition to physical sensations, such as hunger and thirst, the returning soul also appears capable of feeling emotions. Excessive expressions of grief by a widow should therefore be avoided in case the dead husband, or his soul, is so moved by her tears that he is unable to stay away. Conversely, the soul may experience pleasure. The soul of a dead husband who kept knocking on the door of his house was eventually soothed by the sound of accordion music, which he had particularly enjoyed when alive. His widow knew that after he had heard it he would happily depart and not come back again (EW-V Vol-Bel, tape 4, July 11, 1999). In fact, the return home of a soul often seems to be motivated by a strong emotion, either negative or positive. The dead may feel antipathy toward someone left behind and a desire for revenge. A mother-in-law, for example, kept returning home to annoy her daughter-in-law. The daughter-in-law's friend explained to us that their relationship had never been amicable. Every night after midnight the mother-in-law would enter the house and cause a noisy disturbance. To discourage her, the younger woman would attach sprigs of aspen above the lintel of the door, over the porch and the steps leading up into the living quarters (EW-V Vol-Bel, tape 5, July 12, 1997). The bonds of love, on the other hand, especially those between a mother and her children, may equally draw the deceased back home. The following tale provides a typical example of just such an event. The narrator claimed that this was a true story. The incident supposedly took place one cold, clear night when she and her husband were on their way home. A woman stopped them on the road. She was in some distress and wearing only a dress and shoes, in spite of the hard

In addition to a rusting metal wreath, this grave marker bears the remains of the deceased's towel. Note the spoon carefully placed on the grave mound. Smolenets, Arkhangel'sk province, 2010. (Photo by Elizabeth Warner)

frost. She asked for a lift because she was going to a fortieth day remembrance supper being held nearby. The storyteller's husband told her to get in the cart. The woman explained how to get to the village and as they rode up pointed to the first house as her intended destination. She got out and they lost sight of her. As it was now very late, the two travelers decided to ask if they could spend the night at the house, where a number of people had gathered for a commemoration meal. The storyteller explained to their hosts that she was very tired and didn't want to attend the meal in honor of the deceased but would just climb up on the stove to get warm.[4] As she lay there she glimpsed a woman, who sat down by the threshold and began to rock a cradle in which a baby lay. As she rocked she wept. "Was it the woman who stopped them on the road," the narrator wondered. A little boy kept running about near the cradle. From time to time someone would come to fetch him away but he always returned to the same spot. Eventually, the meal was over, the soul of the deceased person had finally been escorted from the house, and the guests had begun to disperse. The narrator climbed down from the stove and accepted a cup of tea. At this point, she informed the master of the house what she had just seen. "Why didn't you tell me?" he asked. "How I wanted to glimpse her again." It turned out that his daughter had died in childbirth. This was the woman who had asked for a lift. She was hurrying to her own fortieth-day memorial supper in order to bid farewell to her children (EW-V Vol-Vash, tape 1, July 12, 2001).

Frequently, the return home of the soul-pokoinik is caused by dissatisfaction with some aspect of funeral rituals or by resentment when its pre-death wishes have been flouted. For example, one woman described a frightening dream or hallucination in which her dead husband appeared before her in the bathhouse. He was clearly angry that she had not made provisions for him to wash on the fortieth day. He stood before her completely naked, with clouds of steam billowing around him. The widow felt his hand on her shoulder and was horrified by the look he gave her. His eyes were dull and glazed: "'Oh God,' I thought. 'But he's dead!'" Then the apparition disappeared (EW-V Vol-Bel, tape 8, July 20, 1997). The dead may object to being buried in the wrong clothing or shoes or (even worse) without footwear. An elderly mother, for example, appeared in a dream to her daughter, who had dressed her in some light-weight slippers instead of the soft, warm, fur-lined boots she had requested (EW-V Vol-Bel, tape 2, July 10, 1999). It is usual, when this occurs, to obey the wishes of the deceased, finding the desired footwear and burying it in, or close by, the grave.

We saw earlier that the manner of preparing the body for burial implies that it will retain some degree of sensory awareness. The same is also true, as we have just seen, of the visiting soul during the forty-day period. It is also the case that its presence in the home is perceived through the senses, although that presence may be limited and elusive. The close proximity of the soul is often detected through sound. Strange noises at night (e.g., footsteps or knocks on doors or windows), particularly in liminal regions of the homestead outside the living quarters of the family, such as a loft or cellar, may all be interpreted as sounds made by the returning soul.[5] News of a death may also be preceded by unexplained bangs and crashes. Sometimes the dead may touch someone they have been close to. As a child, Aleksandra had twice been visited by the "shade" of the collective farm foreman. He did not speak to her but stroked her head and kissed her cheek. She assumed he had come to bid her farewell and she stressed that she had not been dreaming but was definitely awake (EW-V Vol-Bel, tape 5, July 12, 1997).

From the above, it is clear that the presence of the soul of the departed may be detected in dreams or even in reality, as the speaker will often insist. The remarks of one woman who insisted that she had twice seen her dead sister-in-law are particularly revealing in this respect since they illustrate the ambivalence at the heart of what are often perceived as genuine encounters. Instances in which speakers claim to have seen, rather than heard, a returning soul are fairly uncommon, but in the case of Nadezhda, she explained that the "sighting" had occurred in broad daylight and that she had seen her sister-in-law very clearly. However, she later said she had caught this glimpse "out of the corner of my eye" and that this had taken place in the *povet'*, the unheated storage space above the animal quarters—that is, in an area of the house not quite assimilated into the living quarters (FA Mez 17-56, July 21, 2008). Frequently, the dead are seen only by the "inner" eye and in dreams or during sleep—in other words, in a borderline state in which the worlds of the living and the dead may converge. Sight, after all, is the sense by which we most often determine reality: "Seeing is believing!" However, although the soul is not always clearly visible itself, it may leave some visible traces of its presence. In Vologda province a woman related what her daughter had once experienced after the death of her father. It was after midnight on the fortieth day and the bathhouse was being prepared for him. The daughter had just left the house, carrying a bucket of water. She heard the door squeak and the sound of footsteps crunching over the snow. She understood that it was her dead father following behind her, and she called out to him, asking him to stay a while and sit with the family. When she turned around, all she could see was snow scattering. The hand gestures of the speaker indicated departing footsteps (EW-V Vol-Bel, tape 8, July 20, 1997). In this case the presence of the soul was detected by both auditory and visual signals.

Whatever the reasons for the souls' visits to their former homes or the manner of their appearance, and however much they are loved and missed, they are made to understand that these visits must cease upon the passage of forty days. In parts of Arkhangel'sk province, for example, the deceased's plate of food, which remains on the table throughout the memorial meal held on the fortieth day, is often taken to the cemetery and left upon the grave. This may be done on the morning after the fortieth day. In Vologda province at midnight on the fortieth day, the living may give the soul a "send-off" (*provodyat*). Relatives accompany him or her onto the porch of the house, carrying a tray with food and a glass of *kisel'* (see chapter 2 for discussion of this ritual dessert). Or they may accompany the soul as far as the nearest crossroads, carrying its plate of food with them. Any drink is then poured away and the food thrown on the ground to be eaten later by scavenging animals (EW-V Vol-Bel, tape 2, July 10, 1999).

The deceased, or the soul, depending on the term used by individuals, is expected to depart for good at this point. The belief of some that the soul will go to heaven does not seem to contradict the existence of the more physical post-mortem entity that appears to reside in the cemetery. This dualism was clearly expressed in the explanations of one of our interlocutors in particular, a post-Soviet convert to Orthodoxy. Tamara's comments about the supernatural and about funeral ritual were typical of the eclectic intermingling of Orthodox elements, canonical and noncanonical, with other mystical notions characterizing the beliefs of the rural population. What she believed about the fate of the soul after the fortieth day was particularly interesting. She described how the deceased was given a special permit (*prokhodnaya bumaga*), an oblique reference to the prayer for remission of sins placed in the deceased's hand by the priest at the end of an Orthodox funeral service, and how earth, also purchased from the priest, was scattered in the shape of a cross over the body before burial. This was done, according to Tamara, as a way of "requesting the Lord God's acceptance of the person into earthly life [*v zemnuyu zhizn'*]." This was followed by the statement that "the soul flies away to heaven but the body lies down in the earth." As she expressed it, "The Lord God's permission is asked for the body to be accepted there." Of the burial itself, she commented, "We buy the earth from the Lord God. He is commander of the earth too" (EW-V Vol-Bel, tape 2, July 10, 1999). Both for the Russian peasant in the past and the present-day villager, committal of the body to the earth had and still has considerable significance because of its association with the idea of resurrection or rebirth and renewal. According to Christian teachings, man was fashioned by God from earth into which He breathed the breath of life (Genesis 2:7) and returns to earth after death to await resurrection at the Day of Judgment and the reuniting of body with soul. Alongside this, we must also take into account the image of mother-moist-earth in Russian folklore and agricultural ritual, the fertile mother who gives food to sustain life but also generously receives the dead. "How would we have a burial service here? It's only recently that people have become believers. We don't know anything about the cross or fasting. It doesn't matter whether we have a burial service or not. The main thing is to get into the earth. I keep saying, 'All right, let's do it—earth to earth. Just let us get into the earth'" (FA Mez 17-95, July 17, 2008). The extreme importance of burial in earth may be gauged by the fact that it sometimes takes place even when there is no body to bury. When a man drowned, for example, and his body was not recovered, his family made a box into which they put his suit and a tie and "all that was committed to mother-earth" (FA Mez 17-89, July 17, 2008).

Communication between the Living and the Soul, or the Living Dead, in the Afterlife

There seems little doubt that both those who are soon to die and those who will be left behind expect some form of mutual contact to continue after the death. The precise nature of that contact, however, will depend on who initiates it, the bereaved or the deceased, and in either case will be subject to strict control. The dead may also communicate among themselves.

After the fortieth day, the status of the deceased changes, as does their relationship with the living. In the first place, their new domicile is permanently in the cemetery, a border zone between the world of everyday life and the other world of the afterlife, one of the few locations where the paths of the living and the dead may legitimately intersect. Here, the dead act as hosts to their living visitors at their own convenience. The living go there to communicate with their loved ones, both verbally and through actions such as feeding and censing, but they accept the restrictions imposed both by the liminal nature of the venue and by sensitivity to the sad predicament of their hosts. This gives rise to numerous interdictions or restraints on visiting. Thus, cemeteries tend to be avoided after midday and are particularly shunned after sunset. Since the dead are thought to be sensitive, both physically and emotionally, precautions are taken to avoid interrupting their rest and presumed occupations: "Usually we go about ten o'clock . . . because people say you should not disturb the dead. Let them lie" (FA Lesh 17-3, July 9, 2009). Others will stay away from the cemetery on the day after the burial because "everyone says you must leave him in peace" (FA Vash 17-7, July 14, 2000). The cemetery should be visited before lunchtime because, as one interviewee put it, after lunch "they are already busy and we don't disturb them" (FA Mez 17-98, July 10, 2008). Others made statements such as the following: "Don't wake the dead up. . . . Don't wake them. You shouldn't go [to the cemetery] before ten o'clock" (FA Mez 17-89, July 17, 2008); "Some will say that before twelve o'clock the dead walk about but after that they are most likely asleep" (FA Mez 17-24, July 21, 2007).

Verbal communication with the dead, both before and after burial, may be achieved through direct spoken address, the medium of the formal lament (*prichitanie/ prichet'/plach*), or dreams.

As we have seen, in many villages of Arkhangel'sk province grieving visitors to a grave will announce their presence by knocking on the gravestone and greeting the deceased. Knocking to arouse the dead is understood in a way that goes beyond the purely symbolic gesture: "When we get there we always knock. That's the custom here. It's so they can hear. We go up and knock" (FA Lesh 17-32, July 7, 2010). It is assumed that the visitor's message—whether an expression of grief, an invitation to eat, an inquiry about their health, a request, or a complaint—will be heard and understood. Indeed, since they are apparently free to roam, albeit down paths untrodden by the living, the dead may be asked to pass on information, or even objects, to inhabitants of the other world with whom the living cannot come in direct contact. At a village funeral in Azopol'e one of the mourners, whose brother had died in Hungary many years before, described how she had approached the open coffin and asked the deceased to convey greetings from herself and her sister to their dead relative wherever he might meet him during his wanderings—whether "in a foreign land, here in the village, on the open road, or at some crossing of the ways" (FA Mez 17-87, July 15, 2008). Similarly, after the death of her husband, a widow in Roksama (Vologda province) was visited by the daughter of a friend of his who had died two months previously. The daughter explained that her own dead father had appeared in a dream and asked her to send him ten rubles. She had come to ask permission to place the money in the coffin of his friend. The widow agreed (EW-V Vol-Vash, tape 6, July 18, 2001).

As the above example shows, the no-mans-land of dreams permits some limited intercourse between the bereaved and those they mourn. The dead are most likely to contact the living in dreams during the forty-day period after death or while the bereaved are still in a state of mourning. The living, on the other hand, may find themselves transported to the world of the dead through dreams. (This subject is addressed in more detail in chapter 2.)

The dead may also be contacted through the more formal and ritualized medium of lamenting, a tradition that was widespread all over north Russia well within living memory. Elderly women may still be able to perform fragments of laments, but it is now quite rare to hear spontaneous lamenting in its true context, as an integral part of funeral ritual performed beside the coffin or in the graveyard. In laments, as elsewhere in funeral and memorial ritual, although the deceased are named, along with their precise relationship to the lamenter, there is less clarity about the form they now inhabit after the transformative process of dying. Notions of material and immaterial bodies may coexist in one and the same lament. This may be seen, for example, in a memorial lament from the Belozersk region of Vologda province in which the lamenter's dead mother demonstrates her lack of physical substance by not eating the delicious food of the living placed in front of her. The lamenter has noticed that she "does not pick up the shining spoons." Yet when the mother is invited to enter the bathhouse, her daughter clearly imagines a material body in a post-death state of decay, marked by its lengthy sojourn underground: "During these past six weeks your body has become black and your brightly colored clothing stained" (Razova 1994, 177–78). The post-death being is both present and absent, material and immaterial, hungry but incapable of eating. Chapter 3, "The Lament: A Language for Communicating with the Dead," provides an in-depth exploration of the personal experiences of speaking to the dead among different generations of village women in the North.

There can be little doubt that, among the individuals whose practices and notions have been the subject of this research, belief in the continuation of some form of existence for some aspect of the individual after death is undeniable. However, the essence of the envisaged postmortem being is difficult to establish and is often contradictory.

That the soul, or what remains of the deceased apart from the corpse, is imagined largely in material terms seems incontrovertible. While the body of the deceased disintegrates in the ground, a separate "being" sharing his or her features and needs, albeit in an altered way, is formed and continues to exist and live on as long as succeeding generations continue to commemorate it. The deceased in effect becomes a "living" ancestor. This is a concept that deserves some comment as it appears to be at odds with generally accepted definitions of the soul. It seems to have little in common, for example, with ideas about the soul held by philosophers since the time of Plato and Aristotle. It does not seem to be that essence that gives a body life and makes it more than just a physical shell. Neither is it "consciousness," "the mind," or "the brain," to cite the usual terms that appear in debates about the soul today (see, e.g., Goetz and Taliaferro 2011, 152–81).

If we regard this phenomenon from the standpoint of learned religion, the teachings of all the Christian faiths, then we can see that it does not fit well with the statements of Orthodox churchmen, according to whom, for example, God "breathes" life into human beings. In other words, the soul is God's very "breath," a substance quite independent of the body and of a purely spiritual and heavenly nature. According to Christian teachings, the soul is completely immaterial, invisible, and without shape or form. In the soul's new life, which continues after death but is conceptualized as life that takes place beyond the grave (*zagrobnaya zhizn'*) and certainly not in it or near it, the soul will not be completely cut off from contact with those left behind. But, again, this will be a spiritual and not a physical closeness, supported by the prayers and acts of remembrance by loved ones (*Zakon Bozhii* 1998, 408–504). Orthodox Christians also believe in the resurrection of the body and the reuniting of body with the soul at the Second Coming of Christ, but this will be a transformed and heavenly body without physical attributes or desires (*Zakon Bozhii* 1998, 81–90, 684–85). Village mortuary and memorial practice, on the other hand, suggests belief in a soul that is to some extent material and has requirements—for nourishment, clothing, warmth, and interaction with family members—similar to those of the living.

The dichotomy between what Orthodox theology teaches about the soul and the perceptions of ordinary people seems self-evident. In raising it I do not intend to suggest that one form of belief (institutional Orthodoxy) should take precedence over the other or has greater validity; rather, the opposite in fact, since the villagers' stratagems for coping with death and the ways in which they look after their dead and remember them provide the firm foundation upon which life itself is grounded.

With regard to funeral and memorial practice, what happens today in the villages, particularly in the remote North, is the product of many different factors over a long period of time.

Undoubtedly, the Soviet period had a profound effect on the beliefs and practices of ordinary people. Natalie Kononenko, writing of the religious revival in post-Soviet Ukraine, has noted a similar disconnect between canonical and folk Orthodoxy in the villages, where even the priests, many of whom were ordained only recently, were not always entirely sure of the appropriateness of their own views. She also notes the importance of the "tangible" in village funeral ritual and the "very tactile presentation of the afterlife" (Kononenko 2006, 50, 62, 65).

After the revolution churches were destroyed, priests were removed, and their liturgies and sermons were replaced by atheistic and materialist propaganda. Schools were secularized (see Fitzpatrick 1994, 33–37, 204–14 for details of the attack on religion in the villages). Although the extent of religious suppression varied, both across the country and at different times, religious instruction, however good or bad, became a thing of the past, and many communities were left without a priest and a church for the conduct of Christian burial services. This led to the widespread practice, for example, of burial services in absentia (*zaochnoe otpevanie*) (Sokolova 2011, 193–94). The priest of the nearest church would be asked to perform the ceremony without the corpse and to provide a family representative with the funeral attributes regarded as essential by the people—consecrated earth to scatter on the coffin, the paper wreath with its religious symbols for the deceased's forehead, and the prayer of absolution, which was regarded as a form of passport into the afterlife.

The Soviet authorities tended to interfere less in the imbedded structure and what they regarded as the backward practices of rural funerals, particularly in the area of intimate, domestic customs, preferring instead to target the rituals of the workers in urban areas. Nevertheless, efforts were made to exclude any religious content from funerals. "Mystical ideas about the afterlife, about the immortality of the soul and the sinfulness of man" were considered harmful to the physical, mental, and moral health of the people (Nagirnyak et al. 1970, 4). Detailed schemas for the conduct and attributes of Soviet-style funerals and other rituals and festivals produced in the 1960s and 1970s have left a number of traces. The custom of displaying the deceased's work and military medals on a cushion in the coffin, for example, clearly dates to this time. Nagirnyak writes of them as an essential element of the ideal Soviet-style funeral: "Each medal is pinned onto a separate black or red velvet cushion and is carried by one person. ... The people carrying the medals walk in procession behind those carrying the wreaths. ... The honor of carrying the medals is accorded to the most worthy individuals" (Nagirnyak 1970, 231).

However, the main legacy of Soviet interference in the villages was probably to further undermine the already imperfectly understood and variously interpreted canonical Orthodox teachings on such matters of faith and practice as the nature of the soul and the preparation for its departure from this world, while underestimating the tenacity of other ritual imperatives that flourished alongside them in the domestic arena.[6]

Up until the early part of the twentieth century, the peasants of the North, as elsewhere in Russia, mostly thought of themselves as devout Christians, however limited their understanding of Church doctrine. If they had access to a church and a priest, which was not always the case, their funerals were conducted in accordance with Orthodox rite. Preparation for death included confession and the receiving of communion. Prayers were said for the repose of the soul, and narratives about the afterlife echoed Christian teachings about heaven and hell, punishments and rewards. This, however, reflects "ideal" conditions, which by no means prevailed everywhere.

Gregory Freeze has drawn attention to the history, status, and indeed plight of the parish clergy in Russia (see, e.g., Freeze 1983). His translation and publication of Belliustin's *Memoir of a Nineteenth-Century Parish Priest* (Belliustin 1985) showed only too clearly that ill-educated rural clergy, of low social standing and with no financial support, apart from what they could extort from the peasants, often failed to instruct their illiterate parishioners in the most basic core beliefs of their Orthodox faith. Belliustin was far from alone as a representative of the Church in voicing his concerns. The nineteenth-century *Handbook for Village Priests* (*Rukovodstvo dlya sel'skikh pastyrei*) was full of similar complaints in the latter half of the nineteenth century: "The majority of our simple folk either have no understanding of many tenets of the Christian faith or understand them falsely and wrongly" Gr——skii 1860, 133).

The parish register of Verkhneimbatskoe, a village on the River Enisei in the Krasnoyarsk region of Siberia, records the arrival on March 4, 1914, of Father Nikolai Kostik. He was as shocked as Belliustin that the peasants could not even recite the Lord's prayer and "knew nothing of the life of our Savior, Christ." What is more interesting, however, from our point of view, is that the peasants clearly resented his intrusion into their lives and were ready to defend their own viewpoint: "We are Orthodox folk and not some sort of Mohammedans. We know we should go to confession but there is never any time. So don't pester us, priest. You have been appointed so you can pray in our place" (State Archive UNKVD of the Krasnoyarsk Region n.d.). A priest I interviewed in 2003 in Vologda province said something very similar about people's reluctance to engage with the Church as individuals: "In the village there is often one woman regarded by everyone as the 'church granny' (*tserkovnaya babushka*). When she goes to church people give her money to buy candles for them. She believes for everyone. People say 'I don't go to church, but she goes. She always lights a candle for me.' We are performing Orthodox ritual for one person. She does everything for everyone" (EW-V Vol-Bel, tape 3, July 12, 2003). We may agree with Christine Worobec that "faith cannot be reduced to the reading of the Creed and a few prayers and the recitation of the Ten Commandments" (Worobec 2006, 15), but the rural clergy may think differently. The clash here may not be between an "elite" and a "folk" position but rather between two systems of believing, one based on obeying rules and the other based on existential priorities.

In fact, there have always been blurred lines between the Orthodox practices of the clergy and the laity, regardless of what theologians have prescribed. Villagers, as we saw above, have not always been keen to have a priest constantly looking over their shoulders. Across the vast territories of north Russia, where priests were few and far between, dispensation was given for the performance of certain occasional religious services, including funerals and memorial rites, without the presence of clergy, and sometimes the priest was even encouraged to stay away with the gift of "a ram and a *shtof* of vodka" (Bernshtam 2007, 222).

For centuries there was, in any case, a certain amount of cross-fertilization between the ideas of peasants and priests. They were not as separate as some, perhaps, have become today, although it is worth pointing out that the village priests we have met with during our research are not part of an aloof and intellectual elite: they typically live next-door to and in similar conditions to the villagers. In her book about confession in fourteenth to nineteenth-century Russia, based on manuscript penitentials, records of breaches of Orthodox belief, and practice extracted through confession, M. V. Korogodina (2006) provides a valuable source of information on medieval Orthodoxy in the lay population and points out how difficult it was to separate institutional religion from the religion practiced by ordinary people. The people influenced the priests and vice versa: "Since the confessors were themselves carriers of folk beliefs they exerted a latent influence on the formation of concepts, compelling them to change gradually into greater conformity with Christian standards" (Korogodina 2006, 10).

Among the villagers whose opinions we have sought in our research, those who identify strongly with Orthodoxy may offer prayers for the repose of the soul as a spiritual entity, but the desire for a more tangible link with family and kin, here on earth, and a means of achieving that through funeral and memorial ritual, seems to be the dominant concern of all, regardless of their adherence to the teachings of Orthodoxy.

From its earliest stages, the funeral ritual concentrates attention on the body of the deceased. Taken together, many of the commonly observed customs and practices create the unavoidable impression that the body underground, however changed it might be, has not entirely relinquished its grip on life. Providing warm clothes and footwear, making windows in the coffin, censing the grave and leaving food on it, refusing to scatter grain on the grave mound in case it falls into the deceased's eyes, knocking on the grave marker, speaking to the deceased or appealing to them in laments—all reinforce this idea. The soul, therefore, as described in the present research, seems to have two possible forms that are not mutually exclusive. One is that of a postmortem being buried below the earth. At one level of consciousness people understand that in reality the food left out for the dead is consumed by dogs and the vodka by the local drunks. Yet at another, the level of ritual consciousness, there is uncertainty. Asked directly "What do you think? Are they completely dead or not quite?" Galina was clearly at a loss. "I don't really know. I can't say. But it's hardly likely. I think the bones rot" (FA Mez 17-98, July 10, 2008).[7]

Since the appearance above ground of a reincarnated corpse is unthinkable, the deceased acquires a shadowy alter ego that mirrors the body it has left, sharing the material requirements, sensations, and emotions of its partner while remaining essentially immaterial itself. It is capable of movement and of interaction with the living both through the medium of dreams and through what we might dismiss as hallucinations but which are viewed as genuine encounters with loved ones by those who experience them in their life-world.

CHAPTER 2

Ritual Feeding and the Cult of Ancestors

ELIZABETH WARNER

I followed a small group of relatives and friends of a dead man to his grave in the cemetery at the edge of the village and watched as his remembrance ceremony unfolded. Food was removed from a shopping bag and distributed on top of the grave, with a separate dish for the dead man. A lit candle was propped on the dish. Using a small skillet, the widow censed the grave with burning embers. A man laid some sweets and biscuits on the cross at the next grave over, where his mother was buried. I took my turn to enter the enclosure and stood next to the widow, facing the grave with bowed head as I had seen the others do. I ate the proffered piece of pastry and drank the small glass of vodka. As I turned to leave, I heard one of the women leaning on the enclosure fence outside whisper "She drank the lot!" Was this considered *mauvais ton* for a woman? Or had I unwittingly indulged the appetite of the deceased? (EW field notes, Arkh-Lesh, July 7, 2010). The belief that the deceased can receive nourishment through the act of consumption by others is one of the conundrums of village funeral ritual.

This chapter, dedicated to the different ways in which the dead receive sustenance, was inspired by fieldwork I conducted in 2013 in three villages in particular, Vozhgora, Rodoma, and Pustynya, in the Leshukon'e region of Arkhangel'sk province.

In north Russia today the cult of ancestors (*roditeli*) plays a very significant role in village life. It ensures the continuity of family and kinship values and traditions. It acts as a cohesive element in rural communities since funerals are not only private but public occasions, often attended by practically the whole village and conducted to a significant extent by helpers outside the immediate family of the deceased, from the coffin-maker to the women (and sometimes men) who wash and dress the body to the gravediggers and the neighbors who contribute to funeral expenses. It is also the case that, through certain historical and social circumstances, death and the dead are a more familiar and more physically evident phenomenon of everyday life and a more frequent, visible and tangible subject of personal concern than is often the case today in Western societies. Two factors in particular have surely contributed to the pragmatics of death and disposal in the village context.

The first is the degree to which sudden and often violent death is a fact of life in this setting. During my interviews an all-too-common leitmotif of individual biographies has been the deaths of neighbors and loved ones: premature deaths of husbands, the drowning of small children and men out fishing on the treacherous Mezen' river, incidents in which hunters were savaged by bears, and the suicides of young men. The number of elderly women who have buried both a husband and a son or son-in-law strikes one as being disproportionately high. This unusual familiarity with death is endemic and borne out by statistical evidence. Basing his views on statistics from the nineteenth and beginning of the twentieth century, D. A. Komarov suggests that the mortality rate in Russia as a whole during that period was considerably higher than in Western Europe, that it was, indeed, "catastrophically high" (Komarov 2008, 27). Life expectancy among men, especially, has remained extremely low in Russia in the twentieth and twenty-first centuries, although statistics vary. For example, the United Nations list of countries by average life expectancy at birth for the period 2010–15 cites a life expectancy of 64.2 years for Russia (United Nations 2015, 1:190).

The high death rate particularly affects men of working age, and accidents, poisoning, physical injuries, and other unnatural causes are the second most frequent reason for premature death according to the Arkhangel'sk regional Ministry of Health ("Kontseptsiya razvitiya zdravookhraneniya Arkhangel'skoi oblasti do 2020 g." n.d.).

Given the restricted living quarters of the average rural household today, as in the past, the custom of keeping the body of the deceased at home in full view in an open coffin and in very close proximity to the living until the burial has also played its part in the creation of a ritualized framework of coping strategies, ensuring that the physical rather than the spiritual nature of the postmortem being remains at the forefront of the imagination.

One of the most striking manifestations of this awareness of the "physicality" of death is the ritual of feeding the dead. This takes place in a number of locations at different times and is accomplished in a variety of ways. I will comment on the following aspects of feeding: feeding in the period preceding and on the day of the funeral, feeding during the forty days following the death and on special memorial occasions, and feeding in visions of the other world. I will also address the question of feeding the dead indirectly—for example, by using a designated substitute who feeds the dead on behalf of the bereaved or, conversely, by feeding the dead's representatives, such as birds and beggars. Feeding may also be carried out transcendentally, when sustenance is provided merely by thinking about it.

FEEDING IN THE PERIOD PRECEDING AND ON THE DAY OF THE FUNERAL

The issue of nourishing the deceased arises as soon as he or she has been arranged in the coffin although the manner of nourishing has evolved over time and differs from village to village. As we saw from Barsov's comment about the flask of vodka found in a coffin (see chapter 1), in the nineteenth century food was routinely placed together with the corpse and buried with it (Barsov 1997, 1:248). This practice continued into the twentieth century, in some cases as late as the 1970s and 1980s. In some villages of Vologda province, for example, the deceased were still at that time provided with pastries (*shanezhki*), sweets, and grain (Efimenkova 1980, 135). During fieldwork in the Tot'ma region of Vologda province in 1987, I. A. Kremleva recorded the custom of placing a piece of black bread in the coffin "so that the deceased would always be replete" (Kremleva 2001, 671), although whether or not the custom was still extant is unclear. A similar tradition could be observed in Arkhangel'sk province. In the village of Khotenovo in the Kargopol' region, according to material recorded in 1989, some bread and salt, the traditional symbols of hospitality, were positioned under the right armpit of the corpse, along with this injunction addressed to the deceased: "Drink, eat, and don't come scaring us" (Cherepanova 1996, 20). In more recent times offering the deceased food overtly in this way has been superseded by more subtle symbolic acts. In the village of Byche in the Mezen' region of Arkhangel'sk province, for example, a bowl of the traditional funeral dish *kut'ya*, made with rice and raisins, or even a plate of fish, or sweets and biscuits, would be displayed on a piece of plywood laid across the dead person's feet. The idea was that when the mourners approached to bid farewell they could take a morsel of this food as if sharing a snack with the deceased, although in actual fact people rarely did so. When the body was removed for burial the food would be packed away in a basket and taken to the cemetery. By 2008, when this information was recorded, the practice had been more or less abandoned (FA Mez 17-61, July 20, 2008; FA Mez 17-64, July 13, 2008): "We don't need that. In the first place, when everyone is weeping and going backward and forward it could get knocked over and then you've got fish in the coffin and all" (FA Mez 17-61, July 20, 2008). In other villages, however, practices of this nature can still be found. In Rodoma a small portion of food is arranged on a table alongside the coffin. A photograph of a recent funeral in Rodoma in the album of an elderly woman I visited in July 2013 showed a cup of tea with a few biscuits and a plate with a slice of bread on a table close to the dead woman's head. In Vozhgora, on the other hand, a table is often laid in the room where the coffin lies, not more than a couple of feet away, so that guests may eat in the presence of the corpse before the cortège sets off for the cemetery. In theory food is provided for the soul of the deceased, which is believed to remain close to the body during the few days between death and burial.

In general, proximity and/or contact, both emotional and physical, between the living and the dead is maintained while the body remains at home. Although the traditional Orthodox reading of psalms for three days is now rare, except where the Church has been able to restore its links with the more devout elements of the rural community, relatives and friends still spend that time sitting, and indeed often sleeping beside the coffin. As they take their leave of the deceased people speak to them, placing a kiss on the forehead or mouth or touching a hand. They may even ask the dead to deliver a message to the other world by placing a pen and notebook in the coffin so that relatives may write a note. They also place money in the coffin, usually beside the deceased's feet. This is to help pay for the funeral expenses, the greater part of which goes for food. The offering of money, which is removed before the coffin is sealed, appears to be a relatively recent innovation. Previously, it was customary simply to arrive with food such as tea, biscuits, and a bottle of alcohol (EW-A Arkh-Lesh, July 15, 2013). In the present day poorer people still bring food and are not expected to make a monetary contribution. In Vozhgora the explanation given for placing money inside the coffin introduced a metaphysical dimension to the whole notion of feeding. The money is regarded as a form of subliminal payment for the edible treats (*gostintsy*) the dead person must hand over to previously deceased relatives upon reaching the other side: "You are, as it were, sending a parcel (*posylochka*) to your own folk, your relatives" (EW-A Arkh-Lesh, July 19, 2013). In Vozhgora, no one puts money into the coffin of a drunkard because they say he will be denied entry to paradise and won't be able to pass it on. Since the visit of Orthodox missionaries from Moscow to Vozhgora around the year 2000 many of the local people seem to believe that alcoholics (together with suicides, drug addicts, smokers, and others who lead a so-called immoral way of life) should be treated as unrepentant and therefore irredeemable sinners. This suggests there may still be extreme elements within the Orthodox Church that consider denial of Christian burial to such people an appropriate punishment, although officially the Church allows burial even of those who have knowingly "drunk themselves to death," an act of self-harm not unlike suicide. This in turn calls to mind a belief, still extant among the Russian peasantry in the early part of the twentieth century, that inhumation, particularly in the hallowed ground of a cemetery, of those who drank to excess was an insult to the earth and likely to cause various catastrophes, including droughts and other extreme weather conditions, and should therefore be avoided (Warner 2011b, 156). In addition to having a bite to eat before the funeral, it is usual in many villages of the North to have a communal picnic at the graveside after the burial. Although the mourners may seat themselves around the small table usually found in the fenced-in burial enclosure, it is also perfectly acceptable to spread the meal upon the grave mound. In any case a portion of food is set aside at this time for the deceased. Video footage shot by colleagues from the University of St. Petersburg at a funeral in Pustynya, Leshukon'e region (DV 13 Arch-Lesh 230, July 17, 2013), shows the reluctance of the mourners at this point in the ritual to sever the bond with their dead loved one. Mourners stand close to the open coffin, and some kiss the deceased's forehead and touch either the sheet covering the body or the side of the coffin. When the lid has been fixed and the coffin lowered, the grave is filled in while some of the mourners scatter into the pit earth they have picked up with bare hands. Earth is gradually piled up to form a shapeless mound over the grave. A piece of polythene sheeting is spread directly on top of the raw earth mound, and onto this are placed plates of food containing salami, cucumber, sweets, and biscuits. A small glass of vodka and a slice of bread on a saucer for the deceased are positioned at the foot end of the grave while two additional vodka glasses, a tumbler into which a soft drink is poured, and a cup occupy the opposite end. These are to be shared by the mourners, who take their food and

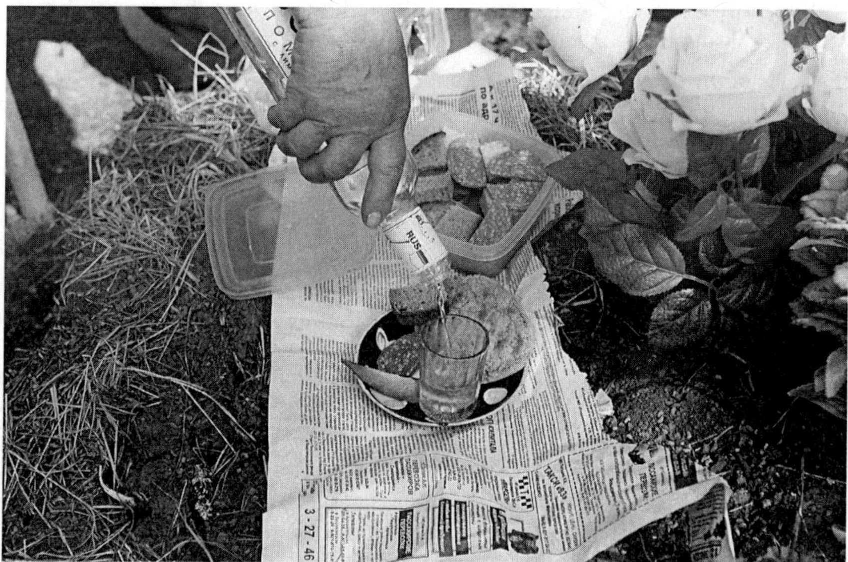

A tumbler of vodka is poured for the deceased during a memorial occasion, and food is arranged on the grave itself. Edoma, Arkhangel'sk province, 2011. (Photo by Elizabeth Warner)

drink while standing in the dusty soil right at the edge of the grave, where the corpse, so recently visible to all, lies only a few feet below them.

It is a general rule for village funerals that while the family and their guests attend the burial in the cemetery, helpers will have been busy at the deceased's home preparing the post-funeral repast. Generally speaking, this will be a generous affair, in accordance with practices by no means exclusive to the northern provinces. In the North fish is generally included in the spread, and although meat is frowned upon in strict Orthodox circles, there is no ban on it. In fact, as I was told, meat is allowed because of the heavy physical work undertaken by some of the male helpers, such as the grave-diggers (EW-A Arkh-Lesh, July 19, 2013). Three dishes in particular have a long association with funerals in Russia: pancakes (*bliny*), the grain-based kut'ya, and the sweet, fruity, gelatinous dessert *kisel'*. Although nowadays mostly made with rice and sugar, like a drier version of rice pudding, traditionally kut'ya was a type of porridge made from whole wheat grains sweetened with honey, to which dried fruits were sometimes added. (For the history and ritual uses of kut'ya, see Valentsova 2004a, 69–71.)

Noting the virtually obligatory presence of kisel' and kut'ya on the funeral table, some researchers have suggested that sweet food is a characteristic, or even preferred, aspect of funeral and memorial repasts (Alekseevskii 2005, 222; Rouhier-Willoughby 2008; Kabakova 2013, 185). M. D. Alekseevskii, for example, associates "sweetness" with productive magic, suggesting, in other words, a link with fertility and well-being. Rouhier-Willoughby suggests the sweets distributed in commemorations brought some pleasure to the mourners and peace to the souls of the dead. Sweets "were symbolically a means to influence the 'sweetness' of the afterlife for the dead" (Rouhier-Willoughby 2008, 196–97). In actual fact, in contemporary villages the presence and distribution of sweets and biscuits on memorial occasions are likely to have a more prosaic explanation. These goods are easily and cheaply available in village shops. When paying a visit in the village, it is usual to bring a few sweets as a gift. Every kitchen table will have a dish of sweets and biscuits to offer with tea, and it is usual to end a meal with them. Offering them in exchange for "remembrance," or scattering a few on a grave when you visit, is a convenient way of nourishing the dead. Kut'ya and kisel', on the other hand, have a well-established and specific role in memorial meals. Kisel' in its original form, although it may have been sweetened with honey, could hardly be considered primarily a "sweet" since it is etymologically connected with *kislyi* (sour), most likely a reference to the fact that the oatmeal, soaked in boiling water, was according to early tradition allowed to ferment (Valentsova 1999a, 496). Fermentation itself was regarded as a magic act with a purifying or apotropaic function (Valentsova 1999b, 498). As for kut'ya, its two main traditional ingredients, grain and honey, have many symbolic connotations in traditional Slavonic usage. Honey can symbolize "immortality, fertility, health, good fortune, beauty, happiness and the 'sweet things' of life" and was also considered the favorite food of the souls of the dead (Valentsova 2004b, 208). In the nineteenth century honey was served in a variety of forms at funeral meals, both as pure honey and as *syta*, for example, a drink made from honey dissolved in hot water. It seems quite likely that honey is more significant in this context than sweetness per se.

In the past the presence of kut'ya was ubiquitous in Russian Orthodox funeral and memorial practices. The theologian S. V. Bulgakov explains his understanding of kut'ya and kisel' in religious terms. The grain in kut'ya is not merely a passive symbol of fertility. It is thought to hold within its death the potential for new life: "Just as generation is contained within the process of the seed's decomposition so too is the process of the body's generation for a future life contained within its decomposition" (Bulgakov 1993, 2:1372–73). The sweetness of kut'ya, according to Bulgakov, supposedly represents the sweetness of eternal life, while kisel', as a food suitable for babies, especially when made with milk, represents the infant phase in which the newborn soul finds itself after leaving the body (Bulgakov 1993, 2:1360). In the North, kisel' is usually served at the end of the meal and marks the completion of its "official" or ritual part. The men are allowed to go outside for a smoke and the closed circle of communion between the living and the dead characteristic of the funeral repast is relaxed.

In addition to food, vodka, a beverage used in a variety of ritual contexts not only by Russians but by the East Slavs in general, was and remains a significant ingredient in post-funeral and especially memorial meals (for further information on the traditional role of vodka, see Tolstoi 1995, 1:392–94). A funeral or memorial meal in a rural setting, or indeed in any part of Russia, is hard to imagine without vodka. A question about whether alcohol was consumed when people came to remember their dead at the cemetery produced the puzzled response: "Why wouldn't they drink? Yes, on the grave, yes. Why would they not drink? For everyone drinks now" (Mez 17-9, 21 July 2007). How much vodka may be consumed without causing offense, however, remains unclear. There are unverifiable but plausible references from past centuries suggesting that excessive drinking was not uncommon at funerals in the North and other parts of Russia. As early as the mid-seventeenth century Adam Olearius's account of his visits to Muscovy mentions alcohol being served at funerals and on memorial occasions. After a funeral, according to Olearius, the mourners "return to the house of the deceased, where they find dinner ready, and where many times they drown their affliction with all other sentiments of mortality in *hydromel* and *aqua vitae*" (Dmytryshyn 1991, 423). Without reference to any particular regions of Russia, A. V. Tereshchenko certainly gives the impression that in the mid-nineteenth century both drinking and feasting on memorial days—he specifically mentions Dmitrii Saturday in October—were endemic among the "simple folk." After the memorial service, feasting took place on the graves, with the assumption that the dead shared in the experience. In conjunction with the many traditional food dishes, Tereshchenko comments that "beer and vodka are essential attributes of remembrance" and that "not to hold a feast over the remains was considered a sin" (Tereshchenko 1848, 3:129).

Bulgakov, from his experience of the Ukraine and the more southerly Russian provinces, wrote in the late nineteenth century of the inappropriate behavior sometimes witnessed at post-funeral meals and encouraged by gluttony and the presence of excessive amounts of strong alcoholic beverages (Bulgakov 1993, 2:1360). More significant for a study of northern customs, however, is Efimenko's information about the peasants in the Pinega *uezd* of Arkhangel'sk province in the latter half of the nineteenth century, who at funerals "eat as much as they can hold and keep on pouring the vodka until they are completely inebriated." Indeed, vodka is listed along with bread, salt, *shchi* (cabbage soup), porridge, and pancakes as one of the chief components of the meal (Efimenko 1877, 136). In the Kholmogorsk uezd of Arkhangel'sk province, however, there was no place for excessive consumption of vodka or for the noise and carousing that accompanied it (Efimenko 1877, 138). Similarly, with respect to a memorial meal in a village in the Sol'vychegodsk uezd of Vologda province, also in the latter half of the nineteenth century, reportedly "there is not usually much beer or wine—a bottle of vodka and a 'bucket' [*vedro*] of beer" (Tenishev 2007, 5 [3]:653).[1] There is clearly some disagreement about this aspect of the funeral in both its historical and contemporary aspects. I. A. Kremleva, for example, refutes the idea that overindulgence in alcohol was a characteristic feature, with abstinence particularly noticeable in the Russian North. According to her, the increased consumption of alcoholic beverages began after the Civil War (Kremleva 2001, 683). Galina Kabakova also writes of vodka being classified as a "sinful" or "impure" product that is particularly avoided today at funerals in the North and East (Kabakova 2013, 184). I. Shangina points out that "on a mythological level" vodka was widely regarded as a "demonic potion" in Russia because of its violent effects on people's emotions and behavior (Shangina 2001, 621). In fact, it is difficult to generalize about this aspect of funeral hospitality today. The Orthodox Church has always been strongly opposed to heavy drinking at funerals and on other visits to cemeteries, and this undoubtedly helped to shape and control popular attitudes. The Soviet authorities adopted the same position, although for different reasons. The Church's renewed disapprobation, in the first decade of the twenty-first century, of alcoholism in the villages, preached during the visits of Orthodox missionaries, may again have reinforced the notion of restraint.

According to informants in Vozhgora in 2013, two or even three small glasses of vodka were considered acceptable for male mourners, but anyone requesting more would be asked to leave the house. On the other hand, I attended a funeral meal in Azopol'e in the Mezen' region of Arkhangel'sk province in 2008 at which a great deal of vodka was consumed.

Generally speaking, an intoxicated state, like sleep or unconsciousness, is a liminal condition that facilitates interaction with the world of the "other." As Mircea Eliade points out, alcohol, hemp, and "magic" mushrooms are among the aids shamans use to enter a state of ecstasy (Eliade 1974, 399–401). On the other hand, one may say that, just as abundant food on the funeral table counteracts the "hunger" of death, so too does drink—in the form of vodka, whose main ingredient is water—counteract the dryness of death: "Life depends upon liquid. From the concept of the 'water of life' to semen, milk, blood, bile, saliva, and the like the consistent principle is that liquid means life while loss of liquid means death. 'Wet and Dry' as an oppositional pair means life and death. Liquids are living: drying is dying!" (Dundes 1981, 266).[2]

The organization of the funeral meal and the behavior of those present contain several elements of interest. First, it is assumed that the deceased, or rather his or her soul, will be present in one form or another. A place is therefore laid for that person, often with a photograph (an innovation of Soviet times) and a lighted candle alongside the place setting to emphasize the individual's "presence." The deceased is given a plate onto which only one spoonful of each dish is doled out as the meal progresses. He or she is also given a drink. The nature and quantity of the drink varies. At the funeral I attended in Azopol'e a tumbler of vodka covered with a slice of black bread was offered. In Vozhgora and Rodoma, on the other hand, it would be normal to pour only a small glass (*stopka*) of vodka for a man and for a woman a wineglass of the "red stuff" (the popular, sweet liqueur made from rowan berries) or, indeed, just a cup of tea.

Many people today cover the glass intended for the soul with a piece of bread, but it is possible that this is a relatively recent innovation. It is not surprising that the soul receives bread along with other types of food. Bread was and remains essential to the Russian table and is truly regarded as the "staff of life." No Russian meal is complete without it. I remember an occasion some years ago when I invited a group of Russian visitors to my home for a celebratory Christmas meal. It would be no exaggeration to say the table was groaning with traditional English Christmas dishes. But one visitor voiced a disappointment that was undoubtedly shared by others: "Isn't there any bread?"

Nineteenth-century ethnographers like Vladimir Dal' have shown that in peasant households bread was treated with the utmost respect. It was considered sinful to drop even a crumb on the floor. Its presence transformed the simple

A place has been set for the dead man, at the head of the table next to the chief mourners, during a post-funeral meal. Azopol'e, Arkhangel'sk province, 2008. (Photo by Elizabeth Warner)

wooden table of the peasant *izba* into a domestic altar, as the proverb suggests: "Put bread on the table—the table becomes an altar: without a scrap of bread—the table is just a wooden board" (Khleb na stol, tak i stol prestol: a khleba ni kuska—i stol doska [Dal' 1957, 811]). In the context of funerals, bread, like the other grain-based foods kut'ya and bliny, has the additional function of combating the destructive influence of death with connotations of fertility and good fortune. The dual symbolism provided by the combination of bread *and* vodka (otherwise known as grain wine [*khlebnoe vino*]) is clearly expressed in another proverb: "Replete on bread and drunk on bread/grain" (Khlebom syty, khlebom i p'yany [Dal' 1957, 802]). S. M. Tolstaya (2012, 412–20) and I. I. Shangina (2001, 611–15) provide more detailed information on the status of bread in its traditional and ritual context while the social and economic role of bread in Russia through the ages is thoroughly documented by R. E. F. Smith and David Christian (Smith and Christian, 1984).

Covering the deceased's portion of drink with bread could be regarded as an apotropaic measure to keep the vulnerable soul safe during the period of transition from this life to the next. In addition to the utilitarian purpose of preventing material foreign bodies from contaminating the liquids, lids have traditionally been seen as providing protection from evil spirits and from the magic of ill-wishers, the effect of whose dangerous spells could supposedly be transferred through the medium of food and drink. Note the following nineteenth-century popular saying in this context: "Leave no vessel for liquid uncovered lest demonic forces settle in" (Nikakoi posudy s poilom ne derzhat' bez pokryshki: vrazh'ya sila poselitsya [Dal' 1957, 819]).

Another noteworthy funeral practice that is still often observed, eating communally from a single dish, was at one time the norm in peasant households. In some villages of the Mezen' region, for example, a single plate containing several larger fish may be laid on the table with the assumption that those present will all help themselves from it. One interviewee contrasted this custom with the modern innovation of funeral meals in the local canteen, where everyone is given a separate plate with an individual portion. In some villages the guests at the funeral meal also drink from one glass. In Keba in the Leshukon'e region, for example, vodka is poured into a single glass given to each individual in turn. Each person in turn stands, remembers the deceased, drinks, and sits down again (FA Mez 17-61, July 20, 2008). Although communal eating and drinking are not practiced everywhere, these elements of the funeral meal underline the connectedness, through death, of everyone present.

One tradition among the East Slavs in general was to only provide spoons at funeral and memorial meals. Forks and knives were not used in case they might injure the fragile soul. Today, in north Russia this interdiction is still observed by some people while others provide forks as well as spoons, but no knives, which, in any case, rarely appear at normal mealtimes in rural areas. Anecdotal evidence suggests that even among urban dwellers the importance of using only spoons at funerals is still remembered. In Rodoma, a funeral in Arkhangel'sk, the regional capital, was recollected by our hosts. After the meal there the men, mainly fellow workers of the deceased, had been allowed to take their spoons home with them (EW-A Arkh-Lesh, July 15, 2013). This custom was known in Arkhangel'sk province in the nineteenth century. In the Kureisko-Sergiev parish of Kholmogorsk uezd, at a funeral meal everyone would be given a new wooden spoon "in memory of the deceased" (Efimenko 1877, 138). The gifting of spoons was a reminder to pray for the soul of the dead person each time the spoon was used (Kremleva 2001, 689). The deceased does not normally receive cutlery at all.

The funeral lunch is only one aspect of the wider Russian tradition of "feasting" (*zastol'e*), which may be organized just for friends or as an element of ritual, such as at weddings and calendar festivals. Like any traditional zastol'e, it is typified by large quantities of food and drink, but there are also significant differences. It is not usual to issue invitations to the funeral meal, for example, whereas the traditional convention of feasting normally requires the giving and receiving of invitations according to a strict etiquette (Morozov and Sleptsova 2004, 213–14). Usually, invitees would be expected to invite their hosts in return, but in the context of funerals return invitations, for obvious reasons, cannot be made. This, however, does not mean that funeral guests are unwelcome at the meal afterward. A woman in Vozhgora remarked that everyone at the cemetery was simply encouraged to attend the meal, with as many as thirty people turning up. If there wasn't room for them all they would have a second seating (EW-A Arkh-Lesh, July 13, 2013). The inference is that the more people there are to eat for and with the soul of the deceased, the better. The same is true for the consumption of food in cemeteries on memorial days. Partaking of the food is vital since "the more *you* eat the more sated *he* [the deceased] will be" (EW-A Arkh-Lesh, July 15, 2013). This may be contrasted with the practice at memorial meals on the ninth and fortieth days after the death, when it is customary to invite only those close to the deceased. There is no toasting during a funeral meal. Drinking to the good health or success of individuals present followed by the "clinking" (*chokan'e/chokat'sya*) of glasses so characteristic of the festive meal in Russia is replaced by a brief eulogy to the deceased, the only participant in the meal with whom it is acceptable to clink glasses. In Vozhgora it was said, although in connection with the fortieth-day meal rather than the funeral, that clinking glasses with the deceased is only permitted to those who are near enough to stretch across the table to do it, suggesting, perhaps, that it is limited to the dead person's intimate family circle, seated near the place set for him or her (EW-A Arkh-Lesh, July 19, 2013). In Rodoma, on the other hand, I was told that anyone who wished to was allowed to do this, addressing the deceased as they did so (EW-A Arkh-Lesh, July 15, 2013).

The post-funeral meal unites the bereaved and also incorporates the deceased as a continuing member of the family and community. A spiritual communion between the living and the dead is achieved through the act of sharing food and drink. However, giving the deceased only a token share of the food rather than a heaped plateful is a sign of his or her "otherness." The deceased has been in some sense "diminished" by the fact of death but, like everyone else present, is still entitled to his or her part of the meal. The idea of receiving one's allotted portion, both of life and the benefits, such as food, that come with it, is an interesting one in Slavonic mythology. The notion of both portion and fate is conveyed by the same word, *dolya*: "Dolya is that part of a certain whole that is allocated to each individual person, and that exists in a state of mutual interdependence with other parts or shares" (Sedakova 1990, 54). While the number of dishes and guests demonstrates the importance of abundance at the funeral table, providing the post-mortem being with what is their due illustrates the importance of inclusion.

The concept of entitlement—what is rightfully mine (*svoi*) as opposed to what belongs to others (*chuzhoi*)—is a powerful one and may be extended to ownership of objects used by or belonging to the deceased. Having been asked why it was customary to take a dead person's walking stick to the cemetery, where it would be laid alongside the grave or propped up behind the grave marker rather than offered to someone else who might make use of it, one of our interlocutors in Pustynya suggested that the deceased would be outraged at the thought of passing the stick on for use by another person: "If you were to walk about with that stick you would dream of that person. He would say 'You are walking with *my* stick. You must not do that. Take your own steed!'" (EW-A Arkh-Lesh, July 16, 2013). For partly this reason, the home or room of a person who has died remains untouched until a whole year has passed. In 2007 in the village of Kimzha in Arkhangel'sk province I found myself living in the empty home of an old woman who had passed away less than a year before. None of her belongings had been removed, including her toothbrush, comb, and soap, which still lay beside the washbowl. Lying in bed one night, surrounded by her possessions, I was awakened by a strange noise, as if someone was beating on metal. At first it was distant, on the edge of the forest, but gradually it came closer until eventually the banging seemed to be on the corrugated roof of the house. It was a very disturbing experience, and when I mentioned it to the village women next morning there were knowing glances. Living in the house so soon after the woman's death, using her bed linen and crockery, was clearly a risky business.

FEEDING DURING THE FORTY DAYS AFTER A DEATH AND ON OTHER COMMEMORATIVE OCCASIONS

In rural north Russia, as elsewhere in the country, ritual remembrance is routinely carried out after the funeral, on the ninth and fortieth days after the death, and on the anniversary of the death. Depending on local or family tradition, graves may also be visited for this purpose on the sixth and twentieth days and on the birthday or name-day of the deceased. Certain days in the church calendar, the so-called ancestor days or ancestor Saturdays (*roditel'skie dni/subboty*), are set aside for remembering all the souls of the faithful departed. These are the Saturday ending Meatfare week (*myasopustnaya*), the second, third, and fourth Saturdays of the Great Fast (Velikii post), the Tuesday of the second week after Easter Sunday (Radunitsa), the Saturday before Trinity Sunday (Troitsa), and the Saturday before St. Dmitrii's day in October. At Troitsa in particular many people make the pilgrimage to the cemetery where their kinsmen are buried (see chapter 5 for more detailed discussion of this practice). Unconnected with the cycle of Orthodox days of special remembrance is Victory Day (Den' Pobedy) on May 9, inaugurated to honor those who perished during the Great Patriotic War.

The fortieth day after a death has particular significance in Orthodox theology: it marks the conclusion of a forty-day-long period of remembrance that echoes the forty days of prayer and fasting by Christ in the wilderness and his ultimate triumph over Satan. The soul during this time supposedly passes through a series of ordeals (*mytarstva*) in the course of which it is shown both heaven and hell, although, according to popular tradition, it can still return to visit its old home. On the fortieth day, however, it must depart this world for good in order to face the individual judgment of its Maker. In rural communities marking the fortieth day with a special memorial meal to which the soul is invited is essential. Although there may be fewer guests at the fortieth-day meal than there had been at the funeral, food and drink are still plentiful. This abundance is not a modern innovation. A correspondent, writing about village customs in the Sol'vychegodsk uezd of Vologda province in the latter half of the nineteenth century, remarked that "No expense is spared for *pominki*." In the village of Ust'e, as he remembered, there lived a poor peasant whose wife had died. He invited the local clergy to the memorial meal for which a "big fat sheep, an extremely fat one" had been specially slaughtered (Tenishev 2007, 5 [3]:653).

As is the case during the post-funeral meal, the soul is fed along with the other guests, although the details of how food is presented differ from one location to another. In Rodoma, for example, the provision of a plate of food specifically for the deceased is characteristic of the funeral meal but not of later memorial meals, where only a glass may be provided. The mere presence of food on the table may be regarded as sufficient evidence of hospitality toward the deceased (EW-A Arkh-Lesh, July 15, 2013). Characteristically, the fortieth-day remembrance meal ends with a formal reminder to the soul of the need to leave its home for good, with the removal from the table of food offerings, which are usually transferred later to the gravesite.

In fact, during the whole of the forty-day period preceding the remembrance meal, food is kept available for the soul, most often in the form of a drink (vodka, tea, or water), with or without food, placed on a windowsill or table near the icon corner. After the fortieth day the food and drink are removed.

These oblations are by no means routinely performed symbolic gestures. The snack is prepared fresh every morning with ritualistic care and ceremony. In Vozhgora in July 2013, I spoke to two recently bereaved women about this custom. One had just lost a husband and the other a sister. Both spoke calmly about funeral ritual in general but became visibly upset while, in the case of the first woman, showing me the deceased man's plate of food sitting on a shelf next to his photograph, and in the case of the other woman, in whose house I was living at the time, demonstrating one early morning the preparation of breakfast for herself and her dead sister. My landlady carefully washed and dried her sister's cup and saucer, placed a few biscuits on the saucer, and poured her a cup of strong tea, just as her sister liked it. In Rodoma a daughter recollected how, after her father died, she would make a thermos of fresh tea every morning and climb the hill to his house to have breakfast with him. "Papa, I've come," she would say (EW-A Arkh-Lesh, July 15, 2013). Food is given as if to a living, sentient person, who would of course expect hot tea and fresh food every day, prepared to his or her own taste. Catering to the deceased's needs in this way is an intimate expression of care and affection, a quasi-religious moment of contact between the dead person and the person who grieves. It is also one way of propitiating the soul and ensuring its good will.

For most of the village people we have spoken to over the years, the destination of the soul that abandons its home on the fortieth day is by no means certain. Although some will say the soul flies away to heaven after the fortieth day, in practice the ritual focus of care for the soul of the deceased is the cemetery. It is here that the most vigorous feeding takes place on days of remembrance: "So, the food you bring is for the soul?" "Yes, it's for the soul." "So, where is the soul then? In the cemetery?" "Most likely it's there, most likely. They are probably even waiting" (EW-A Arkh-Lesh, July 19, 2013). In Rodoma I heard that visiting the cemetery to remember the dead is more respectful than doing it at

Morning tea being prepared for a much-loved sister during the days following her funeral. Vozhgora, Arkhangel'sk province, 2013. (Photo by Elizabeth Warner)

home, and refusing to eat or drink with the dead in the cemetery is regarded as an insult (EW-A Arkh-Lesh, July 15, 2013).

It is worth considering at this point what the act of remembrance means to many of the inhabitants of the rural North. Aside from its primary meaning of "to remember," the verb *pominat'* can refer to the performance of the Orthodox prayer for the repose of the soul (Dal' 1955, 3:272). Similarly, the term *pamyat'* (literally, "memory") may be applied to the memorial service for the dead. Some people will, indeed, say a prayer at the graveside, but they are more likely to express the hope that the earth should be as soft as down for the deceased (*Pust' zemlya budet pukhom*), a sentiment concerning the body rather than the soul. However, the chief significance of memorial occasions and remembering lies elsewhere. Remembering, in its ritual context, is, and has been historically, synonymous with eating and sharing food with the dead. A nineteenth-century informant recollected an incident when a young man, recently returned from his studies at the seminary, was accosted in the street by a woman who invited him to Vladimir the psalm-reader's house for pominki: "Come along, even if you just have a little beer, you'll 'remember' the deceased." To which the young man, who had possibly lost touch with the local customs, replied: "Thank you, but I've already eaten at home" (Tenishev 2007, 5 [3] 653). It is clear that the imperative of combining remembrance with eating is just as strong today: "When you go to the grave you take something. . . . They are pleased. After all they are expecting it and if you come empty-handed—how can you come to a grave empty-handed?" (EW-A Arkh-Lesh, July 16, 2013). For one person in Rodoma, remembering was definitely not just a question of memory but of the need to sit down with a cup of tea or something to eat while doing it: "Yes, I remember. I'll bake something, sit down at the table." She would then make the sign of the cross and ask God to remember her mother and father, her husband, her aunts and uncles, and others close to her who had passed away (EW-A Arkh-Lesh, July 15, 2013). The testimony of one person recorded in Vologda province shows how obsessive this preoccupation with food is. For a whole year after the death of her son, Nina would take food to the cemetery for him. She even took vodka every day. Eventually, her husband complained that more of what she baked ended up in the cemetery than was provided for meals at home. His wife, however, was unrepentant. "Let him eat," she would say (FA Vash 17-109, July 14, 1998). It is taken for granted that no one should enter a cemetery without at least a token offering. Those who go to visit a specific grave will at the same time leave a sweet or a biscuit beside the graves of other relatives or friends. The edible treats from relatives, which the deceased is expected to pass on to those who have entered the world of the dead before him or her, are also a form of pamyat' (EW-A Arkh-Lesh, July 19, 2013).

In 2011, in a village in the Leshukon'e region, I attended pominki organized by Manefa for her husband, on the occasion of his birthday. The grave was newly decorated with brightly colored artificial flowers, which gave it a festive appearance. In the nineteenth century it would have been customary to serve the memorial food at the cemetery on a hand-woven linen towel spread over the grave mound. On this occasion, however, newspaper served as a substitute. Some dishes containing bread, salami, and cucumber were arranged at the head of the grave together with the deceased's portion of food and some vodka in a tumbler. Included with his saucer of food was a piece of *shan'ga*, a type of bun baked for festivals and celebrations and popular in the North, so much so, in fact, that the residents of Arkhangel'sk were in the past jokingly referred to as "shan'ga sellers" (*shanezhniki*) (Dal' 1955, 4:621). The widow had baked the shan'gi on the previous evening, and together with her neighbor we had sampled them in the hot little kitchen in the traditional way, straight from the Russian stove and dipped in a bowl of melted butter, but making sure enough were left for each of the invited guests at the pominki on the following day. One by one, the guests took their place beside the grave, quietly spoke a few consoling words, and remembered the deceased with a sip of vodka and a bite of food. Just before returning home, the widow scattered some grain around, but not on the grave. Visitors to the graveside are careful not to throw grain in the vicinity of the deceased's eyes in case he or she is injured by the flying particles or by the birds that later fly down to peck at the grain. The same consideration for the comfort of the deceased may be found in other methods of distributing food. For example, food is often arranged in the middle of the grave, conveniently close to the folded hands of the deceased lying underground. Sometimes, if no glass is available, liquids may be poured directly into the grave itself, but here again caution is exercised. "Don't pour over the eyes, though," warned one woman, "but here, in the middle. Nothing is put on the eyes, where their eyes are, only in the middle, where the hands are" (EW-A Arkh-Lesh, July 15, 2013). If there is some disagreement about the quantity of alcohol that can be consumed at funerals, its popularity at pominki seems to be less in doubt, with some sections of the population renowned for drinking to excess. Many people disapprove of the "alkies" who take wine to the cemetery: "In my opinion they only go there to get drunk" (EW-A Arkh-Lesh, July 13, 2013). In Vozhgora, some expressed the view that pouring a drink for the dead was a sin and that one should be praying for them instead. The dead who imbibed the proffered alcohol could even become inebriated in the process, I was told. Nevertheless, it is clear from many historical accounts that the consumption of copious amounts of food and to some extent and in some places alcohol as well—in spite of regular assurances from present-day informants to the contrary—should be regarded as a characteristic feature of remembrance days and by no means only in the rural North. Writing toward the end of the nineteenth century of the need to keep cemeteries and their burial enclosures in good order, Bulgakov comments that the construction within cemeteries of booths for the sale of food and drink was forbidden, and establishments supplying customers with hard liquor could be built no closer than forty *sazhens* (one *sazhen'* is approximately seven feet) from a cemetery. Those dispensing porter and beer could be no closer than twenty sazhens. The existence of such restrictions alone indicates that the practice of remembering with alcoholic and other refreshments was widespread and endemic (Bulgakov 1993, 2:1339).

As memorial days approach, the dead, who, as many of the village people believe, can hear, see, understand, and even foretell everything that goes on in the world of the living, may start to become restive and remind their relatives that they are hungry through the medium of dreams. Some may even ask for a specific type of food, as one interviewee pointed out: "One might say, for example, 'I want some fish,' so then you must take them fish." The speaker also provided two graphic examples of the remarkable sensitivity of the dead to the presence of food and drink and their reactions when deprived of it—especially, although not exclusively, on a remembrance day. "You might pour yourself a mug [of tea] and then accidentally knock it over. That means they are asking you for a drink," she said. Then, there was the case of her grandmother, whose grave she had been unable to visit on either the ninth or the twentieth day after the death because she was at home with a sick baby. Her grandmother's "soul" would make its presence felt when the baby was being breast-fed. The young woman could hear the sound of her grandmother rising from the bed on which she used to sleep and the squeaking of her footsteps across the floor. This was not a pleasant sensation. The informant described how she broke into a cold sweat and the baby began to howl and shortly after these incidents fell ill with whooping cough. The old woman was only appeased when her granddaughter promised to visit the grave on the fortieth day (EW-A Arkh-Lesh, July 13, 2013).

Do the people who take food to the cemetery for their ancestors believe that the dead, or their souls, actually eat the food? In our research we never heard reports of corpses emerging from coffins in order to eat biscuits or drink glasses of vodka. On the other hand, we did encounter the widespread practice of pronouncing a greeting to the dead upon entering a cemetery. In the village of Rodoma, it is customary to ring a bell in order to alert the dead to one's arrival and the presence of food. The focus on food suggests a belief that lack of food in this world causes hunger in the subliminal body of the soul in the other world, whether that world is far away or close by in the cemetery. The provision of food, through some peculiar process of osmosis, ensures that the dead

In this village, visitors to the cemetery can announce their arrival and alert their loved ones by ringing the bell. Rodoma, Arkhangel'sk province, 2013. (Photo by Elizabeth Warner)

are satisfied or replete there. Feeding and providing drink to the dead are treated as having a physical effect. As mentioned above, some with whom we spoke reported incidents in which the dead became inebriated or misbehaved, as in the case of one woman's father. She poured him a drink of vodka at the cemetery in Vozhgora, but then her sister had a dream in which the deceased, who had during his lifetime sometimes abused their mother, was again chasing after his dead wife (EW-A Arkh-Lesh, July 13, 2013).

FEEDING IN VISIONS, DREAMS, AND THE "OTHER" WORLD

Tales and legends containing visions of the world beyond the grave, of hell and paradise and the torments of the damned on the one hand and the euphoria of the righteous on the other, were popular forms in Old Russian literature. In addition to these prose narratives, descriptions of the other world may also be found in "spiritual verses" (*dukhovnye stikhi*), a folk verse form with mainly religious sentiments and themes. Some of these were composed in medieval times by devout travelers returning from pilgrimages to the Holy Land. Later, they formed the repertoire of the so-called *kaliki perekhozhie*, wandering holy men and blind musicians who kept the genre alive into the nineteenth century.

By and large, the recipients of such visions were also holy men of one kind or another—priests, monks, or hermits—so that while the entertainment value of the detailed and imaginative descriptions of punishments meted out to the souls of sinners was no doubt significant, their purpose was essentially didactic. Orthodox Christians were shown in graphic terms that the joys of paradise were only offered to those who attended church regularly, prayed, gave alms, and lived a moral and frugal way of life. Drunkards and gluttons, robbers, murderers, suicides, and all the unreformed sinners who neglected the duties of true Christians went to hell instead. The visionary returning from his tour of the other world often brought a cautionary message for ordinary folk. Various combinations of stereotypical motifs and images characterized the geography of these accounts. The landscape of hell, for example, was sterile, without vegetation, a place of darkness and boiling pitch, of bottomless pits and rivers of fire, where the senses were assailed by the stench of burning, the hissing of serpents, and the screams of the tormented. Paradise was sometimes presented as a church. In his vision, the monastic Father Superior Makarii, for example, described a church made of ice from whose altar a spring of water flows, as white as milk. This is the spring of immortality from which the souls of the righteous will drink (Rozhdestvenskaya 2002, 184). In other texts, which A. V. Pigin sees as being closer to folkloric sources, the souls of the blessed live in special "edifices" (*khraminy*) standing in flower-covered meadows (Pigin 1996, 555). The most iconic image of paradise, however, is that of a fertile land or a large garden.

Here, the visionary traveler can find many trees, laden with exotic fruits of all kinds, and an abundance of sweet-smelling and brightly colored flowers, as in the tale of Agapii's visit to paradise (Rozhdestvenskaya 2002, 174). In stark contrast to hell, this is a place of eternal light and perfumed air. Instead of hissing snakes, one can encounter the song of many-hued birds, "some with gold feathers, some with crimson, red, blue, or green feathers, various bright hues and some with feathers white as snow" (Mil'kov 1999, 642).

Among the benefits enjoyed in paradise are an endless supply of exotic food and rivers flowing with milk and honey, or even wine. In spiritual verses about the "Last Judgment" and "Life eternal," those who have lived a Christian life and who have fed and given drink to the poor are promised that they will never go hungry themselves: "In heaven there are chambers filled with light, the dining tables there are laden. / Go to that chamber, all you righteous souls, and eat" (Bessonov 1863, 2, [5]:257). The sinners who end up in hell, on the other hand, are denied food and suffer hunger pangs in addition to their other torments.

In the contemporary village, among the most vivid accounts of the world beyond the grave are those conveyed through the medium of dreams. Dream narrations are often referred to as a specific folk genre that first received serious attention in research by N. I. Tolstoi and S. M. Tolstaya on the Poles'e region, on the borders of south Russia and Ukraine (N. I. Tolstoi and Tolstaya 1979, 63–65; Tolstaya 1999b, 22–23). These narrations may involve either incursions of the dead into the world of the living and their comments about the life they now lead, or, more rarely, visits by the living to the land of the dead. Although sleep itself is a liminal state mimicking death, this particular type of dream was often said to occur while the dreamer was in the state of prolonged and unnatural sopor known in Russian as *letargicheskii son* ("lethargic sleep") or while unconscious, in a faint, or in a coma. At such times the gateway between the realm of the living and the dead, usually closed, is open, permitting the dreamers to enter and return, witness the torments endured by sinners, stroll in the pleasant gardens prepared for the blessed, and chat with deceased relatives (Lur'e and Tarabukina 1994, 23).

The narratives associated with this trancelike state recorded in the twentieth century, according to Lur'e and Tarabukina (1994, 22–26), reveal in their descriptions of heaven and hell a mixture of contemporary elements familiar to the narrators and distant echoes of the eschatological visions of holy men. Typically, they both echo the punishments and rewards meted out after the Last Judgment and retain the moral dimension associated with their medieval forerunners: "Indications of the absence or presence of food in the other world in general separate the sinners from the righteous, those who have been baptized from those who have not. . . . Another characteristic feature which distinguishes

the tormented from the blessed is the absence of clothing" (Lur'e and Tarabukina 1994, 24). E. Levkievskaya also comments that it is the souls of the
righteous who enjoy the abundant food and drink of the other world and sit
at tables "covered with white tablecloths and laden with all kinds of food and
drink" (Levkievskaya 2000, 191).

As imagined in the contemporary village material I have at my disposal,
however, details of the world of the dead in dreams, as in everyday discourse,
tend to be less precise and much less judgmental. It should also be noted that
to those who experience them, these dreams are not "stories" but events that
reveal the interconnectedness of two worlds. The dream is the mechanism by
which the living are allowed a glimpse into that other world, which, in spite of
its "otherness" forms a part of everyday reality in the world of the here and now
and very often reflects that reality in its details. It is also a form of communication that enables the dead to pass on their feelings, wishes, and instructions to
the living.[3] The messages received are deemed relevant to the beliefs and customs of those who receive them. They produce an emotional response and are
acted upon. When a mother appeared to her son in a dream, complaining that
she had been buried without a belt to her dress and that her coffin was facing in
the wrong direction, in other words not toward the East, as is the practice in
Orthodoxy, the coffin was exhumed and turned around and a belt was placed
on top of it (FA Bel 17-51, July 24, 1994).

Both in accounts of dreams and in general remarks, references to judgment
and the destination of good and bad souls, respectively, tend to be sketchy and
hesitant: "On the fortieth day you'll be judged. If you have a lot of sins you'll . . .
you'll suffer but if you don't have many sins then, everyone says, [you go to]
paradise" (FA Kir 17-15, July 14, 2006). Paradise and the kingdom of heaven
may be associated with light and situated up above, whereas hell may be dark
and somewhere down below: "He is in a bright place. . . . They have these bright
buildings, bright" (FA Mez 22-159, July 14, 2009); "People who have not been
baptized or who have been buried without a funeral service, they will not see
the light in the other world" (Kir 17-15, July 14, 2006); "On the fortieth day that's
when the Last Judgment will take place. Everything is decided once and for all.
Before, he [the soul] was flying among the clouds but on the fortieth day he is
brought down and he will be [sent] to the kingdom of heaven or he will—I don't
know what. . . . The kingdom of heaven is when he will be with God, but if he is
sent to hell, you'll suffer there—I don't know. You will burn in fire there. . . . If
you are going to burn in fire, that is probably down below" (FA Kir 17-16, July
13, 2006). Anna, whose son had committed suicide, told of the dream she had
on the first night after his death. She went into the kitchen and saw him there
stoking the stove. The kitchen was full of smoke, and as he had died by hanging

himself, he had difficulty breathing: "He was having a hard time there. [It was] the smoke. He was making the charcoal blaze. The smoke was giving him a hard time" (FA Kir 22-11, July 20, 2006). It is not difficult to recognize the fires of hell in this description and the "fitting" punishment meted out to the suicide, although the setting is entirely domestic. However, the topography of the other world in such dreams rarely seems to reflect a clear-cut division into regions for sinners and for the righteous, while the elements of judgment, reward, and punishment typical of narratives more obviously influenced by Christian teaching are usually absent. The most common setting for the world of the dead is in fact the cemetery, to which the dead have relocated and near which many of the encounters between the living and the dead supposedly take place. As we saw in chapter 1, the notion of death involving a simple change in domicile is introduced early in the funeral ritual with references to the coffin as the new house or living room, specially built for the deceased. In the words of one Mezen' region lament: "We've also made for you a little house of planks, for you, forever, for all eternity" (FA Mez 17a-15, July 15, 2008). The dead themselves clearly regard the cemetery as "home," as in the case of the mother who announced in a dream that she was living nearby "on 1st Coffin street" (FA Mez 22-133, July 11, 2009) or the husband who supposedly phoned his widow from the cemetery to complain that she never called him and then passed on his number to her (FA Mez 22-116, July 22, 2009). In dreams, the dead may be seen living in or renovating a tumbledown house for themselves (FA Lesh 22-141, July 8, 2018). They may ask for money to build a house (FA Mez 22-22, July 10, 2007). Agreeing in a dream to join the deceased in such a home is tantamount to risking one's own death. In Vozhgora a young woman dreamed that her dead husband had built a beautiful house for her. It was painted red and decorated all over like a little toy, but she refused to go with him because she knew her time had not yet come (EW-A Arkh-Lesh, July 13, 2013). In this banal village of the dead, life may be pleasant enough, but the dead who appear in dreams also complain of loneliness, damp, darkness, and especially cold and hunger, those two related discomforts of both this life and the afterlife: "A man who is hungry is also a man who is cold. It is bread that warms not a fur coat" (Kto goloden tot i kholoden. Khleb greet, ne shuba [Dal' 1957, 804]).

In the other world described in dreams, some of the dead have their own tables, and mealtimes may even be organized to some extent. Tat'yana described a dream in which a deceased relative appeared and she heard a sound like a bell being rung, upon which Sashka informed her: "They're calling us to go and eat" (FA Mez 22-159, July 14, 2009). Rimma dreamed that her dead relative had invited her to dine in a restaurant. When they entered, some people were already seated. The restaurant was underground, somewhere among the graves (FA Mez 22-100,

July 21, 2008). However, in contrast with the abundant or inexhaustible quantity of food in the paradise of medieval visions, meals in this more neutral other world are more modest affairs. Furthermore, neither food nor clothing is thought of as a reward for devout behavior or for feeding and clothing the indigent. If the dead look well-dressed it is because, as was and remains the custom, particularly in the case of women, they have carefully chosen their own burial clothes in advance. For their food supplies, on the other hand, the dead are dependent on the generosity and attentiveness of the living, and what they are fed reflects not the esoteric sustenance of the eschatological legends, the strange fruits and the rivers of milk and honey, but the limited, familiar fare of village life, as in the dream of a dead husband seen in the village walking up the hill toward the post office with two loaves of white bread tucked under his arm (FA Lesh 22-58, July 14, 2009) or of a father who appeared before his daughter in a dream and told her that he was going hunting and that a car was coming to pick him up. As the man had not in his lifetime gone hunting or fishing, his quest for fresh meat was in itself thought-provoking. His daughter offered to provide food for the trip. He said he didn't want salami but asked for some "Snezhok" instead: "I would like a drink of Snezhok.[4] They don't give us any of that there" (FA Mez 22-120, July 17, 2009). In another dream, Sofiya saw her dead father and son, who had died within a short time of each other, standing together by the threshold as they set off on their long trek to the other world. The father asked her to fill their rucksack with the rusks of bread she had been drying in the oven (FA Lesh 22-147, July 6, 2011).[5]

Making sure the dead do not go hungry is a significant factor in both funerary practice and in the imagined world of the departed. Food is also used as a bargaining tool in relationships between the living and the dead. Offerings of food or vodka taken to the cemetery, for example, may discourage restless deceased persons from constantly bothering their families. Food helps to maintain a balance between the negatives of death and the positives of life, between taking and giving. If the living sometimes seem obsessive about offering food, the dead too may seem obsessive about receiving it and appear to be keenly aware of its availability, like the father who would come knocking on the window or the walls of the house on the ninth, twentieth, and fortieth days after his death and always at mealtimes (FA Mez 22-54, July 8, 2008). One person had seen her dead daughter in three different dreams, each of which was associated with food, its presence or absence. On the first occasion she saw her daughter in the kitchen at the table washing dishes in a washing-up bowl, while the table itself was covered with freshly baked buns. Next, her daughter was sitting at an empty table—a reproach to her mother for not remembering her with memorial food. In another dream the daughter was eating an egg that had already turned blue. She ate half and her mother tried to finish it but had to give up when she felt ill (FA Lesh 22-58, July 14, 2009). The loss and emptiness of death is clearly expressed in such encounters, as in funerary practices, through hunger and the abnormal appetite of the soul, which can even suck the life from the living.

Implicit in many of the funerary practices and encounters with the dead that involve feeding is the idea that an equilibrium must be reached in meeting the needs of the deceased and the living and a balance between "having" and "not having" what is rightfully one's own. As O. A. Sedakova puts it in her insightful article on the concept of *dolya* (fate, share, or lot) in funeral ritual, we are in the presence of an ethos where importance is attached to "satisfaction with one's own dolya and its corollaries, acceptance and total consumption without appropriation of someone else's dolya" (Sedakova 1990, 60). In the context of inclusiveness and "fair shares," I was interested to note during visits to the cemetery in Lykoshino (Tver' province) on Trinity Saturday and Sunday 2016 that offerings of food such as are to be found on individual graves at this time had also been placed beside the communal war grave of eighty-eight victims of the Great Patriotic War who had died in the military hospital situated in the village at that time. There was a similar scene at another communal war grave of 379 soldiers and officers in the cemetery at Bologoe. By the gateway into the Lykoshino cemetery there was also a large stone slab, possibly the remnant of an old grave, covered with a variety of token food offerings—rice, sweets, and biscuits—deposited by many different people. This was done, as was explained to me, either because someone had been unable to find a specific grave or because cemetery visitors wanted to ensure that no one had been left out.

Disturbing the balance by, for example, failing to provide the share due to the dead on memorial occasions or not remembering them often enough was considered a sure means of provoking a dire misfortune, sickness, or even death, but equally disastrous would be allowing the dead who come to individuals in dreams to sit at their tables like normal living beings. Allowing this might enable the dead to feed not only *with* those they have left behind but *on* them: "Everyone says they will lead you out of the house, they will devour you. . . . They will certainly devour someone from the village" (FA Lesh 22-132, July 17, 2011). An illustration of this point may be found in the account of a dream in which a widow saw her dead husband in the house. Her middle daughter was giving him something to eat and carried on doing so although her mother warned her not to. Later, the woman learned that her daughter had been seriously injured in a car crash (FA Mez 22-149, July 11, 2009). Conversely, the dead who come in dreams bearing gifts, particularly food, augment one's store of good fortune (FA Lesh 22-132, July 17, 2011).

Two dreams that came to my attention during this research illustrate the direct correlation between the amount of food provided for the dead during the process of remembering and the requirements of the dead for sustenance. A young woman from Rodoma described a near-death experience she had had twelve years earlier while lying in a coma after the birth of her son. As she later recalled, during her comatose state she had a vision in which she entered paradise and was struck by the many sweet-smelling flowers there: "It was a real paradise, the fragrance. I couldn't get enough of that perfume." What really drew her attention was a "big, big table," piled high with food, around which many old people she recognized were seated. The old people were feasting on the remembrance offerings people had brought to the cemetery. If anyone visiting the cemetery had shown up empty-handed, she believed, that would mean someone seated at the table would go hungry (EW-A Arkh-Lesh, July 13, 2013). The other dream illustrates precisely this point and was related by Margarita, who heard the story from an acquaintance of hers from Kamenka (a village in the Mezen' region). The acquaintance had confessed to having neglected her mother's grave, and in her dream she saw herself walking to the cemetery, which had big iron gates guarded by a sentry. She told the sentry she had come to see her mother and was allowed to pass. She entered a building rather like a hospital with what looked like wards on either side of a long corridor: "I went into one ward," she said, "and what wasn't laid out on that table! I went into a second ward, where there were only rusks and dry bread. I went into a third ward, the one where I had been told my mother was, and there was nothing but dust there." The sentry told her that her mother had gone out to forage for scraps of food. Margarita pointed out how necessary it was to leave food for the dead at the cemetery when you visit. Sometimes it would be enough just to remember them while you were sitting at the table: "That also gets to them and they are filled" (FA Mez 17-53, July 8, 2008). It is noteworthy that the notion of judgment, characteristic of legends about journeys beyond the grave, is absent here. The welfare of the dead individual is determined not by her conduct in life but by the fulfillment or nonfulfillment of one indispensable aspect of funeral ritual in the rural community—namely, providing food.

FEEDING BY PROXY

Beggars and Almsgiving

The above example shows that merely thinking about the dead while you are eating may be sufficient to provide them with nourishment. Technically speaking, the dead may be fed from a distance at any time. "Sometimes I'll sit down for some soup and I'll remember, for example if I haven't been to the cemetery for a long time" (EW-A Arkh-Lesh, July 13, 2013). It is also possible to sustain the dead by feeding a substitute, such as the beggars and the destitute, who for centuries were the traditional recipients of charitable feeding. One of the earliest references to the ubiquitous custom of visiting cemeteries on Trinity Saturday comes in the mid-sixteenth-century document the *Stoglav* (*One Hundred Chapters*). Here, the presence at this time of street musicians and performers is condemned. Instead of "dancing, clapping their hands, and singing 'satanic' songs," visitors to the graves of their ancestors should behave like Orthodox Christians and be mindful of the poor. They should give alms to paupers and provide them with food and drink (*Stoglav* 1971, 140). Captain Jacques Margeret, in his account of life in Russia in the late sixteenth and beginning of the seventeenth century, also comments on the custom among the "common people," as he terms them, of marking the fortieth day after a death with a meal in the cemetery: "After six weeks they gather on the grave, the widow and some of her main friends, and they bring something there to drink. . . . They eat the viands they have brought, distributing the remainder of what they cannot eat themselves to the poor" (Margeret 1607, 11).

In fact, from medieval times until the early part of the twentieth century, giving alms with the expectation that the recipient would pray for the souls of the dead was a common practice all over Russia, not just in the North or in rural areas. Many different forms of almsgiving have been recorded. Sometimes money was given, but in the villages, giving food, clothing or cloth, or other necessities was much more common. In the Pinega region of Arkhangel'sk province in the nineteenth century, for example, "during funerals anyone who asked was given some money and bread—baked bread or flour or grain." Similarly, on memorial days, in addition to holding prayers and services for the dead on the graves, the peasants would distribute money and baked goods to the poor (Efimenko 1877, 136). In the town of Kargopol' in the Olonets *guberniya* in the nineteenth century, the memorial repast evolved into a meal specially held for beggars.[6] After being fed, the beggars would then receive an additional gift of bread, pies, and sometimes money (Kulikovskii 1894, 3:421). In Vyatka province buns known as "little alms buns" (*milostinka*) were baked specially for remembering the dead and handed out to beggars. Each bun contained a one kopeck piece (Magnitskii 1883, 34).

The importance of almsgiving as part of the Christian way of life was accepted all over Europe, and the indigent had a particular role to play in its proper execution. One might mention the phenomenon of funeral doles, or allotments, known throughout medieval Europe, whereby a Christian would lay aside a sum in his or her will to be distributed to the poor at the funeral with the express command that the poor offer up prayers for the soul of their benefactor

(Roberts 1996, 39). Because Christ Himself identified with the dispossessed, feeding and clothing beggars was seen as synonymous with feeding and clothing Christ, a gesture believed to encourage divine gratitude and a subsequent remission of sins. As we saw above in the message of spiritual verses, only those who had given generously to the poor could expect to be rewarded with the plenitude of paradise. The same moral may be found in Russian folk legends such as "Brother of Christ" ("Khristov Bratets"), in which Christ, disguised as a beggar, in rags and covered in sores, reveals to those who receive Him with charity the joys of paradise awaiting them after death (Afanas'ev 1990, 57–65). It is also the case that, although most beggars were either genuine unfortunates down on their luck or professional scroungers, a faint odor of sanctity clung to the notion of destitution, no doubt in recognition of the few holy men who voluntarily gave up their worldly possessions for a life of prayer and poverty. The beggars, then, interceded, as it were, between the giver of alms, God, and the souls in the afterlife. In Russian culture, the perception of the beggar as an intermediary figure, positioned between the world of the living and the world of the dead, was especially strong. Mendicants were often also wanderers, spending a lifetime on the road, without homes or families. They existed outside the parameters of normal society. (Further analysis of these aspects of the traditional role of the beggar may be found in Shchepanskaya 1995, 110–176 and Levkievskaya 2004, 408–11.) Because of their liminal status, beggars were often asked to perform tasks associated with the dead, such as digging graves or washing corpses, in addition to offering prayers and reading psalms over the body (Shchepanskaya 1995, 131). It is important to note that almsgiving was not an entirely altruistic activity but depended on maintaining a balance between the giver and the receiver. The beggar was empty and "naked" in his rags and required both filling and covering. The donor, according to the principle "Give and it will be given to you . . . good measure will be put into your lap" (Luke 6:37) expected recompense in the afterlife or, indeed, in this life. In Arkhangel'sk province, for example, in preparation for sowing, the peasants would pray for a good harvest to give "food for the beggars and profit for us" (Levkievskaya 2004, 409). For their part, the souls received relief from suffering.

The tradition of almsgiving and feeding beggars on funeral and memorial occasions continues in parts of the North to the present day. During the Soviet period the practice declined since it was regarded as irrelevant in the new economic and religious climate. However, the rural economic collapse following the demise of the Soviet Union has led to considerable poverty, exacerbated by alcoholism and, to a lesser degree, drug abuse. Speaking of the large numbers of guests expected at a funeral meal, one woman commented: "Those bums [*bomzhi*] who are hungry, they'll definitely turn up" (EW-A Arkh-Lesh, July 13,

2013).[7] Such direct links with the charitable acts of the past are now relatively rare, and although the name "alms" (*milostynya, milostynka*) has been preserved, both the nature and the purpose of almsgiving itself have evolved. For instance, although food may be offered to the village poor or the very elderly in the belief that they are closer to those who have already passed into the next life, almsgiving in its contemporary form is not necessarily limited to the indigent, and the link with the spiritual welfare of the soul in the other world has largely been lost. In Vozhgora, Rodoma, and other villages of the Leshukon'e region, giving gifts with the specific request that the dead should be remembered by the recipient is still carried out routinely but is attached to the physical requirements of the deceased, particularly for food. Thus, if a bereaved relative cannot visit the cemetery in person, she may give alms in the form of food: "You can buy sweets or biscuits and just give them [to someone], or, for example, the boys who run about round here—I'll buy sweets and distribute them to all of them and ask them to remember my papa and mama. Everyone knows our name. . . . So I pass them round. In this way they [the dead] are fed too" (EW-A Arkh-Lesh, July 13, 2013). The commercial availability of sweets has made the process of asking people to remember much more convenient. According to information recorded in 2006 in the Kirillov region of Vologda province, it had been customary on memorial occasions in earlier times to offer guests a spoonful of kut'ya from the communal bowl with the request to remember the soul of the deceased sinner. Nowadays, however, people may take a few sweets if they are offered, and some of them will remember and some will not: "I'll take a few sweets. Nowadays they are in the shop. People will leave a bag of sweets lying on the counter for remembering. Take one and remember. They leave them on the counter. . . . Well, no one can be bothered to walk around, handing them out. But the old women, they'll take some and go where their neighbor is buried. Remember, remember. They'll give some sweets or something there" (FA Kir 17-2, July 20, 2006).

Aside from food, alms also took the form of gifts of clothing and cloth. Beggars would be given the clothing of the deceased, for example, or a specially prepared roll of cloth, cut to the exact length of the corpse and containing a pie or money, would be handed to the first person encountered by the funeral procession (Lysenko and Komarova 1992, n.p.). Today, in exchange for remembrance, close relatives and funeral helpers, such as the women who wash and lay out the corpse, may receive various gifts of cloth such as a blouse or headscarf, sheets or duvet covers, and especially towels. In Russian mythology thread, tow, yarn, and ultimately the cloth and clothes spun and woven from them have magical significance as mediators between this world and the world of the dead. Thread and its derivatives have had, and still do have in some respects, symbolic relevance in all the major transitional rites—of birth, initiation, marriage, death, and magical acts connected with them (Maslova 1984, 8–109; Lysenko and Komarova 1992, n.p.; Krinichnaya 2004, 476–92). N. A. Krinichnaya has underlined the importance of woven items, such as cloth, towels, and headscarves, as metaphors for the "road which links the worlds of dead ancestors and their descendants." Some of the most obvious symbols of travel or transfer were the handwoven linen towels that in the past were hung from the window of a peasant house where a death had occurred, in order to provide a pathway for the departing soul (Krinichnaya 2004, 481). From the above it may be seen that some of the traditional aspects of almsgiving have been lost, while others have been retained, particularly the roles of food and cloth. Both food and cloth are given with the express intent that the deceased should be remembered; the recipient of the gift assumes the role of intermediary between the bereaved in this world and their dead ancestors in the other. In the form in which these traditions survive, these intermediaries in most cases offer the souls relief from hunger and other material want rather than relief from punishment for their sins. The question of feeding may not be referred to directly but is implicit in all requests to remember. By extension, the need to remember can even be attached to gifts made by individuals long before they have actually died. One woman we interviewed commented that when using an object gifted by someone who is deceased, one should always remember that person. For example, she claimed that she always invoked her mother-in-law with the words "May she enter the kingdom of heaven and may the earth be like down upon her" when lying down to sleep or when changing the set of bed linen her mother-in-law had given her for her sixtieth birthday (EW-A Arkh-Lesh, July 16, 2013).

Feeding Birds and Remembrance

Finally, I will add a few words about birds, their role in the process of remembrance and association with food. In Slavonic mythology as a whole, birds are often seen to have a connection with death. They may symbolize death itself (Tolstaya 2000, 77) or may act as intermediaries between the worlds of the living and the dead. Birds may carry messages—for example, forewarning of an imminent death. In Arkhangel'sk province in the nineteenth century it was said that if a raven was heard cawing on the roof of a house where someone was sick, then that person would surely die. Similarly, if a swallow were to fly in an open window there would be a death in the house that year (Efimenko 1877, 135). Such beliefs survive in contemporary Russia. A man from the Mezen' region recollected how, after he had been to visit his father, who was seriously ill, he had heard a blue tit tapping on the window and knew that something was wrong. A few days later he received a telegram informing him that his father had died

(FA Mez 17-53, July 8, 2008). Black birds and nocturnal birds are particularly singled out as harbingers of death and misfortune. In folk belief birds are also among the forms assumed by the soul.

In Russian and other Slavonic mythologies, there are many different metaphors for the soul. It is sometimes represented as an indefinable entity, indistinct and nebulous like mist or invisible like air. On the other hand, it may take on a material body that is sometimes anthropomorphic (a small child, for example), but more often zoomorphic (a mouse, a bird, or an insect) (Tolstaya 1999a,162–67; Tolstaya 2000, 76). Tolstaya has suggested that whether the soul is described in its immaterial or material form may to some extent be determined by the chronology of its position in funeral ritual: "Insects and birds, as well as mice, most often embody the soul in the period up to the fortieth day, that is before the final departure of the soul for the other world. . . . Less frequently do the souls of the dead take these forms when visiting their living relatives at later times of remembrance" (Tolstaya 2000, 72). In north Russia, birds may indeed be mentioned as metaphors of the soul during the forty-day period. Recollecting the death of her little brother when she was still a child, an old woman described how the youngsters would keep running up to the coffin where he lay, hoping to see his soul flying down: "We'd look and look . . . but no soul flew down, no little bird flew down. We thought the soul was a little bird" (FA Mez 17-85, July 13, 2008). However, the symbiotic relationship between birds and the souls of the dead is also much in evidence during the later stages of remembrance. I was struck by one particularly vivid reference to bird-souls in connection with a May 9 Victory Day ceremony. Valentina had been reminiscing about the Great Patriotic War, the terrible loss of life and all the men who had not returned home. Asked where souls go after death, she said it was possible they flew up into the sky and turned into doves. Then she described what she had seen once while standing beside the war memorial on Victory Day, listening to the names of the war dead being read out. She had looked up into the sky and seen two cranes flying overhead: "'Oi,' I said, 'Those are someone's souls flying in. Probably our fathers have flown in. No one knows where they lie,' . . . I said. 'The little geese [*sic*] are flying. They [the dead] know they are being remembered'" (EW-A Arkh-Lesh, July 15, 2013).

In addition to taking food for the dead to the cemetery, it is very common to take grain or seeds of some kind or crumbs of bread to scatter in the vicinity of the grave, specifically for the birds. When asked why they scatter grain, people will often say it is for the crows, but in my experience pigeons or doves are more likely to be seen pecking near the graves, since they feed on grain while crows are more interested in the sandwiches and pieces of salami left behind on the graves by mourners. Crows, like ravens, are more often associated in Russian and Slavonic folklore and folk belief with the dark side of death and misfortune (Gura 1995, 436–37), and it is therefore unlikely that they have a more specific function as substitutes for the souls of dead loved ones. However, as birds of ill omen, they may sometimes figure in folk beliefs as the alter egos of the unnatural or unclean dead, such as sorcerers. Nevertheless, for some people birds in general are clearly regarded as host bodies for souls, and this provides a more focused rationale for feeding them. As Lidiya commented: "Well, the little birds, well an ordinary bird flies, so maybe it's the soul of someone who is lying in the ground. The soul is in that bird" (FA Mez 17-74, July 15, 2007). She also, however, provided a second common explanation for the scattering of grain. It is done so that the birds can remember—in other words, so that the birds can perform the same function as beggars or other recipients of alms and gifts. "Sometimes I take seeds," explained Nina, "sunflower seeds, but not the roasted ones, or rice. . . . Our mother was very fond of those seeds. You must have some bread as well, biscuits, sweets. You must have everything." As she presented these offerings she would call on the birds, asking them to "fly down, and remember my dear mom" (FA Mez 17-20, July 15, 2007). In this example a link is established through a favorite food between the dead woman and the birds, so that, once again, eating (or pecking the seeds) while remembering becomes a form of proxy feeding of the dead. This idea may be expressed more explicitly. Pressed to explain why the birds had to peck the grain, another person said she didn't know, but "for example, people have brought it and they say it is so that the dead person will be sated [*chtob on byl sytoi*]" (EW-A Arkh-Lesh, July 15, 2013). The same effect can also be achieved more remotely when birds, which are believed to pass freely between the worlds of the living and the dead, fly up to heaven after they have eaten their fill of grain and inform the souls that they have been remembering them, suggesting, in effect, that they have eaten on their behalf (FA Vash 17-16, July 25, 2001).

Funerary ritual in general is not susceptible to sudden and extreme change. This is particularly the case in north Russia, where even today many outlying villages have little direct contact with centers of urban civilization because of poor roads, lack of transport, and extreme weather conditions at certain times of year. The disasters of the twentieth and twenty-first centuries, beginning with revolution and ending with the economic meltdown of the early 1990s—along with the plummeting birth rate and high suicide and accident rates—have ensured that the traditional rituals of death have retained their power and integrity.

It is generally accepted that funeral rituals in Russian village culture as a whole have two basic aims—to ensure the passage of the deceased into the other world and to safeguard the living during this transitional period. In fact, the situation is much more complex, particularly with regard to food and feeding, which clearly have a crucial role in the rural North. Indeed, I would go so far as to say that feeding associated with remembrance is the key element of funeral ritual.

Ensuring that we, and those who depend on us, have enough to eat and drink is a fundamental human requirement. For the people who have provided the material for our research, it is an obligation that continues beyond the grave, and its purpose is to guarantee the continued survival of their close relatives and more distant kin in the next world. Food seems to flow along an invisible umbilical cord linking the living and the dead and reflects a strong reluctance to accept death as the absolute end of life.

There is a strong belief, perhaps strengthened by familiarity with death and intimate contact with the dead, in an afterlife with distinct material as well as nonmaterial dimensions. As we saw in chapter 1, the soul is imagined as having physical characteristics. Therefore, provision is made for the deceased's material requirements in life beyond the grave. Examining photographs of a funeral in Rodoma, I noticed a number of small packages in the coffin. These turned out to be all the medications the deceased had been taking at the time of his death.

The dead are thought to have both emotional and physical needs. Their return in the dreams of the living may be motivated by the dead's loneliness and desire to seek out a companion, for example, but more often they are thought to visit the living because they are suffering from cold or hunger. In funeral laments, by contrast with dreams of paradise derived from or influenced by medieval literary sources, the afterlife often lacks both food and warmth. In the words of one funeral lament, "Were you not afraid, had you no fear of entering mother-moist-earth? For it is cold there, and there is hunger there" (FA Mez 17a-1, July 27, 2007). This premise lies behind the practice in parts of the North of dressing the dead warmly for burial in winter and also behind the universal practice of providing food.

It is also the case that life in the other world is often imagined as mirroring life in this world. Provisioning the dead may be regarded as simply an extension of normal life beyond the world of the living: "You have had a drink yourself. Your soul should also have a drink" (FA Mez 17-64, July 13, 2008). The same logic also applies to clothing. The dead must be dressed according to the conventions of the living, wearing all the usual garments according to etiquette and the demands of the world to which they are traveling. Thus, missing garments, or garments thought to have been rejected by the deceased, sometimes require replacing, most often through the services of an intermediary. For example, if a man is buried without his hat, a boy might be given the hat to wear (EW-A Arkh-Lesh, July 15, 2013), or if the deceased complains in a dream about the shirt in which he has been buried, a man might be given a replacement to wear (EW-A, July 7, 2013). By wearing the garments of the deceased, intermediaries are thought to be able to reconnect the dead with their belongings.

Feeding the dead may also be regarded as an act of compassion since it relieves their hunger pangs. The well-being of the dead is clearly perceived as depending upon whether or not they are fed, how much they are fed, and how frequently. This in itself, however, seems to reflect a wider moral imperative to "do good," or act in a positive way in order to elicit reciprocal beneficial acts, or to reverse a negative. Acting badly, on the other hand, such as starving your parents and grandparents, is believed to bring about not only harm to the dead but also retribution to the living. This philosophy, often encountered in the rural mentality, is reminiscent of our own homilies: "Do as you would have others do unto you," "What goes around comes around," "Tit for tat," and so on. Bad things are expected when the dead are obliged to fast: "Of course they won't be sated. They won't have any good intentions toward you. They'll have evil intentions" (EW-A Arkh-Lesh, July 16, 2013). That hungry people in general are best avoided is reflected in many Russian proverbs and popular sayings: "A full stomach slumbers, a hungry one is wide awake" (Sytoe bryukho spit, golodnoe na slukhu sidit [Dal' 1957, 804]); "Fear no one more than a dog which is full or a man who is hungry" (Nikogo tak ne boisya, kak sytoi sobaki da golodnogo cheloveka [Dal' 1957, 805]).

At worst, the hungry dead may demand a living sacrifice. Extreme cases of this are vividly demonstrated in nineteenth-century folk tales about flesh-eating or blood-sucking revenants—the restless dead, suicides, and sorcerers denied a Christian burial (see, e.g., in Warner 2011b, 168–71). However, these are merely aberrant examples of the demands made by the dead in general. It is still widely believed, for example, that when the head of a household dies he may at the same time steal the family's cattle or chickens (Golubkova 2002, 207–9). The deceased may even come for a member of his family: "If the dead man is not at the table [i.e., not given his portion at a memorial meal] he may do something, he may take someone away with him from this life" (EW-A Arkh-Lesh, July 17, 2013). The reverse is also true: "If you remember and do your duty by the deceased then they will support you when required" (FA Bel 17-71, July 15, 1994).

The experiences of one woman are a good illustration of this "something for something" balancing act of doing and receiving good or ill. On the one hand, she meticulously remembered her dead parents and had good relations with both of them. On one occasion, when she needed to visit her child in a hospital in Arkhangel'sk, she appealed to her mother for help, asking her to send a car, since it was dark and too far to walk. When she went out into the road a car appeared and she was offered a lift to the hospital. She believed that her parents had somehow sent the car because she had been a dutiful daughter (EW-A Arkh-Lesh, July 13, 2013). On the other hand, after the death of her grandmother she missed visiting the grave on several important memorial days. The grandmother became angry and consequently the woman's baby son fell ill (EW-A Arkh-Lesh, July 7, 2013). This kind of trade-off between the living and the dead makes feeding and other forms of remembrance apotropaic acts in which ensuring that the dead are content, rest peacefully, and have no wish to harm the living amounts to self-preservation.

On a more abstract level, feeding the dead may also be seen as a major factor in restoring the equilibrium destroyed by death, replacing a negative with a positive, lack with abundance, hunger and (in its most extreme form) famine and drought with drink and food. The subtle balancing act between giving and taking, fullness and emptiness, which characterizes various aspects of traditional patterns of behavior in Russia, and which is particularly evident in funeral ritual, is well-illustrated by V. A. Dashkov's nineteenth-century description of a memorial meal in Olonets province. This was a special meal to which all the ancestral dead of the village were invited and in which all the living villagers took part. It was only held in years distinguished by a bountiful harvest and offered not one but three tables of food, one on the porch, a second in the anteroom or storage space (*seni*), and a third in the living room of the house where the ceremony took place. This profusion was offset by the empty stomachs of the hosts, who fasted before the meal, and by the hunger of their dead visitors (Dashkov 1842, 213–14).

Finally, one might say that between the living and the dead there is a symbiotic relationship underpinned by the shared experience of eating. At the cemetery, refusing to partake of the memorial food is not an option because "the more you eat, the more will he [the deceased] be filled" (EW-A Arkh-Lesh, July 15, 2013). Perhaps this provides the answer to the question I posed at the beginning of this chapter—was swallowing a whole glass of vodka at the graveside a positive act or a negative one? In general, women who drink alcohol to excess are frowned upon in Russian village culture. Nevertheless, I have often accepted a glass of wine or sweet liqueur from an elderly village woman who was glad of my company and my interest in her life, as well as the opportunity to enjoy a discreet drink with a visitor, so I do not think my action would be condemned. I like to hope that the dead man was pleased to receive an unexpected extra portion of vodka.

During any visit to a cemetery, biscuits or sweets are placed on the cross or scattered on the grave. Edoma, Arkhangel'sk province, 2011. (Photo by Elizabeth Warner)

The Lament

A Language for Communicating with the Dead

SVETLANA ADONYEVA

From the time of the first scholarly records in the middle of the nineteenth century until well into the twenty-first century, the main features of funeral and memorial practices in Russian villages have remained largely unchanged and differ considerably from funeral rituals in towns, where care of the dead has been handed over to the medical profession and commercial funeral services. The tradition of lamenting at funerals and on memorial occasions was only preserved in the villages.

The first significant records of the lament, a form of song-recitative that constitutes its own folkloric genre, were made by P. N. Rybnikov (Rybnikov 1864, 3; Rybnikov 1867, 4). Rybnikov named the genre *zaplachki* ("weeping songs," from *plakat'*, to weep, cry, or lament). However, in his major collection of northern laments, E. V. Barsov (1872, 1) used a different term, *prichitaniya* (from *prichitat'*, to wail or lament), and this became the accepted designation. The women who performed laments were known variously as *voplenitsy* (howlers), *prichetnitsy* (lamenters), or *plachei* (weepers).

Today, only on very rare occasions—perhaps when a village woman has traveled to town in order to bid her last farewell to a relative—will lamenting be heard in an urban setting. I was present on one such occasion. In the St. Petersburg City Hospital several rooms are set aside for people who wish to take their leave of the deceased. In one of these an elderly woman was weeping and lamenting beside a coffin. While this was going on the other people present were obviously dismayed and uncomfortable and clearly had no idea how to react to this ecstatic outpouring of emotion. Indeed, in towns, beginning with the gentry, the practice of lamenting died out centuries ago. Peter the Great abolished keening at the funerals of members of the royal family at the beginning of the eighteenth century. By the nineteenth century, as was the case with many other folklore genres, lamenting survived as an active element only in peasant culture.

Before my first experience of hearing a lament performed in its proper village context I had, of course, like all students of folklore and ethnography preparing for fieldwork, read the relevant textbooks on the subject. From these I learned that there were wedding laments (performed by the brides at weddings as late as the 1930s), funeral and memorial laments, and recruit laments, which accompanied young men setting off to do military service. Laments of the latter sort were still being recorded in the 1940s when village women saw their menfolk off to fight in World War II. Despite the strict division of laments into these three separate categories, in 1984 in villages along the Sukhona river in Vologda province I heard laments performed for the first time and realized that though they might differ by subject matter, they were linked by a similar style of intonation during the performance. Each locality has a different lamenting "voice," a combination of melody and rhythm, but within the locality the "voice" remains the same, whether the lament is performed at a funeral, at a wedding, or at the leave-taking of army recruits. After her first public performance of a lament, at her own wedding, a woman became accustomed to this particular register and was able to apply it in different situations.

LAMENTING DURING A FUNERAL

In order to show the place occupied by lamenting at a funeral, I will begin with a brief outline of funeral ritual drawn from our field materials recorded in Vologda and Arkhangel'sk provinces.

As soon as a death has been established, the body of the deceased is "made ready" (*obryazhat'*). It is washed, dressed in the clothing prepared for the occasion, and laid out on a bench. Lamenting begins as soon as the corpse has been washed and dressed. A woman born in 1918 in the Leshukon'e region of Arkhangel'sk province told us: "So, the deceased is lying there and you are sitting beside the coffin and you weep over the body:

> Ох ты, ясненько-тошнехонько,
> Ты сердешно мое дитятко,
> Это, мило ты моя, ладушка,
> Ты пошто нас оставила?
> Ты на кого нас бросила?

> Okh, I am so sick at heart,
> My darling little child,
> My own dear darling.
> Why have you left us?
> Into whose care have you abandoned us?

Then they go on, lamenting and lamenting. They lament and cry and all the people cry. If someone doesn't know how to lament they sit there anyway and listen. They cry, but just with tears, not using their voice" (FA Lesh 17a-3, July 8, 2009).

Lamenting takes place again on the third day after the death, when the body is removed from the house. The lamenter accompanies the funeral procession, lamenting at the village boundary and beside the grave. Until the fortieth day the deceased's home remains unlocked and a shot of vodka or a cup of tea—together with a pie, a spoon, and a fork—is left in the front corner of the living room next to the icons, as people believe that the deceased may reenter the house during that period. On the ninth, twentieth, and fortieth days relatives go to the cemetery in order to "bring home" the deceased. The lamenter invites him or her in and seats the deceased at the table. A woman born in 1923 in the village of Tsenogora in the Leshukonʹe region described how, on the ninth day, the deceased should be invited for a meal:

> Подуйте, ветры буйные,
> С южной стороны, с северной.
> И с восточной, и с западной . . .
> Раздождитесь мелки дождички.
> Размочите сыру землю.
> Ты откройся тогда, гробова доска.
> Разпахнитесь белы саваны.
> Вы откройтесь очи ясные.
>
> Blow, stormy winds,
> From the south, from the north,
> From the east and from the west . . .
> Little rain showers scatter your rain
> And soak the damp earth.
> Then open up, coffin lid,
> Unravel, white winding sheet.
> Bright eyes, open wide . . .
> (FA Lesh 17a-7, July 15, 2009)

The lamenter herself does not take a seat at the table but approaches the icon corner where, it is believed, the deceased will be sitting and addresses her lament to him. On the fortieth day the remains of the memorial meal, together with the table it was laid on, are carried from the house onto the street, the deceased is led outside, as it were, to continued lamenting and accompanied to the edge of the village, with an icon borne alongside. On these special memorial days floors in the house are washed and the bathhouse is heated.

According to the Belozersk tradition in the northeast part of Vologda province, the bathhouse is still regarded as a location where memorial practices, including lamenting, may take place:

> This is what happens in the villages. The bathhouse is heated on the Friday before an "ancestral Saturday."[1] Whether you wash or not it's heated on Friday. Me, for example, I'm used to heating the bathhouse on Monday or Sunday. But when there's an ancestral Saturday I heat it on Friday. You take clothing and a towel for your ancestor into the bathhouse. You leave it for about fifteen minutes. . . . Then you say, well, more like lament: "Dear ancestors come and have a wash." That's all. Then you shut the door and wait for twenty or twenty-five minutes and then everyone else can come and wash. (FA Bel 18-508, July 10, 2002)

Some Old Russian homilies against paganism condemn the performance of bathhouse memorial rites, including heating the bathhouse for the dead, producing steam, and hanging up clothing and a towel (Gal'kovskii 1916, 1:202–3). Clearly, these same customs appear in contemporary records, but unlike in Vologda province, in the villages of Arkhangel'sk province no mention is made of lamenting in the bathhouse.

The preceding general outline, compiled from the accounts of various informants, allows us to see the place occupied by lamenting in village funeral rituals from the end of the twentieth century to the beginning of the twenty-first.

THE PERSONAL EXPERIENCE OF LAMENTING

The following description of specific moments in the ritual was recorded in 1998 in Vologda province from interviews with one individual, Evstoliya Konstantinovna Tekanova, in the village of Maeksa on the shore of Lake Beloe. Her narrative provides us with a greater understanding of how laments are generated in concrete situations and allows us to see the deeply personal relationship between the lamenter and what is happening in the course of the funeral. The text has been considerably shortened as Evstoliya was a very prolific lamenter:

> I didn't learn how to lament. I would just speak out about my sorrows from the bottom of my heart. They lay out the deceased on the table. People begin to gather and then they start to lament. Everyone who can, laments—the wife, the sister, the cousins. For three nights they sit round the deceased. You'll sit down to lament more than once during that time and people come in to listen and have a cry. Oh! It's tough. You speak out about anything that comes into your head, all your aches

and pains, your troubles, your grief, your pity. When my father died I lamented
like this:

Уж подойду я, сиротиночка,[2]
—ой, заплачу:
Уж я ко углу ко переднему,
Уж ко столу да ко дубовому,
Уж я ко телу то ко белому,
Уж ко языку безответному . . .
Уж(ы) ты скажи, да тепла пазушка,
Уж(ы) ты куда да снарядилося,
Уж(ы) ты куда да сподобилося?
    . . . Уж(ы) сама знаю, сиротиночка,
Уж(ы) ты куда да снарядилося:
Уж(ы) ты во матушку сыру землю . . .

Well, I will go, little orphan girl,
(Oh! How I'd weep)
Well, up to the front corner,
Up to the oaken table,
Up to the white body,
Up close to the tongue which answers not . . .
Tell me, my dear protector (*tepla pazushka*)
Where are you going now, all dressed up,
How did you deserve this honor?
Well, I know myself, little orphan girl,
Where you are going, all dressed up,
You are on your way into mother-moist-earth . . .

I could lament a lot but I must stop. I would lament for two hours. . . .
I'm missing a lot out, leaving gaps. You couldn't listen to it all. I lamented over
my husband, over my sons. That was my lot as a woman. . . . The tears come
of their own accord. I go to the cemetery and lament. My mother used to say:
"Go any time, even if its late, or later in the morning. It's never a sin to 'cry'
your grief."

In the literature on the subject laments are described as an improvisatory
genre. Set themes, word combinations, and poetic images are all part of the performer's repertoire. However, although Evstoliya herself may also have thought
of the lament as a form of improvisation, she revealed the limitations of such an
assessment by continually checking that her laments were being "correctly"

recorded. Recollecting how she lamented over her brother, who died young, she corrected herself several times in her efforts to remember word for word the text she had pronounced at the funeral as she addressed her sister-in-law, her brother's wife: "Take a look, white swan. . . . No, that's not right! Take a look at your dear husband . . ." Of importance for her were not the poetic formulae but the deeply personal situation in which they were being pronounced. Again, in her lament about the death of her brother, she reminded his widow how her considerate husband used to get up very early but never woke her up, and this, in turn, caused her to remember her own dead husband who also "always saw the sun rising":

При тебе [о муже], да добра голова,
Я не знала, сиротиночка,
Откуда солнце поднимается,
Куда красное девается.

When you [her husband] were alive, my dear,
This [widow]-orphan never knew
From which direction the sun rises,
Nor where the beauty sinks.

I didn't think about getting up early. It didn't worry me. He was up and about. That's how it was with us. He would get up early. He saw the sun rise while I went on sleeping. That was in my lament for my own husband too. Oh! the pity of it.

Remembering how she addressed her dead son during her funeral laments, Evstoliya probably did improvise, drawing on her reserve of images and expressions, but that did not conceal the extreme nature of her personal suffering:

They were taking the coffin out and I was lamenting:

Уж вы держите да двери за скобу,
Не отпускайте да сына милого! . . .
Приходи, Сережа миленькой
Уж ко мне, да сиротиночке,
Уж ко мне, да горькой матушке!
Уж не завешаю окошечек,
Не закутаю воротичек.
Буду ждать, да дожидатиси,
Из окна в окно бросатиси

Hold tight to the door latch,
Don't let my dear son go out! . . .
Come to me, Serezha my darling.
Come to poor, orphaned me,
To me, your grieving mother!
I won't draw the curtains over the windows,
I won't lock up the gates.
I will wait and wait until you come.
I will dash from window to window . . .

While I was lamenting everyone present was weeping. I saw nothing around me, not the people, no one. Pity tormented me and grief. They had to hold me up while I lamented. Lament! Lament for your dear ones! How sad I am for my son. . . . Along with your tears some harmful poisons leave your body.

Evstoliya also remembered how lamenting is done on special memorial days, when it is customary to remember the dead at home, at the cemetery, and in the bathhouse:

The bathhouse is heated up. People bring clean underwear and hang it up on the clothing rail for the deceased.

Уж приходи ты, добра голова![3]
Уж стопила да парну баянку . . .
Уж дам чистую перемывочку
Уж за твою-то за добротушку,
За твою да за ласкотушку.

Come in now, my dear,
The steamy bathhouse has been heated . . .
I'll give you clean linen,
For the sake of your little kindnesses,
For all your tenderness . . .

You invite them into the bathhouse and you weep and say it all.

Lamenting at the cemetery by her son's grave, she begs him to come back home with her where a memorial meal has been prepared for him:

Уж раскрой ты да очи ясные!
Ты раздайся, да мать сыра земля,

Уж расколись-то гробова доска,
Уж ты повстань-ко мило дитятко,
Ты услышь меня, горюшицу,
Ой уж во сегодняшний Господний день!
Уж напекла я, наготовила
Уж для тебя, да гостя милого, . . .
Уж ты пойдем-то да пожалуйста. Что, там все наготовлено . . .

Open wide your bright eyes!
Break asunder, mother-moist-earth.
Coffin boards, split apart.
Stand up, my darling child.
Hear me, your grieving mother,
On this, the Lord's day!
I have baked and cooked
For you, dear guest . . .
Please, let us go together.
Everything has been prepared ready . . .

As we learn from the performer herself, the description of the road to the cemetery, although it makes use of various conventional images of the genre, in fact corresponds to reality: "In winter when we lament we say, 'Trample the white snow, lay down fresh footprints. . . .' I lament on the road to the cemetery. It's unbearable. In the summer we say, 'Trample the gray sand,' because the soil in our cemetery is sandy."

In Evstoliya's village, in addition to the special memorial days, the dead person was remembered on Easter Monday and at Christmas, although on that day there was no lamenting. There was no lamenting when graves were visited on Trinity Sunday either: "No one weeps on that day because the whole earth rejoices."[4] On memorial occasions when the deceased's presence was expected at table Evstoliya would lament as follows:

Погляжу я, сиротиночка,
В передний угол, да на лавочку,
На место благочестивое.
Уж как сидит да гость любимый там.
У его у теплой пазушки
Ложичка не подымаетсе,
Стопочка не выпивается . . .

As an orphaned woman, I will turn my gaze
To the front corner, to the bench,
To the place of honor.
My beloved guest already sits there.
But my dear protector does not lift his spoon,
Does not raise his glass . . .

She goes on to explain how they would place a little three-cornered table in the front corner and set out a shot glass with vodka and a plate for the deceased and then, when they sat down to their own meal, they would begin to remember and to lament:

If the mother, sister, or aunt of the deceased are present they will definitely have to lament. When you've had a cry your heart seems lighter, as if a stone has been rolled away. When you speak, you feel you can almost see them. Of course, people believe that when you are lamenting they [the dead] can hear you. At the memorial meal we serve fish dishes, some smoked fish or fried, and we must have *olad'i*. The last, "farewell" dish is *kisel'*.[5] We chant prayers. On the fortieth day we say the "Lord's prayer." Then, we go outside to the front corner by the entrance, opposite the porch, and we lament there. This is the last lament, when we bid the deceased farewell and tell him not to come home again. We do this by the front corner, although some people may go a bit further away:

Ой уж(ы) как пошел, да тепла пазушка,
Дорогой да гость возлюбленной,
Уж он пошел, да не обвернется,
Уж он пошел, да не оглянется! . . .

Oi! Uzh(y)! My dear protector has departed,
Our dearly beloved guest.
He has departed and will not turn back,
He has departed and will not glance behind!

That's how it all is. We go out onto the street. We take his food on the plate and the shot glass, go up to the front corner and lay everything on the ground.

Once an old woman offered to "take away" Evstoliya's anguish, but she refused: "I will go on weeping, and pitying, and remembering," she said. She also refused to lament for people she didn't know. "You don't know what to say. You'd make yourself a laughing stock. Anyway, you wouldn't have the heart for it. It's only for your own folks" (SA field notes, Vol-Bel, July 17, 1998).

Village women who married after 1930 no longer had the experience of lamenting at their own weddings since traditional village weddings became a rarity after collectivization. Their first experiences of lamenting came with the "woe" (*gore*), or deep grief from personal loss, that came with the burial of their parents, husbands, or children. Most women told us they had not learned how to lament deliberately. On the other hand, we often witnessed how older women who were performing a lament for us would draw in their grown-up daughters so that they could learn while it was taking place.

LAMENTING IN EXTRA-RITUAL SITUATIONS

Some of the women we interviewed described how lamenting may arise outside the normal "collective" context of funeral and memorial rituals. For someone who is lamenting, the traditional verbal formulae used for describing emotions transform speech from a spontaneous conversational mode into an organized, poetic mode: "Oi, my grief is enough to fill the blue sea! I'll go out. I'll get dressed. I'll go out into the street. I'll sit down in the street. Oi, my grief is as high as a mountain. Oi! A river of tears runs between the mountains" (FA Bel 17-115, July 6, 2002).

In the following interview Lyudmila, an informant born in 1926 in the village of Pogorelets, describes how, in the late 1930s, her mother would lament for Lyudmila's father at home and outside the ritual situation, when something happened to remind her of her loss. Memories of these occasions clearly made a profound and lasting impression on the daughter.

> I remember my mother lamenting because she was left with four [children]. My father died. How she wept. . . . He died in the autumn and after that we went down into our winter quarters and then in May we came back up here [into the summer *izba*].[6] How she would lament. As soon as spring came she would start wailing: "Then lovely spring came, the spring waters began their flood, the wide rivers began to flow, the geese-swans flew down," and then, "Everyone else went off to do their hard work, to earn their keep. And I alone, sad and grieving, am without a partner. Who will provide for me? How will I raise my children?" It was like someone reading from a poetry book. I was eleven at the time but I still carry those words in my heart, yes, I do. (FA Mez 17a-2, July 18, 2007)

Another woman in the Mezen' region, born in 1935, told us something similar. She had heard her mother lamenting during the war after she got the news that her husband had been killed at the front. Now, she herself laments at the funerals of relatives. From her story, it is clear that for her mother the lament provided a means of addressing her dead husband. It was her mother's way of speaking to him:

Dad was killed at the front and, well, he hadn't finished building our house. After work my mom would come home, sit down on the threshold and begin to lament. She took it very badly. He was killed at the front in 1944. News of his death arrived on the sixteenth of July. So, she would come home from the haymaking. . . . It was a collective farm, they worked without wages.[7] There were four of us children. With granny that was five, and the pension we got for him was only seven rubles. So, she'd come home from the haymaking—and how they worked! It was dreadful . . . from sunrise to sunset. She'd come home and the house wasn't finished. There wasn't even a door. She'd sit down on the threshold and begin to lament, addressing him like this:

Ты венчальна моя мила ладушка,

Ты . . . восхоже моё красно солнышко.

Ты куда нас оставил, ты куда нас покинул, спобросил?

У меня стадышка-то немалые,

У меня детушки-то недорощены,

Недорощены, недоподняты,

Умом-разумом не наставлены,

Твёрдо на ноги не поставлены. Вот . . .

Золота моя гора осыпалась,

Медовая река повытекла,

Восковая свеча растаяла. Вот . . .

Накатилась на меня туча грозная,

Накатилася, навалилася—

И её ветрами не проносит,

И её снегами не рассекает,

Её дождями не промывает. Вот . . .

И как я буду тебя забывать-то?

Я во сне ли буду засыпаться

Или водой холодной буду отпиваться?

И как я буду . . . жить, детей-то ростить?

My dear, my beloved husband,
   . . . My rising sun.

To what fate have you left us, cast us off, abandoned us?
My flocks are not small.
My little children are not grown-up.
They are not grown-up, not yet raised.
They have not been taught common sense yet,
Not shown how to stand on their own two feet. That's how it is . . .
My mountain of gold has crumbled.
My river of honey has all dried up.
My waxen candle has melted away. That's how it is!
A storm cloud has rolled onto me,
Has rolled onto me, fallen upon me,
And the winds cannot carry it away,
And snow falls cannot cleave it,
And heavy rain will not wash it away. That's how it is!
And how shall I ever forget you?
Will it happen as I close my eyes in slumber,
Or drink the cold water of forgetfulness?
And how will I live, how will I bring up the children?
(FA Mez 17a-1, July 27, 2007)

This woman had learned how to lament from her mother. The day we interviewed her turned out to be a day of remembrance for her cousin who had died, and we were able to record her own lament for him. From our long conversation with her it was clear that listening to her mother as she wept on the porch of their house had been her first major experience of listening to laments, and it had made a profound impression on her. In spite of the fact that these laments were performed outside the ritual situation of a funeral, the mother was nevertheless lamenting in a liminal state of "orphanhood," reflecting her transition from the status of wife to that of widow. The daughter remembered her mother's lament word for word, and formulaic expressions drawn from it later formed the basis of her own laments, performed in the context of funerals.

INITIATION INTO THE STATE OF "ORPHANHOOD"

At this point it is appropriate to consider the social parameters of lamenting. The village funeral ritual is a form of initiation into the state of "orphanhood" (*sirotstvo*). By contrast with its dictionary definition as a person who has lost one or both parents, the word "orphan" (*sirota*) in the language of the lament describes an individual whose social status has changed as a consequence of the death. The husband becomes a widower, the wife a widow, the children orphans.[8] A wife may call herself an "orphan" as she sits down on the "orphan's" bench to lament over her dead husband:

> Моя милая ты ладушка,
> Накажи-тко деткам миленьким
> Про меня про сиротиночку . . .

> My dear darling one,
> Explain to my little children
> What has happened to me, the poor orphan . . .
> (FA Bel 17a-10, July 23, 1997)

A mother who has lost a son may call herself an orphan:

> Я повыйду, сиротиночка,
> Я на площадь на широкую,
> Опущу я свой весел голос
> Ко могилушке глубокия.
> Буду звать я, дозываться
> Своего да сына милого.

> I will go out, little orphan that I am,
> Into the expanse of the cemetery.
> I will send my comforting voice
> Down into the deep grave
> And call out and my call will reach
> My dear son.
> (FA Bel 17a-13, July 10, 1993)

Daughters lamenting for their fathers, mothers for their sons, and wives for their husbands may all equally apply the definition "orphan" to themselves. In other words, in the context of the lament the meaning of the word orphan is expanded beyond the notion of children who have lost their parents to include anyone who has suffered a deep personal loss, who has experienced the death of parents, children, a wife, or a husband. In those cases when we asked women for an example of how a lament is performed "in general," rather than asking them to remember their own laments linked to their personal situations, we were presented the following kind of text, with no use of "orphan" to indicate the lamenter herself, no real names, and none of the other terms of address that define a precise relationship between the lamenter and the deceased (such as *lada* [my beloved husband] or *semeiyushka* [head of the family] for a dead husband or *dityatko* [dear little child] for a dead infant):[9]

> Подойду я поблизехонько
> (там по имени называют мать ли, кто ли)
> Сяду рядом порядешенько.
> Ты куды да нарядилоси?

> I will go up very, very close
> To . . . (they will name the deceased, the mother, or whoever it is)
> And I will sit down next to her, right beside her,
> [and ask] Where are you going all dressed up?
> (FA Bel 17a-18, July 16, 1993)

Women who are relatives of the deceased but whose status will not change as a result of the death avoid using the designation "orphan" for themselves during their lamentations, in spite of the fact that the term "Poidu ya, sirotinochka" (I will go, little orphan) is a widely accepted rhythmic formula for beginning laments. They may use alternative expressions to describe themselves such as "poor thing" (*bednushka*), "sorrowful little soul [literally, dejected little head]" (*kruchinnaya golovushka*), "poor grief-stricken one" (*bednaya goryushitsa*), and so on (Adon'eva 1998, 63–83).

The women who come to lament at funerals, as our records from 1990 to 2015 clearly show, have already had the experience of "becoming orphans," whether literally, after burying their parents, or following the death of a husband. The woman who laments for the first time in her life at a funeral is the one who is being orphaned at that precise time. The funeral ritual invests a specific group of people with the new status of "orphanhood" and the corresponding change in social roles. In the prerevolutionary village this status was distinguished by certain legal, material, and social characteristics.[10] In the Soviet period and later, the status of orphans was more concerned with particular ritual functions and rules of behavior (for the ritual functions of orphans see Trofimov 1999, 25–26). The continued existence of a special "orphaned" category was suggested, for example, by something we noted in our research throughout the Belozer'e region of Vologda province: women who demurred when we asked them to sing a song almost invariably cited the loss of parents, children, or a husband as the reason: "I don't sing, I have had too many sorrows." Even today, children are regularly reminded of the special status of orphans when they are told not to enter their neighbors' houses unless explicitly invited: "You have no business in other people's homes. You are not an orphan after all!" The imperative for orphans and widows to seek charity is reinforced by the desire of donors to distribute food among beggars and orphans on those special days when ancestors are remembered, according to a tradition still encouraged by the Orthodox Church. On one occasion, in the village of Ferapontova in Vologda province in 1993, one of our informants, as she opened the door, immediately invited us to come in and join her at a table laden with pies. It transpired that we had arrived on a memorial day. On that day everyone always made pies and distributed them among the indigent, orphans, and itinerant beggars so that everyone would remember the ancestors together. Our unexpected arrival on that day qualified us for the role of itinerants. Women in the Mezen' region told us about the custom of "secret almsgiving" when, after the war, their grandmothers or mothers would send them out with a cloth bundle containing some food to the home of someone who had lost a close relative. They had to leave the bundle on the porch, making sure that no one saw them.

The interdiction against widows' participation in public amusements of any kind still makes itself felt today. If a widow has been heard singing a frivolous song, for example, or has been seen at a festival or has even been out visiting too often, her social peers are likely to show their disapproval, at least behind her back. On the other hand, widows and orphans feel an obligation to attend the funerals of close relatives, kinsmen, and neighbors. After the initiatory experience of loss, the boundary between the living and the dead remains open for those who have suffered it. Lamenting is a way of connecting to the ancestors on memorial days, or indeed any other days, when the bereaved feels the need to bemoan her fate or seek solace. On the fortieth day after a death, in Loida in the southwest part of the Belozersk region, after the memorial meal it was customary for everyone to go outside to send off the deceased, but in contrast to previous memorial days, they would not go to the cemetery but accompany them only as far as the village boundary, where the lamenter would show the deceased how to mark the spot where they could meet again:

Попрошу я, сиротинушка,

Как тебя, да родитель-матушка,

Заломи-ко ты заломочку

На пути, да на дороженьке.

Как уж я то, да сиротиночка,

Как уж я то порастоскуюся,

Как приду-то на заломочку,

Поговорю да с родитель-матушкой.

I, your orphan child, will ask you,
I will ask you, my own dear mother,
To mark a place on the path, on the road.
Mark it with a break in a branch,
So that when I, your orphan child, feel sad,
I can come to the break
And talk to you, my own dear mother.
(Razova 1994, 186)

Time and again during interviews our informants would refer to the secluded places they had chosen for lamenting on their own—the vegetable garden, a field, a hillock in the forest, the cowshed.

After she has performed her first lament in public at the funeral of the person whose death has made her an "orphan" (e.g., a husband, mother, or father), a woman becomes a fully legitimate participant in all the funeral and memorial rituals that follow, with the right to make use of her "lamenting voice." I believe this explains certain facts noted by folklorists in recruit laments recorded in the Pechora region of northwest Russia and the Pudozh region of the Republic of Karelia, also in the North. Laments for the young men leaving the village for the front in 1941–45 were mainly performed not by their young wives, as one might have expected, but by their widowed mothers (Bazanov 1962, 10–44). In other words, widows were lamenting over their orphaned sons. One of the consistent themes of recruit laments is the appearance of the dead father at the farewell ritual (*provody*) for his son:

Ды по сегод(и)нешному деницьку
Уж(и) ко теби, рожоно дитятко,
Дак приходил(ы) кор(ы)милец-батюшко . . .
Уж самы знаем, самы ведаем—
Нет кор(и)мил(и)ца света батюшка.

Today was the day,
My own dear son,
Your father-provider came to you . . .
But we know ourselves, we know full well,
Your dear father-provider is no more . . .
(Adon'eva 1998, text No. 99)

"Orphan" versions of the wedding ritual can be found all over the Russian North.[11] The brothers B. M. and Yu. M. Sokolov, who were recording folklore in

Vologda province in the first decade of the twentieth century, commented about one particular performer of laments, Marim'yana Ivanovna Medvedeva: "She is famous in the district as a talented weeper [*plakusha*] and knows a mass of laments and songs. . . . The sincerity of her laments can be explained by her early marriage. She was forced to marry against her will. By that time her father was no longer alive. For several days before the wedding she 'would go out into the street to call her dad' who would, as she said, have stood up for her" (B. Sokolov and Yu. Sokolov 1999, 1:177–78).

I heard a performance of this type of lament by an orphan-bride in 1983, during my very first folklore expedition—to the Velikii Ustyug region in the eastern part of Vologda province—and it was a completely new experience for me. I was in conversation with a woman of about sixty years of age. Describing for me the wedding ceremony she had gone through as a young woman, she mentioned that she had lamented during the wedding, and I asked for more details. She told me that she was escorted to the street door of the house (it is customary in Russian villages for the wedding ritual to take place in the bride's home), and the door was then flung wide open in front of her. At that point she began her lament, addressing her dead father who had come, or so she supposed, to give his blessing for her marriage:

> Ой да под окошком колотится,
> Ой да за скобу забирается,
> Ой, да по стене пробирается,
> Ой, да вот идет ко мне батюшка,
> Ой, да и несет-то мне батюшка,
> Ой, да как на правой на рученьке
> Ой, да платьице подвенечное,
> Ой, да на левой на рученьке,
> Ой, да платьице умиральное,
> Ой, а кабы взять-то мне девушке
> Ой, да платьице подвенечное . . .
> Да осудят люди добрые . . .
> А платьице умиральное брать мне не хочется . . .

> Oi! Someone is knocking at the window.
> Oi! Someone is reaching for the latch.
> Oi! Someone is creeping along the wall.
> Oi! It is my papa, who is coming to me.
> Oi! On his right arm my papa bears
> Oi! My wedding dress,

Oi! And on his left,
Oi! He bears my burial gown.
Oi! If I, young girl that I am, take the wedding dress . . .
Oi! Then good folks will censure me . . .
Oi! But I do not wish to take the burial gown . . .

I asked the woman if she would perform the lament for me and furthermore requested that she use the full lamenting voice rather than just speaking the words or using a simple recitative. She looked at me doubtfully and asked if I was quite sure that was what I wanted to hear, but she agreed anyway. By the second phrase of the lament we both had tears running down our cheeks. The sound of the lament had such emotional force that, as I listened to it, I was unable to hold back the flood of feelings. When she finished the lament, the performer turned to me and asked in a perfectly calm, untroubled voice: "Well, how did you like it?" I was shocked and understood then that behind the ability to lament lay not only feelings but also a special skill, that of manipulating the feelings of others. "Orphanhood" provided both the skill for lamenting and the right to manipulate the feelings and sensibilities of the listener (SA field notes, Vol-V Ust, July 15, 1983).

Initiation into a state of "orphanhood" upon losing a parent, husband, or child and lamenting over them guaranteed a woman the right to address the world of the dead in public and to make ritual contact with the ancestors. From that moment the initiative for undertaking memorial activities and ensuring that they were conducted properly lay in her hands. A woman from Belozersk (b. 1930) told me that on memorial days she believed she had an obligation to "remember" in the bathhouse all her deceased relatives as well as the ancestors of her first husband.

An understanding of how the world beyond the grave operates was within the competence of "orphans," as was a talent for poetic meditation and mystical insight into the realm of death. One of the tasks of lamenters, as the ritual unfolded, was explaining the principles of this realm to the uninformed "newly deceased." For example, on one occasion a widow lamenting at the funeral of her young nephew explained to the deceased what was going to happen to him beyond the grave:

Ты пойдешь, да мила ладушка,
В дальнюю дороженьку,
За леса да за дремучие,
За болота за зыбучие,
За озера да глубокие,

За моря да за широкие.
Там ести сторожа
Да ести верные,
Караулы ести крепкие.
Не отпутсят тебя, ладушка
На родимую сторонушку.

You will set off, my dearest dear one,
Down a long road,
Past the deep forests,
Past the shifting marshes,
Beyond the deep lakes,
Beyond the wide seas.
In that place there are guards,
Trusty guards
And doughty sentinels.
They will not let you return, my dear,
To your own land.
(FA Bel 17a-10, July 23, 1997)

THE LAMENTING "VOICE": A GIFT AND AN OBLIGATION

If the text of the lament is a communication addressed to the dead, the act of performing the lament provides the channel of communication itself, the link between the living and the dead. Not everyone is capable of achieving this.[12] Practically all the women we have interviewed who are involved in some way with funeral and memorial lamenting, whether as performers or as witnesses, have told us that not all women are good lamenters: "God made us all, but he didn't make us all equal," commented one interviewee about having a gift for the language of laments (FA Mez 17a-5, July 10, 2007).

The combination of ideas about altered conditions (spiritual exaltation or poetic ecstasy), knowledge of the world "on the other side," and mediation between the living and the dead is not something exclusive to the Russian tradition. The ability to act as intermediary between the living and the dead presupposes a considerable knowledge of the world of the dead. The priest P. A. Florenskii, in his critique of Paul's Letter to the Philippians, wrote that dying is a matter requiring experience and preparation:

A person dies only once in a lifetime. If he has no experience, therefore, he may have an "unsuccessful" death. Man does not know how to die and his death fumbles its way to him, in the shadows. However, death, like any activity, demands skill. In order to have a completely successful death one must know how to die, one must acquire the skill of dying, one must "learn" the art of dying. For that, however, it is necessary to die while yet alive, under the tutelage of experienced people who have themselves "already died." . . . For the uninitiated, life beyond the grave is a completely new country, in which he has difficulty orientating himself, into which he is born, like a baby, without experience or guides. For the initiated, on the other hand, this country is familiar. He has already been there, has already looked around it, albeit from afar and with the guidance of experienced people. . . . As the ancients said, the map of the other world is known to him and he knows the names of things in the world on the other side. (Florenskii 1996, 167–68)

The participants in a funeral may be divided into those who are being initiated—that is, those acquiring the status of orphans—and those who already have that status and experience to do the initiating. The rest of the village community perform the role of witnesses or spectators. As our own observations and photographs from the second half of the twentieth century affirm, funerals traditionally involve the whole village.

When called upon to weep over the grief or woe of others, lamenters are in a position to draw on their own experience of suffering: "Grief torments, grief obliges you to weep" (Bazanov 1943, 28). In standard Russian, the word *gore* may be used to refer to grief, sorrow, or misfortune in many contexts. In the colloquial parlance of the north Russian peasantry, however, the term has a more precise meaning. It is used to indicate the social and psychological experience of personal loss, a state that may be better illustrated in English by the more poetic or folkloric term "woe," with its connotations of lamentation, deep distress, and affliction. Gore does not normally have a plural form, but the expression "many griefs" or "many woes" (*mnogo gorei*) is used to refer to the many deaths a woman may have mourned in her lifetime.

Women have persistently, and indeed consistently, explained to folklorists that the ability to lament is connected with coming to know "woe," and that woe itself is the subject of which the lament speaks. According to A. K. Nosova, from the village of Ust'-Tsil'ma (Komi Republic, north Russia), "Your woe cannot be entirely wept away, nor spoken away, nor lamented away." She demonstrates this point in her lament:

Я горюха ли—горе злочастное.
Я злочастное да горе злыденное
Я со всех злыдень да верно сграбила,
На себя горе да я положила.

Monstrous woe, woe malignant,
Malignant and wicked woe,
Some calamity I surely raked in from everyone
And heaped that woe upon myself.
(Bazanov 1943, 28, 35).

Bazanov provides another example: "Matrena Grigor'evna would go out to her work in the field and she would remember her fate, remember her father. She would go behind a weeping willow bush and begin weeping her woe. Woe teaches you to weep. Whoever has suffered more will weep more. When woe passes, you'll forget. When woe contrives it, you'll weep again" (Bazanov 1943, 42–43).

It is worth pointing out the lexical and grammatical complexity of the term *gore* in the language of lamenting. The woman performing the lament, for example, may refer to herself as *gorepashitsa* (plougher-up of woe), *gorenoshitsa* (bearer of woe), *goregor'kaya* (bitterly woeful one) or by any number of derivatives or diminutives of the noun *gore*. She can, for example, be *goryukha*, *goryusha*, or *goryushinochka*. Note also the following case of the word acquiring a verbal form: "How the 'orphan,' the bitterly grieving one [*gore-gor'kaya*], pines or, cries woe [*gorekue*] for her darling little child" (*Slovar' russkikh narodnykh govorov* 1972, 7:34).

To have passed through the experience of woe is the only way of acquiring the gift of lamenting. To lament is to communicate, articulate, or "speak" woe rather than speak *about* it: "You don't need to learn it or listen to anybody. Your own woe is just something you tell." Woe is "put into words," "given voice," or "unleashed" in the laments:

Ой, дак вместе думушки вы,
Ой, да думы подумайте,
Ой, дак вместе горюшко,
Ой, да вы поразмыкайте . . .

Oi, Together, think,
Oi, Think your thoughts.
Oi, Together, unleash woe.
(FA Bel 17a-30, July 12, 1995)

In laments woe can be the subject of an action: "woe will come," "woe will teach," "woe will pass," "woe will have its way." The possible localization of woe within a temporal or spatial framework is not a poetic device. Woe is a particular condition that characterizes breaching the frontier between the realm of death and life —including the time and place where this occurs: "Bitter-woe is being lived-through somewhere." The individual who takes this condition upon herself makes it her own internal condition. She is "in woe" (*v gore*). The only and essential way of ridding oneself of woe is to "weep it out" (*vyplakivanie*), "unleash it" (*razmykanie*), "plough it up" (*razpakhivanie*), "live it through" (*izzhivanie*). The lamenter's authority determines her capacity to perform her rite and use the language of lament to control both her own and other people's suffering. The ability to "unleash woe" or "give woe its freedom" is connected to the lamenter's own personal qualities and experience of woe. The process of living through a state of woe and acquiring the gift of turning it into verse represents crossing a threshold beyond which she achieves a new perspective on her own past life: "Oi! Earlier there were such lamenters. They would all remember what sort of life each had had and would tell of it in their woe" (Adon'eva 1998, text No. 68).

The Georgian philosopher Merab Mamardashvili noted that the funeral lament "is not intended to make us feel sorry but to create in us the structures of memory" (Mamardashvili 1990, 16). Relating the circumstances of another person's life as if it were their own, experienced lamenters act as narrator-interpreters. The ability to see and feel another person's emotional state as if it were their own is the gift revealed through the experience of "living through" their own personal woe. T. I. Ornatskaya writes about two types of lamenters, corresponding to my earlier division into those being initiated (i.e., lamenting for the first time) and those already initiated:

> The majority of women are passive carriers of laments: they are able to lament only when grief is present. . . . The laments of such women are a form of personal poetry, subjective and concerning only their private grief, the grief of a single family. . . . The second type of lament-bearer is less common. These are women who can lament both about their own and about other women's grief. . . . These "wailers" by vocation were always especially valued by their community as conveyors of the thoughts and misfortunes of the "orphaned," as sensitive interpreters of another's grief. A considerable part of their success, furthermore, is due to the fact that they were usually women whose own life had given them cause for lamentation (spinsters, widows, and orphans), a circumstance that endowed them with the ability to enter into another person's grief. (Ornatskaya 1969, 14–15)

N. Shaulich, writing of the Serbian lamenting tradition, also comments on two different types of lament: *tuzhenie* is a well-thought-out, structured, and melodious performance, while *naitsan'e* is an elemental and often disjointed outpouring of grief that resembles recitative (Zaitsev, E. Shaulich, and N. Shaulich

1993, 383). Shaulich points out that the older the lamenters were, the more the social dimension took over from the personal in their laments. Their views on life and death were already formed. They had their own philosophies of life, and their laments for that reason would modify into epic narrations (Zaitsev, E. Shaulich, and N. Shaulich 1993, 385). A similar phenomenon was noted in a Russian description of laments for soldiers setting off for World War I in 1914:

> Usually, an elderly lament-performer is invited for the whole day. . . . The old woman must be very familiar with the way the ceremony of "bidding farewell" is organized and with the corresponding rituals and laments. Sometimes she laments herself, but also occasionally passes on the words of the laments to the other weeping women. . . . In contrast to the female relatives, who bring many personal elements into their laments—condolences, grief, and inner pain—she explains to those present the noble aim behind the call-up of soldiers going to war. . . . She depicts how warriors fight and die for the fatherland: "As the soldiers fight these great battles the dark forests bow down to the ground, the savage beasts flee in terror and the little birds fall down from the commotion." (Ul'yanov 1915, 4–9)

This lamenter uncovers for her listeners a scene unfolding far beyond the limits of ordinary understanding, revealing, first, her own particular social status, which gives her the right to speak of someone else's moral duty, and second, the gift of "seeing" in a special way.

The laments of those in the process of initiation and the laments of those already initiated, while sharing the same poetic-rhythmic form, are substantially different. The various ritual positions occupied by the participants in the funeral-memorial complex are stated unambiguously by experienced performers, who always make clear the status of the woman on whose behalf the lament is being performed. For example, the outstanding and much-fêted north Russian lamenter recorded by E. V. Barsov, I. A. Fedosova (1831–99), who performed her laments in an extra-ritual situation before an audience in St. Petersburg, would always identify the intended recipient of each lament and the relationship between the lamenter (i.e., the bereaved woman she was depicting) and the deceased. In her "Lament for the Village Elder [*starosta*]," for example, where the lamenter is the village elder's wife (*starostikha*), she was essentially demonstrating how a widow wails for her husband. In her "Lament for the Clerk," the wailer is presented as *kuma*—that is, a person related to the deceased by marriage, not by blood. In the case of a lament for a man killed by lightning, a neighbor is the one who wails. In other words, the relationship between the deceased and the lamenter has a marked effect on the manner of performance (Barsov 1997, 1:231, 237, 202).

The person being initiated into the state of orphanhood is assigned a specific ritual role, as are other participants in the funeral, but in contrast to others taking part, the "newly orphaned" adopts a role with life-changing implications. The task of the ritual procedure is to ensure that the newly initiated orphan rejects the self with which she previously identified and accepts her new self. The orphan neophyte must not only reject the life-world she inhabited before, but experience its destruction.

For the village community, right up until the end of the twentieth century lamenting was regarded as an essential funeral practice: the funeral ritual had to be carried out "correctly." The lamentations of neophytes, however, were evaluated according to a different scale. Lamenting over the deceased was necessary for the completion of the ritual, but the ability of any given widow or daughter to perform it varied. The process of initiation was always an ordeal, and helpers or initiators had an obligatory role in it. At village funerals elderly women were obliged to perform laments, while newly initiated orphans would play their parts to varying degrees, depending upon how well or badly they were able to cope with the ordeal imposed upon them by fate and their social group.

The new orphan must learn to accept and understand the break with her old life. This process is reflected in the speech patterns and symbols of the lament form. In a one-sided dialogue the neophyte questions the deceased but receives no answers:

Ой, поспрошу я только беднушка:
Ой, тебе што не прилюбилосе,
А тебе што не приглянулосе . . .

Oi! I will ask you, unfortunate creature that I am,
Oi! What was it you disliked,
What was it displeased you . . .?
(FA Bel 17a-10, July 23, 1997)

Ты на кого меня, родитель, оставил,
Ты на чье большо великое желаньице?
To whom have you abandoned me, father?
Who will want the heavy task of caring for me?
(FA Bel 17-112, July 16, 2002)

The questions insinuate that the responsibility for the predicament in which she now finds herself lies with the person she addresses (i.e., the deceased):

Ой, тебе што не прилюбилосе,
А тебе што не приглянулосе,
Ой, тебе денюшки ль не полныи,
Ой, али хлебы не довольныи.
Ой, ты оставил молоду жену . . .

Oi! What was it you disliked,
What was it displeased you?
Oi! Were your days so empty,
Oi! Was my bread not tasty enough,
Oi! So that you left me, your young wife? . . .
(Adon'eva 1998, text No.3)

The lamenter entering orphanhood emerges as a figure who has suffered the consequences of her interlocutor's decisions, something that makes her ritual role different in principle from that of other lamenters who merely interpret what is taking place. The information she wants, as indicated in her questions, is very precisely targeted. She wants to know about herself and wants the deceased himself to tell her:

Ты куда нас оставил, ты куда нас покинул, спобросил?
У меня стадышка-то немалые,
У меня детушки-то недорощены,
Недорощены, недоподняты . . .

 In what place have you left us, where have you cast us, abandoned us?
My flocks are not small,
My little children are not yet grown-up,
Not yet grown-up, not yet raised . . .
(FA Mez 17a-1, July 27, 2007)

The question "Why did you die?" is addressed to the deceased, who of course cannot answer for reasons beyond his or her control. At the same time the speaker accepts that she is probably somehow to blame for having been abandoned: "Of what am I guilty? Where did I go wrong?" This particular interrogatory form of address is determined by the problem the ritual must solve. First, the newly orphaned lamenter must be alienated from her former life-world, and second, through the agonizing process of initiation, she must be inducted into the new one. From the point of view of the neophyte, what takes place is the establishment of the new world and her place in it:

И как я буду тебя забывать-то?
Я во сне ли буду засыпаться
Или водой холодной буду отпиваться?
И как я буду жить, детей ростить?

How will I begin to forget you?
Will it happen as I close my eyes in slumber?
Or when I drink the cold water of forgetfulness?
And how shall I live, how bring up my children?
(FA Mez 17a-1, July 27, 2007)

The laments of the newly initiated convey the lamenters' confusion about what is happening to them, and this state of disorientation is conveyed, for example, by enumerating objects that have lost their usual function. The widow, gazing at her home, which was once so familiar, now sees only a prison in which she is incarcerated (Barsov 1997, 1:37). The passage of time is also disrupted: "Now time grows shorter. It has rolled in upon itself" (Razova 1994, 175). The normal order of things has been destroyed:

Уж(и) во твоей-то высокой горёнке[13]
Уж(и) будё в том ды уг(ы)лу пустёшенько,
Уж как в другом(ы) да холоднёшен(и)ко,
Уж как в третьём-то снежки белыи,
Уж как в четвёр(ы)том пець кирьпицьная,
Уж(и) пець кирьпицьная, холодная.

Uzh(i) in your lofty living room
One corner will be empty,
Another corner will be chilly.
In the third corner there is white snow
And in the fourth a brick-built stove,
A brick-built stove which is cold.
(Adon'eva 1998, Text No. 5)

The transformation of the world begins with the life-changing event the lamenter has experienced and the sentiment "everything I know about the world no longer corresponds to what I see." L. G. Nevskaya, researching the poetic characteristics of laments, noted the rather consistent theme of the deconstruction of various elements of the home (Nevskaya 1997–98, 51–66). A house half-built, tasks unfinished, and objects incomplete are all used as metaphors of widow-hood. During a wedding feast the following lines might be sung to a widow:

Это чья в поле нива
Стоит без огороды?
Это чьей новый терем
Стоит без верху строен?

"Whose cornfield stands unfenced in open country?
Whose new house stands with the roof unfinished?
(Kolpakova 1973, 197, Text No. 405)

These recurring images reflect the lamenter's experience of her disintegrating world. The lamenter describes what she observes but does not have the key to unlock the meaning of her observations. The lament creates the verbal exposition of the contradiction that has arisen between life and its social projection. Through the medium of the initiation ritual and through the experience of grief, a fact of external reality, death, is transformed into an internal fact of personal fate.

LAMENTING AMONG WOMEN OF DIFFERENT GENERATIONS

We have recorded and continue to record laments from village women of different generations. It is difficult to make precise generational divisions, but in general terms we are speaking of women born during the periods 1899–1916, 1917–29, and 1930–50.[14] When the lamenters were born is relevant since it determined what role their improvisational abilities would play in their lives and what kind of relationship they would have with the dead.

The oldest generation of the women we have interviewed consists of those born at the end of the nineteenth to the beginning of the twentieth century, between 1899 and 1916. I met women of this generation during my expeditions of 1983–99 to Vologda province. These women were born into extended peasant families, where it was customary to be brought up by one's paternal grandmother, the matriarch, or *bol'shukha*. The head of the family was the paternal grandfather, whom the whole household obeyed. This generation of women of peasant background in Vologda province received a traditional upbringing and training; took part in the church festivals when members of the wider family came to visit; were christened as babies; observed the fasts; and went to communion with their parents, at least during the big church festivals. As children they were present at weddings and funerals, heard the laments sung by their elders, and repeated them when they played at weddings and funerals with their friends of the same age. Their youth was spent in villages whose community life was as yet untouched by the ravages of Soviet power. They were given in marriage according to the "old way," with match-makers and everything decided by the parents. By the time collectivization began in the 1930s, these women were already married. During the collectivization period the process of dekulakization dispossessed the heads of households, the so-called *bol'shaki*, who were men in their forties to seventies, along with their large families. These men were the fathers and fathers-in-law of our first generation of women, whose husbands then inherited the role of head of the family after the devastations of the 1930s and were taken away to fight at the front, as were their young sons. These events were wept over in memorial laments. It was the women of this generation who "attained their majority" (*vstali v bol'shinu*)—that is, became responsible for maintaining the family—during the war years of 1941–45. Their experiences of life, born out of the upheavals of the 1930s, the difficulties of the war years, and the hungry years that followed, had taught them the need to preserve the rules and conventions taught to them by their elders. It was from the women of this generation that we recorded the greatest number of laments. Their adherence to the funeral ritual and their insistence on lamenting over the deceased were in large part a personal protest against the Soviet regime, which condemned their activities as "women's blubbering." The women spoke of learning how to lament as a skill they specifically chose to maintain. Anna Andreevna Pozdnyakova (b. 1907) explained it as follows: "If you can, feel free to lament, if you can't . . . You have to know how to lament but nowadays there are few who do lament." When asked who had taught her, she replied, "I taught myself. In the old days everyone lamented and we would listen. If I understood and paid attention, then I would learn. But someone else might not pay attention, so she would not know anything" (SA field notes, Vol-Bel, July 13, 1993). Another informant, Ekaterina Vasil'evna Krylova (b. 1914), said much the same thing: "Not everyone is capable of lamenting. I taught myself. My sister was good at lamenting. When you're little you pick things up, you learn to prepare beforehand, learn which words to start with. When you are grief-stricken you'll learn soon enough" (SA field notes, Vol-Bel, July 16, 1993). Conversing with the dead was a way of expressing the religious conviction that all the dead were alive. Against the background of the widespread Soviet anti-religious campaign of the 1920s and 1930s, funeral lamenting was considered an act of transgression.

In 1962 V. P. Bazanov and A. P. Razumova published their volume of north Russian laments. It contained laments recorded between 1942 and 1945, during World War II, in the Ust'-Tsil'ma district of the Komi Republic on the Pechora river. The folklore group went first to Ust'-Tsil'ma, the administrative center of the district, where they were able to record laments, in most cases as they were actually being performed for menfolk who had been drafted. Later, in 1944 and 1945, respectively, the researchers continued their work in the Transonega (Zaonezh'e) and Pudoga regions of the Republic of Karelia, in territories recently freed from German occupation. The authors told the following story about one of the women who performed for them: "Anis'ya Mikhailovna Fedulova was sixty-two years old and from the village of Koskosalma. In 1938 M. M. Mikhailov recorded two laments from her—'Lament for My Husband Setting off for the War' and 'Lament for My Daughter.' The lament for her husband, recorded in 1938, was her recollection of how she had seen her husband off to the First World War. In 1941, when the German occupying forces attacked our country, she saw her son off to the Great Patriotic War" (Bazanov 1962, 28). In August 1944, a telegram arrived in Koskosalma, informing Fedulova of the death of her son. They recorded the lament, which was her reaction to the bitter news. According to their account, she performed the lament "while gazing at her son's photograph." However, on the same day that they recorded the lament for the son who was killed, they heard her singing the following *chastushki* as she worked:[15]

Пойду-выстону на гору,
Я увижу белый гроб.
От войны немецкой дитятко
В сыру могилу лег.
Что я, что я расплясалась,
Что развеселилася.
Не мое ли мило дитятко
Домой сулилося.
Что я, что я расплясалась,
Что на пляску повело,
Не мое ли мило дитятко
С войны домой идё.

I will go up the hill to groan my fill.
I will see the white coffin.
All for the German war, my dear boy
Laid himself in the damp grave.
Why did I, why did I dance,
Why did I make merry?
Was it not my own dear boy
Who was promised a homecoming?

Why did I dance,
What drew me into the dance?
Was not my own dear boy
Returning from the war?
(Bazanov 1962, 28)

What is particularly interesting here is Fedulova's use of two different linguistic-stylistic registers when addressing the fact of her son's death. When talking only to herself, even on this most painful of subjects, she used the form of the chastushki. When addressing her dead son, using the photograph as a substitute for his living presence, she did so through the medium of the lament.

Women born in the period 1917–30, after the establishment of Soviet power, were, in contrast to their mothers, by and large brought up "in the Soviet way." On the one hand, they did inherit some traditional pieces of information about village life. They listened to lullabies and fairy tales. They heard their mothers lamenting as their fathers and brothers went off to war. On the other hand, they attended Soviet schools and were exposed to the core message of atheism. The story of their lives was a tale of work, war, famine, and heroism. If they were lucky, all of this was preceded by a happy prewar youth filled with sewing or spinning bees, meeting up with girlfriends, and flirting with young men. The credo they lived by was an astonishing mixture of Soviet ideology and traditional village life. The Soviet worldview made itself felt in any official dealings, as for example in their relationship with the collective and state farms, but in their private lives and relations with neighbors, they adhered to traditional beliefs (e.g., in magic and the supernatural) and patriarchal practices. Having been brought up by their pre-Soviet grandmothers, these peasant women preserved the vertical structure of command typical of the patriarchal family. They obeyed their mothers-in-law, whatever the nature of their relationship with them. Laments recorded from women of this generation were most often addressed to their parents. Lamenting over parents was regarded as a personal duty and a show of respect for the values of the previous generation. Sometimes their mothers would ask them to learn to perform laments for them:

My mother—she was eleven years old when *her* mother died. My mama, when she knew she was dying she said to me "Anyutka, when I die compose a lament about me." "Oi, *matka*, when it happens, how could I?" . . . She would have taught me but of course I couldn't. . . . But she was so insistent that I brought in an old woman [to perform the lament instead]. She carried out her wishes for a lament. I brought in an old woman. I couldn't do it myself. I didn't lament. I have two older sisters but they didn't lament at all either. (FA Syam 17a-6, July 17, 2005)

I have recorded other cases where a mother orders her daughter to perform a lament. A woman born in 1925 told how her mother asked her to be sure to remember and pronounce a few words in the language of a lament. Her mother said: "When I'm dead and you're walking back or driving back to the house from the funeral, from the cemetery, say these words, if you can't weep them— 'No longer is our day-time protector with us, no longer is our night-time spell-maker with us.' That bit you must learn by heart, girls. When I'm buried weep that bit" (FA Lesh 17a-18, 17 July, 2010).

The village women we interviewed who were born in the 1930s and later were rarely able to lament. Their childhood and youth were passed in the years following the end of the war. Many women of this generation born during the war or in the years immediately after were orphans, or the illegitimate children of war widows. They grew up with a Soviet education, Soviet songs, and Soviet films. This third generation of women depended largely on the state for approbation, whereas for the second generation this was only partly the case. The women born in the 1930s were likely to have lovingly preserved all of the decorations, medals, and certificates they had received. This generation experienced the revival of the wedding ritual, which retained some superficial prerevolutionary aspects, although the church wedding was replaced by registration at ZAGS (Department of Registration of Civil Statuses). In essence, however, these state-sanctioned ceremonies bore little resemblance to the traditional arranged marriages of the past. While accepting various traditional Soviet ways of doing things, women of this generation nevertheless faced a dilemma when it came to overt expressions of sorrow. Their mothers and mothers-in-law would beg them to observe the tradition of lamenting when they died. However, the ecstatic nature of the funeral lament was at odds with the accepted Soviet way of expressing one's sympathy to those who had lost a loved one. Offering condolences was regarded as sufficient. As for the bereaved themselves, they were now expected to either sit in sorrowful silence or weep quietly, and lamenting in public was now seen as embarrassing. Lamenting was an overt declaration of belief in life after death and a world beyond the grave. It openly demonstrated how one could talk to the dead. Some women of this generation told us how they would sometimes lament when they visited the cemetery on memorial days or remember their dead loved-one in a secluded spot. In 2007 we recorded a conversation with a mother and daughter in the village of Tsenogora (Leshukon'e district, Arkhangel'sk province). The daughter, Valentina Aleksandrovna (b. 1960), said of lamenting, "No, I don't want people watching me, don't want to be seen. But I can do it when I'm on my own, just by myself." Her mother, Angelina Danilovna (b. 1938), said much the same thing: "I'll go to the gravestone on my own. I'll sit down and I'll speak and speak, speak and speak out all I have to say. But I feel uncomfortable when people are around" (FA Lesh 17a-15, July 11, 2010).

The voice of the lament is intended to be heard by the dead. However, even those who are unable to communicate with the dead by lamenting still have the ability to talk to them, as one can witness in Russian villages today when village women enter a cemetery and speak directly to their loved ones. The place for these conversations is the cemetery, although if the body is not buried there, as, for example, in the case of soldiers killed in the war, the conversations may instead take place by an obelisk or war memorial. By speaking to the deceased, a woman incorporates that person into her own life and circle of relationships. The dead are interlocutors from whom she expects sympathy and to whom she may relate her sorrow. Elderly village women go to the cemetery to commune with dead family members and neighbors and inform them of relevant events through live conversation.

During our research, we were often invited to accompany these mainly elderly women to the cemetery on memorial days and could observe for ourselves how the women would gradually make their rounds to all the graves. First they would visit the graves of people close to them and "remember" with some food and a tot of vodka, and then they would visit their neighbors' graves, where they would typically place out some food or scatter grain for the birds. They would also chat with the dead, telling them what was happening with their families and in the village. To give one example, in 2010 Nina Vasil'evna (b.1936) invited our group of folklorists to accompany her to the cemetery in her village in Arkhangel'sk province. She approached the fence surrounding the graves of her close relatives, went through the gate, and knocked loudly on the cross over the grave: "Oi, Vitalii Fedorovich, are you comfortable lying there, sleeping there? Pavlik, dear son. Do you think you left us at the right time? [she weeps]. Oh you!!! You were so young, just forty-two! How do you think such a thing could be borne, how could I get over it?" Then she turned to her companions: "Oi-Oi-Oi! That's how it is when we come here. And they just lie there, stretched out, with nothing to think about any more." She was weeping as she spoke and laid some sweets and biscuits beside the cross (FA Lesh 17-59, July 7, 2010).

We do not know precisely how much the dead hear as they listen to a lament, but we do know with certainty what knowledge the living receive through the practice of lamenting. Those rare occasions in the twentieth and twenty-first centuries when we have witnessed lamenting during a village funeral have shown us that this is indeed the case. In 2016 we witnessed the funeral of an elderly woman in Melogora village in Arkhangel'sk province. During the ritual farewell beside the coffin there were speeches, addressed to the gathering of relatives and friends, about the dead woman's commitment to her family and her contributions to society. Every speech ended with the same ritual phrases: "Sleep in peace, Tat'yana Petrovna, may the earth be as down upon you." But while the dead woman's coffin was still in the house an old woman, a neighbor, approached it, sat down, and began to lament, addressing only the deceased. She spoke not only about the deceased's past but also about her present and her future. She asked Tat'yana Petrovna to pass on greetings to her parents when she met them: "When you meet my parents, tell them about me. Tell them to come and fetch me as soon as they can." The lamenter did not envisage the dead woman as being either asleep or resting under the earth. Soon she would be in the realm of the Lord and there she would meet the lamenter's parents. As the lament proceeded the demeanor of all those present began to change. The dead woman's grandsons who had been standing stiffly, and seemed to have no idea how they should behave, suddenly began to weep. Others present listened attentively to what the lamenter was saying. She said the dead woman's death had been quick, which meant she had earned a "good" death. In contrast to the speech makers who had praised the woman's past merits, the lamenter spoke of them in the present tense: "You are worthy of a good death. You are in a fit state to meet the Lord. You are well-prepared" (DV 16 Arch-Mez 134, July 25, 2016).

Even today laments carry important messages to the living. Firstly, they show how it is possible to live in a world where death means not the end of existence but merely passage into another world. This world is situated not in a different time (the past) but only in a different place, so that contact with the dead, therefore, is also possible. Secondly, laments teach that the life-world of villagers, in spite of the disruptive changes and innovations they have experienced, still presupposes reciprocity, loyalty, and duty in relations between the living and the dead. And thirdly, laments are instrumental in the structuring of memory. Through laments the widows and all the "orphaned" will come to know those forms and characteristics of the dead which should be preserved in imagination and memory.

CHAPTER 4

The Cross, the Birch, and the Kawasaki Motorbike

The Visual Rhetoric of Russian Rural Cemeteries in the Twentieth and Twenty-First Centuries

ELIZABETH WARNER

In recent years the importance of visual images in our daily lives has increased exponentially, with a corresponding growth of attention to the significant role of visual messages in the communication of meaning. The volume of publications in the field of visual rhetoric is now very extensive, with a preponderance of works, as one might expect, on obviously visual artifacts—films, photographs, video games, web design, advertising products, maps, architecture, street signs, and so on. Spaces, on the other hand, have received less attention, with studies focusing on places largely connected to public rather than private discourse and with a considerable emphasis on the presentation and manipulation of images in a political, ethnic, or gender context. Semiotic studies of spaces often focus on a predominantly urban environment, as in Scollon and Wong Scollon's analysis of both the signs and symbols of such public venues as city streets, shopping malls, restaurants, and the workplace, together with the interpersonal communications taking place within them (R. Scollon and S. Wong Scollon 2003). Museums, which mold our perception of our own and other cultures through their visual displays, have been a particularly popular subject of research (Ragsdale 2007, 2009a, 2009b; Dickinson, Blair, and Ott 2010). More relevant to the present focus on visual messages as they relate to Russian rural cemeteries are memory places associated with death—monuments and memorials for the victims of war, terrorism, and atrocities (Blair, Balthrop, and Michel 2011; Paliewicz and Hasian 2016); memorial parks and complexes; historical battlegrounds, particularly those associated with World War II and the US Civil War (Spielvogel 2013). On the other hand, these, like museum displays, are mainly concerned with the presentation, and indeed shaping—in accordance with the prevailing mindset or political agendas of their civic and national guardians—of public rather than private memory. Elizabethada Wright has written of rural cemeteries in New England, but in a historical context, reflecting on how the cemetery has provided a rhetorical space for the voices of social groups otherwise largely excluded from public memory, such as African Americans and white women. For these groups the cemetery "allows memories forgotten in other locations to survive" (Wright 2005, 51). Ol'ga Matich broke new ground in the 1990s with her investigation of the burial practices of the Russian criminal mafia fraternity, drawing on visual images exalting wealth and power and death-defying physicality on the extravagant grave markers of mafia foot soldiers and bosses in cemeteries in Moscow and Ekaterinburg (Matich 1998, 75–107).

My own purpose and approach in this chapter concentrate on the cemetery as a place of private rather than public memory. In previous chapters emphasis has been on the attention paid to the dead—what is done by the living to and for the deceased, both as "body" and as "soul"—and on the ways in which those left behind maintain contact with those who have passed on. The cemetery has been seen as the "new home" of the dead. It is, however, also a place the living can not only visit but create and shape to their own requirements. As will be seen, the individual's aesthetic conceptualization of the deceased's new home can be just as susceptible to external pressures, whether political, religious, financial, or social, as other aspects of daily life.

A BACKWARD GLANCE

In considering the visual aspects of Russian rural cemeteries in the twentieth and twenty-first centuries it is worth remembering that many are actually not that old. Even the smallest and seemingly insignificant rural cemeteries in my own country, for example, may chart many centuries of the locality's history through the names of both ordinary and illustrious families buried there, together with the clergy of the parish—whether these are recorded on simple headstones or more elaborate stone or marble tombs. Yet similar cemeteries in Russia, which have not enjoyed such a peaceful history, rarely contain graves predating the revolution or even from the period before World War II. Many old cemeteries disappeared altogether during the massive changes and upheavals of the twentieth century. During the Soviet era, amid scant regard for the feelings of local inhabitants or respect for the dead, some cemeteries were covered in concrete for the convenience of mechanized collective farms or bulldozed and built over with new roads and housing complexes as towns expanded into the countryside. Others were lost when churches and monasteries were transformed into workshops and warehouses or pillaged and abandoned to the elements. Local authorities had some rural cemeteries moved away from locations near villages, supposedly on health grounds, so that it is quite common to find villages with both old and new cemeteries. In Kimzha (Mezen' region, Arkhangel'sk province), for example, which I visited in 2007, the remnants of the old cemetery—a scattering of ancient crosses with no sign of actual graves—could be seen in what was by then nothing more than a large open field skirted by Soviet-era farm buildings and outhouses, while the new cemetery was hidden in the forest some distance from the village. On the outskirts of Yuroma in the Leshukon'e region of Arkhangel'sk province, which I visited in 2009, there are several abandoned burial areas, the exact parameters of which have been obliterated by time. The church that used to stand in the center of the village was knocked down in Soviet times, and the road into the village runs through where the cemetery used to be. Accidentally exhumed bones still occasionally turn up by the roadside.[1]

However, it is also the case that impermanence and decay were natural characteristics of rural cemeteries in the more distant past. We can build up a reasonable impression of their appearance in the nineteenth century by examining their depiction in visual artworks. Such cemeteries may be seen, for example, in the following: Vasilii Perov's *Old Parents at the Grave of Their Son* (1874) and *A Scene at the Grave* (1859), Aleksei Korzukhin's *Remembrance Day in a Village Cemetery* (1865), Aleksei Sovrasov's *A Village Cemetery on a Moonlit Night* (1887) and *At the Cemetery* (1884), Konstantin Makovskii's *A Child's Funeral*, and Isaak Levitan's *Above Eternal Rest* (1894), among others. Even allowing for any romantic artistic exaggeration of these desolate scenes, it is clear that the cemeteries depicted were shapeless, unstructured spaces for the burial of the dead, roughly hewn from the surrounding countryside and lacking in any obvious visual appeal. In the mounds of earth covering the dead, also weed-strewn and haphazardly spaced, in the simple wooden crosses already displaying the ravages of time, it is difficult to see any visual aesthetic or rhetorical information beyond the simple reminder of the individual's return to the earth at death and the message of resurrection to eternal life offered by the Church and symbolized in the crosses. In literature too—Turgenev's *Fathers and Children* and Pushkin's *The Stationmaster*—country cemeteries are often depicted as gloomy and neglected places. "Like almost all our cemeteries," writes Turgenev of his hero Evgenii Bazarov's final resting place, "it presents a sad spectacle: the ditches surrounding it long overgrown with weeds, its gray wooden crosses leaning over and rotting beneath their once-painted roofs, the gravestones all askew as if someone was pushing them up from below. Two or three sparse-leaved little trees barely provide an inadequate shade, sheep wander unchecked over the graves . . ." (Turgenev 1956, 196). In *The Stationmaster*, the narrator visits the grave of an old acquaintance, the keeper of a provincial post-house who drank himself to death after the disgrace and disappearance of his only daughter: "We came to the cemetery," he comments, "a bare and unfenced space, with a scattering of wooden crosses, lacking the shade of a single tree. In all my life I never saw such a miserable cemetery." A black cross with a brass icon stuck in a sandy mound marks the stationmaster's grave (Pushkin 1949, 6:144). It is interesting that both Turgenev and Pushkin comment on the "nakedness" of these places, without the softening effect of vegetation or the protection of fences. A similarly depressing picture is revealed in the rare surviving photographs of rural cemeteries at the end of the nineteenth and beginning of the twentieth century.

Between 2006 and 2016 I visited and photographed many village cemeteries in the northwestern regions of Russia as part of my ongoing research into traditional aspects of funeral ritual. Until 2013 I concentrated on villages located in Vologda and Arkhangel'sk provinces. Between 2013 and 2016 the focus of my attention moved to the more westerly Pskov, Novgorod, and Tver' provinces. This chapter is based on my own impressions and photographic records. I begin with my impressions of archetypal village cemeteries in remote areas of Vologda and Arkhangel'sk provinces between 2006 and 2013.

Crosses and Posts, Obelisks, and Stars

Here and there in a few cemeteries it is still possible to see the remains of stone slabs from nineteenth-century or very early twentieth-century burials, covered in moss and lichen, half-buried under the grass, with barely discernible inscriptions. In 2009 in Selishche (Leshukon'e region, Arkhangel'sk province) I noticed several such stones dating to the early 1900s. Their sole ornament was the Orthodox three-barred or eight-ended cross and the Old Slavonic inscription "The King of Glory" (*Tsar' slavy*) cut in stone above a simple statement to the effect that "Under this stone is buried the body of servant of God Irina . . . / Nikolai . . ." followed by the dates of birth and death. One stone adds that the deceased was a "defender of the faith" (*veroispovedatel'*). Names were given in full—Christian name, patronymic, and surname. In other words, the presentation of the gravesite fully conformed to the sole requirements of the Orthodox Church, which remain the same today (i.e., a cross, full name, and dates). However, such relics of a distant past are rare. The major visual impression provided by the cemeteries I have visited in the Russian North has been the large number of graves marked by crosses, of which Vologda and Arkhangel'sk provinces in particular present a remarkable variety. Some of these are obviously new, raised in the post-Soviet period, but many others are clearly considerably older. A few even appear to be survivals from an era of the most violent anti-Christian persecution. In Azopol'e (Mezen' region, Arkhangel'sk province) in 2008, for example, I noted a small wooden cross bearing only the message: "The remains [*prakh*] of Anastasiya . . . 1935." The bottom part of the old cross had clearly rotted away, and what was left of it had been nailed to a newer post.

There are many plain wooden three-barred crosses and crosses with "roofs," which are particularly characteristic of the Russian North. Their sloping roofs have the utilitarian function of protecting the cross beneath from rain but are also one of those elements of funeral and memorial custom related to the notion of the grave as the new home of the deceased's soul. Many are painted, as apparently they were in Turgenev's day too, presumably in part as a protective measure against decay. The colors are surprisingly bright and mainly in the blue or green hues that became popular in Soviet times and were used for the wooden or metal fences surrounding gravesites as well as for crosses.

The Mezen' region of Arkhangel'sk province has long been famous for its tall, elaborately carved crosses, usually made from hard-wearing larch, which weathers to silvery-gray. I have seen numerous old examples of these in the cemeteries of Azopol'e, and Kimzha. The Old Slavonic bas-relief lettering that adorns them is aesthetically beautiful and also contains religious texts in superscripted, abbreviated form. Such crosses placed at the foot of a grave proclaim: "Lord, we adore Thy cross and glorify Thy holy resurrection" (Krestu Tvoemu poklony-aemsya Vladyka i svyatoe voskresenie Tvoe slavim). Simple crosses of wrought metalwork painted with silvery-gray metallic paint can be seen in cemeteries all over the northwest provinces I have visited and are, indeed, ubiquitous in cemeteries across Russia. These more obviously reflect the style and limitations of the Soviet period and may be seen on many graves dating to the 1950s–80s.

Crosses with "roofs," Kimzha, Arkhangel'sk province 2007. (Photo by Elizabeth Warner)

I particularly remember the grave of a nineteen-year-old boy I photographed in July 2009. According to the faded ceramic plaque with his photograph, he had drowned in 1958. The rusting metal cross to which the plaque was attached rose from a tangle of weeds and wildflowers in an abandoned cemetery near the village of Yuroma in Arkhangel'sk province. I was interested to note that, although more than fifty years had passed since the death, wreaths of artificial flowers lay on and around the cross. From their condition I would guess they had been placed there not long before and most probably at Troitsa, two months before my visit. This abundance of crosses seems at first glance paradoxical. The Soviet campaign of terror against the Orthodox Church is well-documented (see Pospielovsky 1984 and 1987) and needs no detailed comment here. As a result of its atheistic stance between the late 1920s and the invasion of the Soviet Union by Fascist Germany in 1941, the state had largely succeeded in dismantling the mechanisms that allowed the Orthodox Church to function. Believers were denied access to the Christian message, and to places where they could congregate for worship, through the demolition and desecration of church buildings, the removal and destruction of icons, and the execution or imprisonment of priests and monks. Participation in religious festivals and pilgrimages, the veneration of shrines, the baptism of children, the wearing of a cross, and many other examples of overt Christian practice attracted harsh penalties. Funerals were no longer conducted by priests. During the Great Patriotic War, it is true, an accommodation was reached with the Orthodox Church, providing some toleration of religious observances and a relaxation of the relentless punitive war against those who still followed their faith. In return, the Church made a considerable contribution to the patriotic war effort. The next debilitating wave of anti-religious activity took place during the premiership of Nikita Khrushchev (1958–64). No doubt, in different places and at different times, acts of anti-Christian vandalism took place in cemeteries or objections and difficulties arose when the bereaved asked for a cross to be made in a local workshop. In spite of all this, however, it would seem that anti-religious barbarism did not extend to the wholesale removal or banning of that fundamental Christian symbol, the cross, from cemeteries. Icons, on the other hand, displayed in small boxes similar to reliquaries and attached to crosses in northern cemeteries, were often forcibly removed. Those that survived into the later years of the Soviet era, when the value of icons as objects d'art was again recognized, were often stolen by scavengers. During the Soviet period even city cemeteries retained their crosses. Not long before his death in 1980 the Soviet writer Leonid Martynov described the Vostryakovskoe cemetery in Moscow in his poem "S ulybkoi na ustakh" ("With a Smile on My Lips"). In the poem the sky above the cemetery is a "void" (*pustota*)—suggesting, perhaps, not only the absence of clouds but the absence of a heavenly afterlife—

while the ground beneath is "covered in crosses" ("I vsya zemlya v krestakh") (Martynov 1986, 666).

This impression is also confirmed by photographs of rural cemeteries taken during the Soviet period. In 2012 I was conducting fieldwork in Vozhgora (Leshukon'e region, Arkhangel'sk province) when an archive of five hundred rolls of photographs belonging to the local teacher and amateur photographer Yurii Alekseevich Galev (1929–2006) was discovered by members of the group. Many of his photographs of village life, including those of funerals, date to the 1960s–80s. One, dated 1978, shows three village men struggling in deep snow to carry a newly made large and heavy wooden cross through the village to the cemetery, followed by the mourners carrying a coffin. The scene raises involuntary associations with images of the Road to Calvary. Another depicts the raising of a similarly large cross over a newly dug grave. Many of Galev's other photographs of funerals show a proliferation of different crosses in the cemetery and Orthodox crosses marked on coffin lids.

Deliberate acts of desecration were, by and large, limited to the graves of the clergy. In Lykoshino (Bologoe region, Tver' province) in 2016 my companion pointed out a section of the old cemetery that had contained the graves of priests. Originally the graves were marked by large, handsome, wrought-iron crosses, but then, as she put it, they were "liquidated." Those crosses were thrown away, and the ground was used for new burials.

In spite of the obvious Christian symbolism of the cross, it should be remembered that for many people continued use of crosses in cemeteries did not represent a challenging declaration of faith but rather served to simply mark burial sites. Although people may have continued to go there for private prayer or to visit their dead, the cemetery was not a place of worship like a chapel. This was even more true once funeral obsequies largely ceased to be carried out by priests. Hidden away, often some distance from the village, cemeteries were, and remain, the territory and home of revered dead ancestors and social spaces in which the living and the dead could communicate, through speech—lamenting or simple conversation—through touch—stroking or knocking on the grave marker by way of greeting, sitting on the grave mound—or through the act of "sharing" or offering food.

A different fate befell other crosses in the North that occupied a more prominent position, both literally and metaphorically, and that performed quite different functions. Monumental carved crosses were sited high above riverbanks, on hilltops, in open fields, at crossroads, and even outside houses or in other highly visible locations. Some had specific objectives. They acted as markers for fishermen making for the shore or were dedicated to the well-being of cattle, the protection of fields, or the enticement of fish into the fishermen's nets. But whatever their function, all were sacral objects. They were raised originally for many different reasons—to commemorate the death of a loved one, to honor a saint, or to offer thanks for an escape from drowning. Some are described as votive crosses (*obetnye/zavetnye*) used for making promises and fulfilling vows, a practice that continues to the present day. In fact, since the 1990s many new crosses have been erected, some of them to replace old ones removed in Soviet times or to mark the position of a chapel destroyed at that time. In Zaozer'e (Mezen' region) in 1990, it was said that a woman on her own initiative paid for a cross to replace one that had been thrown into the river by the Soviet authorities. Her gift came with a prayer that her son and other serving soldiers should return safely from war (FA Mez 15-35, July 14, 2008). More surprising is the fact that the folklorist N. P. Kolpakova mentioned in her field diaries that in the late 1950s (i.e., after the death of Stalin) some crosses were restored, including one that a woman in Yuroma replaced after having a dream about it (Kolpakova 1958). In addition to votive crosses, some of the old crosses were especially venerated (*poklonnye*) and occupied a place in private worship similar to roadside chapels or the icon corners in peasant homes. In fact, such crosses, when erected by individuals outside their homes, were sometimes positioned before the "front" corner. Inside the house, this was the icon corner where prayer took place. Some crosses bear a carved effigy of the crucified Christ, who in many cases is wrapped in white cloth because of the perception among some village women that Christ must feel the cold and should therefore be clothed (FA Mez 15-1, 2007, July 10, 2007).

Votive crosses are easily recognizable from the quantity of clothing and other objects draped upon them. Gifts in the form of embroidered or gaily patterned towels are brought as an expression of gratitude or to invoke a favor. Sick people bring items of clothing corresponding to the locations of their physical ailments and in new condition, albeit having been worn or at least having come in contact with the person's body. Children's toys may be left there. Offerings of coins can also still be seen today, pushed into cracks in the old wood or spread along the larger cross-piece, although nowadays, in order to prevent the coins from being stolen by drunkards, people may prefer to take them to the nearest chapel. Schoolchildren bring exercise books and leave notes requesting success in exams. Women pray for the return of a lost cow. Food—bread, biscuits, sweets, and so on—is also sometimes left.

Whatever their precise function in different villages, there is no doubt that for the villagers these crosses have always had a religious meaning, although few today understand the Christian messages carved in Old Church Slavonic upon them. The dialogue taking place in the vicinity of these crosses is not between the living and the dead, as in the cemetery, but between the worshipper or supplicant

Alongside this votive cross in the cemetery is a box filled with shoes from people with bad feet. Azopol'e, Arkhangel'sk province, 2008. (Photo by Elizabeth Warner)

and a divine entity, a personal and anthropomorphized divinity, however vague some people may be about its specific nature. In the absence of a church, whether this was because the village did not have one or because it had been destroyed by the communists, people would come to these crosses to pray. Through prayer and offerings, a pact would be made between the human and the divine. In Pogorelets (Mezen' region) a villager had been very offended when some men came and removed their cross, which had fallen down, and re-erected it "without any sort of blessing" near the cemetery. This arbitrary choice of location was unacceptable: "The old ones had put it up, you know. They believed, they prayed, they knew where to put a cross up but you see . . . The old folk put it up because we didn't have a church then but there had to be somewhere you could pray and they chose a place that the Lord . . . well it's a godly place, so to speak. God has these places where people can pray and the Lord helps them" (FA Mez 15-9). I remember an impressive votive cross on the edge of the cemetery in Kimzha (Arkhangel'sk province), lavishly decorated with wreaths of artificial flowers and draped with items of clothing. A separate box contained shoes.

In a village in the Mezen' region a woman was asked why there were no offerings attached to a large cross outside a house, a cross that had somehow survived Soviet aggression: "We have a chapel," the woman explained. "Now we can go to the chapel." She described how people "who need something" take items to hang up there. Someone who suffered from headaches might take a headscarf, for example (FA Mez 15-15, July 18, 2007). In other words, the new chapel had replaced the old cross, just as crosses in the past were a substitute for chapels.

I would suggest that the different functions of crosses determined their fates. The crosses over graves in cemeteries were clearly viewed as less threatening to the Soviet authorities than crosses at which "religious" behavior could be openly observed, to which people traveled from distant villages as if to a place of pilgrimage, and which could attract large numbers of visitors on particular religious festivals. Although crosses of this type did survive in and around a number of villages in the North, many more were knocked down and smashed by Communist Party activists. In Tselegora in the Mezen' region the villagers removed all the crosses from the village as demanded by the chairman of the collective farm, but apparently without opposition, relocated them to the cemetery, or more precisely, as they said, took them "to the ancestors." Paradoxically, these particular crosses were finally chopped up during World War II by evacuees who had no firewood (FA Mez 15-16, July 18, 2007).

It would be a mistake, however, to imagine that the Christian cross was the only type of grave marker common in remote Northern cemeteries. Whatever the extent of tolerance of or antipathy toward the cross as grave marker at various times in the history of the Soviet Union, a gradual process of secularization took place over the years, and other grave markers such as the obelisk appeared in most cemeteries. Obelisks in particular became the obligatory form for the graves of Party members. The proliferation of the obelisk form in European monumental architecture is usually associated with increasing interest in Egyptian architecture and cultural artifacts following Napoleon's Egyptian campaign, and already by the end of the eighteenth century obelisks in stone or granite with pyramid-shaped domes were becoming popular throughout Europe as tributes to notable people and particularly to military heroes. The most famous example in Russia is probably the granite obelisk with an eagle mounted at its apex designed as a memorial to the great victor of the Russo-Turkish war (1787–91), field-marshal Rumyantsev, and raised in St. Petersburg on the military parade ground, Field of Mars, in 1799. In 1818 it was moved to Vasil'evskii Ostrov, on the other side of the river Neva, where it can still be seen in the middle of a little park known as the Rumyantsev Garden. During the nineteenth century impressive obelisks were popular adornments on the gravesites of the wealthy—their size and prominence in one part of Highgate Cemetery in London, for example, earned it the title of "Egyptian Avenue." As can be seen from the remains of nineteenth-century tombs, the cemeteries of Moscow and St. Petersburg did not escape the fashion for obelisks. However, the design of obelisks marking graves in the rural cemeteries of the North, as indeed elsewhere in Russia, bears little resemblance to these grandiose relics of the past, and the source of their inspiration can be found in the twentieth century. After World War I, Russia, because of the revolution and civil war that followed it, did not participate in the proliferation of war memorials, great and small, erected in so many cities and tiny villages alike in other countries of Europe. A popular shape for such memorials was again the obelisk. In the Soviet Union it was not until after 1965—when, during the premiership of Brezhnev, May 9, Victory Day, became a grandiose national day of remembrance for those who fell in the Great Patriotic War—that the wholesale construction of memorials began across the land. Situated at some strategic point in the village, very often, and for obvious reasons, next to the site of the former church, these simple stone, brick, or even wooden constructions, crowned with a five-pointed red star, the symbol of the Soviet army, became the rallying place for politicized public remembrance of victory, a place for propaganda and speeches as well as private tears. They were echoed by the appearance of obelisks in cemeteries, made of white- or gray-painted metal or unadorned wood topped with a red star (or sometimes a pointed finial) and often bearing the portrait of a young man in military uniform. Not all obelisks necessarily mark the graves of soldiers or bear reference to the Red Army, however. The shape became familiar, and a surprising number of these carry small crosses, rather than stars, at their apex, just as it is possible to find crosses to which a star has been attached.

A noticeable number of graves in north Russian cemeteries are marked only by a wooden stake, shaped on two sides to form a sloping point at the apex. Some of these today have a purely utilitarian function. The poor, sandy soil quickly begins to settle into the grave pit, making it impracticable to erect a heavy, permanent memorial immediately after the burial. This is usually only done after a year or so has passed. The stake is then removed and buried nearby or hidden behind the new cross. There are numerous grave markers of this type, on the other hand, that have clearly been in position for many years. Substantial in size, with "roofs" like many traditional crosses, with names and dates etched into the surface or bearing ceramic portraits of the deceased, they have a look of permanence. In fact, this form of grave marker with numerous variations has a long history in the Russian North. D. K. Zelenin, referring to the nineteenth and first years of the twentieth century, comments that with such markers it was common to attach a cross to the summit (Zelenin 1991, 351). I have only recorded one such post with a cross on top (in Azopol'e) for a burial dated 1958. It is possible that during the Soviet period the familiar shape was retained but not always with a cross.

Finally, there are numerous, virtually identical and probably mass-produced metal grave markers of unusual shape—an irregular quadrilateral, not quite a trapezoid, with no two sides the same length and no two sides parallel. This disconcertingly indefinable form with no discernible relationship to the established rituals of death suggests an attempt to provide a grave marker reflecting a particular Soviet aesthetic concept. Its antecedents may be found, I suggest, in the geometric styles in modernist interior design that became popular in the 1960s during the time of Khrushchev.

In spite of the innovations mentioned above and the gradual replacement of wooden crosses with the more fashionable metal ones, these remote northern cemeteries still contain much that would have felt familiar to Turgenev, or even Pushkin, and the artists who were their contemporaries. True, there is plenty of vegetation, as most cemeteries are situated in forest clearings rather than at the edge of a village, but there is little sense of order or organization, with graves dotted haphazardly across an ill-defined space bordering on wilderness at its outside edges. Maze-like pathways between graves follow no logical course, obliging one to constantly backtrack. Ancient grave markers poke through long grass and wildflowers, redundant wooden crosses and bits of fencing lie propped against trees. Moss, grass, and lichens sprout on sandy grave mounds. Many abandoned graves and indeed whole cemeteries are in the process of returning to nature.

A Soviet-era grave marker, Vozhgora, Arkhangel'sk province, 2013. (Photo by Elizabeth Warner)

On the other hand, in addition to the new types of grave marker mentioned earlier, the Soviet era saw the introduction of several significant changes in the visual aspects of these cemeteries. One of these has been the increasing use of wreaths at funerals and the proliferation of artificial flowers at both funerals and memorial occasions. Driving for the first time in July 2010 into Leshukonʹe, the administrative center of Leshukonʹe region, our group of researchers was struck by a strange sight. At the far side of an open field was a long line of brilliant color, surely not a tropical garden in the Far North! Later inspection revealed a cemetery where wreaths, bouquets of artificial flowers, and unusual, tall containers specially made to display other floral tributes adorned graves and fences with a riot of dazzling color. Village shops now have a section where such items may be bought. The strident, clashing kaleidoscopes of flowers in every shade of pink, red, purple, yellow, and turquoise was somewhat startling to our eyes, which were used to more subdued and subtle tones. However, these colors fall naturally within the aesthetic tastes of those who chose them. The interior decoration of the many village homes I visited in the North from the late 1990s revealed a similar penchant for extravagant color and patterns, on wallpaper, curtain material, bedspreads, pillowcases, wall hangings, handmade rugs, oil-cloth tablecloths, decorative tea towels, and the like. The notion of color coordination is completely absent. A similar enjoyment of color can be seen in items of dress, housecoats, aprons, headscarves, knitted socks, and mittens.

The introduction of wreaths into village funerals was not so much concerned with the creation of a beautiful effect. Wreaths came with ribbons proclaiming the givers' sympathies and relationship to the deceased. Wreaths given by family members or friends are one thing, but many of the wreaths were supplied by the village soviet (*selʹsovet*) or the collective farm management, for example. Contributions of this kind conveyed something of the status of the deceased and his or her role as a member of a "collective" rather than of a village community. They had a similar function, I would suggest, to the presentation of long-service medals or certificates of merit for outstanding work on the farm and were also in keeping with the secular graveside eulogies that had replaced the burial service.

Another change to the appearance of cemeteries in Soviet times, and one that might have impressed Turgenev, who complained about sheep being allowed to wander over graves, can be seen in the proliferation of fences or railings around both individual graves and family plots. As a result of their unregulated growth, cemeteries themselves were rarely bounded with a fence or wall. The local woman who accompanied me to the cemetery at Piruss (Borovichi region, Novgorod province) in 2016 pointed out, as a particularly unusual feature, the remains of a stone boundary wall and a large gateway, with brick pillars that had lost their wrought-iron gates and above which rusting, blue-painted metal "cupolas" exhibited a crudely drawn Orthodox cross and the word "Entrance."

Although railings were common around the graves of the wealthy in urban cemeteries in the nineteenth century, they were virtually unknown in rural cemeteries where peasants were buried. Gradually, wooden fencing, similar to the picket fences around vegetable gardens in the villages, was introduced. In the latter part of the twentieth century wrought-iron fences and crosses were popular. These fences were usually painted blue—faint traces can still be detected on the decaying posts of abandoned graveyards—while metal railings were often painted with gray metal paint. The same tradition is maintained today although various shades of green and turquoise are also widely used. There is no one answer as to why the fences appeared. One commonsense reason given by local people is that they protect the gravesites from damage by foraging livestock, like Turgenev's sheep. In Soviet times a privately owned cow or horse could not be grazed on land belonging to the collective farms. In the northern summers, cattle may still be deliberately grazed in the forest, where it is cooler. In any case, cows and horses, not to speak of the many stray dogs, today roam free and in the absence of fencing may not encounter any obstacles to entering a cemetery. The sites of votive and other venerated crosses are similarly protected. There is a perceived danger not only that cattle will trample the ground around them but that they may damage with their horns the wood and the garments and other votive offerings hanging there (FA Mez 15-2, July 7, 2007). On the other hand, a fenced and gated area, inside of which may be found a bench and table where family members gather at particular times to remember their deceased loved ones, is also a visible sign of "ownership," and plots containing generations of one family are jealously guarded. Enclosing an area also underlines the notion of the deceased's new home having been prepared in the "village" of the dead, the cemetery, and supports the status of the cemetery as a place for private socializing on special days of remembrance.

Last, but by no means least, a very significant change to the visual impact of cemeteries during the Soviet period was the appearance of photographic images on grave markers. In the absence of more sophisticated devices, ordinary photographs, framed or boxed in, were featured in memorials that can still be seen today. I particularly remember a rather faded black-and-white framed photograph of a homely, elderly woman who died in 2004, pictured clutching her pet dog. Mostly, however, in the cemeteries I visited in Vologda and Arkhangel'sk provinces one could see photoceramic plaques, usually oval in shape, showing either black-and-white or color images. By and large, these plaques are small, with a simple "head and shoulders" likeness of the deceased facing the camera. It is noticeable that those portrayed are plainly dressed in everyday clothes, and their appearance largely reflects the age at which, according to the dates shown on the grave markers, they died. Elderly women are almost invariably depicted wearing a headscarf, as was customary outside the domestic interior, a practice still observed in many parts of the conservative North. Occasionally, the portrait of a young soldier or sailor in uniform can be seen.

It is extremely difficult to know when these memorial plaques first made their appearance in Soviet-era cemeteries in the North. I have not recorded any earlier than the late 1950s (although that certainly does not mean that earlier examples do not exist), and many of those in my photographic archive from the region date to the 1970s to 2000s. However, the technology for bonding a photographic image onto various hard surfaces has been available since the middle of the nineteenth century. In 1854 two French photographers, André François Bulot and Joseph Marguerite Cattin, invented a process for fixing a photographic image on porcelain and enamel. The image was glazed and then fired at a very high temperature (Heinz Henisch and Bridget Ann Henisch 1996, 125). According to Ronald William Horne, by the late nineteenth to early twentieth century this type of memorial portraiture, promoted by the Italians, was becoming especially common in the cemeteries of southern and eastern Europe (Horne 2004, 64). His research into early twentieth-century memorial portraits in the Holy Cross Cemetery in Colma, California, revealed that a large number of such portraits were in fact to be seen on the graves of immigrants from these regions. Horne also comments that he had noticed an especially high concentration of portraits in the Slavonic section of the cemetery (Horne 2004, 30). It would seem likely that the trend for memorial portraiture arrived in Soviet Russia through growing familiarity with the Slavonic countries of postwar eastern Europe, including the former Yugoslavia, which, because of its more relaxed economic policies, eventually became a familiar "near-abroad" holiday destination for many Soviet citizens.

The appearance of these photographic plaques in the cemeteries of the Russian North is significant in a variety of ways. Being able to see a likeness of the deceased on every visit to a gravesite no doubt helps to preserve the memory of that person for the bereaved. As time passes, the portraits may also acquire a wider significance as historical artifacts, inviting us to enter and explore the lives of individuals representative of a specific culture, in a specific place and time. Whether intentionally or not, they also offer a secular alternative to the faces of the Savior, the Mother of God, or saints on the small icons often used to adorn graveyard crosses in pre-Soviet times. In 2013, in a village of the Leshukon'e region, an elderly widow showed me photographs of the funeral of her husband, who had died the previous year. She remembered that when her grandmother died in 1945 a small icon had been attached to her grave marker.

No one had prevented her family from doing this. Then, when thieves began to steal the icons from their niches in the crosses, people started to replace them with photographs (EW-A Arkh-Lesh, July 15, 2013). This sensible solution nevertheless indicates a move toward secularization when it seemed acceptable to replace a sacred image with a human one. These faces on grave markers also suggest a "reinstatement" of the physical persona of the deceased that, in turn, enhances the process of interaction between the living and the dead, an integral part of religious practice in the villages.

THE RURAL CEMETERY TODAY

Grave markers are as subject to fashion and to technological advances as any other artifacts. Over the past decade or so, even in isolated village cemeteries far from urban centers in Arkhangel'sk province it became noticeable that a new type of monument was becoming increasingly popular—the granite slab. In 2015 and 2016, I traveled to Tver' province to investigate birch tree engravings on grave markers of this type. My research centered on eight cemeteries serving the villages of Lykoshino—which has an old and a new cemetery—Mshentsy, Vypolzovo, Berezaika, and Turny in the Bologoe region and Piruss in the Borovichi region of the neighboring Novgorod province, together with the cemeteries of the small towns Bologoe and Borovichi. All of these revealed elements of what I had come to regard as the "traditional" cemetery in the North: old wooden and Soviet-era metal crosses and metal trapezoidal shapes—some blue and turquoise, some still silvery, and some rusting away—together with the occasional obelisk. The older sections of these graveyards in particular were still disorganized, with graves scattered randomly and separated by long grass and weeds.

In fact, there is nothing to stop a bereaved family today from continuing the simple traditions typifying the rural cemeteries of preceding decades, but it is clear that few do so, judging by the predominant style of new grave markers. Although one can see new crosses (which are sometimes integrated into the main body of the monument) in what has become the favorite material for grave markers, black granite, they are greatly outnumbered by other more "fashionable" designs.

Nowadays, grave markers usually consist of three main sections: an upright headstone (*stela*) placed on a base (*postament*) and a curbed surround (*tsvetnik*) where flowers may be planted. The shapes and designs for grave markers are largely standardized (indeed, they may be described as "classical" or "traditional" on the websites of funeral directors) so that, in spite of a considerable amount of individual choice over the type and quality of stone, the shape of the headstone, and the placement and style of ornamentation, cemeteries are beginning to develop a somewhat more uniform appearance. This is particularly true

Elizabeth and Anastasiya Gavrilenko explore the sprawling cemetery in Vypolzovo, Tver' province, 2016. (Photo by Father Vasilii Kukushkin)

in the newer sections, where geometric shapes and angles; a sense of sharpness, hardness, and shininess; and the color black predominate. These flat, upright, unchanging urban blocks are somehow out of kilter with the "organic" nature of the old wooden and metal crosses and the untended, grassy margins with which they share common ground.

Eternal Memory

One of the reasons for the increasingly changing visual profile of cemeteries since the 1990s is the proliferation of privately run businesses offering comprehensive funeral services that include the provision of memorial stones. Great emphasis is placed by these companies on the longevity and hard-wearing properties of the material to be chosen for the grave markers, with natural stone and, more often, granite and marble being the obvious first choices. Granite, in particular, is advertised as having the most longevity and as being able to withstand any amount of battering from the weather. Although much cheaper monuments of molded concrete and various types of artificial stone are also available, their susceptibility to damage and decay, leading to expensive repairs and replacements, is clearly stated. The same argument is used to promote the more expensive hand etching of designs onto the gravestone rather than the cheaper use of computerized laser technology, which produces a shallower and therefore more short-lived cut. The monument, and by association, the memory of the deceased person, is intended to "last forever." So many grave markers now contain a message to this effect: "Your memory is always alive" (Pamyat' o tebe vsegda zhiva); "We remember, we love, we grieve" (pomnim, lyubim, skorbim). A bright shiny stone that does not seem to deteriorate with time may offer an antidote to the notion of death as a matter of loss and decay. It presents a clear contrast to the rickety impermanence, poor materials and workmanship, and lack of "style" in the typical Soviet-era rural cemetery.

In terms of memory, the stone has two main functions. It constitutes a personal promise that we, the living, will retain the deceased in our memory, and it serves as a public, material memorial raised to honor the dead individual. The solidity of these memorial tablets runs counter to the sense of impermanence and instability many have experienced in their lifetimes, with families broken and reshaped by Soviet ideology and war or dispersed in post-Soviet economic upheavals. The stability of stone markers seems to deny the fragility of human memory, which, realistically, may not last more than a few generations. In all the cemeteries surveyed for this research, alongside well-tended graves were many others that had clearly been abandoned as families moved away and villages emptied. In the Bologoe town cemetery swaths of abandoned graves with rusting fences lay hidden under chest-high grasses and purple hollyhocks, growing wild.

The notion of raising an expensive monument to a person of modest family and nonheroic status is certainly a new development. Serving as a contrast with the unpretentious and uninformative grave markers of the Soviet rural cemetery and a far cry from the dominance of the "collective" in the social conscience, the present-day grave marker is a paean both to individual choice for the bereaved and to the value of the deceased as an individual. It is also a reflection of growing spending power and, as far as the more elaborate monuments are concerned, a way of demonstrating wealth publicly: "People have just got rich so they began to put up monuments. Before, there were just little crosses" (EW-A Tver'-Bol, June 16, 2016).

The Portrait Gallery

The smooth, polished surfaces of grave markers are blank pages that may be filled with virtually any message or conceit, depending on the desires and means of the bereaved and consistent with the norms of public decency. In general we may say that the grave marker nowadays is likely to contain the following elements: a cross etched into the marble or granite upright, a name and dates of birth and death, a portrait of the deceased, and a decorative device. This can range from a simple motif such as a flower or candle to a complex laser etching of a detailed landscape or object, sometimes situated on the reverse of the stone or, where the grave is large, on the flat slab covering the grave. In addition, there is usually a message of some sort. In the case of Orthodox burials, the Church recommends a quotation from the Scriptures, such as, in the case of one stone I saw, "Blessed are the pure in heart for they shall see God." More often the inscription is an expression of grief and love for the deceased. It may also take the form of an epitaph or a poem written for the occasion. Among all these informative and decorative items, the dominant position is often held by the deceased's portrait. Even though Marcel Proust, in the famous passage about madeleines in *Swann's Way*, shows us that memory can be unlocked by taste and smell, I have found in interviews that the strongest triggers of memory are usually visual. In chapter 1, I described the custom of taking photographs just before the departure for the cemetery, when family members gathered close to the open coffin and recorded their "last look" at the deceased. Although postmortem photographs of the deceased are less fashionable than they used to be, there is in general a relatively relaxed attitude toward photographing funeral and memorial occasions. Inquiries about funeral practices in the households I have visited over the years almost invariably led to the production of the family "funeral" album, which in turn opened up discussion of one of the most important aspects of traditional village life, the family unit itself, with its complex internal relationships and its wider kinship genealogies. Photographs of children and grandchildren, birthdays, weddings, and jubilee celebrations followed on from photographs of graveside scenes and memorial meals. In many homes photographs of parents, grandparents, and other family members are displayed on the walls of living rooms, often grouped together to form large tableaux.

Today, a portrait of the deceased is a virtually obligatory part of the grave marker, whether it is displayed on a modern granite slab or a traditional cross.

Although basic photoceramic plaques, such as may be seen on older graves, are still being produced, the arrival of digital photography in the late 1990s, combined with the development in the twenty-first century of new laser technology capable of transferring larger and more complex images onto stone, has transformed memorial portraiture and the decorative aspects of grave markers in general. Portraits have become larger and more eye-catching as well as less formal. Interestingly, the desire for the more elaborate portraiture offered by laser etching appears to have had a particular appeal to Russians, although examples can be seen all over Europe and the United States. In Alexis Madrigal's short essay on laser-etched gravestones in the Washington Cemetery in Brooklyn, New York, a cemetery worker comments that the new fashion was in fact introduced to the cemetery by the Brooklyn Russian immigrant community (Madrigal 2011).

According to strict Orthodox protocol, the only memorial on the grave of an Orthodox believer should be a cross, a reminder of Christ's sacrifice and of the promise of bodily resurrection. The deceased should be positioned facing the cross placed at his or her feet. However, it is now more common to signify a Christian burial with only a small cross engraved on the top left- or right-hand corner of the upright stone, vying for attention with the usually larger portraits of the deceased and many other graphic designs. In effect, rather than contemplate the cross of resurrection, the deceased now contemplate themselves as they were in life. As I mentioned earlier, the simple wooden post or cross placed at the time of the funeral is often left hidden behind the new grave marker since nothing should be removed from a graveyard. I have also seen graves where the original photograph or drawing used to produce the etched portrait has been left alongside it.

Writing of memorial and postmortem portraiture, Jay Ruby comments: "Photography's amazing popularity over the last century and a half is undoubtedly due to its capacity to help us remember people, places, and events. It provides a witness—one thought to be unimpeachable and permanent" (Ruby 1995, 1). The "life-like" qualities of photographs clearly do act as an *aide-memoir* in cemeteries, creating the illusion that the deceased is somehow still with us. Fixing the physical image of the deceased is particularly relevant in a culture such as that of rural Russia, where, as noted in earlier chapters, loved ones maintain a close "physical" relationship with the dead. Nevertheless, the notion of the body suggested by the ubiquitous presence of ceramic and etched images of the deceased is by no means a simple one. Clearly, what is envisaged during the rituals of contact and communion is not the corrupting body underground. Nor is it likely to be the incorruptible body promised to the Orthodox believer after the resurrection. The graveyard body-soul lies somewhere in between and is neither solid flesh nor wraith; still, it possesses a definite "physical" presence. For this reason, no doubt, cremation, while allowed by the Church (albeit with some reluctance), is not regarded favorably by village women.[2] It is more difficult to "re-imagine" a body that has been reduced to ashes before it arrives in the cemetery. The ambivalent nature of those buried in the cemetery and the relationship between them and the grieving relatives was well expressed in the comments of women with whom I spoke in 2016 from Lykoshino and the surrounding villages. One told me how she would report all her news to her loved ones in a sort of one-sided conversation. Another always said "Hello!" as soon as she arrived at the grave and would ask the deceased how things were with them. The photographs of the deceased were mentioned as a form of replacement for the dead person, making communication easier.

Photographs concentrate the memories of mourners toward their loved ones, acting as conduits through which messages from the living pass to the dead. This idea is reinforced by the custom of placing a shot of vodka with a piece of bread over it in front of a photograph or portrait of the deceased on the grave, where it remains for forty days following the death. The women gave many different and sometimes contradictory reasons for the custom, practiced for generations and imbibed with their mothers' milk, of offering food and drink to the dead. Some of the explanations were as follows: they were leaving items such as biscuits, sunflower seeds, and grain for the birds, who represented the souls of the dead; the food was for poor people who would eat it and remember and name the deceased, thus providing comfort to the dead similar to prayers said in church; the deceased loved sweet pancakes and little pies, so his relatives left these treats for him to enjoy. One woman protested that, on the contrary, the food offerings had nothing to do with the deceased person's favorites while another dismissed the custom altogether as nothing more than a pagan sacrifice. They were all reluctant to take food home from the cemetery, so an unfinished bottle of vodka might be left for the local down-and-outs while a glass poured specifically for the deceased was regarded as his and his alone, and no one else would dare to drink it (EW-A Tver'-Bol, June 16, 2016).

The act of placing the offering of food and drink in front of the portrait clearly demonstrates the role of the photograph as alter ego of the deceased. To what extent, though, can this photograph be the "unimpeachable witness" referred to by Ruby?

Making the Grave Beautiful

It is perfectly understandable for the bereaved to wish to preserve the good memories they have of a departed loved one, to remember the deceased in the fullness of life rather than dwelling on the darkness and emptiness of death. And in fact, the facial or bodily image presented on the grave marker has little to do with death. Particularly when viewed as part of a pictorial scene, it is almost a fictional recreation of the person, reflecting what the bereaved relatives prefer to remember and ignoring any effects of illness and aging in the cases of those who were old when they died. It is noticeable that the deceased is often depicted at an age considerably younger than that achieved by the time of death. Here, three women discuss the photograph one of them chose for her father's grave: "My father was eighty-seven when he died, but in the photograph I had made, he is forty. That's because I remember him as a young man. He was full of energy, handsome, healthy, so why show old age? No! I showed him as he was when he was young, healthy, and handsome." "After all," agreed one companion, "an old person is not very pretty. . . . Sometimes they age to such an extent that you simply don't recognize them. Especially if someone has been ill for a long time. They just look different so people try to [show them] in middle age." A third woman had actually replaced an earlier photograph on her mother's grave because it showed her as an old woman wearing a headscarf: "I made her young too" (EW-A Tver'-Bol, July 16, 2016).

The image on the stone represents a frozen moment only, an image chosen by the living to show the loved one at his or her best, smartly dressed with tidy hair, smiling or solemn. The image aims to evoke pleasant memories and command respect, even admiration, whether viewed privately or publicly. This representation is thus one aspect of a wider objective, the creation of a burial plot with aesthetic appeal. Referring to the fashion for stone monuments, Tat'yana remarked, "You want to provide your parents/forebears/ancestors [*roditeli*] with the best, you understand? I think what I did was so it would be beautiful there" (EW-A Tver'-Bol, June 16, 2016).

One indication of the desire to "beautify" gravesites is the proliferation of floral bouquets and designs. While fresh flowers are difficult to obtain and expensive, not to mention short-lived and available only during a limited season, artificial flowers can be bought even in small villages, and they stand up well to the harsh climate. After graves have been cleaned and tidied at Troitsa, new bouquets replace the old and sometimes remain in situ until the following year. In every cemetery I visited in the Bologoe region at Troitsa in 2015 and 2016, virtually every grave was bright with the exuberant colors that appeal to the artistic tastes of the local people. Gazing at this wild profusion of color, it was easy to imagine that so many bouquets had simply been picked at random from the great variety I saw on sale at the entrances to cemeteries. This is very far from the truth, however. Women who were asked which preferences they had when choosing flowers to lay on a grave were quite clear that their selections were made with care and purpose, and they were even prepared to defend their choices when companions disagreed. One preferred pink, light blue, and red flowers but did not like yellow or white ones because they were not showy enough. Another loved bright colors, especially for her mother's grave. Yellow reminded her of sunshine. For her father, on the other hand, she would choose something darker—lilac, perhaps, or claret-colored. Yet another considered soft colors most suitable for a woman's grave and pointed out that white was considered to be the color of purity. By and large, women chose "what their hearts desired," as one said.

Although there appeared to be no hard and fast rules among the women, picking the right flowers to lay on a particular grave certainly involved some thought and a variety of considerations—personal preferences, the symbolism of certain flowers, associations with particular hues, the appropriateness of particular flowers or colors for men's graves versus women's graves, and so on.

Lilies of the valley, rarely seen on graves in any case, were said to be unsuitable for a man's grave, being tender flowers suggesting youth and more suitable for the grave of a child or a young woman. Carnations, on the other hand, could be regarded as a "male" variety of flower. In general, carnations and roses were considered to be the most popular flowers both in bouquets and in the small flower emblems that embellish the gravestones themselves, engraved or etched toward the lower edge of the front face of the stone. Roses were seen as a "symbol of love" and would typically be requested by a husband for his wife, or vice-versa, while children, it was thought, would be unlikely to suggest a design of roses for the gravestone of their parents (EW-A Tver'-Bol, June 16, 2016).

My own observations in local cemeteries confirmed that gravestone floral motifs are indeed predominantly either carnations or roses, particularly the latter, and that both kinds of flowers may be found on the gravestones of males as well as females, although carnations predominate on the graves of men and roses on the graves of females. Many of the newer gravestones today commemorate both husband and wife, the grave having been updated after the most recent death. In these cases it is not unusual to see a sprig of carnations next to the portrait of the husband and one of roses beside the wife.

As far as bouquets of flowers are concerned, the chance to exercise one's personal tastes, although important to those who decorate the graves, is only possible because of the proliferation of floral choices available today and must be a fairly recent phenomenon. Older women recalled how, on the way to the cemetery when they were young, they would pluck a few flowers from the meadows to lay on a grave—bluebells, daisies, wild pinks. The first artificial flowers, as they recollected, probably began to make their appearance about forty years ago. Some of the women talked about making paper roses in school. I too remember similar amateurishly made garlands in Russia and still have one I bought at the Danilovskii market in Moscow in 1976! The now-faded, stylized pink "roses" with green leaves threaded onto a wire support were cut from scrap paper, the remains of lines and print still visible on the reverse side, and dipped in wax to preserve them. The "sophistication" of today's offerings is a far cry from such simplicity, but sophistication and choice come at a price. The women I interviewed grumbled at the high cost of flowers today, a consequence of burgeoning consumerism and the market principle of supply and demand now rampant in the funeral trade. The provision of flowers, wreaths, and monuments was described as a money-grabbing enterprise, "the most profitable business" (EW-A Tver'-Bol, June 16, 2016).

What seems to motivate the impulse to create visual beauty on burial plots, and indeed, for whose benefit is it created? According to my observations, three kinds of beneficiaries, of differing levels of importance, come into play. In third place are casual visitors, or those who have come to visit other graves. In small, closely knit communities these may well be acquaintances or neighbors of a particular bereaved family, so there is a social imperative to maintain standards. An untidy grave suggests abandonment by the deceased's relatives, a matter for censure. A well-tended grave, on the other hand, shows that the deceased is still remembered and loved.

In second place are the grieving members of the deceased's close family. One of my interlocutors suggested that flowers and monuments, and even toys on a child's grave, helped to create a more beautiful, cheerful, and even "lifelike" ambience that can make visitors feel less sad and less afraid: "It seems like we are visiting the living" (EW-A Tver'-Bol, June 16, 2016).

In first place are the dead themselves. In the previous remark about "visiting the living," we may find the essence of the impulse to beautify, which is to give pleasure to the dead who are also in some sense "living" and in some way "present." Flowers are taken as gifts to the dead in the same way one would take gifts to the living, with the conviction that the gifts will afford pleasure and reflect the trouble the giver has gone to. Beautifying the grave here, in this world, ensures a corresponding sense of beauty *there*, in the other world of the dead.

Pondering this abundance of floral tributes and the way in which many rural cemeteries seem to merge with the natural world, I was reminded of a passage in Boris Pasternak's novel *Doctor Zhivago* in which the author reflects upon the multitude of fresh flowers, whole bushes of white lilac, surrounding Zhivago's coffin in 1930s Moscow, as his relatives and friends came to bid farewell. The flowers served perhaps as compensation for what was necessarily missing—the familiar rituals of Orthodoxy, preceding and following his death, and the voices of the psalm-singers where his body had been laid out:

> The kingdom of plants can easily be thought of as the nearest neighbor of the kingdom of death. Perhaps the mysteries of transformation and the enigma of life which so torment us are concentrated in the green of the earth among the trees in the graveyard and the flowering shoots springing from their beds. (Pasternak 1958, 439–40)

The Living and the Dead Conjoined

For the people whose opinions and beliefs formed the bedrock of this book, the notion that the living and the dead and the worlds they inhabit remain linked together in an essential way is axiomatic. The existence of this link, in its various manifestations, was a recurrent one in discussions I had with women in the Bologoe region about various aspects of their beliefs and practices concerning the dead. As I have said, one function of the memorial portrait on the grave is to facilitate this link. Large rural cemeteries can be very disorientating. One widow complained that she often got lost and was unable to locate her husband's grave—until, that is, she called out his name. Then she would suddenly catch sight of him, peeping out from behind a tree. In other words, his portrait on the grave marker acted as a guiding beacon. Dreams in which the dead communicate with the living were also offered as proof of the link. In one dream, for example, a dead woman complained to her sister that she could not breath because a heavy birch tree had fallen across her grave. The sister was immediately galvanized into action. The horse was harnessed to a cart, a chainsaw was brought, and the tree was sawn up and removed (EW-A Tver'-Bol, June 16, 2016).

In chapters 1 and 2, I argued based on interviews with village women that it was endemic in the rural population to believe both in a direct link between the dead and the bereaved and in a concrete "presence" of the deceased in graveyards. The dead were thought capable of seeing, hearing, expressing feelings and preferences—in short, of having consciousness. Time and again these beliefs manifested themselves in behavioral patterns and in casual remarks about the dead. They affected decisions regarding the choice of grave markers. Those approaching death often made requests that suggested belief in a sentient afterlife, and those who felt duty-bound to honor those requests revealed similar beliefs in their actions. A daughter, therefore, followed her mother's dying wish not to erect a heavy stone on her grave: in life her mother had found lying under a sheet difficult enough, and she would surely suffocate under the weight of a stone (EW-A Tver'-Bol, June 16, 2016).

Belief that the dead can hear, feel, and have opinions and preferences regulates the etiquette of visiting graves in rural villages to this day. Greeting and bidding farewell, touching the crosses and monuments, kissing the photographs and respecting visiting hours (best before lunchtime) are all part of normal cemetery behavior. The dead are spoken to as if they have maintained their knowledge and understanding of the world they have supposedly left behind. A teacher, for example, described how she would complain about the bad behavior of a naughty pupil when she walked past his granddad's grave. On one level of consciousness people understand very well that their loved ones are dead and buried, but on another they strive to keep them close and maintain a link with them. They are concerned for their dead, always alert to their physical needs and to those deprivations and even sufferings occasioned by the straightened circumstances in which they find themselves. Even when imagined in an otherworldly location, well beyond the confines of the cemetery, the dead are still a prey to the physical sensations of the living body. In discussions about the clothing provided for the dead, footwear is often mentioned as an essential element. A person buried in the wrong footwear, or inadequate footwear, is likely to be distressed. I have often wondered why, beyond aesthetic reasons, footwear was considered to be so necessary. It was another of those questions I posed to my endlessly patient interlocutors in the Bologoe region. The answer was to be found in a somewhat literal interpretation of the Orthodox belief in the ordeals through which the soul must pass on its long journey to judgment.[3] On the arduous forty-day trek between worlds, "barefoot is bad" because "it's uncomfortable," and "if they were barefoot they would wear out their feet." The correct footwear could help to alleviate physical pain and discomfort in a metaphysical situation. Women, therefore, are not buried in high-heeled shoes because they are difficult to walk in.

The Home of Ancestors: Past, Present, and Future

As we have seen, the portraits displayed on crosses and gravestones have a number of different functions. In many cases the portraits themselves and their accompanying attributes, the symbols and written tributes surrounding them, to some degree reconstruct the most important characteristics of the deceased, such as work or profession, personality and interests. The gravestone may show quite literally the public or private face of the deceased. In this respect I noticed an interesting trend. Almost all the visual references to the profession of the deceased, at the time of death or long in the past, are military. I noted very few signs of civilian occupations—a pen-nib symbol presumably indicated a writer, a man shown with a telephone pressed to his ear may have been a businessman or a local official. By contrast, there are many portraits of men in army or naval uniforms, usually proudly displaying medals. Naval uniforms are distinguished by their anchor and chain motifs, which also appear etched on gravestones. A star, hammer, and wrench motif suggests the grave of a military engineer or sapper, a badge in the shape of "wings" that of an aviator. There are also pictorial etchings with more precise information about the nature of a man's service. The grave of a submariner, for example, is distinguished by an etching of a submarine emerging from the waves and that of a pilot by a small plane disappearing into the clouds.

The presence of these military uniforms and emblems has of course been influenced by memories of the fate of so many members of the armed forces killed during World War II and memorialized in cemeteries all over Russia. The cemeteries I visited in Vypolzovo, Lykoshino, and Bologoe all contain communal military graves and memorial complexes that become a focus of attention on Victory Day. In Vypolzovo, near the old war graves there are other, more recent private burials of military personnel. However, grave markers showing the deceased in uniform can be found in most cemeteries and are not connected to specific memorial sites.

Some of those commemorated in this way are veterans of the Great Patriotic War; others are victims of the Soviet-Afghan War or the two Chechen wars. Still others have simply served a period of time in the armed forces. Until 2006 compulsory military service in the Russian Federation lasted two years. It was subsequently reduced to eighteen months and later to one year. Virtually every adult male buried in the cemetery will therefore have been conscripted at some time. From the portraits it is tragically clear that some died very young. I noted the portrait of a seventeen-year-old youth in a seaman's uniform and an elaborate monument erected in memory of a cadet from the Mozhaisk Military-Space Institute in St. Petersburg. On one side of his gravestone is the portrait of a young man in uniform, on the other a detailed engraving of the Faculty of Topography and Cartography at the Mozhaisk Institute (formerly the Antonov Military-Topographical College, founded in 1822), where he studied. According to information from local people who know this cemetery well, the monument was commissioned by the institute. Another monument to a very young soldier displays the medal he received for "fulfilling his international duty in Ethiopia."

Among the more startling militaristic images I noted were the inscription to a "Don Cossack," the words picked out in gold over two similarly gilded crossed swords, and the depiction, on the reverse side of another monument, erected by the Ministry of Defense, of two armed rocket launchers aggressively pointing skyward.

A number of crosses and gravestones carried an additional military emblem, the so-called George ribbon (Georgievskaya lenta), which has become a familiar attribute of the Victory Day celebrations that had taken place only a few weeks before my visit in 2016. One monument in particular drew my attention. Three members of one family are commemorated by a marble plaque bearing the symbol known as the Bowl or Chalice of Hygieia, widely used in Russia, as elsewhere, by the pharmaceutical and medical professions. The George ribbon tied around the cross on the top of the monument suggested, perhaps, that one of the three must have had some military experience, possibly in a medical unit.

The distinctive black and orange stripes of the George ribbon echo the black and yellow of the ribbon of the imperial award for exceptional bravery in action, the Cross of St. George, instituted by Empress Catherine II in 1769. In Soviet times the black and orange version became familiar as part of the Order of Glory (Orden' slavy), awarded mainly to noncommissioned officers, and of the medal "For victory over Germany in the Great Patriotic War 1941–45." Although the striped ribbon was a well-recognized symbol of victory in Soviet times, it did not become a major component of Victory Day celebrations until the twenty-first century. Its present-day popularity was launched in 2005 as a project for the sixtieth anniversary of Victory Day.[4] In addition to its role in preserving collective respect for and memory of the nation's heroes, the George ribbon has become popular in expatriate communities around the world, where it has been associated with Russian nationalism. It has been worn by demonstrators supporting Russian interests in the Baltic States and Ukraine and other countries formerly part of the Soviet Union or in its sphere of influence, where its use has become a matter of controversy.[5] It has even made an appearance in the UK and Ireland. On May 9, 2016, I happened to be in Cork in the Republic of Ireland. Like other passersby I was suddenly startled by a cavalcade of cars driving at speed around the quiet streets of the center, their horns blaring loudly and with George ribbons flying from their antennae. On Victory Day the ribbon is pinned to clothing, tied on handbags, or attached to cars. Even pets may sport a ribbon. Various explanations may be given for hanging the ribbon on the graves of war veterans: "On the one hand these offerings to the dead, like ritual food or clothing and household items, are usually explained as satisfying the needs of the dead ('the deceased requests it'). On the other hand, the George ribbon on a grave, like a red star in some cases in Soviet times, identifies the deceased as a member of the armed forces" (Arkhipova 2017).

The use of military symbols, uniforms, and medals draws attention to the sacrifices and achievements of husbands, fathers, and brothers in the line of duty and service to country and is closely bound up with notions of status and family honor. It marks a resurgence of pride in the rank and achievements of individual family members: "So they depict a medal or he's a soldier in uniform, a general or—what else do they write?—a major-general. . . . Once, they would have written a 'collegiate assessor' but now . . . we have someone buried in the cemetery who today has the rank of general . . ." (EW-A Tver'-Bol, June 16, 2016).[6] It is also, I think, symptomatic of the growing spirit of nationalism in Russia and reminiscent, in its appreciation of "service," of Soviet times when funeral processions with official wreaths, brass bands, and graveside speeches rewarded workers who had been loyal to the mechanisms of the Soviet state. It was not unusual for the state to pay for an elaborate monument, honoring particularly appreciated individuals, a practice that, from the description of several of the monuments referred to above, still survives today. In the homes of elderly villagers, framed certificates recognizing excellence on the collective farm or long service are still proudly displayed, and military and civilian medals are brought out to show the visitor and given a prominent place in open coffins.

Like these somewhat public tributes to rank, bravery, and honorable service, many more intimate references to the deceased also follow certain clearly delineated patterns. As one wanders among the graves, one's attention is constantly attracted by detailed pictorial etchings of rural landscapes. Although they may vary in some details—swans swimming or geese flying, sunshine or clouds, a weeping willow or water lilies, a bridge, boats drawn up on a grassy bank—they clearly represent a generalized and somewhat romanticized vision of the Russian countryside, identified always by the linked features of water—in the form of rivers, lakes, and streams—and trees, a pine forest on the horizon and the inescapable birch trees lining the riverbanks. Occasionally, a small, traditional wooden house or the cupolas of a church may be glimpsed. Of course, these pictures include elements of reality and in some cases have clearly been adapted from photographs. Yet in their generic similarity they are mainly significant for their symbolic value as indicators of the beloved homeland and the natural place within it of the deceased. Similar art, which corresponds to popular taste, is often bought as a gift or souvenir to beautify an interior and can be seen in people's homes, in paintings or wall hangings. Taken together, the motifs appearing on the gravestones—the natural world with its rivers and birch trees, the homely wooden houses, and the little churches—represent a paradigm of "Russianness" dear to the hearts of the bereaved and offered subliminally to those who have been deprived of it in death. Embedded within some of these quintessentially Russian landscapes are bucolic scenes of fishing and hunting for wildfowl. The deceased is imagined following his favorite pastime, fishing from a rowboat, casting a line from the bank, or following his gundog through the reed beds in search of wildfowl.

In this engraving on the back of a gravestone, the deceased is imagined in an earthly paradise where he enjoys a day's fishing. The fallen tree is a typical symbol of death. Vypolzovo, Tver' province, 2016. (Photo by Elizabeth Warner)

These are not the only passions or hobbies depicted in the gravestone etchings. Young men are often pictured with their treasured guitars, but a more common favorite possession is a car or motorbike. Such complex attributes are open to a variety of questions and interpretations. A motor vehicle, especially one that is powerful and costly, like the Kawasaki and Yamaha motorbikes shown on some grave markers, is a symbol of status or wealth, of proud ownership, or even of aspirations and dreams. In one cemetery the full-size portrait of an eleven-year-old boy caught my eye. On one side of the tall, black granite stone, dressed in a suit with fashionably baggy trousers, he stands with hands in pockets, legs akimbo in an attitude of boyish bravado. On the reverse side of the stone, the portrait is stranger and very disturbing. Against the backdrop of a dark sky full of clouds, the boy, dressed in motorbike leathers but *without* a helmet, rides a motorbike down an empty road. The front wheel of the bike is raised in the air as if the bike is about to fly off the stone, straight at the observer. The image is accompanied by the words, "Like an angel, up into the sky you soared [*vzmyl*]." One wonders, could the boy actually have had such a possession or only dreamed of having it? Or was the bike associated directly with his tragic, early death? It is worth mentioning that the boy's family are Roma (commonly called Tsygane in Russia). Roma family graves, I was told, tend to be more elaborate and flamboyant than Russian graves. This was certainly the case in one of the cemeteries I visited in an area where there is a large population of this ethnic minority. In the Berezaika cemetery (Bologoe region, Tver' province), some portraits showed the deceased at full height or even larger than life-size, the young men posing nonchalantly in front of their cars. Members of this ethnic group in Russia, as elsewhere, have a reputation as horse breeders and traders, and although mechanized transport has largely replaced the role of the horse in everyday life, horses may still be used to transport a coffin to the cemetery. Images of horses were also incorporated into the wrought-iron fences enclosing some gravesites so that those buried within were characterized by both traditional and mechanized forms of transport.

Drawings of motorbikes can mostly be seen on the graves of young men who died in their twenties, and it is natural to wonder how many of them were killed in road accidents for which Russia—with its reputation for drunk-driving problems and poorly maintained and unpaved roads in rural areas, combined with a macho attitude to driving—has a particularly bad record.

Although it would seem strange that anyone would create a visual reference to the manner of a loved one's death, I remember an occasion in 2013 in Rodoma, a remote village in Arkhangel'sk province, when I photographed the grave of a truck driver who died in a road accident. The steering wheel that had been placed on his grave was a tribute to his profession, but at the same time it was a material link to the manner of his death.

An open road, sometimes empty and disappearing into the distance, with birch forest on either side, and sometimes showing a solitary vehicle—a car, motorbike or even a truck—appears on a number of gravestones and can obviously be read simply as a metaphor for departure and death, the motor vehicle subconsciously envisaged as the modern equivalent of the angel conveying the soul to heaven.

The vehicles themselves, though, are far from metaphorical. They are depicted realistically and in great detail, as can be seen from the etchings of Kawasaki and Yamaha motorbikes. One young man, who died at the age of twenty-five, is depicted together with his three hundred horsepower Kawasaki Ninja bike, from which he was clearly inseparable, even in death, as the poem on the other side of the stone reveals. His friends imagine him riding the bike in heaven and hear the roar of its engine in rain and thunderstorms: "We simply know it's you, racing down the roads of paradise." As if he has become some new patron saint of bikers, they invoke his protection "from misfortune and crashes."

It is striking that symbols of status; prestigious occupations; possessions such as motorbikes, which suggest adventure, mobility, and freedom; and enjoyable outdoor pursuits like fishing are, by and large, shown as the preserve of men. This clearly reflects the deeply patriarchal nature of the society and the clarity with which gender roles are defined. Many women have served with distinction in the Soviet and Russian armies, but I have not seen a single depiction on a gravestone of a woman in uniform and have recorded only one reference to a woman's profession. Her epitaph mentions that she was a postal or telecommunications worker (*svyazistka*) in addition to being a wonderful mother, grandmother, sister, and friend. The associations found on women's graves usually have to do with their roles as homemakers. For example, a portrait on a grave might be juxtaposed with a typical village house, complete with vegetable garden. I have also come across women photographed holding pet cats or dogs, against a starry sky, or in a flower-studded meadow, all images chosen to suggest an imagined relationship with femininity.

Whatever one may think of the disparity between expressions of patriarchal status on one hand and matriarchal homeliness on the other, the designs of contemporary gravestones play a part in a wider picture of the fundamental importance of the cult of ancestors in traditional Russian mortuary practice. In terms of memorialization, nowadays it is clear that the simple recording on a grave marker of a person's name, date of birth, and death, regarded as adequate by the Orthodox Church, is not always regarded as adequate by bereaved families, whether or not they regard themselves as Orthodox. The opportunity to add visual and verbal reminders of those interred has been greatly enhanced by new technologies. While excessive flamboyance and expenditure may be frowned upon, the provision of more information about the deceased is welcomed. These are the graves of "ordinary" people whose "ordinariness" and relative anonymity is no longer always acceptable to their relatives and friends. Their monuments are no less significant for their families than the carved tombs, statues, and busts that graced the graves of the privileged and famous in the distant past.

It is important for people to know who exactly is buried in the grave, and monuments with visible embellishments that offer faces, uniforms and medals, images of figures engaging in popular male pursuits or leaning on the hoods of their hard-earned automobiles—or even shown with a mug of coffee, a cigarette, or an adored pet—provide that information much more efficiently than a name and a date: "How I enjoy, for example, going to the cemetery now and again . . . maybe to tidy the graves or something. Oh! We can walk all about the cemetery and you read and see the faces . . . and there are so many interesting ones and ours is an old cemetery. When we were there last time, there's a man buried there who even has three George crosses! Well, it's just interesting. Sometimes you'll see a familiar name, maybe someone you know, and you begin to . . . and you'll dig up something really interesting . . ." (EW-A Tver'-Bol, June 16, 2016). Portraits and pictures encourage children, who are introduced to graveyard rituals from an early age, to ask questions about the dead and learn about their kin and the importance of remembering and honoring them.

The gravesite has implications for both the living and the dead. As far as the living are concerned, the cemetery is the home of their forebears. All those I have visited, whether in the North or the more westerly provinces of Pskov, Tver', and Novgorod, are distinguished by the number of graves, grouped together, belonging to members of one family, and very often, since the latter half of the twentieth century, fenced in to form a single unit. Family members who have died in the city or abroad are frequently returned to the village of their family origins for burial alongside their own people. In some cemeteries, as in Lykoshino, for example, space is now limited, with fresh burials taking place on the site of old ones in preference to a place elsewhere, with more room but with no connections to other family members. Looking around these cemeteries today, one is struck by the number of new grave markers commemorating more than one deceased: a husband and wife, a father and son, a mother and two sons, or several generations of one family. It is self-evident that in most cases the present memorial was erected many years after the first death, presumably because earlier there had been no opportunity, or perhaps no possibility of commemorating the deceased in the desired manner. The contiguity of portraits where there are multiple burials creates a sense of the generations being reunited. One stone in Piruss, for example, shows two brothers who died, aged nine and twenty-three, respectively. In fact, they died twenty-four years apart, the one born in the year after the first brother died. They never saw each other in life but are united in death. Similarly, another stone portrays a husband and wife and their two daughters, whose deaths span fifty years (1958–2008). Early on in the Soviet regime there was a deliberate policy of breaking down the old class divisions, of leveling society to its lowest common denominator before reintroducing other social distinctions of a different kind. This policy was directed not only at the aristocracy, intellectuals, and rich entrepreneurs but also at the largest social group of the population, the peasantry. Its effects on traditional peasant life and culture have been well-documented (see, e.g., Fitzpatrick 1994). Before collectivization and the policy of dekulakization in the 1930s, community life in the villages was regulated not by class considerations but by family and kinship bonds, which played a significant part in economic, agricultural, and social affairs such as the arrangement of marriages. Families took pride in genealogies stretching back centuries, and ties were complex and interwoven. The heads of families, the patriarch *bol'shak* and the matriarch *bol'shukha*, had clear-cut roles within the household and the wider community, each in control of a different sphere of influence. Dekulakization may have uprooted and dispossessed families, depriving them of status, but it did not manage to destroy pride in family or the importance of kinship, both of which retained their place in funeral ritual. Who needs the information recorded today on gravestones? The answer to questions like this is unequivocal—children and grandchildren, closely followed by all family members and, indeed, anyone interested in tracing the history of their own community. The value of understanding and appreciating genealogies was only broken during the Soviet period and especially during the Stalinist repressions, when many people were afraid to talk about the history of their own families. Today, matters of ancestry and kinship have once again become elements of social discourse and practice, and even "vanity and pride" in one's forebears, as one person remarked, is again permissible.

Most monuments that proclaim pride in the status and achievements of the deceased in these rural cemeteries refer to military honors, but communities are nevertheless aware of other types of worthiness that could and should be celebrated. For example, women from nearby villages called my attention to a whole "dynasty" of teachers buried in the cemetery in Turny (Tver' province). Why should a teacher who had been officially recognized for services to education not have a special monument?

Earlier in this chapter, I commented on one explanation I was given for the number of enclosed gravesites, that the fences would stop animals from trampling the graves. However, it is much more likely that maintaining a space for multiple generations of one's own family is the chief aim behind creating these enclosures. This particular topic aroused some passionate comments and was clearly close to people's hearts. Many felt strongly that all the relatives, if possible, should be buried together in one plot of the family's choosing: "One old fellow has picked out a place for himself. He's already dug in his cross. He's still alive, hale and hearty, but he's already got a place with a cross, so that no one else can occupy it" (EW-A Tver'-Bol, June 16, 2016). Maintaining one's private space is becoming more problematical today as many cemeteries are already overcrowded. Fences are erected with the prime objective of keeping strangers out. The burial of a stranger on or too close to one's chosen spot can raise hackles and lead to heated arguments: "I had a stranger's burial foisted on my place. They put up a fence, the swine" (EW-A Tver'-Bol, June 16, 2016).

Although the living are responsible for the general appearance and aesthetic embellishment of cemeteries, the dead too are perceived as having an interest in how the gravesite will look. When a grave is made beautiful, it is done at least in part for the benefit of the dead. Relatives offer the dead a look at objects that were of interest to them in life, such as toys and the walking sticks often placed alongside or behind graves in Arkhangel'sk province, or the depictions of floral bouquets, motorbikes, houses, medals, churches, fishing boats, and lakes surrounded by birch trees. Describing the design she had chosen for her mother's gravestone, Tat'yana remarked that she had chosen a church with four cupolas, each with a cross, because, although her mother was not a churchgoer, she had been a believer. She herself loved the picture, with its neat little church and birch tree, and was convinced that her mother too would be pleased with it (Tver'-Bol, June 16, 2016).

Inscriptions and epitaphs on gravestones are almost always addressed specifically to the deceased as if they were present to read them: "You left this life too early"; "We shall miss you eternally, but for ever remember you"; "Sleep, dear one, you are our pain, our wound"; "On earth we shall pray for you, while in the heavens you will pray for us"; "May the earth lie on you like down. All your relatives and friends are grieving for you"; "How sad your life was so short, but you will be remembered forever" (see also Gromov 2010, 30–33).

The Cross and the Birch: Religious and National Symbols on Grave Markers

In the rural and small provincial cemeteries that have provided the visual material for this study, there are still many old crosses. There are also more recent monumental granite crosses and small crosses, and occasionally crucifixes etched onto the front of grave markers. In most cases these are not the dominant emblem. Their presence often has the feel of a nod to convention, overshadowed by other images, such as portraits or landscapes. Apart from crosses, a few other symbols with religious significance recur. These include doves, angels, saints, or other figures connected with Orthodoxy, along with churches, which are occasionally representations of well-known structures, such as the Iverskii monastery in Tver' province, but more frequently function as component parts of imaginary rural landscapes.

OF DOVES AND ANGELS

Neither of these two religious symbols is particularly prolific in the cemeteries I have researched, but they do occur. Based on the message of the Scriptures (see, e.g., Luke 3:22: "and the Holy Spirit descended upon him in bodily form, as a dove, and a voice came from heaven, 'Thou art my beloved Son; with thee I am well pleased'"), the dove in Orthodox and Christian iconography generally has become the symbol of the Holy Spirit. On the other hand, the occasional depiction on gravestones of doves flying up into the sky or the dove-shaped finials painted with silver metal paint, which I saw adorning the fence posts at one gravesite, are more likely to reflect one of the traditional beliefs about the soul discussed in chapter 2. According to this, birds such as doves, pecking the grain left in cemeteries as a form of remembrance, are either themselves souls that have taken the shape of birds or creatures that travel between earth and heaven and may be in contact and communication with the souls of the dead.

In Orthodox tradition, angels, too, traverse the spaces between the worlds of the living and the dead. They have the task of carrying or accompanying righteous souls to heaven and are often depicted in this role in icons or frescoes of the Last Judgment. Angels of this type occasionally figure among the decorative etchings of gravestones. More frequently, angelic figures are to be found on the graves of children, in response to a common belief that small children, being entirely without sin, may be transmuted into angels upon death, although Orthodoxy does not actually teach that toddlers are free of sin but rather that they do not yet properly understand the nature of sin.

"Baby angels" in the form of etchings, statues, or doll-like figurines were clearly designed to appeal to the viewer with the sweetness and innocence of little children, to evoke sympathy and even raise a smile. The plump, winged babies reclining on clouds—sleeping, bearing floral garlands, holding candles, or clasping their hands in prayer—bear little or no relationship to the beautiful yet aloof and mysterious androgynous figures with magnificent wings depicted on icons. The latter variety of angel, through the use of color and symbols, such as the cross and sword carried by guardian angels, is clearly defined by rank, character, and function. The whimsical winged babies are rather descended from the *putti* known in the art world from the fifteenth century, the most famous of which are probably the two cherubs lying on clouds in Raphael's fresco known as the "Sistine Madonna." The facial expressions and hand positions of Raphael's cherubs were clearly reflected in one of the gravestones I viewed in a monumental stonemasonry showroom in Borovichi. On the whole, on the gravestones of children such images replace the usual portrait of the deceased.

THE CANDLE, THE ROSE, AND THE CROSS

Lit candles, usually positioned along the lower edge of the stone, are among the most popular designs etched on grave markers. In Orthodox tradition, as in the Christian faith generally, the light of the candle is a symbol of Christ, the "Light of the World," but it also has many other meanings and complex uses. Candles form an indispensable element of church services, with specific functions in baptismal and marriage ritual, during the administering of extreme unction, and at funerals. Four candles are placed around the coffin of the deceased in a symbolic representation of the cross, and the mourners at a funeral also carry lit candles, signifying the divine light of God. Many Russians today, who may not be regular churchgoers, will nevertheless enter a church to light a candle for the good health of a loved one or to comfort the soul of the deceased. On days of remembrance, such as Troitsa, and on regular visits to the grave of a relative, the bereaved will often light a candle to place in the grave mound or close by.

We have already noted the popularity of roses among the floral designs on grave markers. The commonest flower Russians choose as a special gift, bearing the universal connotation of "with love," roses may be depicted as sprigs of one or two stems or, in rare cases, in the shape of a garland. Sometimes they figure as attributes of angels. They can often be seen juxtaposed to candles. The combination of roses winding around an Orthodox cross seems a little odd. Roses have long been associated with Catholic Marian devotion: Mary herself is symbolized as the "immaculate" white rose, and the prayers of the rosary are envisioned artistically as a garland of roses. The Orthodox veneration of the Mother of God differs in many respects from the Catholic cult of Mary, and this is particularly evident in its iconography, which lacks the rose symbol. It seems likely that the proliferation of roses, especially when shown together with a candle, and more especially a cross, may have something to do with the influence on cemetery aesthetics of funeral bureaus and the providers of monumental stonemasonry. In one workshop I visited in Borovichi in June 2016 several of the stones on display for sale would have been more to the taste of Catholics. One of these showed a Madonna-like figure, hands clasped and holding a rosary, bowed in prayer over a candle set between two roses. A member of staff at the workshop explained that the artists chose their designs from the internet and that these particular "icons," as she described them, had been standing there a while. Earlier, as she told me, people weren't educated enough to know the difference. Anyway, a Catholic would occasionally ask for a gravestone (EW field notes, Nov-Bor, June 14, 2016).

In the advertising patter of funeral bureaus the flowers growing around a cross are, however, devoid of any religious significance. While the cross itself is seen as embodying the Christian message, the rose, "queen of flowers," is envisaged as a quintessentially female motif, suggestive of "feminine" characteristics and virtues, of beauty, love and tenderness.[7]

One particular design feature in which a cross and a rose are combined shows a rose climbing the outer edge of the stone and arching out protectively over the top to encompass both the cross and the life-like portrait of the deceased woman. The shape of this design mirrors one of the most popular pieces of memorial art in all the cemeteries I visited in connection with my research. Here, we find not a rose but a birch, and this device can be said to rival the Orthodox cross in terms of its popularity and significance as a gravestone motif. Indeed, the Church has adopted the birch as an attribute of the Great Feast of Troitsa. The complex symbolic role of the birch tree in Russian folklore, rituals, and beliefs will be developed more fully in the following chapter on the Semik-Troitsa festival.

THE BIRCH

Among all the decorative motifs on grave markers, and not only those drawn from the natural world, the birch predominates. It takes a great variety of forms, from various artistic renderings of leaves, twigs, and branches (some with dangling catkins) to complete trees embedded within naturalistic or symbolic landscapes. In the philosophy of websites advertising the engraving of grave markers, the seemingly frail and slender birch with its delicate foliage is, like the rose, envisaged as a particularly female symbol suitable for the graves of girls and women (see the previous note).

In reality, birch trees are extremely popular emblems that can be seen just as much on the graves of men as on those of women. However, it is true that the birch has long been identified as a female image, beginning with folk poetry and continuing through the popular songs and poetry from the Soviet period right up to the present day. Its commonest embodiment is as a slim and beautiful young girl, an image often used to suggest vulnerability. However, more relevant to its popularity on gravestones is the fact that the birch is also a symbol of sorrow. Nikolai Klyuev, in a poem written in 1913, "Is it true, friends, that somewhere in the world there is a wondrous land?" ("Pravda l', drugi, chto na svete est' chudesnaya strana?"), describes in the starkest terms the desolate landscape around a dying village. Its fields are empty, its cottages decaying. Here, the tousled birches with their bowed heads seem more like the mourners at a funeral than beautiful young girls (Klyuev 1969, 218–19). In the course of the twentieth and twenty-first centuries, through many poems and songs, the grieving birch became firmly entrenched in the national psyche as the symbol of a country weeping for its dead soldiers and as a patriotic grave marker. In the 1960s every Russian was familiar with the popular song "Do the Russians Want War?" ("Khotyat li russkie voiny?"), with words by the poet Evgenii Evtushenko. "Do the Russians want war?", the song asks. As Evtushenko suggests, the birch trees and all the Russian soldiers lying in their graves under those trees might have an answer to that question (Evtushenko 1962, 42).

More recently, with the growth of nationalism, the stress on patriotic education, and the fervor surrounding Victory Day, there has been a resurgence of poems about the war and the need to remember the sacrifices made. And in these too the sorrowing image of the graveside birch is highly visible. Typical of this trend, for example, are Nata Romanchenko's poem "Softly Weeps the Birch over the Soldier's Grave" ("Tikho plachet bereza nad mogiloi soldata"; Romanchenko 2007) and Vladimir Oliinyk's "The Soldier and the Birch" ("Soldat i bereza"; Oliinyk 2015).

In this context, the popular design in which the trunk of a birch tree, complete with roots and branches, is constructed as an integral part of the headstone, becomes more than a mere decorative feature. Like the rose bush I mentioned earlier, its branches at the apex form an arch over the portrait of the deceased. The overall effect is to suggest a protective function for the birch. Sometimes the presence of the tree beside the grave is merely suggested by delicate fronds of birch drawn as if they were reaching down onto the stone to gently touch the deceased's shoulder, like a comforting hand. In one example I saw, the portrait of the deceased was embedded in and supported by the stump and branches of a birch tree, molded in concrete, almost as if the two, human and tree, were joined in a symbiotic union. The small crosses engraved on the front of the gravestone tend to be covered by or enmeshed in the tracery of branches. In cases where the temporary wooden cross planted at the time of the funeral remains visible behind the new granite stone, here too there is a sense that the old Christian "tree" has been overshadowed by the newer image of the birch tree.

Like the open road, the birch tree can also be used to symbolize death itself. A branch of the tree may be shown as chopped off or broken away, just as a life may be "cut short" in the "storms" of life. Birch trees also appear in epitaphs: "Sleep in peace and we shall brush our tears away. May the birch trees rustle above you." As a naturally occurring part of the Russian landscape, birches are, as a matter of course, well represented in the many rural scenes depicted on gravestones, but a single tree alongside a portrait, or a solitary birch with drooping branches on a lakeside facing the setting sun, suggests a direct relationship between the symbol and the deceased. Garlands of artificial birch leaves may also be seen, twining around the fences and railings surrounding burial sites, while on the Saturday and Sunday of Troitsa week graves and graveside crosses are decked with bunches of fresh leaves.

One of the most popular designs for grave markers is a composition containing three significant elements: the portrait, birch trees, and a religious symbol. A typical design for molded concrete gravestones, for example, consists of three equally balanced pictorial elements—a church with three "onion" domes designed as a bas-relief in the center of the stone, the deceased's portrait fixed to the front of the church, and the birch tree overhanging the ensemble. Time and again, in a variety of forms and combinations, one sees the juxtaposition of these three visual motifs, suggesting a union of the divine (Orthodoxy), the deceased individual, and the natural world represented by a tree that symbolizes Russia itself. The birch is now inextricably entwined with patriotic love of homeland and its characteristic landscapes.

On the question of why birch trees are so ubiquitous on grave markers, I leave the final word to one of the village women whose ancestors lie in the cemeteries that provided the material for this research: "Well, because, you know, all the same, I think it is the soul of the Russian people, yes. And the birch, its

These molded gravestones display the common combination of portrait, church, and birch tree. The tree with its broken branch (symbolizing death) frames the edge of the stone while its overhanging branches shelter the occupant of the grave. Lykoshino, Arkhangel'sk province, 2016. (Photo by Elizabeth Warner)

branches hang down, you understand. Yes, really it's a sort of sorrowful tree. It can be cheerful too, and at the same time, you understand, it seems to be sheltering them there. I don't know, that's what it's like. And it's sad and all. Well, I have a gravestone like that here. I have a birch tree . . . That birch tree—well, it's the soul of the Russian. It is our tree" (EW-A Tver'-Bol, June 16, 2016).

Elizabethada Wright writes of the American rural cemetery, "The stability of this space seems not only controlled by the rural cemetery corporations, but by the visitors themselves. These cemeteries were and are beautiful gardens. They were structured for people to walk through, look at and internalize. One important goal of these cemeteries was for visitors to go and contemplate life and death, to see the beauty of order and to emulate this order" (Wright 2005, 59). The same could be said for many rural, or indeed urban cemeteries in my own country, England. However, nothing could be further from the general aspect of most rural cemeteries in Russia. In smaller villages, particularly in the more isolated regions of the Far North, the overall impression is normally one of disorganized space, with graves in the older sections packed together, difficult to access, and sometimes difficult to find, even for close relatives. Where space is lacking, the dominance of burial in Russian culture, as opposed to cremation, also contributes to overcrowding. At Troitsa, it is true, individual families will make efforts to tidy graves and trim grass and weeds. In larger cemeteries, near small towns or administrative centers, particularly in newer sections, the site may appear more orderly, but there is no guarantee of this. There are various reasons for these differences. One of these may be lack of any overall control of cemetery etiquette, such as by a church or an administrative center. Rural cemeteries in Russia are not planned spaces but have grown organically in response to the needs of individuals. If they often seem neglected, this may be laid at the door of rural decline and emptying villages. However strong the imperative to visit and look after the graves of ancestors, many people will be prevented by circumstances from doing so.

Unlike the cemeteries described by Elizabethada Wright (2011) that were designed in the nineteenth century as green spaces for the pleasure as well as the convenience of the population, these cemeteries have never been venues for country strolls. That is not their purpose. At certain times of day, they are even shunned for fear of disturbing the dead and only liven up on special memorial days such as Troitsa. The Russian climate, especially in the North, is also a deterrent to visiting for pleasure: snow in winter, mud and flooding in spring, and mosquitoes in summer can complicate matters. The space itself has a different function—as the home of the dead, as a place for communication between the living and the dead, and as a meeting ground for relatives and friends of the dead. The lack of places to walk together on the one hand and the ubiquitous presence of tables and benches within the graveside enclosures on the other demonstrate where the focus of attention is to be found.

In the course of the twentieth and twenty-first centuries, the face of the rural cemetery has of course visibly changed. In spite of the many crosses in Soviet-era cemeteries, the gradual move toward secularization brought with it a stronger emphasis on the material nature and requirements of the deceased, or the soul. This was exemplified in the increasing dominance of the photographic and/or etched portraits of the dead on grave markers. Contrary to what one might have expected, it is a trend that has accelerated during the 1990s and 2000s, encouraged by the commercialization of funerals and the resurrection of notions about the importance of family and individual status. The effects of advertising, the availability of choice, and the demands of fashion have penetrated even isolated villages. The natural processes of decay are being replaced with the hard-wearing symbols of supposedly everlasting memory. Even in locations that in other respects may not be economically thriving, displays of wealth are not hard to find in, for example, the full-length depictions of the deceased on large, complex memorials. Ol'ga Matich has commented on this phenomenon with regard to the graves of rich mafia bosses in the 1990s. Not only the grave markers themselves but the attributes of the deceased depicted on them, such as Rolex watches or the keys for a Mercedes, are, according to Matich, an open demonstration of the power of money (Matich 1998, 75–107). As far as the graves of more ordinary people are concerned, the motivation for ostentatious monuments may be somewhat different. I was particularly struck by the grave of a young couple in one cemetery. All the visual signals suggest a tragic, accidental death, very shortly after their wedding. The pictorial representation of the couple shows them dancing at what is probably their wedding reception, the young girl in a décolleté dress, her head flung back, full of life, in the exuberance of the dance. The huge monument also contains a large sculpted cross and a statue of an angel, surely an effort by the despairing parents to provide for much-loved children the maximum that could both be imagined and afforded. The social and psychological imperatives behind such choices are reflected by the advertising methods of organizations providing funeral services. The monument for an old person with few relatives does not have to be expensive or ostentatious since there is no point in trying to "pull the wool over someone's eyes." On the other hand, "if the deceased was a young person, had many friends and relatives and met an untimely end, then an overly ascetic approach to the design may cause bewilderment among visitors to the cemetery."[8]

The visual signs of cemeteries are multifaceted and may mean different things to different viewers. In a cemetery the Christian cross may be no more than an "essential," conventional detail on a headstone. But its biblical carvings might serve to remind the true believer of the promise of salvation. The votive cross replanted in a cemetery may be seen as a focal point for dialogue and bargaining between the human and divine while the cross over a grave may not. Interpretations of symbols and visual signals are always open to a certain amount of subjectivity. Suzie Wong Scollon, for example, cautions us about the pitfalls of relying too heavily on our own assumptions when taking part in "intercultural communication," when we are in "spaces that are in some way 'not our own'" (Scollon and Wong Scollon 2003, x). A salutary example of this followed one cemetery visit, when I asked why there were so many gaudy, artificial flowers on the graves. They would not have been my personal choice, and my remark was a little disparaging. "We are different people from you," was one comment. "Probably our soul is different too." For the people who had placed them there, the flowers were beautiful—the more flowers, the more beautiful and the more pleasure for the living and the dead.

My own interpretation of military uniforms, medals, and especially George ribbons as attributes of grave markers may also differ substantially from those who chose them and whose aim was probably to underline the valor and patriotism of their relative. Such symbols do, however—in the same way as Soviet-era obelisks did in cemeteries and in village gathering places where once a church stood—seem to introduce a whiff of public, even political discourse, into an otherwise private setting. The symbolic significance of the birch tree as a dominant visual component of many grave markers also appears to go far beyond its aesthetic appeal, its presence affirming the essential Russianness of the deceased over and above his or her common humanity.

CHAPTER 5

The Russian Semik-Troitsa (Trinity) Ritual Complex

A Deconstruction of the Public and Private Faces of Ritual, or "A Festival of Life and Death"

ELIZABETH WARNER

THE ORIGINS OF THE FESTIVAL

The Semik-Troitsa ritual cycle is one of the most complex and enduring in Russian traditional culture. It is both a religious and a family festival. It is also closely linked to the agrarian life of the village, and from its beginnings has been a factor in the formation of national identity.

A major aspect of Troitsa is its association with care and remembrance of the dead. But despite this focus, the festival does not dwell on the darkness of death but rather allows death to take its place within a never-ending cycle of dying, regeneration, and resurrection both in the natural world, with its changing seasons, and in the world of humans, marking beginnings and endings both real and spiritual. These multiple, intertwined themes are the subject of this chapter.

As there is room for some confusion over nomenclature, it is worth pointing out that Troitsa in the Russian Orthodox Church falls on the fiftieth day after Easter, corresponding in time, therefore, to Pentecost in the Western church, which marks the festival of the Holy Trinity a week later. In the Eastern Church Troitsa is one of four Great Feasts, second in importance only to Easter.

Pentecost, which celebrates the descent of the Holy Spirit upon Jesus's disciples on the fiftieth day after his crucifixion, and the Feast of the Holy Trinity, which honors the fundamental Christian doctrine of one God in three persons—Father, Son, and Holy Spirit, made manifest at Pentecost—both hold a major position in all the Christian churches. Pentecost is often described as representing the beginning of the church of Christ on earth. However, the Russian Orthodox Church marks the occasion in a distinctive way, starting with celebrating the Festival of the Holy Trinity on that day. The Russian celebration of Pentecost evolved over time, but much of its essential meaning became subsumed in the following Day of the Holy Spirit, while Troitsa developed into a hugely popular national religious festival centered on the veneration of Andrei Rublev's famous icon of the Trinity painted for the Church of the Holy Trinity at the Troitse-Sergiev monastery near Moscow, most probably between 1422 and 1427 (Bunge 2007, 74). The icon addresses a subject already common in iconography—the visit described in the Old Testament of three enigmatic male figures to Abraham as he sat among the oaks of Mamre (Genesis 18, 1–2). The earliest depiction of this subject known in the West is a fresco dating to the first half of the fourteenth century (Bunge 2007, 24). From the form most closely mirroring the biblical text, known as "the Hospitality of Abraham," the theme underwent numerous transformations over the centuries. The biblical text refers only to "three men," one of whom is addressed as "the Lord." By the eleventh century there had emerged a new Byzantine interpretation of the three central figures depicted on the icon, suggesting that they represented the Holy Trinity. This new iconographic type was well-known in Russia before Rublev came to paint his icon and may have been known to him from Feofan Grek's fresco in the Church of the Transfiguration of Christ in Novgorod (Bunge 2007, 33–34). According to Bunge, Rublev's rendering of the theme was quite unique. His detailed analysis of the icon suggests a significant shift of emphasis from the central figure of the Son to that of the Spirit on the right. Rublev's masterpiece may be read as "a depiction in color and shape of the Johannine account of Jesus' Farewell Discourse, which is completely shot through with the mystery, now being revealed, of the Triune God" (Bunge 2007, 103). In other words, "It is the sending of the person of the Holy Spirit, who came from the Father through the Son and owing to the self-sacrifice of the Son, which we commemorate at Pentecost, as John alone has described for us" (Bunge 2007, 105).

St. Sergii of Radonezh, the first abbot of the Troitse-Sergiev monastery, is regarded as the greatest of Russia's spiritual leaders, the founder of a great monastic tradition. He played a crucial, formative role in the country's religious, political, and cultural life from the middle of the fourteenth century, when as a newly consecrated monk, he chose to follow the holy and isolated life of a hermit. Possibly as early as 1337, on a hillside deep in the forest not far from the town of Radonezh, he and his brother built a wooden church dedicated to the Holy Trinity in response to a prophesy made at the time of his baptism. In time, this formed the nucleus of what was to become one of the greatest monastic settlements of Russia, the Troitse-Sergiev monastery (Malakhova 2014, 64, 77–90, 131–37). A place of religious devotion and a repository of culture and learning, the monastery attracted pilgrims ranging from tsars to peasants and hailing from every corner of Russia. Two major historical events were instrumental in solidifying the monastery's importance in Russian life. The first was St. Sergii's call for the warring Russian princedoms to unite against a common foe, Mamai of the Golden Horde. St. Sergii's blessing and inspiration ensured a victory for the Russian army under the command of Grand Prince of Moscow Dmitrii at Kulikovo in 1380, a battle that broke the stranglehold over Russia of the Mongol-Tatar yoke, preparing the way for Russia's eventual freedom and changing the whole course of Russian history. The second event was the grueling sixteen-month siege during the Polish-Lithuanian Intervention between 1608 and 1610, when St. Sergii bolstered the monastery's heroism, according to legend (Malakhova 2014, 374), through a series of powerful visions. St. Sergii's spiritual messages, the cultural-political role of the monastery of the Holy Trinity, and Rublev's Pentecostal vision of the Holy Trinity all became inextricably linked with notions of unity and national identity. In its essence, Rublev's icon, in terms of both its circular composition and its spiritual focus on the "oneness" of the three angelic figures representing the triple persons of the Godhead, is also a clear symbol of unity. Rublev's icon, particularly after its endorsement as the official model for future icons of the Trinity by the Council of One Hundred Chapters in 1551 (*Stoglav* 1971, 128), became an essential attribute of the Troitsa festival.

The significance of Troitsa as a peculiarly Russian festival and a cornerstone of national spirituality was aptly identified by Pavel Florenskii, who wrote of the Day of the Holy Trinity as "A liturgical creation of a specifically Russian culture and, even more precisely, a creation of the Venerable Sergii. Let me remind you that this festival was unknown in Byzantium, just as, essentially, Trinity chapels and Trinity icons were unknown. . . . The festival of Pentecost, formerly in the place of what is now Trinity Day, was a historical festival without overt ontological significance. In Russia from the fourteenth century it began to reveal its ontological essence, becoming the festival of the Holy Trinity" (Florenskii 2007, 62–63).

The Troitse-Sergiev monastery became a focal point for royal religious devotion, thus cementing its extraordinary significance in the religious and cultural life of Russia. According to Giles Fletcher, ambassador of Queen Elizabeth I to the Russian court, Irina Fedorovna, the wife of Tsar Fedor Ivanovich, would make a pilgrimage there on foot every year, accompanied by a massive retinue of "five or six thousand women attending upon her, all in blue liveries and four thousand soldiers for her guard," to pray to St Sergii "to make her fruitful, as having no children by the Emperor her husband" (Fletcher 1966, 88–89). During the Trinity period in particular the monastery attracted royal visitors: "On the Wednesday of the seventh week his Majesty made the journey to the Troitse-Sergiev monastery in order to pray. Tsar Petr Alekseevich entered the cathedral in the second quarter of the twelfth hour" (Novikov 1789, 11:142).

TRINITY SATURDAY

The significance for Christianity of the descent of the Holy Spirit upon Christ's disciples at Pentecost is often described in terms of birth and new beginnings, the start of a new epoch in the relationship between God and man, the dawn of the Christian church, and the mission of its adherents on earth. In such a context it seems almost perverse, at first glance, that one of the dominant aspects of the Semik-Troitsa period is remembrance of the dead in ways officially sanctioned by the Orthodox Church and in less canonical private memorial rituals in cemeteries. However, there is no contradiction here in Orthodoxy for the transformative power of the Holy Spirit promises renewal to the dead as well as to the living.

Prayers for the dead are a constant feature of Orthodox worship, but two days in the year are dedicated specifically to remembrance of all the faithful Orthodox deceased, including the nameless and unknown dead, whose departure from this world was not marked by the usual Christian burial rites. These two days, known as "universal ancestor Saturdays" (*vselenskie roditel'skie subboty*), are Meatfast Saturday, which precedes the Sunday Day of Judgment, with its message about the fate of souls at the second coming of Christ, and the Saturday before Troitsa.[1]

Although members of the congregation may ask the priest to commemorate relatives and friends in prayer during the requiem service, which often follows vespers, the services on Trinity Saturday are essentially devoted to prayers for the faithful dead in general; "All our forefathers, our grandfathers and great-grandfathers, from the first to the last" (Bulgakov 1993, 1:673). Prayers include people of all ages, men and women of all social classes, and those long dead whose names may have been forgotten and who have no one left to mourn them. Included too are those deprived, for one reason or another, of a normal Christian burial, many of whom in earlier times would have been deposited on the territory of an *ubogii dom*, or paupers' graveyard: "Those who have died at sea, or on land, or in rivers, or springs, or lakes, or the mouths of brooks . . . in the wilderness or in towns . . . who were burned by lightning or killed by frost, or by any wound . . . who became food for wild beasts and birds of prey and serpents . . . who died from venomous bites or were swallowed up by serpents, or trampled by horses" (Bulgakov 1993, 1:673). These prayers for the repose of the soul and relief from the torments of hell are immensely detailed and virtually all-embracing, excluding only those who have died by their own hand while of sound mind. According to the theologians, the grace of the Holy Spirit, which descends at Pentecost, infusing all with new life, should be a gift for all the faithful, both living and dead (Bulgakov 1993, 1:673). This same sentiment may be found in the "kneeling" prayers attributed to St. Basil the Great, spoken on Trinity Sunday while the whole congregation, together with their priests, kneel or prostrate themselves on the floor of the church. In the third prayer God's mercy is invoked not only for the souls of the righteous but even for those imprisoned in Hades, so that their suffering might be alleviated (Bishop Alexander [Mileant] 2001). One might say that on Trinity Saturday an official line was drawn under the differences separating those who died of natural causes at home and with the blessing of the Church from those who died suddenly and without due preparation, who died "a death that was not their own" (ne svoeyu smert'yu) and who, in the popular imagination, were considered "unclean" and capable of harming the living. At Troitsa, the end, as it were, became a new beginning.

SEMIK

In the context of unnatural death and "unclean" corpses, Semik (from *sem'*, seven) the Thursday preceding Troitsa in the seventh week after Easter, had a very special function in Russia as a calendar date dedicated specifically to the remembrance of the dead who fell into this category. The day was marked by visits by affected families to the graves of their unfortunate relatives. A map showing the distribution of this practice at Semik, provided by T. A. Agapkina, shows that, at one time, it was well-known in the northeastern, western, and central provinces (Agapkina 2002, 311).

In Russia, traditional attitudes toward and treatment of those who had died an untimely death differed significantly from the norm. In medieval times this included a reluctance to bury them in the ground, as was demanded by the Church, for fear of incurring the retribution of "holy" earth and the consequent destruction of crops (see Warner 2011b). Instead, these dead were often carried off and left lying above ground, far from human habitation, in the open countryside, in forests, or in ravines. A rough cairn of stones or branches was sometimes built over them, giving rise to the designation *zalozhnye*—that is, corpses that were "blocked up or fenced in with planks or stakes" rather than buried, according to Dmitrii Zelenin's definition (Zelenin 1994, 251). Although with the passage of time and continual pressure from the Orthodox Church burial nevertheless eventually became accepted, the old fears were not forgotten, leading, in times of drought or other climatic disasters, to the illegal exhumation of suspect corpses. From the many examples provided by Zelenin, it is clear that even in the late nineteenth century, rural communities in parts of Russia still had recourse to such extreme measures when the need arose: "Over the past century hundreds of village men have fallen victim to this conviction and, digging up *zalozhnye* from their graves in times of drought, have gone to prison for it" (Zelenin 1994, 254).

In towns, where indigence, lawlessness, and drunkenness produced a significant number of corpses that could not be given a Christian burial for a variety of reasons, the Church found a different solution to the problem.

Of Russian mortuary customs in the seventeenth century Samuel Collins wrote as follows: "If anyone dies without confession and extreme unction, he is denied Christian burial. Such as are killed or frozen to death are brought into the *zemsky precaus*,[2] an office for that and many other trials, and there they are exposed to view three or four days; if any own them they are carried away, if not they are sent to the *Bosky* or *Boghzi Dom* which is a great pit in the fields arched over, where they put an hundred or two hundred, and let them rest till midsummer and then the popes go and bury them and cover them with earth" (Collins 1671, 21–22). Once, during the time of Lent, Collins himself witnessed the gruesome sight of many bodies, some of which were already horribly mutilated and partially eaten by dogs, being transported to this place by sledge (Collins 1671, 23). Although Collins refers to midsummer, the practice he describes took place annually on two particular occasions, sometimes on October 1, the Feast of the Protecting Veil of the Virgin (Pokrov), but most commonly at Semik, which fell sometime in the summer months of May or June, depending on the date of Easter. The establishments he describes were based on the idea of the "potters' field," set aside near Jerusalem for the burial of deceased foreign pilgrims to the temple. These were the forerunner of paupers' cemeteries and burial grounds throughout Europe. It is perhaps not without significance, given the polluted nature of the corpses dispatched to these places of temporary disposal, that the original potters' field was supposedly bought by the chief priests to whom Judas Iscariot gifted the thirty pieces of silver he had received for his betrayal of Christ before committing suicide by hanging himself (Matthew 27:5–7).

Collins was by no means the only early visitor to Muscovy to note the manner in which Russians dealt with the unidentified corpses of the many victims of violence, self-harm, poverty, disease, alcohol abuse, and the merciless winter climate who were brought in to the *zemskii prikaz*. The dates June 17, 18, and 19 were singled out by Johann Georg Korb, secretary to the Austrian ambassador at the court of Peter the Great, as the days in 1689, during his stay in Moscow, when the bodies of those who had suffered a violent death were finally interred, "whether they had perished by the executioner's hand, by order of the authorities or by the hand of robbers" (Korb 1867, 74).

Known by a variety of names—*ubogii dom* (paupers' house), *skudel'nitsa* (paupers' graveyard), *zhal'nik* (place of sorrow, from *zhalet'*, to be sorrowful)—these equivalents of the potters' field had a very long history in Russia. One of the earliest references may be found in the *Sofiiskii vremennik* (the chronicle compiled in the St. Sophia cathedral in Novgorod) for 1474 (Snegirev 1883, 6). It tells of a devout man who at Semik regularly went to one of the "paupers' houses" to buy candles and *kanon*, more commonly known as *kut'ya*, the dish of grain mixed with honey offered to mourners at funerals and on memorial occasions. Then, together with others, he would gather the accumulated bodies, bury them in a newly dug grave pit, cover them at last with earth, and pray for their souls.

It is clear from surviving accounts that there were many such places, particularly in Moscow, and that the large number of corpses mentioned by Collins was not exceptional and had multiple causes. The Orthodox Church was rigorous in its refusal to provide a Christian burial in consecrated ground to those who died an untimely death without confession and absolution. These included many beggars and itinerants, a population with no fixed address and therefore no affiliation to a parish church, as well as the indigent with no relatives to care for them at the end and no money of their own to pay for the services of a priest or a Christian funeral. For these unfortunates, who, like unbaptized infants, ended up in the ubogii dom through circumstances largely beyond their control, a burial service was finally held at Semik. For more specific categories of deceased, which varied down through the centuries, even this small comfort was denied. Korb, in his description of the execution of the Strel'tsy (Musketeers) who had rebelled against Peter the Great, remarks that "there was no priest there to give spiritual support, as if the convicted were unworthy of this religious ritual" (Korb 1867, 226). In general, the bodies of unrepentant executed criminals, suicides, and those who died during the commission of heinous crimes were usually disposed of unceremoniously and certainly without a burial service. Korb notes that this fate befell any malefactors impaled for insulting the tsar (Korb 1867, 74). Even if their bodies were permitted onto the territory of the ubogii dom, they were kept apart from those whose death was merely unfortunate until, also at Semik, they were removed for burial in forest or field (Snegirev 1883, 8). The decisions of religious and judicial bodies regarding the disposal of certain categories of cadaver at the ubogii dom were reinforced by the common superstition that the bodies of those who died unshriven, particularly in the case of evil men and great sinners, should not be committed to the ground in case the earth, regarded as holy, should react with violence to the perceived insult. One of the most notorious villains in this respect was the pretender Dmitrii Otrep'ev, who had been responsible for the Polish-Lithuanian Intervention in the struggle against which the Troitse-Sergiev monastery had played such a pivotal role. Several historical accounts of the disposal of his body in May 1606 describe disturbances in the natural world, including snowfall and devastating frost. As his body was driven to the ubogii dom on the territory of the Pokrov monastery in Moscow by an angry, cursing mob, a terrible storm raged. Shrieks and howls were heard coming from the open grave pit, and his corpse was flung from one side of it to another "by an invisible force." Unworthy of a place even in the paupers' house, Dmitrii's body was removed and burned (Snegirev 1883, 4).

At Semik devout Christians gathered at the ubogie doma to provide the unclaimed corpses with the funeral rites and prayers of which they had so long been deprived. Winter frosts undoubtedly helped to preserve bodies left lying for months. The grave pits often had roofs to shelter them from the weather, and in some places bodies were stored in underground chambers. Sometimes ice was used to help delay the advance of corruption. Nevertheless, it is difficult to imagine the horrors and danger of infection faced by the devout as they recovered the bodies from the pits with their bare hands, wrapped them in shrouds, laid them in the coffins they had brought as an act of charity, and deposited them in newly dug communal graves, which were then covered over with earth before a funeral service was held to offer up prayers for all those buried there (Snegirev 1883, 10). Since many of those who ended up in the ubogie doma were unidentified and therefore nameless, prayers for the repose of their individual souls, which would normally be carried out by the priest at a funeral or requiem mass, could not be said. This was and remains a serious matter for an Orthodox Christian since the comfort of each soul after death depends on the prayers of the living. Possibly, as the historian Nikolai Karamzin suggested, it was believed that God heard the prayers of those who attended these mass burials and knew Himself the names of the unfortunates for whom they were offered up. He also points out that, apart from the names, the nationality and faith of the deceased were also usually unknown and that the ubogie doma were used for the burial of foreigners (Karamzin 1819, 7:219–20), recalling the purpose of the original potters' field outside Jerusalem.

Snegirev, in his article on the ubogii dom at the Pokrov monastery, decries the notion of some foreigners that bodies were taken there and stored until the spring because the frozen ground made interment difficult. In the sixteenth century one of these foreigners was Giles Fletcher, who wrote: "In Winter time, when all is covered with snow and the ground so hard frozen as that no spade nor pikeaxe can enter, their manner is not to bury their dead, but to keep the bodies (so many as die all the Winter time) in an house, in the suburbs or outparts of the town, which they call *Bohsedom*, that is God's house, where the dead bodies are piled up together like billets on a woodstack, as hard with the frost as a very stone, till the Springtide come and resolveth the frost" (Fletcher 1966, 106). It is possible that the weather provided an additional impediment to the earlier burial of the many unclaimed corpses in a system lacking the necessary institutions for dealing with such a problem. However, the mass burials at ubogie doma at Semik were above all prompted by the approach of Trinity Saturday.

The importance of the funeral services carried out in the ubogie doma at Semik is attested by the official grandeur and ceremony attending them. Records from the late seventeenth century show the extent to which they were organized by the patriarch himself. Each year he would designate senior figures of the church to conduct the funeral masses: bishops and archbishops, archpriests, abbots, and Fathers Superior of Moscow's most renowned cathedrals and monasteries—including the Pokrov monastery, mentioned above; the Vysoko-Petrovskii; and the Svyato-Danilov and Spaso-Andronikov monasteries (Novikov 1789, 11:143–616). From the churches a religious procession—literally, a "procession of the cross" (*krestnyi khod*)—would make its way to the place of burial (Sakharov 1885, 2:194). "Processions of the cross" were (and still are) organized for special festive occasions, the priests dressed in bright robes appropriate to the particular day and carrying embroidered banners, richly decorated crosses, and icons. The combination of colorful spectacle and solemn liturgy attracted large crowds of onlookers, including many beggars, who were given alms with the understanding that they would pray for the souls of the unfortunates being buried that day (see chapter 2 for commentary on the significance of beggars in Russian memorial ritual). This strange mingling of dark with light, of the macabre with the entertaining, was a characteristic feature of Semik as, on a wider scale, the preoccupation with death intertwined with the affirmation of life that was characteristic of the Semik-Troitsa period in general.

Snegirev describes how, in the Mar'ina Roshcha district of Moscow, when the crowds of devout gravediggers had completed their gruesome task of interment at the paupers' graveyard, they would wash their hands in a nearby river and make their way to the popular Mar'ina Roshcha pleasure garden, situated in a grove of trees where the traditional Troitsa fair was held. Here, they would throw off their sorrowful mood and begin to enjoy themselves, taking part in traditional Troitsa customs such as plaiting birch garlands for fortune-telling (Snegirev 1838, 3:102).

Ubogie doma survived as an institution until the mid-eighteenth century. Officially closed down by the Empress Elizaveta in 1753, they survived here and there into the nineteenth century (Tul'tseva 1999, 636). The first proper cemetery for the indigent in Moscow was opened in 1758 on the site of the former Mar'ina Roshcha *bozhedomka* (another name for a paupers' graveyard). Paradoxically, the cemetery, which eventually closed in the 1930s, was then turned into a children's play park and later became the Festival Park, as it is still known today (see "Festival'nyi park v Mar'inoi roshche" 2008). This was by no means an isolated incident. In the 1930s, for example, during the construction of the Moscow underground railway, the cemetery containing the communal graves of more than seventeen thousand military and civilian victims of World War I was closed, tombstones were removed, and the graves covered over to form a park (Krotov and Dyatlova, n. d.). During the Soviet period, respect for the sacral nature of death appears to have been suspended by officialdom.

VISITING FAMILY GRAVES AT TROITSA

Throughout Russia, the Semik-Troitsa period, whether in towns or villages, has traditionally been a time for remembering familial dead just as much as those lying in unmarked graves. Remembering one's kith and kin on Troitsa Saturday has long been an important part of religious and secular observance. However, the precise manner in which this is accomplished reflects a variety of different concerns. These may be religious, canonical and noncanonical, or social, both private and public, in nature. Although the dead may be remembered in any place, in practice, and certainly in the village context, this is done predominantly in cemeteries and is a potent reminder of the sense of continuity between living and deceased family members so important to Russians. Although Trinity Saturday may be regarded as the "official" day for such cemetery visits, cemeteries are also frequently visited on Trinity Sunday, on the following Day of the Holy Spirit, or even, although less commonly, on the next Sunday, the festival of All Saints (Vsekh svyatykh) as, for example, I found in the village of Poreche, Tver' province, in 2015.

According to T. A. Agapkina, among the East Slavs in general, Troitsa visits to the cemetery in the past shared a number of characteristic features including a requiem *litiya*, censing the graves, having a meal and crumbling bread and eggs upon the graves, and distributing food as alms (Agapkina 2002, 306).

In one of the earliest references to such customs, Adam Olearius describes a cemetery visit in Moscow on Troitsa Saturday, or "Whitsun eve," as he calls it, which fell on May 24, 1634:

The churchyard was full of Muscovite women, who had spread the graves with handkerchers, whereof the corners were fringed with silk of several colors, upon which they laid dishes full of fish, broiled and fried, custards, cakes and painted eggs. Some stood, others kneeled, making divers questions to their kindred, weeping over their graves and expressing their affliction with dreadful howlings. . . . The priest, attended by his clerks, walked up and down the churchyard, having in his hand a censer into which he ever and anon cast little pieces of wax, to cense the sepulchers. The women named to him those of their kindred whom they would recommend to his prayers, pulling him by the surplice to be served one before the other. The priest did this devotion very slightly and with so little attention, that he was but too well paid with the piece of copper they gave, so far was he from deserving the provisions they brought him, which his clerks had a care to secure for the advantage of their master. (Olearius 1662, 1:5–6)

Since the end of the Soviet era, priests have reappeared in the cemeteries on Troitsa Saturdays. The kind of graveside keening heard by Olearius has become a rarity, but colorful repasts are still de rigeur. On Sunday, June 8, 2014, I was present with the family and friends of a colleague at their Troitsa remembrance gathering in the cemetery at Zakline (Dno region, Pskov province). All were dressed in their Sunday best. The table and the benches in the burial enclosure were covered with white cloths, and the food had been carefully chosen as for a special meal, with tasty open-faced sandwiches, salamis, fresh salad, vegetables and fruit, jars of choice pickled mushrooms retrieved from the cellar, bags of large expensive chocolates, and plenty of vodka. In addition, food not intended for the living was laid separately on surrounding graves and small tables. There were biscuits, large amounts of sweets in foil and paper wrappers, sandwiches, savory pastries, slices of apple, bread and butter—in other words, a selection of what was being consumed by the families.

The subject of food offerings is a complex one that permeates funeral ritual in Russia. Chapter 1 illustrated how the gesture of giving food is seen as emphasizing the material substance of the post-death being. Chapter 2 showed the fundamental role of feeding in funerary practice. In this chapter, other aspects of feeding are explored, particularly as they function as part of a system of reciprocal "gift-giving." For most people leaving food and drink on or near graves for the ancestors is like fulfilling the obligations of guests toward their hosts. After all, entering a cemetery is like entering someone's home: "It's as if we come as guests to visit the dead and we bring them sweet things (*gostintsy*) as a gift" (EW-A Pskov-Dno A13, June 11, 2014).

As anyone familiar with Russia will know, the exchange of gifts, or the giving of gifts, is very much a part of Russian traditional behavior. I remember an occasion a few years ago when I was bidding goodbye to my landlady in the village. I regarded her conversations with me and the photographs she allowed me to take of her remembrance rituals as a precious gift. All I could give in return were a few impersonal souvenirs of England. However, this threw Zoya into a panic. She dashed back indoors and returned with a pile of her own knitted gloves and household linen, insisting that I choose something. Reluctantly, I picked out a linen towel and was mortified to find that it had been a gift to Zoya from her (now deceased) mother. For Zoya, however, this was perfect. Her relief was palpable.

The exchange of gifts is a way of maintaining a proper balance in relationships so that no one loses out and no one feels beholden to the other person. It was very evident in Soviet times when doctors, nurses, teachers, anyone from whom a favor might be asked, or anyone whose good will was sought or had been demonstrated would receive gifts, mainly in kind, from grateful patients, pupils, and so on. This practice still continues to some extent, particularly with regard to the medical profession. Vasilii, a resident of the village Lykoshino in Tver' province, told me, "If we go to a dentist, not privately but on the health service, we usually take some expensive coffee, we take sweets, cognac . . . or maybe some delicacies." In the gift-bringing to cemeteries there is an element of unstated propitiation. As was made clear in chapter 2, the dead too are capable of responding positively or negatively to the presence or absence of gifts. It is interesting in this context to recall Marcel Mauss's influential work on the obligation to give, receive, and reciprocate gifts (Mauss 2002). Although Mauss is dealing with mainly economic and legislative issues among what he terms "archaic" societies, it is not difficult to see similarities with the gifts offered to the dead and the contract between giver and receiver that such gifts imply in Russian funeral ritual: "The thing that is given produces its rewards in this life and the next. Here in this life, it automatically engenders for the giver the same thing as itself: it is not lost, it reproduces itself; in the next life, one finds the same thing, only it has increased. Food given is the food that in this world will return to the giver; it is food, the same food, that he will find in the other world" (Mauss 2002, 72).

The table of remembrance (*pominal'nyi stol*) on Troitsa Saturday in the Church of the Nativity of the Most Holy Mother of God, Belaya, Pskov province, 2014. (Photo by Elizabeth Warner)

The giving of alms, charitable distribution of food to beggars and the indigent in return for prayers for the dead, is in general a key element in Orthodox tradition. Giving food as alms at Troitsa takes several forms. It can be taken to the church on Saturday and placed upon the "table of remembrance" (*pominal'nyi stol*). In fact, most churches have a place available throughout the year for gifts of food brought by parishioners. Food may also be taken to the cemetery or given, directly or indirectly, to certain individuals.

At the Troitsa Saturday service I attended in 2014 at the Church of the Birth of the Most Holy Mother of God in the village of Belaya (Dno region, Pskov province), there was a table piled high with bread, biscuits, cakes, sweets, bags of sugar, apples and oranges, and many other items. In Orthodoxy it is accepted that prayer may help to alleviate the suffering of individual souls punished for sins committed on earth. In this process the consumption of food while praying may have a special function. Instead of monetary donations, parishioners are encouraged to bring offerings of food to the church for the clergy with the express wish that prayers for a specified soul will be said while the priest partakes of the proffered food. The supplicant may enclose a note with the name of the person who is to be remembered in this way. In the words of one rural priest: "It's a meal for the repose of the soul (*zaupokoinaya trapeza*) when, through food items or a meal, we solicit prayers for our dead. We give money, that's usual so to speak, but well, today it can take this other form, people distribute sweets, good chocolates, biscuits. They give them on behalf of someone, for a name, they name the person. The idea is there should be a meal or food items, by means of which a person simply solicits mercy" (EW-A Tver'-Bol, June 18, 2015). One might also remember again the role of kut'ya as a memorial food. During a funeral service it is traditional to have a bowl of kut'ya on a table to be shared among the mourners afterward. Through food the living and the dead are brought together again.

The link between eating and the welfare of the soul is often reinterpreted by parishioners in a much more literal way. There are undoubtedly those who view the food on the table of remembrance as an indirect way of actually feeding the dead: "They say our ancestors also want people to bring something for them to eat" (EW-A Pskov-Dno A1, June 9, 2014). Someone may dream of a deceased relative who complains of being hungry and may even specify what kind of food she or he requires. The dreamer will be motivated to place that particular food on the table of remembrance in the church. The act of remembrance accompanied by the gift of food is sufficient to assuage the hunger pangs of the deceased.

A similar idea was expressed by an elderly interlocutor who had been ignorant of these practices when she was young. Nowadays, however, she always took food with her to church on an ancestor Saturday. She knew that you had to cross yourself and ask the Lord to remember the deceased and that the food was given to people who were supposed to remember as well. More important, however, was the knowledge that the deceased could see that their relatives had brought food for them and would therefore consider themselves fed. If she took nothing, on the other hand, her mother, father, or brothers would go hungry (EW-A Tver'-Bol, June 16, 2015). Some of the food taken to the church as a form of charity is usually intended for the clergy and helpers in the church. The rest is distributed to poor families, to children's homes, or to the elderly or sick in the hope that these recipients too will offer a prayer for the dead. The benefits of giving in this way affect not only the souls of the dead and the receivers of gifts but also the donors: "It will count on our behalf for something, somewhere" (EW-A Pskov-Dno A14, June 11, 2017).

Historically, beggars and itinerants had an important role in the giving and receipt of alms, but perhaps surprisingly, we can still find examples of this in more recent times in Russia. In Tver' province in 2015 I heard about a husband and wife team who in the 1960s used to walk from village to village collecting alms: "They sang prayers, people gave different things, bread, pies. People were a bit afraid of them. They would come into the house, cross themselves and begin to sing a prayer" (EW-A Tver'-Bol, June 17, 2015). Mendicants like these, reminiscent of the itinerant singers of spiritual verses of an earlier age (*kaliki perekhozhie*), must surely have been a very rare sight at that time, given the official attitude to overt demonstrations of religiosity. Yet the presence of vagrants and the indigent at funeral and memorial occasions continues to the present day, and I have recorded information about them (mostly negative) in villages of Arkhangel'sk, Pskov, and Tver' provinces. In Dno (Pskov province), for example, where there is relatively high unemployment, poor families will still occasionally appear at funerals and on days of remembrance, and people will give them food. According to some informants, members of the Roma community sometimes go to the cemetery if they know a lot of food has been left there and collect something, if only a few sweets for the children (EW-A Pskov-Dno A14, June 11, 2014). In Tver' province it was mentioned that children and people from poor families who perhaps "knew no better" were allowed to take food (EW-A Tver'-Bol, June 17, 2015). Similarly, and not so long ago, in spite of the fact that they were scolded for doing so, small boys from the surrounding villages would cycle up to the cemetery in Lykoshino at Troitsa, after everyone had gone home, in order to collect sweets and biscuits. They were not allowed to take them home but had to eat them in situ. This is not likely to happen today, I was told, now that sweets are readily available and affordable for most people (EW-A Tver'-Bol, June 18, 2015). I myself watched a shabbily dressed man wander from grave to grave around the cemetery in Lykoshino at Troitsa. From his appearance and gait, he might have been mentally ill or under the influence of alcohol. He was picking up food and stuffing it into an old rucksack. The extent to which any of those who take food of any kind from cemeteries still reciprocate with prayers is debatable. Furthermore, the people who leave the food are more likely to do so for the benefit of deceased family members rather than as an act of charity to others. Not everyone approves of the possibility that strangers may come and remove it. Frequently, bread and even eggs, which are taken to the cemetery at Radunitsa and at Troitsa, are broken apart or crumbled rather than being placed whole, ostensibly so that the birds can peck at them more easily. When I raised the topic of taking food offerings from the cemetery with village women (Tver' province), one person in particular strongly disagreed that it was acceptable. The dead needed their eggs, so breaking them up would prevent the unemployed, for example, from coming along later to collect them (EW-A Tver'-Bol, June 15, 2015). The same speaker agreed in principle that if a child ate something or a bird pecked at something left in the cemetery, that counted as remembering the deceased: "But we didn't bring it for them. We brought it for the deceased, but these others kind of took it away from them. . . . Yes, indeed, we brought it for someone dear to us and then they come and take it from them" (EW-A Tver'-Bol, June 17, 2015). The same sentiment may be expressed about wild strawberries growing in the cemetery. To pick them is a sin because they are "not ours" but belong to the dead (FA Bel 17-123, July 19, 2002). Such comments remind one of the intimate, caring nature of the bond between the living and the dead that expresses itself in the way people interact with them: "Well, when we've arrived at the grave, like now, we gather, we remember, you understand? You take a pie to eat and you say, 'Dad, get up and eat with us' . . . and so on. Then you'll crumble a pie on the grave and you'll say, 'Little birds of the forest remember servant of God Arsentii.' We'll sit for a while and talk. It's like we're calling him to join the chat, in our imagination" (FA Syam 17-2, July 10, 2005).

Apart from alms or gift giving, there are several other aspects of ritual "feasting" at Troitsa that deserve attention. Many people nowadays comment negatively on the excessive eating and drinking that has become more and more typical of graveside conviviality at Troitsa since the mid-1990s to early 2000s. In chapter 2, I indicated that large amounts of food had the function of sating and satisfying the dead. This is also true of food served on calendric festivals of memorialization, but as far as Troitsa is concerned, there are other additional factors at work.

Troitsa today is an important social and, indeed, national event, the dominant time for significant family reunions all across Russia. It has therefore become an occasion for the large-hearted hospitality for which Russians are famous: "Every year we all gather at Troitsa, even those who live far away. . . . It's just the custom for everyone to go to the cemetery at Troitsa. You can just stand for a while and remember. . . . It's just the custom for everyone to meet up. In fact, there are people there you haven't seen for years. . . . They come there to fill themselves with drink and food, the way Russians do. You have to pour a drink for a specific [dead] person or put a sandwich down for them. That's necessary. But it's more than just remembrance that goes on. It's a blowout and when it's over people cart themselves home and it's 'Lay the table.' How it all ends after that is nobody's business. Why?! But if you don't do it you'll be criticized" (EW-A Pskov-Dno A9, June 10, 2014). A similar comment was made about funerals in the village, where the number of guests and the quantities of food prepared have reached gargantuan proportions. In a sense, the cemetery at Troitsa has become a public space where graves and visitors alike are open to scrutiny. Before guests arrive, graves are cleared of debris and weeds, fences and gates are painted, fresh earth or sand is scattered, flowers are planted, and wreaths of bright-colored artificial flowers are placed all around. A thorough cleaning of graves, homes, and village streets before Troitsa is a well-established tradition in Russia. It recognizes the sense of new beginnings both in nature and in the history of the Church, but all the same, an untended grave is also a matter for community comment and censure.

The overgenerous provision of food and drink was also described to me as normal at the festival of All Saints, which some villages celebrate after Troitsa. On this day too, baskets laden with food and drink are taken to the cemetery and glasses of vodka for the deceased men of the family are placed by the crosses at the foot of graves. For some people, remembering is more likely to be carried out by means of a glass of vodka and its accompanying snacks than by prayers. This in turn can lead to misbehaving and unpleasant scenes, raised voices, and people falling asleep and being left behind at the cemetery. Older residents, some of whom remember more restrained practices in earlier times, commented unfavorably on inappropriate amounts of food abandoned in the cemetery after celebratory meals. One person reported seeing barbecued meat, fried fish, onion and dill—in other words a full meal—left behind (EW-A Pskov-Dno A14, June 11, 2014).

I have heard several priests express the view that overindulgence in alcohol and misbehaving in cemeteries at Troitsa is a by-product of anti-religious measures during the Soviet period. In the 1970s, for example, in order to frustrate any attempts to celebrate Pentecost by attending church on Trinity Sunday, buses were even provided by city authorities to convey people en masse to the cemeteries on that day, providing an opportunity for a free excursion without the restraining presence of clergy. A village priest (not a native of the region) whom I interviewed in Tver' province in 2015 had vivid memories of a secularized Troitsa from his childhood experience of visiting an Orthodox cemetery in the Chuvash Republic. He described the scene as nothing more than a drunken orgy, a real "pagan" funeral feast (*trizna*), dominated by alcohol and abundant food and, in his opinion, lacking any sense of a Christian act carried out for remembrance of the dead (EW-A Tver'-Bol, June 18, 2015). It is worth remembering, however, that the Soviet authorities, far from encouraging alcohol abuse, waged war against it. There were three major campaigns against alcohol abuse—in the 1950s, in the 1970s, and during the so-called "Gorbachev campaign" from 1985 to 1990. An act was passed in 1958 by the Central Committee of the Communist Party banning the sale of alcohol in the immediate vicinity of establishments such as factories, schools, hospitals, airports, stations, and any places of leisure where people gathered in large numbers (see "Anti-alkogol'nye kampanii v SSSR" 2020).

Another priest I interviewed in Pskov province in 2014 also recollected rowdy behavior in the cemetery beside his church at Troitsa. He was open about the Russian weakness for alcohol, which could lead to a completely unacceptable "drunken shindig" (*p'yanka i debosh*), as he put it, with singing and even accordion music. Over the past twenty to thirty years, however, as he informed me—in other words, since the end of the Soviet period and the revival of Church influence—people had begun to behave in a more or less civilized manner (EW-A Pskov-Dno A15, June 11, 2014).

When assessing comments such as these, it should be remembered that ways of celebrating and respecting the dead may be understood in different ways by different people. As Huntington and Metcalf have commented, "Even where custom calls for restraint, it often happens that the pleasure of a reunion of family and friends bubbles up amid the prescribed hush" (Metcalf and Huntington 1995, 24–25). In the Belozersk region of Vologda province, Anna, interviewed in 1996, commented that it was usual to take a bottle of wine with you to the cemetery at Troitsa, although she herself did not drink or offer drink to the dead. She remembered that people would take an accordion with them and there would be dancing "right on the graves" (FA Bel 17-33, July 13, 1995). References such as this and the remarks of my priest friends given above require further elucidation. First, it should be remembered that the Russian rural population in particular still retains a remarkable sense of closeness to their deceased relatives. They visit the dead in what is essentially their new home, greet them, speak to them, offer them food, share the joy of Easter with them by bringing Easter eggs, and greet the coming of summer with them by sprucing up the gravesites and laying flowers and sprigs of birch. The dead are not feared and remain a part of the community. Seen from this perspective, singing and enjoying yourself beside the graves at Troitsa and on other memorial occasions seems less incongruous and has a long history in Russia. That mourning may swiftly give way to merriment is attested by the sixteenth-century *One Hundred Chapters* (*Stoglav* 1971, 140), which condemns the behavior of visitors to cemeteries on Trinity Saturday who, having finished their lamentations, called for the street musicians to come and entertain them and began to "jump and dance and clap their hands and sing their devilish songs." In the first decade of the twentieth century, N. Ivanenko recorded a virtually identical scene in a village of the Dmitrovsk *uezd* of Orlov *guberniya*. On Troitsa Saturday the peasants set off for the cemetery with vodka and pies. The priests who conducted graveside requiems were given a pie each instead of money. The peasants sat on the graves, drank vodka with their piece of pie, remembered their dead "with kind words," and then, before setting off home began to sing and dance and clap their hands, keeping this up the whole way back to the village. Outraged, Ivanenko remonstrated with an older woman who excused such apparent irreverence by pointing out that "we held a requiem, we remembered the deceased, now we have to cheer them up, otherwise they will be offended" (Ivanenko 1910, 4:326). The peasants in Orlov guberniya were clearly singing *chastushki*.

These humorous verses are created when people gather for a festive occasion. They are accompanied by accordion music, and dance and would seem, on the face of it, to be completely inappropriate in the presence of death. Nevertheless, there are chastushki specially created for graveside performance. The singing of so-called "funeral-memorial" chastushki has been recorded in the Arkhangel'sk and Vologda provinces of the Russian North in the twentieth and twenty-first centuries. Such chastushki were recorded, for example, in 1993, 1994, and 1995, during the folklore expeditions of the Russian Institute for the History of the Arts (St. Petersburg) to the Ust'ya region of Arkhangel'sk province. A short two-part videorecording of Troitsa customs was shot in the villages of Siniki (1994) and Slobodka (1995). In the film, family groups of men, women, and children are seated on benches in the fenced-in enclosures around their relatives' graves, with white tablecloths spread on the tables and laid with copious amounts of food and bottles of vodka. The women are mostly wearing headscarves and are smartly dressed, as they might be for an outing. There are at least three accordionists present, all male. Both women and men sing the chastushki or "remembrance songlets" (*pominnye pisenki*), as they are sometimes called, all of which make reference to someone they wish to remember—a daughter, mother, or brother. In one example a dialogue takes place between a grieving mother who knows in her heart "that the grave will not split open" to release her child and the dead daughter who comforts her and accepts her fate. Although the four-line structure and the simple melodic line of this unusual musical form and its accordion accompaniment are obviously based on those of the chastushka, the manner of performance and the emotional timbre of the sound are not. The voices are harsh and completely devoid of the exuberance and light-heartedness typical of the chastushka, holding a suggestion of the intonation usual in funeral laments. The singers wear somber expressions, and their gestures—a bowed head, a hand covering the eyes, weeping—clearly signify grief. One woman, after her song about her mother, stretched out face-down upon the grave. A man straddled the grass-covered grave mound, conversing with his deceased relative, and then began to play the accordion. There seems little doubt that these performances were an accepted ingredient of memorial ritual and provided a form of catharsis for the bereaved.[3] As S. R. Kuleva, whose research is based primarily on twentieth and twenty-first century material from the Ustyug region of Vologda province, has noted, these have a similar function to laments and share with them some formulaic motifs (Kuleva 2003, n.p.). Svetlana Adonyeva has also commented on the use of the chastushka as a way of expressing grief when the full lamenting voice is considered inappropriate (see chapter 3).

It is easy to imagine that after a period of ritual gravity, the presence of an accordionist, food, and alcohol might encourage a lightening of the atmosphere and the singing of the more usual chastushki intended for entertainment. Not all graveside "revels," or graveside music can be dismissed as mere tipsy boorishness but may in some cases have formed an integral part of funeral and memorial ritual.

It is very difficult to ascertain the extent to which Troitsa as a major religious festival was properly remembered and its traditions upheld in different parts of Russia during the long period of Soviet rule and in spite of the Soviet determination to uproot it. It varied in different regions and villages and depended on a variety of circumstances: the waxing and waning of anti-religious campaigns; the strength of family commitment and memory; and, to a considerable degree, whether or not there was a functioning church anywhere in the vicinity. Not all churches were destroyed or remained closed throughout the Soviet period. The Church of the Birth of the Mother of God in Belaya, for example, lost several of its priests during the repressions of the 1930s, was closed in 1940, and turned into a tractor repair workshop but reopened in 1941, under the protection of the Nazi occupiers, remaining open throughout the war. In spite of extreme hardships, exacerbated during the period of persecution inaugurated under Khrushchev in 1958, the church survived (Klishina 2011, n.p.). In my experience, in the Russian North one factor in particular determined the importance of Troitsa in the memories of the local rural population: whether or not it had been the patronal festival of the village, which meant that it was inextricably bound up with the entirely secular pursuit of entertainment and relaxation with family members and friends from the surrounding villages.

What is clear, however, is that after the beginning of the twenty-first century, it became increasingly popular for large numbers of people to travel long distances, sometimes even from abroad, in order to congregate with kith and kin beside the graves of ancestors at Troitsa. "Fancy! It's just like at the Kremlin," exclaimed one elderly woman, describing the scene outside the church in Belaya, "Cars, cars, expensive cars" (EW-A Pskov-Dno A12, June 11, 2014). According to another (Syamzha region, Vologda province), "there are many, many cars for two days. They arrive on Saturday and on Sunday there's a load of them near the cemetery. Many people drive there. After all, people are brought for burial there from the whole *volost'* [a small administrative division]" (FA Syam 17-63, July 11, 2006).

The reason for this phenomenon is not just the reestablishment of church authority, although the televised presence of state and local dignitaries in church at Easter and Troitsa has played a part in popularizing these occasions. Since 1990 rural Russia has been experiencing the latest of several massive waves of exodus from the countryside that have occurred during the twentieth and twenty-first centuries. The early years of collectivization witnessed a major population movement from the country to the towns, reaching 12 million people between 1928 and 1932 (Fitzpatrick 1994, 80). In order to stem uncontrolled depopulation of the countryside, an internal passport system was introduced in 1932. However, the hemorrhaging of the rural population did not stop there. Although freedom of movement for many became restricted until the issuing of passports to all rural dwellers from the 1970s, others were able to leave to continue their education, find work in factories, or join the army (Fitzpatrick 1994, 94–100). Then, World War II removed a generation of young men from the villages. More recently, lack of employment and other opportunities, particularly in the more remote rural areas, have brought about mass immigration to the cities, leaving many villages with only an ever-decreasing population of old people and deserted houses. Yet nostalgia for a lost way of life, for community and family bonds, including those with former generations, remains a powerful stimulus for Russians. Among the elderly, many will continue to live in their villages only in the summer months, spending their winters in the towns with children and grandchildren. But many of these same people will expect to be buried in their home cemeteries, so for some people, the need to tend graves persists in spite of the dwindling population. The ideas deeply rooted in the Russian psyche—the institution of the extended family, the patriotic yearning for native places, and the notion of *zastol'e* (the convivial, ritualistic gatherings of guests around a laden festive table)—all have combined to make the village cemetery, especially at Troitsa, one of the major venues for prearranged family reunions. More prosaically, perhaps, it should be remembered that Troitsa is not only an important date in both the church and the traditional calendars, but representing as it does the beginning of summer, it offers the first real opportunity for large al fresco gatherings on a major "ancestor day." Thinking about how to answer the questions "Why gather at Troitsa?" and "Why lunch in the cemetery?," an acquaintance in the Dno region referred to a conversation she once had with a local teacher who was occasionally visited by her former pupils. One young man could only return to the village in winter because of his job. "I only see the dead. I don't see the living," he complained and only managed to meet up with his old classmates when he changed his work schedule to have time off at Troitsa. As far as lunching at the cemetery was concerned, she laughed: "Well, where else can we go? Everything else has closed!" (EW-A Pskov-Dno A8, June 10, 2014). In Soviet times the usual venue for large gatherings on festive occasions, for concerts, films, dances, and so on, would have been the clubhouse, but many villages no longer have such facilities. The cemetery has become the communal space where families and whole communities can meet together.

TROITSA AS A VILLAGE FESTIVAL (*PRAZDNIK*) IN RURAL RUSSIA IN THE TWENTIETH CENTURY

Major festivals, such as Troitsa, always had many different functions and many different intertwined aspects, social and intimate, secular and religious. Each village held its own annual patronal or chapel (*prestol'nyi/khramovoi*) feast day. Some celebrated the patron saint of the local church and others a religious emblem, such as a particularly venerated icon. Many villages, however, held their festival on days of wider significance in the church calendar: the Annunciation (Blagoveshchenie); Ascension Day (Voznesenie); Troitsa; and the following Monday, the Day of the Holy Spirit (Dukhov den').

These festivals were not purely or even predominantly religious occasions so much as major events in village life that helped to cement family and community relations. Because of the large numbers of people they attracted, they were often simply referred to as *sezzhie* (i.e., "assembling" or "gathering" festivals). The festival seasons (spring to summer or autumn to winter) were a time of constant movement between villages; exchanges of visits between relatives, kinsmen, and friends; and an associated round of feasting and merry-making. Because people often had to travel a considerable distance, some festivals continued for several days.

The revolution and particularly the later 1920s and 1930s brought drastic changes to the profile of village festivals. The destruction of churches removed the focal point for many village gatherings. Worship at Christmas, Easter, Troitsa, and other feast days was either banned or actively discouraged: "Earlier on we, how shall I put it? We were forbidden during the Soviet regime to have festivals like that. Medosii's day is religious. . . . Same with Petr's day [*Petrov den'*]. In Tot'ma region when the Tot'ma folk set out [for the festival] the militia would arrive to stop them celebrating Petr's day. The people wanted to. But then there was no way you could celebrate any of these, you had no right to have a good time feasting. Just work, work" (DAu 1-13 Vol. Syam, August 6, 2007, (2)).

In spite of prohibitions and restrictions, many villages did manage to cling to their old traditions. People treasured the original names of the festivals and did not entirely forget them. Anna, from a village in the Leshukon'e region of Arkhangel'sk province, recollected how, when she was about six years old, her two uncles, after their return from the war, had taken her to a festival in the village of Keba, which was a distance of fourteen to sixteen kilometers. She managed to walk part of the way herself, and her uncles carried her the rest of the way. They stayed with relatives for two days (FA Lesh 18-164, July 11, 2011). Householders in the different villages took it in turn to entertain guests, and the women were expected to provide generous hospitality. The following description from the village of Nikulinskaya in the Syamzha region of Vologda province shows both the eagerness and determination with which people looked forward to the festivals, even in the days of extreme austerity after World War II, and their enjoyment of whatever food they could get together:

> Troitsa was in Sholoty and Petr's day in Rezha. People would go—nowadays no one worries about their footwear—but sometimes we went without our shoes. You had to get to the festival. Someone would give you something. Someone [would give] a headscarf, maybe someone a dress, whatever they could. There was nowhere to get anything, there was nothing after the war. So you would take it with you, not in bags, you'd tie it up in a headscarf, any kind, shabby or worn, and you'd get to the village. When you could see it, you'd wash your feet and put on your shoes and off you'd go. Then you'd visit someone. People would come to my festival—a number of girls would come and they'd spend the night and I would give them something to drink and some food—and then you would go there and visit one of them. You would go visiting. You would have lunch somewhere. It was really good. The young folk would tuck in to the food. (DAu 1-83 Vol. Syam, August 29, 2006)

Indeed, the huge losses of the war years suffered by village communities made people all the more determined to reestablish any surviving family and community links. There is no doubt that in spite of the original religious basis of many festivals, including Troitsa, eating, drinking, meeting family and friends, and having a good time together were major objectives: "We drank, sang, and ate until we couldn't take any more! [*Pili, peli, eli do otvala*]" (FA Lesh 18-156, July 7, 2010).

The festivals also had a more serious side, playing a significant part in the regulation of family, community, and intercommunity contacts and relationships. In addition to visiting the graves of ancestors, the villagers looked forward to the future, to match-making and the creation of new generations. Youths and girls approaching marriageable age were given ample opportunities to get to know their counterparts from other villages while mothers enjoyed the spectator sport of spying out future daughters- or sons-in-law.

There was considerable rivalry among would-be suitors at these gatherings, with demonstrations of male bravado often escalating from jeers and foul language to overt violence. Gangs of young men from opposing villages would march into battle with their accordionist at the head of the procession, playing in a particularly provocative manner known as "combat style" (*pod draku*). These ritualized fights were known all over the country and were a significant component of village festivals at least until the 1950s. The root causes of these conflicts were not hard to find: "They fought over girls. . . . They fought less at Pokrov than they did at Troitsa. They would get drunk and of course a drunk man doesn't give a damn" (DAu 09-041 Arch-Mez, July 10, 2009). Not infrequently, since the young men armed themselves with knives and stakes, the battles between villages ended with serious injuries and even death. I am indebted to a colleague in St. Petersburg for the following account of events at the annual Troitsa festival related to him by his father, who, in the 1950s was the accordionist for a village in the Kalyazin region of Tver' province. By evening it was mainly young people on the street:

> Gradually, the whole strolling mass [*gulyan'e*] split into two groups at opposite ends of the village. Each one had its own accordionist. My father was one of them. The groups walked towards each other singing provocative and offensive chastushki. It was a bit like a "rap" battle. They knew a lot of chastushki and particularly esteemed the ones that "hit home," emphasizing the physical shortcomings of a rival. They walked and taunted until their emotions were at "white heat." At the head of each group, as before, walked the accordionist with the singers while those at the back were fetching their lead-tipped whips and knives and ripping out fence pickets. My father said they fought ferociously in the early 1950s. They crippled and even killed people in fights like these. . . . Without a fight it wasn't considered a proper festival. (information received by email April 6, 2015)

Although vestiges of the former village patronal festivals survived into the mid-twentieth century, their decline was visible and irreversible. This was attributable to two major factors. One was the reduction of village populations, already a serious problem after Stalin's insistence in the 1930s that workers were more needed in industry than on the collective farms (Fitzpatrick 1994, 96). The flight from the countryside escalated after the collapse of the Soviet Union, with wholesale closure or running down of local industries, such as farming, fishing, and forestry. This trend has only continued since then, leaving many villages with only small populations of elderly people: "Who can go traveling? In the first place the river has silted up. Then, someone might need gas. Girls, do you see anyone here who works? There's no one. . . . Earlier, girls, we were all on more friendly terms. Very friendly. . . . There used to be 480 people here. . . . Now, some people don't even say 'hello' to their neighbor. They just live here. There are only fifty of us now" (FA Lesh 18-176, July 7, 2011).

A second factor was deliberate—religious persecution and the determination to impose a Soviet ideology and instill Soviet values. Whereas in the past festivals were private family and community occasions arranged by the experienced older householders themselves, the Soviets wanted to organize and control both work and leisure themselves and turn traditional holidays into more passive public spectacle. For this reason they emphasized the village club or cultural center, as opposed to the church, as the hub of activity and organized events in which the main roles were orchestrated and scripted by Party activists or appointed workers from the cultural sphere (*kul'trabotniki*). In the old days, when people worked for themselves, they could arrange their leisure time accordingly, but in the collective and state farms time off was very limited. There was no question of not working on religious festivals and very low tolerance for absenteeism after several days of visiting (*gost'ba*), feasting, and drinking.

Destroying and deforming village religious festivals amounted to an assault on religious values and practices as well as on the structures and conventions of village community life. By the postwar period more supposedly relevant Soviet celebrations, such as May Day and Victory Day, had been introduced, while other festivals were renamed, and the dates on which they would have been celebrated previously were sometimes reorganized. Troitsa was renamed the Festival of the Birch.

THE TROITSA BIRCH TREE: FOR THE LIVING AND THE DEAD

New Life and New Beginnings

Because its new leaves appear early, it has become axiomatic to associate the birch with nature coming alive again. Many researchers have stressed the connection of the Semik-Troitsa festival and particularly its birch tree motif with agrarian ritual and fertility rites (see Propp 1963, 58–62; Anikin 1970, 55; Sokolova 1979, 188; Zelenin 1991, 395).

Vladimir Propp considered the week preceding Troitsa to be "the main festival dedicated to the cult of vegetation" (Propp 1963, 58). Whether or not there was an actual vegetation cult based around the birch tree, notions of fertility and regeneration formed a leitmotif of the early summer period, and the birch was a dominant attribute in customs intended to encourage these.

A major aspect of traditional activities in the weeks around Troitsa in the nineteenth and early years of the twentieth century related to courtship and marriage. The imagery of Troitsa songs—with their pairings of ducks and ganders, male and female swans, little red berries and green nut trees, and the central motif of the solitary little birch tree and the daring young gallant who embraces it—all resonate with the prospect and invocation of wooing, marriage, and new life. In Troitsa songs the birch tree is more than a mere poetic symbol. It is rather the hypostasis in nature of the girls who sang the songs. Imagined as a young woman of the same age, she mediates between the girls and their fate, linking this world and the world of the supernatural, creating and revealing the future through magic. A similar image of the birch tree can be found in the lyrical songs and laments of wedding ritual. As N. P. Kolpakova writes of bridal imagery: "Most often she [the bride] is a lost little dove, a slender birch tree, a swan left behind by the flock, all well-established images of folk poetry standing for innocence, youth, and weakness" (Kolpakova 1973, 254). As a single birch tree, unreachable by any path, insulated from the cries of geese and swans, she hears only the song of the young nightingale, her suitor Ivan (Kolpakova 1973, 93–94). As her father hands her over to her new husband, she likens herself to the "white birch tree, torn up by its roots" (Efimenkova 1980, 343).

At Troitsa it was customary for girls of marriageable age to weave garlands, mixing birch leaves with flowers. These garlands were eventually cast upon a nearby river or pond, and as they floated away, they were used to make predictions about each individual girl's future. The predictions touched on whether or not the girl would soon marry, the direction from which her suitor might come, whether he would be faithful, whether he would soon forget her, or whether he pined for her. A garland that sank might predict that a girl would remain unmarried that year or that she might even die. In addition to these garlands, circlets of leaves were formed by plaiting together the ends of birch branches, which were left for a few days to see whether or not they would wither. Each girl would then inspect the condition of the one she had made and foretell her future from it (for more detail on fortune-telling with garlands, see Sokolova

1979, 190–93; Pashina 2006, 64–68). Young women also kissed through these circlets of birch, vowing eternal friendship, a ritual act known as *kumlenie* (cf. *kuma*, a bosom friend), which consolidated the notion of sisterhood at a time of transition between girlhood and womanhood, spring and summer. Another practice in some parts of Russia was to cut down a birch tree or a large branch and dress it in female clothing—or simply adorn it with token ribbons, colorful headscarves, or beads—in order to form a centerpiece for the dancing and singing and the feasting of revelers. Later, the girl-tree was divested of her finery and destroyed, cast out into the fields, or more usually flung into the local river or pond (Maksimov 1994, 381–82; Sokolova 1979, 188–99).

The extent to which these more complex games and customs involving the birch, popular in the nineteenth century, survived into the twentieth century varied from region to region, although in general there was a marked decline as the ritual significance of various practices became less relevant and was gradually forgotten. Nevertheless, some village people in both Vologda and Arkhangel'sk provinces retained memories of the "girl-tree" witnessed in childhood before World War II. For example, in the Onega region of Arkhangel'sk province, according to a woman born in 1906 and recorded in 1981, girls would gather in a meadow and cut down some birch saplings. Three were placed in front of each girl and scraps of cloth were then tied on the trees (FA Onezh 18-38, July 18, 1981). While conducting fieldwork in Vozhgora in 2013, I was shown a place on the edge of the forest, the site of a votive cross to which offerings were brought and at which notes imploring assistance of various kinds were left. For many years this and the hillside upon which it stood, a popular venue in living memory for summer festivals, with singing and figure-dancing, had been a favorite gathering place for women at Troitsa. The birch trees lining the approach were covered in bits and pieces of fabric and ribbons, both white and colored.

Even if the birch trees were not decorated or particularly anthropomorphized, they clearly continued to form an important component of Troitsa traditions in the North. A woman from the Velikii Ustyug region of Vologda province remembered that they used to bring birch trees back to the village and create a sort of corridor between them leading from the street to the porch (FA VUst 18-6, July 16, 1983). "At Troitsa," according to another, "it was essential to have a birch tree standing beside the house" (DAu 1-123 Vol. Syam, August 6, 2015). Usually, the windows received special treatment, each one having its own tree in front of it, in some cases even two, when trees were arranged in a double row (FA VUst 18-16, July 11, 1983). After the leaves withered and the festival was over, the trees were often, as in the more distant past, thrown away into the river (FA VUst 18-22, July 9, 1983).

However, throughout Russia it is the decorative use of birches that has proved the most enduring tradition. An acquaintance originally from the Dno region of Pskov province told me how, when she was a child in the 1940s and 1950s, little birch saplings would be cut down and nailed crosswise on the outside of windows and on the porch and by the front door, while smaller branches were placed inside the house in the spaces between windows, behind photograph frames, and on the stove. She was particularly struck by the pervasive fragrance of the young vegetation. The sheer scale of such domestic ornamentation was a recurring feature in people's memories: "The whole village was crammed full of little birches, such was the reverence for the birch tree at Troitsa" (EW-A Pskov-Dno A10, June 10, 2014); "Even the Communists had birch branches in their houses at Troitsa" (EW-A Tver'-Bol, June 16, 2015); "On the Saturday, on the eve [of Troitsa] I would go into the forest. Behind my house we had a very good vegetable garden and beyond the house there was a bit of a marsh with some woodland. I would break off bits from the birches and stick them everywhere—beside the icon, the windows. We had simple village windows—I'd stick them at the windows, in doorways, in the yard. I'd put those birches everywhere." Today, Pelageya lives in the same village but in a more modern house less conducive to the nailing of birch branches about it, but "all the same," she said, "I had some here in a vase and there are still some birches in my chicken run although they've withered now. That's the custom" (EW-A Tver'-Bol, June 16, 2015). Nowadays, domestic ornamentation with birch is on a much more modest scale. Walking around the villages of Bologoe region in Tver' province not long after Troitsa, I could see sprigs of withered birch still stuck beside front doors and on garden gates. Eventually, the birch twigs would be burned in the stove or thrown into a river, but they were not supposed to be thrown away carelessly, just anywhere. This suggests that the Troitsa birch trees have retained something of their earlier magical significance.

In fact, the Troitsa birches, positioned by the windows and entrances to the homestead, still have an apotropaic function, protecting it from evil forces during the transitional period between spring and summer. The birch tree is well known in Russia, as elsewhere, for its medicinal uses. Every part of the tree, from its leaves to its roots, is thought to have health-giving properties, and its talismanic reputation was no doubt enhanced by this knowledge. The birch is widely regarded as a quintessentially "pure" tree. The dried leaves from the birch switches prepared for use in the bathhouse, and sometimes fresh leaves, were used routinely in village funerals as a filling for the pillow and to line the bottoms of coffins. This practice continues in many places to the present day "because [birch] is holy, pure. And you need to put things that are pure in with the deceased" (FA Bel 17-33, July 13, 1996).

A graveside offering of flowers and sprigs of birch, Berezaika, Tver' province, 2016. (Photo by Elizabeth Warner)

Birches for the Dead

Earlier, I commented on the custom of taking refreshments to the cemetery during memorial rituals in the Semik-Troitsa period. These were not the only gifts deposited on or beside the graves of loved ones. T. A. Agapkina has indicated that among the Slavs in general there existed in the past a variety of customs between Easter and Troitsa involving the decoration of graves with greenery and flowers (Agapkina 2002, 309). In many regions of Russia, the custom of depositing sprigs of birch on graves is still very much alive. I noticed this particularly during fieldwork in Pskov and Tver' provinces. In the Bologoe region of Tver' province the custom was particularly in evidence. In three cemeteries I visited in June 2015, several weeks after Troitsa, virtually every grave contained twigs with already withering leaves. In some cases the twigs had been pushed straight into the soil on top of the graves, and in others they were simply lying on or at the side of the grave or had been placed in vases. Many people prefer to utilize for this purpose birch foliage broken from the large branches or saplings with which churches are adorned at Troitsa and which have received the blessing of the priest. A friend who is a priest in Vologda province pointed out that Troitsa is referred to in church books as "flower-bringing day" (*tsvetonosnaya*) and that in his experience bouquets of flowers and branches of birch are brought into the church specially for the blessing and taken home, where they are dried and kept beside the icons until the following year. This is the same practice I noted in the Bologoe region. Taking offerings of birch to the cemetery, particularly when the stalks are pushed into the grave itself, has more than a purely aesthetic purpose. The intention is to let the dead know that it is Troitsa and that they too are participating in the festival. It is a way of sharing Troitsa with the deceased. In other words, the gifting of birch, like the gifting of food, is a gesture of inclusion, in this case joining the living and the dead in the joy and redemption of Pentecost. The apotropaic function of the birch, its connotations of purity and its many links with ideas of transition from barrenness to fruitfulness, are also significant. Placing birch on graves is a reminder, to the dead as well as to the living, that death is both the end of one life and the beginning of another.

In addition to the presence of birch twigs on the graves, I noticed that the headstones on a substantial number of graves in all three cemeteries I visited in the Bologoe region bore engraved images of birch trees, sometimes as components of complex symbolic landscapes illustrating death and grief, so that the birch tree had acquired a perpetual presence and significance on the grave (see chapter 4 for more detailed discussion of the birch tree emblem).

L. Lobkova illustrates the link between the birch and remembrance of the dead or the souls of the dead in material from the Plyussa region of Pskov province.

A gift to the deceased of Troitsa birch twigs pushed into the grave mound, Lykoshino, Tver' province, 2016. (Photo Elizabeth Warner)

Here in the nineteenth century, for example, the villagers would create special pathways at Troitsa for the returning souls of the dead to follow, by sprinkling red and yellow sand in the road. They would then cut branches of birch from their own fields or patches of forest and position them under the windows of their homes, one branch for each member of the household who had died. When girls broke off birch twigs for their garlands they would lament and call to deceased family members in the belief that the souls of the dead could alight on the birch trees (Lobkova 2000, 36–37). The birch is a many-faceted symbol. It may reflect new beginnings and change in nature and the lives of the living, but does not exclude the dead, for whom change and resurrection are also promised.

In the course of the twentieth and twenty-first centuries the birch tree began to acquire new connotations. Its female persona began to evolve into a symbol of Russia itself.

FESTIVAL OF THE BIRCH: AN IMAGE AND A FESTIVAL TRANSFORMED

I asked a number of women why so many of the grave markers in cemeteries I had visited in the Bologoe region bore engraved images of birch trees. Since none of them had noticed this feature before, the question produced a lively discussion and a variety of answers. It was said that "the tree is beautiful," "people just like it," and "maybe it's because birch trees are our Russian thing." Both the material and the metaphorical significance of the birch for Russians were identified. It was not only the favorite tree, it was also very useful. It had medicinal properties. The sap provided a refreshing drink. It could be used for firewood. Leafy switches of birch were used in the bathhouse. But above all, the birch was associated with Russianness and recognized as a symbol of Russia (EW-A Tver'-Bol, June 16, 2015).

The widespread acceptance in Russia today of the "female" birch tree as a symbol of the native land (literally, the birth land [*rodina*] or Russian motherland [*matushka Rossiya*]) is a concept rooted in Russian literature and art. But in fact, it only really began to make its mark in the twentieth century, evolving rapidly during the latter half of the century and becoming deeply entrenched in the twenty-first.

It would be difficult for any Russian describing the Russian countryside to avoid mentioning birch trees, and naturally, they can be found scattered through the lyric verses of most nineteenth-century Russian poets. Mostly, however, they appear there as favorites in a familiar landscape rather than as explicit symbols of the native land. There are a very few possible exceptions. In this context we might mention Aleksandr Pushkin, for example. Describing his 1820 tour of the Crimea in a letter to A. A. Del'vig, Pushkin wrote of his great astonishment when, after crossing a mountain ridge, the first object he saw was a northern birch tree! "My heart nearly stopped," he wrote. "I began to feel homesick for my dear north" (Pushkin 1937, 13:250). Yet, although the poet is clearly remembering his homeland here, he chooses to call the birch tree "northern," rather than "Russian." Nor do birch trees in general have a particular place in his poetry. Mikhail Lermontov's accolade of 1841 to his native land, "Rodina," expresses his love for the beauty of its landscape and the characteristic features of its "sad" villages. His gaze is captivated by the "pair of whitening birch trees" on a rise in the middle of a yellow cornfield (Lermontov 1936, 2:100–101). Much closer to what later became an indissoluble bond in the popular imagination between the birch tree and the country where it grows abundantly, however, is Petr Vyazemskii's poem "The Birch Tree" ("Bereza") of 1855. Largely because of ill health, Vyazemskii spent a great deal of time abroad in the 1850s and in 1863 moved permanently to the spa town of Baden-Baden in Germany, where he was to spend his final years. "The Birch Tree" is written from the point of view of an exile for whom a birch tree in the forest is not merely a reminder of home but a voice that speaks to the soul, like a letter from one's "dear mother." Here, Vyazemskii openly calls the birch tree the "mark" (*kleimo*) or symbol of Russia and gives it a new identity, no longer that of the innocent maiden, as in folk poetry, but of Mother Russia (Vyazemskii 1862, 164–65). The sentimental tone of Vyazemskii's poem and its clear-cut division between the notions of "home" and "abroad," the "familiar" and the "strange," also became typical aspects of later songs and verses. The birch tree was to become a territorial marker, a feature of a specifically Russian and even Slavonic landscape, in both its material and symbolic sense.

Esenin and the Birch Tree

Mikhail Epshtein has suggested that changing perceptions of the birch tree and its place in the "national landscape" as a symbol of the whole country may be largely attributed to the popularity of the poetry of Sergei Esenin (1895–1925) (Epshtein 1990, 247).

There is no doubting Esenin's love for the land of his birth. However, the inspiration for his greatest poetry derived from a very particular, selective view of the contours and denizens of this land. Although he uses the term native or birth land frequently, it is not always the case that he has in mind the wider geopolitical entity of Russia/Rossiya. Essentially, he saw himself as a child of Rus', the holy Russia of medieval times, distant echoes of which he imagined in the archaic way of life and traditions of his rural childhood in Ryazan' province. Esenin's deepest affection and descriptive skill were reserved for what he knew best from his early years, the village where he was born and its surroundings, an idealized landscape that appealed to his readers and has been repeated endlessly by his followers and imitators into the twenty-first century.

Tree imagery plays a particularly significant role in Esenin's lyric verse, and it is true that the birch is mentioned frequently. Like many trees, including the maple, rowan, lime, apple, willow, fir, and pine, it is an integral part of his rural surroundings, as in "The white birch beneath my window" ("Belaya bereza pod moim oknom"). On the other hand, in its anthropomorphic form, it has a precise visual and symbolic presence that owes much to the folk poetry of the Semik-Troitsa period. It represents the young, unmarried girl, the little "birch-tree bride" (*berezka-nevesta*), as he calls it. Several of Esenin's poems make direct reference to the traditions of Troitsa, traditions with which, as a village lad, he was no doubt personally familiar. Fortune-telling with garlands, for example, is the subject of one such poem in which the collapse of a garland in the water is interpreted as an omen of death: "Above the weir the rushes began to rustle" ("Zashumeli nad zatonom trostniki"; Esenin 1970, 1:48). In his poem "Trinity morning, the morning canon" ("Troitsino utro, utrennii kanon"), Esenin refers to the custom of gathering flowers and greenery at dawn on Troitsa morning (Esenin 1970, 1:49). During the "kneeling prayers" of St. Basil the Great at the morning service, members of the congregation would shed a few tears into the fragrant bouquets and later "sweep" the graves of the dead with them in token of the healing, comforting, and regenerative power of the foliage. According to L. A. Tul'tseva, "the tears symbolize the waters of oblivion as linking threads between those praying and the other world, the world of ancestors" (Tul'tseva 2014, 27).

To what extent, then, do Esenin's birch trees match those of the much later birch tree festivals, and why did his vision of Russia retain or acquire such resonance in the patriotic discourse from the second half of the twentieth century to the present day? What relationship, if any, do these idealized trees have with the dead?

In tune with other so-called peasant poets of the day, like Nikolai Klyuev, and artists such as Mikhail Nestorov, Ivan Bilibin, and Viktor Vasnetsov, Esenin projects a vision of Russia that looks to its imagined glorious past for its inspiration, to Holy Russia with its saints and icons and holy pilgrims. In the landscape he describes, one can see the cupolas of churches and hear the distant sound of church bells pealing through the birch trees on Troitsa morning. Esenin imagines himself as one of the holy men who could still be seen, and not long before were a familiar sight, on the roads of rural Russia, the monks and pious laymen on pilgrimages to distant monasteries and shrines, the beggars who received alms in return for their prayers for the dead, the kaliki, or traveling bards with their "spiritual verses"—all images of people passing through a country rather than living a stable, entrenched existence. Although Esenin's love for Rus' was inspired by his childhood and youth in the village of Konstantinovo in Ryzan' province, he did not remain there to share the hard life of the peasant, but abandoned it for the fame and benefits of the city. As an adult, on his very infrequent return visits to his native village, he knew himself to be a stranger, caught in the tragic dichotomy between a quasi-religious love for it and a recognition of his fundamental alienation from it. Predictably, it was not the contradictions in Esenin's vision that caught the imagination of his admirers and followers. It was the way he looked back with regret to a romanticized, preindustrial, pastoral past imbued with great cultural significance and a conservative, almost mythical religiosity. The foundations for the later "cult" of the birch tree were in part built upon Esenin's unconditional love for and exile from what it represented. However, World War II, significantly known in Russia as the Great Patriotic War, was probably the catalyst by which Esenin's Russia became the landscape of the Russian "soul" and the white birch trees outside every window the stereotypical image worth fighting and dying for. His poems, often in handwritten copies, became treasured items for many Russian soldiers in the front lines of battle (Safonov 1995). Ilya Ehrenburg commented in his memoirs about how, during the war, young lieutenants "straight from school" treasured his poetry (Erenburg 1966, 8:367).

The dismantlement of the pious, patriarchal, rural Russia familiar to Esenin as a boy continued during the Soviet period long after his death. The sound of church bells and the sight of church cupolas were virtually eradicated. In the 1930s collectivization and the campaign against kulaks wreaked havoc with the interconnected social and economic structures of traditional village life. During the Great Patriotic War villages were ravaged by occupation and lost a high proportion of their population at the front while those who remained suffered starvation and deprivation. From the 1940s onward, but especially between the 1960s and 1980s, a flood of emotional patriotic poems and songs were produced, inspired by memories of village childhoods and a faraway homeland. In these verses the birch tree's role as a symbol of the nation became endemic (Leleko 2009, 335–39).

A quintessential addition to this type of verse is the well-known, popular poem "The Birch Tree" ("Berezka"), by Yakov Zakharovich Shvedov (1905–1984), written at the front in 1943. It reveals many of the patriotic themes commonly associated with the birch in the twentieth and twenty-first centuries—nostalgia for the countryside left behind (in his case after conscription into the army); the birch as the alter-ego of Russia, which must be defended to the death; the birch as the guardian of the graves of soldiers; and the birch tree and its physical and/or spiritual identification with Russians. Shvedov's sense of union with the tree is such that the wounding of a tree on the battlefield is experienced as a personal trauma: "A shell struck the birch-tree's trunk. / It seemed as if it was striking me" (Snaryad udaril v stvol berezki/A pokazalos' chto v menya). The "apotheosis" of the birch is confirmed at the end of Shvedov's poem by his creation of what seems like a new eternal Trinity. Wholly secular in nature, it consists of the birch, the sun, and Russia, "which live and shall for ever live" (Narovchatov and Khelemskii 1970, 464–65). The post-Soviet period witnessed what many of our interviewees in the northern provinces have described as the "death" of the village. It is unsurprising, therefore, that poems similar in sentiment to Shvedov's earlier work have continued to be written (see, e.g., the song "Birch trees" by the popular poet and songwriter Mikhail Vasil'evich Andreev).

The Festival of the Birch: A Soviet and Post-Soviet Reinterpretation of Troitsa

Ways of celebrating calendar customs, particularly those closely connected to religious festivals, began to change dramatically during the Soviet period. Some changes were the inevitable result of evolving social, political, and economic conditions—the changing role of women, the increased influx of rural dwellers into the towns and urbanization in general, the gradual development of mass media, the imposition of a state-run education system, and so on. However, questions regarding the importance of public holidays in the formation of the national consciousness and what exactly should now be celebrated, and how and by whom, arose very early in the life of the Soviet state and became a matter of official policy and campaigns. Decisions were made from 1917 onward to create and promote holidays in keeping with Bolshevik ideals, praising the successes of the revolution and the achievements of Soviet heroes and workers and celebrating military and political events of significance to the new regime, such as the anniversary of the October Revolution. Family rituals—christenings, weddings, and funerals—acquired "Red" equivalents (Rolf 2013, 41; Lane 1981, 67–88). Long-established calendar traditions, particularly those popular in rural communities but bound up with religion or the product of what was considered to be ignorance and superstition, were actively discouraged, suppressed, secularized, and renamed. The social and cultural functions of churches were replaced by the work of clubs and cultural centers, which became one of the main platforms for what Christel Lane, one of the earliest and most comprehensive Western commentators on Soviet manipulation of popular rituals and festivals, refers to as "cultural management and political socialization in modern industrial society" (Lane 1981, 11). "Cultural management," however, had many facets and went through several phases. By the end of the 1950s and more especially during the 1960s and 1970s, although anti-religious activity continued, official attitudes to traditional culture had begun to change direction. Writing about and studying popular customs, rituals, and festivals became acceptable again, and a number of serious scholarly works in that field appeared (see

Chicherov 1957; Propp 1963; Sokolova 1979). However, they all presented calendar ritual as solidly and more or less exclusively based in the work cycle, needs, and hopes of the agriculturalist, playing down the Christian contribution to such festivals and stressing their archaic, pagan roots. Education about the past, about the origins and meaning of ritual practices, became a tool for state propaganda. In her book about calendar rituals among the East Slavs, V. K. Sokolova approves the application of ethnographical knowledge to new state-sponsored festivals: "We must take from the rituals their aesthetic and theatrical side. That will make the festivals more varied and more interesting. It will give each one its own special character and will facilitate their more successful absorption" (Sokolova 1979, 4). The views of such "experts" clearly influenced the development of public calendar festivities, including the Days of the Village, which replaced many of the former patronal festivals, including Troitsa, in the latter half of the twentieth century. The celebrations of the Shrove (Maslenitsa) and Troitsa periods, with their obvious links to the Orthodox calendar, became prime targets for the modernizers. The former was renamed Farewell to Winter (Provody zimy), and the latter the Festival of the Birch. In 1965 Elizaveta Nagirnyak and her coauthors published *New Festivals and Rituals* (*Novye prazdniki i obryady*), an obvious response to the demand for greater relevance in public festivities.

Nagirnyak writes of the current "conditions of acute ideological struggle" (Nagirnyak, Petrova, and Rauzen 1970, 103)—in other words, the battle for hearts and minds—that lay behind the need to create and encourage new festivals. She offers a choice of numerous and varied components for what is essentially the reinvented Troitsa festival, but the overriding impression is of a celebration devoid of spontaneity and controlled and regimented from beginning to end. The ideological aims of the festival are stated unambiguously. It is designed to replace not only the religious significance of Troitsa but also its social significance in the lives of ordinary folk. The official part of the festival, with its speeches from the tribunal, is designed to emphasize the efforts and successes of collectives and individual workers, who are invited to take their place on the stage and receive "sashes of honor" (*lenty slavy*; Nagirnyak, Petrova, and Rauzen 1970, 106). Apart from encouraging the workforce, the new festival propagated other ideas. It was to be a "patriotic and lyrical" event (Nagirnyak, Petrova, and Rauzen 1970, 101). Love for the native land and praise for its heroic exploits, communist ideals, and the nobility of the Russian character are proclaimed in all the many entertainments suggested by Nagirnyak—from the repertoire of choirs to the dramatic scenes based on Soviet history and the exhibitions of art and photography. In all this, the birch tree had a special place as the appointed "mistress of ceremonies" for the whole festival. The birch was one of the attributes of the festival that characterized efforts to amalgamate traditional elements with the new. A birch tree decorated with ribbons and garlands, for example, was to form an aesthetic centerpiece. A large number of the recommended poems and songs for the festival were about the birch, which by this time had a firm grip on the popular imagination as a sentimental image and symbol of Russia. Perhaps it is not an exaggeration to suggest that the new festival facilitated the "politicization" of the birch tree. Far from being an intermediary between young girls and nature, as previously suggested by agricultural rituals, the birch had become an intermediary between the authorities and the workers. It had become a "character" in the life of the Soviet Union, as presented to the audience in historical tableaux, a witness to and even a participant, albeit a silent one, in the great and terrible events that had shaped it. The tree's role as intermediary between the living postwar generations and their war dead was shown, for example, during a scene about the Great Patriotic War when the tree provided a hiding place and shelter to a wounded soldier; in another scene, it acted as a "guard of honor" over the body of a dead hero (Nagirnyak, Petrova, and Rauzen 1970, 107). This combination of sentiments has continued, in one way or another, to define the ideological framework of the birch tree festivals to the present day.

One of the most detailed and interesting accounts of the new Soviet Festival of the Birch I have seen appears in an essay on Troitsa traditions published on the internet on February 26, 2014, by Tat'yana Komissarova and Dmitrii Smirnov. Information for it was gathered by ninth-grade students and staff from the comprehensive school in the village of Turan', Vetluga region, Nizhegorod province. The research was carried out with the aim of preserving the memories of the oldest members of the community and of encouraging people to take part in the revival of customs enjoyed by previous generations. Significantly, before it was destroyed during the Soviet period, the Church of the Holy Trinity had been an architectural landmark in the village, and Troitsa was the village's patronal festival. During the 1950s mass festivities were organized as a replacement for Troitsa but eventually gave way in the 1970s and 1980s to the Festival of the Russian Birch, otherwise known as the Day of the Village, a special day for workers on the collective farm. One old resident recollected the activities organized at the village clubhouse—speeches about the achievements of the workers, presentation of diplomas and prizes—followed by a concert. Outside there was a market, along with games, singing, and the recitation of poems, all involving the birch ("Traditsii Troitskogo obryada v sele Turan'" 2014). Elsewhere, the festival could be considerably less elaborate. I am grateful to a colleague from St. Petersburg who wrote to me on April 6, 2015, with the following recollections from his Soviet childhood:

I witnessed the Festival of the Birch in the most distant regional center (of Kaliningrad province), Krasnoznamensk, on the border with Lithuania, 330 kilometers from Kaliningrad. The festival unfolded as follows. On a large meadow near a river a stage was constructed out of planking and this was decorated with chopped-down birch saplings. Tents and kiosks were erected round about. In one tent there was a free cartoon film show. In the kiosks food and alcohol were on sale. Various amateur groups of artistes performed on the stage. I have a vague recollection that the festival was opened by some important bloke representing the province, someone everyone was wary of, probably the secretary of the provincial committee, not the chief. All this was called "The Festival of the Russian Birch" and it took place roughly between 1975 and 1977.

Typical of these revamped Soviet festivals was the imposition of an alien ideology and the intention to edify through entertainment. Uniform, bland, carefully structured, and regulated "performances" organized by *kul'trabotniki*, personnel specifically trained to conduct educational work in the cultural sphere, were invented to supplant the rich, diverse, self-regulating, and undisciplined festivities that had been deeply embedded in the psychology of the rural population and in the social, gender, and generational groupings in which they had arisen.

Interestingly, birch festivals have continued to survive in the post-Soviet period, retaining many features of their Soviet antecedents. Initiated as before by workers in the spheres of education and culture, they mostly take place in town squares, open-air museums, and national parks, as well as in the playgrounds of schools and kindergartens. Representatives of city or regional authorities are often present. Although some attention may be paid, especially in village settings, to ethnographical features typical of a particular region, there is a tendency to present a homogenized folkloric experience with troupes of musicians and dancers from various parts of the country, artisans demonstrating crafts, balalaika and accordion players, stalls selling festive foods, and an eclectic mixture of "traditional" activities. These may include decorating the birch tree, presenting it with colored eggs, making and wearing pretty floral garlands, dancing figure dances, playing traditional games, and wearing folk costumes. The cult of the birch tree and its role in traditional ceremonial events has developed into a particular phenomenon in the late twentieth and twenty-first centuries. These festivals in honor of the birch (for which the endearing diminutive form *berezka* is often used) are nowadays organized throughout the country at Troitsa. The birch is fêted as a beloved symbol of Russia and a focus of patriotic feelings. The events serve the purpose of reacquainting people with their historical roots and preserving—or indeed, restoring—aspects of Russia's cultural heritage, albeit in a romanticized and sanitized fashion. In other words, the Troitsa festival has to some extent developed into a politico-cultural phenomenon, part of a countrywide incentive to reawaken and consolidate a sense of national identity and values. As Klaus Roth has pointed out, the utilization of folklore by states and other elitist organizations, the "cultural experts," as he puts it, for precisely this purpose, has been common enough since the eighteenth-century Enlightenment and has become very evident in parts of post-Socialist Eastern Europe (Roth 1998, 2:69–70). This aspect of the Festival of the Birch is particularly noticeable in scripted versions specifically designed for the entertainment and edification of children, which encourage affection for the tree, for Russian nature, for the children's home region (*malaya rodina*), and for Russia itself. Throughout the verbal narrative of the festivals in general there is an ideological subtext that reinforces certain ideas of patriotism based on the link between Russia and the birch tree. Drawn from an eclectic range of sources—ethnographic and imagined, folkloric, historical, literary and musical—they predicate authenticity and claim their origins from the distant past, from customs that are quintessentially Russian and/or Orthodox, although in fact they are mostly superficial reconstructions of disparate elements detached from the place and purpose they once had in people's lives.

In a sense, Russia has been inventing and reinventing itself since 1917. The Troitsa birch tree festivals today are a way of redressing the loss of identity and purpose caused by the social and political upheavals of the past two decades in particular. For some Russians the Festival of the Birch provides a way of reconfirming "who we are," "what we are like," and even "what is ours." The beloved birch has become so entangled with the idea of the Russian nation, with the heart and soul of Russians, that some people, including one of my interlocutors from Pskov province, seem unaware that birch trees also grow elsewhere: "But over there, abroad, there aren't any of these trees. You don't see them. . . . All the same, we are people with a great heart. Birches are the symbol of human purity. . . . Every Russian unquestioningly loves the birch tree" (EW-A Pskov-Dno A10, June 10, 2014).

It is interesting that the Festival of the Birch, a Soviet invention that did not enjoy immediate popularity in rural communities, where it was intended to oust both the Christian celebration of Troitsa and its many other associations for village people, seems to have found its true mission as the Soviet period moved toward its end and the post-Soviet period began. Paradoxically, it returns us full circle to the origins of Troitsa and the role of St. Sergii in the formation of the Russian national identity.

THE GREENING OF THE CHURCH AT TROITSA

Troitsa is a festival celebrated by families and whole communities. It is a church festival and a secular festival. However it is experienced, it reveals in its themes and symbols the same underlying preoccupation with life, death, and resurrection. I once asked a village priest why Russian Orthodox clergy wear green vestments at Troitsa. "The color green itself," he replied, "the color green in Orthodox iconography has the meaning, that is it has the spiritual meaning of life. It is life. That is, it is the color of the holy spirit. Green is the color of the holy spirit" (EW-A Tver'-Bol, June 18, 2015). Green is also the color of the natural world as the cold of winter retreats and new life stirs in the vegetation of early summer. The imagery of Troitsa reveals a symbiotic relationship between rebirth in the Church, in nature, and in mankind: "Branches and flowers are brought to God as the first fruits of spring-time renewal but at the same time they serve as symbols of the Church of Christ which, since the revelation of the grace of the Holy Spirit, has burgeoned like the lily in the hymn and denote the renewal of human beings through the descent of the Holy Spirit" (Bulgakov 1993, 1:682).

Since the collapse of the Soviet Union, the resurgent Orthodox Church has reclaimed its festivals, and today Troitsa is celebrated widely and joyously. For centuries it had been customary to deck the churches for the day of Pentecost with greenery, tree branches showing the young leaves of early summer, and bunches of flowers from members of the congregation. Although any trees or bushes may serve the purpose, the birch has become the tree of choice in Russia, particularly in those regions where it grows abundantly. This emphasis on greenery makes explicit the connection between the Christian Pentecost and the Jewish Pentecost, the festival of Shavuot. According to Scripture, it was when Christ's disciples had gathered to celebrate this festival that the descent of the Holy Spirit took place. Shavuot is a harvest festival ("You shall keep the feast of ingathering at the end of the year, when you gather in from the field the fruit of your labor" Exodus 23:16) that takes place fifty days after Passover. In thanksgiving for a successful harvest, farmers would take baskets of the first fruits of their fields to the temple in Jerusalem. Shavuot also celebrates the Torah, the day when Moses received the Ten Commandments on Mount Sinai. Today, partly in recognition of the festival's link with vegetation and partly as an echo of the legendary blossoming of flowers on the summit of Mount Sinai before God's revelation to Moses, many synagogues and Jewish homes are decorated at Shavuot with green branches and flowers, such as roses.[4]

Through the use of greenery the churches of the Old and the New Testament are linked. The theologian S. V. Bulgakov speculates that the room in which Christ's disciples celebrated Shavuot may well have been decorated with greenery.

If the Jewish Pentecost looks back, however, using "first fruits" as an offering of thanks for a harvest successfully gathered in, the Orthodox Pentecost looks forward, with gifts of verdure that serve as a symbol of hope for the coming harvest and the renewal of life after the death of winter.

It is difficult to be precise about the origins of the custom of using birch trees and/or greenery in general as a source of ecclesiastical decoration and ritual significance in Russia, but certainly by the seventeenth century it was well-established in the public, religious-state appearances of the tsar himself. According to Zabelin's account of the daily life of Russian tsars in the sixteenth and seventeenth centuries (Zabelin 2000, 1 [1]:449), it was customary for the tsar to attend mass in the Uspenskii cathedral in Moscow at Troitsa. Carried before a procession of boyars (members of the nobility) was a small rug with a bouquet of flowers and a pile of leaves, stripped for this purpose from the branches of trees. The patriarch had a similar offering, which was presented to the tsar. Then, after the mass, when the Trinity vespers began, leaves, flowers, and grasses were combined, sprinkled with rose water, and strewn on the floor by the tsar's place in the cathedral, while a similar covering was prepared for the patriarch. There are a number of interesting observations in this early description. The leafy mixture referred to by Zabelin was intended for a precise location and function. The Trinity vespers include three distinctive prayers, composed by St. Basil the Great. These are the lengthy "kneeling prayers," during which members of the congregation are expected to kneel and bow low or prostrate themselves on the floor. In accounts contemporaneous to Zabelin's description, this was referred to as "lying on leaves" (*lezhat' na listu*; see footnote in Zabelin 2000, 1 [1]:449). The covering of vegetation on the floor makes kneeling more comfortable. The utilitarian purpose of layering grass and leaves upon the hard floors of churches has not been forgotten today. A priest in Vologda province described to me how the nuns used to prepare two shaped bundles of grass for his use at the Troitsa service, one to kneel on and the other to support the prayer book during his reading of the kneeling prayers. The exchange of leaves between the tsar and the patriarch suggests an acceptance of the unity brought about by shared power and responsibilities, religious and secular. It is worth noting that Zabelin's account, although accurate in its information, is in fact a paraphrase of entries from Nikolai Novikov's eighteenth-century compendium of historical documents, which includes descriptions dating to the latter half of the seventeenth century (Novikov 1789, 11:142–52). From the number of references in these descriptions to the use of leaves, we may infer that it was an established practice. However, although leaves were distributed around the cathedral, as well as in the places of the tsar and the patriarch in front of the iconostasis, there is no suggestion of the lavish decoration with whole birch branches or even saplings that came to characterize Trinity services by the nineteenth century. The festive and opulent nature of these services comes rather from the descriptions of the tsar and his entourage dressed in all their finery and the gold vessels contrasting with the white draperies and hangings over the miracle workers and the tombs (Novikov 1789, 11:151). Possibly these were references to the tombs of metropolitan bishops and patriarchs lining the side walls of the cathedral and the four reliquaries with the bones of the miracle workers Petr, Ioana, Filipp, and Ermogen.

Further information in Zabelin's account concerning preparations for Trinity Sunday in the cathedral in 1679 reveals the scale of the enterprise. The boyars sent their servants into the patriarch's forest to chop branches from all kinds of trees. The men were to acquire carts from the peasants and form convoys, one consisting of twenty-five carts and the other of twenty. The branches were to be tied in bundles, two hundred to each load (Zabelin 2000, 1 [1]:449). Contemporaneous to these accounts is an observation made in 1698 by Johann Georg Korb, then in Moscow as secretary to the Austrian ambassador Guarient, that at Pentecost "The Russian priests bless shrubs and the leaves of trees" (Korb 1867, 177).

Since birches are among the first trees to produce new leaves in summer it is probable that they were used in these early examples of Troitsa rituals, although there is no specific reference to birch trees in the seventeenth-century texts, and it would appear that leaves rather than whole branches were used. The later emphasis on birch trees and their increasingly dominant role in the decoration of churches suggests a wholehearted acceptance of the popularity and significance of birch in traditional ritual and a fusion of secular and religious imagery. The themes of death, resurrection, and renewal were illuminated in the great church festivals of Easter, Ascension Day, and Troitsa while folk tradition, as we saw, marked these themes in its own way.

My personal experience of Troitsa relates to fieldwork in and around the village of Belaya in Pskov province in June 2014. On Troitsa Saturday morning a cartload of culled birch saplings was drawn up by the side of the church. When its load was dragged onto the porch it looked as if a river of greenery was flooding the church. The morning was spent in trimming and positioning trees and branches, work enthusiastically undertaken by the priest himself. During the service on Sunday the interior of the church was almost hidden under a veritable forest of leaves. This was no mere decorative effect but a recognition of and absorption of the outer world of nature into the inner world of the church. In Russian mythology there is recognition, both on a physical and a metaphysical level, of inner and outer spaces, of "one's own" territory and the spaces of other worlds. There are, for example, clear divisions between the human world and the world of nature. Far beyond the safety and familiarity of the village homes and their neighboring fields is the forest, an outer dimension with different rules of behavior, a world controlled by spirit beings. The "other" world of the dead exists alongside the world of the living but also in its own separate space (see Warner 2011a for further discussion of "inner" and "outer" spaces).

Troitsa took place during a period of vigorous regrowth in nature and for that reason may be regarded as the time "most propitious for contact between 'this' world and the 'other'" (Agapkina 2002, 309). The regenerative spirit of Troitsa affected the dead as well as the living, according to the beliefs and practices of Slavonic peoples in the past. Souls were allowed to escape the other world of the dead for a brief home visit at Troitsa and liked to settle in the branches of birch trees. Among the Russians and the East Slavs as a whole there were many Troitsa customs and beliefs that connected greenery, including the leaves and boughs of birch, with the souls of the dead. T. A. Agapkina refers to the tradition in Pskov province of placing birch saplings outside houses according to the number of people who had died there and of sprinkling sand on the ground in the shape of ladders to facilitate the reentry of the dead to this world. In the Zaonezh'e region of northwest Russia (now Republic of Karelia) doors were left open for the souls' return. It was also the custom in the North to sweep debris from the surface of graves so that the dead could see out. Each family member would provide a sprig of birch from which a broom was fashioned (Agapkina 2012, 306–7). The transformation of churches into green spaces at Troitsa also reflects the link with the dead since they are reminiscent of paradise, the abode of blessed souls mentioned in the "kneeling" prayers of St. Basil, and imagined in the tales of visionaries, the drawings of folk engravings (*lubki*), and the dreams of village people as a verdant and sweet-smelling garden.

The obligatory removal of decorative greenery in the week following Troitsa was the equivalent of "seeing off" the soul after a death: "The destruction of the ritual greenery was the final act in the rituals of the Troitsa cycle. The greenery that had decorated homes, the wreaths and bouquets of flowers, the ritual trees and branches, the Troitsa birch, were cast away in secluded places, burnt, thrown into water or carried to the cemeteries" (Vinogradova 2000, 201).

In Belaya on Troitsa Sunday the whole congregation, following their priests, processed once around the outside of the church, every person carrying a sprig of birch. As we filed back into the church—bowing our heads to pass under Rublev's icon of the Trinity, held aloft over the entrance—I was reminded of passages from Ivan Shmelev's memoir of his boyhood in Russia in the 1880s. He vividly captures the flavor of the Troitsa festival with its multiple messages. In his home every room had its share of birch branches: "There were birches everywhere by the icons. There were birches in the corners, even in the hall, as if it was no longer a house but a grove. And it smelled like a green grove" (Shmelev 2012, 104). Of the Kazanskaya Church at Troitsa he writes: "We couldn't

Birch saplings adorn the church in Belaya, Pskov province, 2014, as the congregation kneels during the prayers of St. Basil the Great at the Troitsa Sunday service. (Photo by Elizabeth Warner)

see anything in the doorway because of the birch trees. Everyone bumped their heads and parted a way through. We entered as if into a grove of trees" (104). Shmelev captures the aesthetic characteristics of Troitsa, the dominance of lush foliage, the appeal to the senses, the transfiguration of spaces, and the idea of a world newly come alive. The room in his home with its mantle of greenery over the icon of the Holy Trinity seems to contain "something alive." In the church the faces on the icons peering though the leaves are like those of living beings (102, 104).

The Orthodox Church recognized and welcomed the sensory experience of Troitsa through the fragrant flowers and leaves that filled the churches: "The visible world and the sensory world celebrate, for on this special day Holy Church, when it decorates its temples with branches, conjoins, one might say, its own temples with the temple of nature, recalling man's original state in Eden and prefiguring his future state on Sion, when there will no longer be temples of the senses, for everything will become one temple" (Borisov 1872, 1:454–55).

Theologically speaking, according to one of my priest correspondents, "[Troitsa] is interpreted as a renaissance of life, victory over the state of death [*mertvennost'*]." According to Hapgood, "The trees and flowers, the tokens of the renewal of Nature in the Spring, typify also the renewal of mankind through the indwelling of the Holy Spirit" (1965, 246).

The Semik-Troitsa period represents a time of multiple ritual practices with many regional variations, the individual elements of which have evolved together with naturally changing patterns of daily life or the dictates of history or politics. It has, by and large, involved all segments of the population, from urban to rural, from peasants to tsars. It is an exemplar both of life-cycle ritual, with its funeral and memorial themes, and of agricultural ritual, with its early summer focus on awakening nature and the hope of coming fruitfulness. Its motifs are drawn from the intertwined beliefs and values of both the Christian and the secular, the world of the agriculturalist and the world of ordinary Russians today who have found a way to reconnect with their sense of Russianness through the symbol of the birch and its festival. It is no accident that the Festival of the Birch, as an offshoot of Troitsa, was one of the few popular celebrations reframed by the interests of the Soviet period that acquired a lasting impact. (For Sovietization of calendric rituals see Lane 1981, 130–39.)

In spite of its varied sources it is not difficult to identify those elements of the Troitsa festival that have retained their primary significance for Russians. Overcoming death and celebrating life—which may be symbolic (as in the life-affirming descent of the Holy Spirit upon the living and the dead at Pentecost) or actual (i.e., centered on the regeneration of the natural world as personified by the birch tree)—were and remain the dominant leitmotifs of Troitsa week. Troitsa is the name day of the forest and the earth. At Troitsa, it is said, "the earth itself rejoices." Upholding this life-death-life continuum is central to funeral ritual. These themes of regeneration and continuity are ideally reinforced by the various acts of *memoria* that typify the Troitsa festival and are one of the means by which Russians remember and renew their kinship with past generations. These include the communal burials of the nameless indigents that used to take place at Semik; the Trinity Saturday service, with its prayers for all the Orthodox dead, known and unknown; and the priest's reading of the diptychs with the names of deceased individuals known to the congregation. For Russians, knowing and naming one's own familial dead, knowing where they are buried, being present where possible at the bedside of the dying, were and are of great significance. In this excerpt from a lament for her husband, killed in the Russo-Japanese War, the widow's pain centers not so much on the fact of his death but on its circumstances, for he laid down his head

Not on a soft bed,
Not on a high pillow,
Not under a warm blanket,
But on the bloody battlefield.
For his bed, he had

Cold mother earth,
For his pillow, small bushes of broom,
For his blanket, weapons and a heavy kit-bag
(Chistova and Chistov 1960, 304).

The festival of Troitsa today is a unifying and positive element in Russian society. It reinstates (and even to some extent reinvents, as we saw in the case of the Festival of the Birch) things of value lost during past repressions and depredations—on the one hand, the right to express one's faith and beliefs, whether in churches or at gravesides, and on the other, the traditions and conventions of village communities that had ensured through their ritual gatherings the continuity of family life. Mass family visits to cemeteries and picnics beside the graves, so popular and widespread today, have acquired a particular resonance in reestablishing, against a background of decay and depopulation, the enduring relationship with the idea of "home," both the native village and the graveyard resting place of ancestors.

The historian O. G. Oexle has pointed out that remembering is more than just a function of memory. It is understanding how the past may be made present through remembering: "Remembering can therefore be defined as the conscious reproducing of the past in the present" (Oexle 1976, 80). The medieval practice of naming the living and the dead in prayers and liturgies, identified by Oexle as a memorial act in which a social group or a community defines and confirms itself as a group (86), would seem to have its parallel in Russia today.

CHAPTER 6

The Story of the Eternal Flame

Ritual Memorial Sites of the Soviet Era

SVETLANA ADONYEVA

I well remember how, when I was little, I was fascinated by the concept of an eternal flame and wanted to understand how it was possible for a flame to be unextinguishable. Expressions such as "eternal fire," "bottomless purse," or "bottomless pit" suggested the presence of something supernatural. I imagine most people were baffled as children by the notion that something could exist for ever and ever. I even recall the irritation in my parents' voices when my questions about the eternal flame wouldn't stop: "How can it *never* go out? Will the snow not put it out? . . . or the rain . . . or the wind?" Together with this memory comes another from my childhood—Leningrad on a dull, cold day, with a light rain falling; my father in his gray felt hat; balloons everywhere; and the eternal flame. It was a November 7 parade marking the anniversary of the Great October Socialist Revolution. Everyone was obliged to go, with groups of coworkers walking along together. My father and his colleagues were marching in a single column that had set off from the Vasil'evskii ostrov district, where the metallurgical plant where he worked was situated, and was making its way to Palace Square (Dvortsovaya ploshchad'), where the party bosses would deliver their speeches from the tribune. Eventually, the crowd began to disperse toward the open ground of the Field of Mars (Marsovo pole),[1] where there was a more relaxed, holiday-like atmosphere in the park surrounding the memorial to the heroes of the revolution, with that unquenchable fire leaping from its central plinth.

My curiosity about the history of this symbolic flame was aroused during a visit to Volgograd (formerly Stalingrad) in 2000. My diary entry for October 3, 2000, reads as follows:

I am sitting on a bench not far from my hotel, enjoying the hot sun, which is definitely no longer hot in Petersburg. This is the first time I have been in this town but everything in it seems surprisingly familiar. I grew up in Leningrad, in the backyards of Stalinist times, so the scrolls and pilasters of Stalinist classicism in the buildings here are quite familiar. The only things that surprise me are the colors and the light. Everything looks the same but has the appearance of an over-exposed photograph. The image fades in the brilliant white of the southern sun. The Central Children's Park where I have deposited myself is practically empty. In the middle of the park is an obelisk built of artificial cobblestones. It's made of plaster or some such thing and bears the laconic inscription—Yakov Serman. Who was he? I have no idea. Behind a row of berberis bushes, sparsely planted alongside some bare wooden notice-boards—perhaps they used to carry notifications about people who had died or been honored—someone is walking to and fro. I take a look—a flasher!! On the central alley just opposite me a middle-aged woman and an old biddy in a headscarf are sharing scandal about a neighbor. I have a sense of dé ja vu. I am sitting in a park from my childhood.

In Soviet times Parks of Rest and Culture all looked very similar. They displayed the same banal ideological and educational messages—an ugly monument to some obscure sportsperson or Soviet hero, placards with portraits of shock workers (*udarnik truda*), bulletin boards. Now that none of that had any relevance I could relax. I almost felt nostalgic. The park even had a certain retro-charm.

After the park I strolled down the main street, Leninskii prospekt, toward the Square of Fallen Warriors (Ploshchad' pavshikh bortsov). In the middle of the square, which honors those killed during the Civil War, there is an obelisk with a granite memorial holding another eternal flame. I saw that some school children had formed a guard of honor beside the flame and was rather taken aback to realize that in the year 2000 this essentially Soviet ritual still continued. In the Soviet Union the widespread construction of war memorials, particularly obelisks and memorials containing an eternal flame or torch, began toward the end of the 1950s. It became customary to invite the most outstanding grade schoolers or cadets to form guards of honor. They were always smartly dressed in school or cadet uniforms, and it was considered a great privilege to be chosen. In fact, as I learned later, this custom was being reinstated—or indeed, introduced for the first time—in many towns in the early years of the new millennium and continues to the present day.

My next objective was the memorial complex Mamaev Kurgan (Mamai's burial mound),[2] situated on the rising ground where the battles for Stalingrad took place during World War II. Under the ground are the communal graves of around thirty-five thousand soldiers killed in those battles. Mamaev Kurgan struck me as being both huge and virtually "uninhabited." The great sweep of land on which the complex is constructed, the gigantic statue of the Motherland—a warrior-maiden with upraised sword, summoning her subjects into battle—the enormous hand emerging from the floor in the Hall of Military Fame (Zal voinskoi slavy) bearing aloft a flaming torch, together with the many monuments of gargantuan proportions, all seemed designed to dwarf and dominate the human visitor. The intrinsic "emptiness" of gigantic structures of this kind, which have never had a utilitarian function (or which long ago lost their original purpose), may easily be filled with symbolic or cult significance.

I was astonished not only by the absence of any obvious practical purpose for the outsized construction but also by the massive expenditure that had evidently gone into its creation, and this against the background of the general asceticism of Soviet architecture typical of the 1960s. Why had the Soviet state committed such exorbitant funds to such an apparently useless object? What caused such extravagance for a place of mourning?

My main question, however, was as follows: How and why had the tradition of the eternal flame been created in Russia? I could find no parallels to explain it in Russian folklore or ethnography. Some ethnographical similarities may be found in the custom recorded in the nineteenth century known as "warming the dead" (*gret' pokoinikov*). This took place just before Christmas when the peasants lit bonfires in their yards and "remembered" their ancestors. "The peasants are convinced," commented D. K. Zelenin, "that alongside them, although invisible, their forefathers too warm themselves at the bonfire" (Zelenin 1991, 401). Another memorial custom associated with fire was the lighting of a bonfire near a cemetery after a funeral had taken place. It was kindled with the wood shavings left over from the making of the coffin. People would jump over the flames in the belief that this would help to overcome their fear of the dead (Razova 1994, 168–69). The closest parallel I could find in Orthodox ritual was the custom of lighting lamps and candles beside the relics of saints and on the graves of venerated holy men. In addition to the devotional candles of Orthodoxy, Nina Tumarkin has suggested the "heroic images" of the ancient Greek Olympic games as possible antecedents or that the flames themselves are symbols of "life in all its dissonant complexity" (Tumarkin 1994, 126). However, none of these examples bring us closer to an understanding of the cultural and ideological significance of the eternal flame. Explaining the sense and function of a symbolic act by searching for its prototype does not, in any case, allow us to understand the point of an act, the need for that particular act in a given historical and social context. In 1918 the Soviet regime relegated funeral affairs to the civil and domestic sphere and death became merely a question of "civil status" (Sokolova 2011, 187–202; Sokolova 2018, 74–94). In other words, the dead were nothing more than decaying corpses to be disposed of. From an atheistic point of view, they could never be the recipients of any kind of message. Why did the atheistic regime need this symbolic project, and what kind of social action took place in these ritual arenas?

THE FIRST RITUAL ARENA OF THE SOVIET ERA

It occurred to me that the lighting of the first eternal flame might be associated with the construction on the Field of Mars of the first piece of memorial architecture after the October revolution. However, although ideologically sound, this idea turned out to be factually incorrect.

After the February revolution of 1917 a pressing question arose: where to bury the many hundreds of victims of the vicious street battles and clashes with the tsarist police. This became the subject of lengthy debate, and many different sites were proposed. One proposal would have involved removing the Alexander Column in order to bury the corpses, those "victims of tsarism," at Palace Square, right in front of the windows of the Winter Palace.[3] In the end, the Field of Mars was chosen as the burial ground, and in March 1917 the bodies, which had lain unburied for almost a month, were finally laid to rest there.[4] This was the first ceremonial public burial to be carried out in Russia that broke the rules of ecclesiastical custom, dispensing with a funeral service, crosses over the graves, and even a cemetery.[5]

The writer Ivan Bunin described the procedure as follows:

I saw the Field of Mars, upon which, like some traditional act of sacrifice to the revolution, there had just now been enacted the comedy of the funeral for those heroes who had supposedly fallen in the cause of freedom. What need was there for this mockery of the dead, for depriving them of a decent Christian burial, for nailing them in coffins that were for some reason red, and, against all natural instincts, interring them right in the middle of a city of the living! The comedy was played out with total lack of thought, and after insulting the modest remains of these unknown dead with their high-flown rhetoric, they proceeded to dig up and trample this magnificent square, disfiguring it with burial mounds and sticking tall, naked posts all over it, draped with long, black strips of cloth. Then, for some reason, they fenced it in with wooden palings, hastily nailed together and no less disgusting in their barbaric simplicity than the posts. (Bunin 2000, 157–58).

The decision at the beginning of the 1920s to undertake the reconstruction of the Field of Mars was prompted by the pressing need to replace the temporary burial ground and place of remembrance described by Bunin. In fact, the new memorial arena was to be the first major project of Soviet architecture.

IMMORTALITY AND ETERNAL MEMORY

In the middle of September 1918, A. V. Lunacharskii, who was at the time commissar for education, wrote the following to Vladimir Il'ich Lenin regarding the proposed memorial to the heroes of the revolution: "Here are some of the inscriptions I have thought up myself, if you are interested. 1. Those who fell in a great cause are immortal. Those who laid down their lives for the people, who labored and struggled and died for the common good live forever among the people. 2. Since not all heroes who shed their blood in the struggle for freedom were known by name, the human race honors the nameless. To honor and remember all for many years to come this stone was erected" ("Lunacharskii-Leninu" 1971, 80:82). Lunacharskii's words provide the key to understanding the significance with which this cult edifice under construction was to be endowed: those who died for the common good were immortal. The common good had become a holy objective, and the normative response to that objective was self-sacrifice. Immortality would be guaranteed through the memory of those who came after and would be humanity's reward—"the human race honors them"— for accomplishing it. The word "immortality" in this context takes on a new meaning that can easily be gauged by comparing dictionary entries. If we look, for example, at Vladimir Dal''s nineteenth-century dictionary we find that the primary meanings for "immortality" (*bezsmertie, bezsmertnost'*) are given as follows: "Not susceptible to death, a property, characteristic or quality of the undying, the eternally existing or living; the spiritual life, unending and independent of the flesh." As a secondary meaning we find: "The habitual, extended memory of a person on earth, according to his merits or works." Similarly, "immortal" (*bezsmertnyi*) is defined as "undying, living eternally, gifted with a spiritual life," with the secondary meaning of "unforgettable, living on in the memory" (Dal' 1955, 1:73). In 1948 the first volume of the *Dictionary of the Contemporary Russian Literary Language* (*Slovar' sovremennogo russkogo literaturnogo yazyka*) was published, after a long delay because of World War II. This seventeen-volume dictionary became the gold standard, the arbiter of meaning in the Russian language for all educators, students, academics, writers, and members of the general Soviet public. While not ignoring more historical meanings, it specifically pushed to the forefront those that had the greatest contemporary currency and reflected the ideological transformations that had taken place since the revolution. Furthermore, its illustrative material began with examples from contemporary, rather than classical literature. Here, the primary definition of "immortality" is as follows: "Eternal existence in people's memory, being unforgettable" (*Slovar' sovremennogo russkogo literaturnogo yazyka* 1948, 1:427). In other words, this is an echo of the shift in meaning envisaged by Lunacharskii.

By way of illustration, the dictionary provides examples from characteristic Soviet literary works, including the following: "Almost above the snow by now, the young girl, barefoot and pushing her slender body onward, walks forward into immortality (M. Aliger 'Zoya')." Margarita Aliger's poem describes the apotheosis of Zoya Kosmodem'yanskaya, the schoolgirl partisan executed in occupied Russia by the German army in 1941. For this work the writer was awarded the Stalin Prize in 1943. A further example from Maksim Gor'kii's novel *The Mother* (*Mat'*) states the postrevolutionary ideal of "immortality" even more clearly: "I believe, comrades, in the immortality of honest people, in the immortality of those who gave me the happy chance to live the beautiful life I live now." The final example for the entry on immortality is a historical reference to the lyric verse of Aleksandr Pushkin—prescribed reading in Soviet schools. Pushkin, it is pointed out, prized gaining immortality through his art above the eternal life of his soul.

A second definition of immortality is given as "eternal existence, the never-ending being of matter." "Immortal" is defined as "remaining forever in people's memory; unforgettable, retaining an eternal significance, as in 'Lenin is with us, immortal and majestic' ('Lenintsy,' *Mayak*)." The notion of an immortal soul is mentioned at the end of the entry without further commentary (*Slovar' sovremennogo russkogo literaturnogo yazyka* 1948, 1:427).

The new notion of immortality transformed it into an act independent of the individual's personal fate or choice. Instead it became the result of external evaluation of the individual by society.

FROM THE MEMORIAL SQUARE TO THE ETERNAL FLAME

The work of reconstruction on the Field of Mars involved creating a square with a monumental wall around the graves of "the warriors of revolution." The architect I. Fomin was responsible for the design of the square as a whole while the wall was designed by L. Rudnev (Bartenev and Batazhkova 1983, 218). Right in the middle of the memorial was a flower bed in the shape of a star. According to one version of the memorial, which was not used in the end, there should have been an obelisk in the center. The unextinguishable, "eternal" flame would appear on the burial ground only forty years later, in autumn 1957. Its establishment, however, would have the same aim as that formulated earlier by Lunacharskii— that is, to guarantee eternal life through the memory of succeeding generations:

> To mark the fortieth anniversary of the Great October Socialist Revolution and with the aim of immortalizing the memory of those who fought for the revolution and fell for the freedom of the people, the Executive Committee of the Leningrad Soviet [Lenispolkom] of Workers' Deputies passed a resolution regarding the

construction of a grave slab incorporating a lamp with an unextinguishable flame on the place of burial, on the Field of Mars, of the victims of the Great October Socialist Revolution, the project to be designed by the architect Maiofis. (*Byulleten' ispolkoma Lengorsoveta deputatov trudyashchikhsya* 1957)

It is interesting that the initiative for the construction of the flaming lamp seems to have come entirely from Leningrad. The official opening took place on November 7 while the resolution of the Leningrad executive committee received a mention in the bulletin that came out after the event on November 30. Only one newspaper (*Leningradskaya pravda*) published a piece about the event, and that was on page 8:

> Comrade Spiridonov (First Secretary of the Leningrad City Party Committee) proposed the lighting of the eternal, unextinguishable flame, symbol of the great torch of the proletarian revolution, in memory of those warriors who gave their lives for the revolution. P. I. Kulyabko, the oldest Communist Party member in Leningrad (she has been a member since 1898) and V. N. Smirnov, secretary of the city committee of the Komsomol, approached the center of the Field of Mars and lit the eternal flame on the granite slab. ("Vechnyi ogon' na Marsovom Pole" 1957, 8)

The mythological and ritual development of this innovation took place in the 1960s and later. With the help of a torch lit from the flame on the Field of Mars, the fire was transferred and used to light many other memorials and communal gravesites, for example in the Piskarevskoe and Serafimovskoe cemeteries in Leningrad in 1960 and 1966, respectively. These places contained the mass burial sites of civilians who died of starvation in Leningrad during the blockade. When, in 1967, the memorial Grave of the Unknown Soldier was unveiled in Moscow, the torch that set ablaze the eternal fire there was also lit from the fire on the Field of Mars: "The heroes of the revolution have been joined by the heroes of the Great Patriotic War. Carrying on the tradition of the eternal flame symbolizes the immortality of the heroic deeds of those generations who fought for the idea of the victory of socialism" (Kalinin 1986, 8).

In Russian funerary ritual there is a particular category of dead, those who have died a death that was "not their own" (*ne svoeyu smert'yu*), or who died before their time. This category was first analyzed in depth by Dmitrii Zelenin (Zelenin 1911, 354–424) and was one of the themes addressed in the preceding chapter on Troitsa customs. During the Soviet period, with the proliferation of memorials for those who died in revolutions and wars, marked by the symbol of the eternal flame, it is clear that we are dealing with a new type of untimely death, one that granted the status of sacrificial holiness.

The basis for marking out these "fiery" spaces was the assumption that these dead understood the teleology of their own deaths. They died "for the common good," represented by the victory of socialism. The fact that in reality this was not always the case is simply a matter of common sense. The victims of the "victory of socialism" included the citizens of Leningrad who died of hunger and cold during the siege by the German army (1941–44). It is difficult to see how their deaths could be regarded as a freely chosen acceptance of suffering in the cause of socialism. The same could be said of the deaths of those killed on the street during the February revolution of 1917.

P. Vail' and A. Gennis have pointed out that in the 1960s, during the proliferation of war memorials across the territory of the USSR, alongside the established view of the Great Patriotic War as a war to prevent the destruction of the world's first socialist state, another version began to gain ground. The war was presented as a struggle against universal evil: "The people's war evolved into a holy war, into a matter, not merely of state, or historical importance, but into a mythological event, like the battle between the gods and the titans" (Vail' and Gennis 1998, 91). I should mention that, in fact, the war had already been referred to as "holy" as early as 1941 in the words to a song by V. I. Lebedev-Kumach for which A. Aleksandrov composed the music. "There's a war on, a people's war, a holy war" (*svyashchennaya voina*). The Great Patriotic War was referred to as holy because of the faith in the triumph of socialism that provided its ostensible underpinnings. It is interesting to note the change in emphasis applied to the various meanings of *svyashchennyi* and *svyatoi*, which may be translated as "holy" or "sacred" depending on context, from prerevolutionary to Soviet times. The nineteenth-century dictionary by Vladimir Dal' does not define *svyatoi* (which can also mean "saintly") as a religious term, taking this as self-evident, and by far the majority of the dictionary illustrations relate to what is regarded as pure and holy in the spiritual sense—the Holy Spirit, the saints, the Holy Fathers, the martyrs, and so on. A secondary meaning for "everything that is cherished and dear, connected with truth and the good" produces "the holy fatherland" (*otchizna*) and "sacred duty" (Dal' 1955, 4:161). On the other hand, in the dictionary edited by D. N. Ushakov and compiled in the 1930s, although references to the spiritual dimensions of these expressions are by no means absent, each example is offered as a "religious term" or a term used in "the Christian cult." In this matter Ushakov's dictionary presumed or even imposed upon its readership a narrower and more secular field of understanding. References to subsidiary meanings for *svyatoi*, for example ("what is revered, dear or cherished," what is "majestic in its mission" or of "exceptional importance," what is "unshakeable, indestructible") are greatly increased, with illustrations from Soviet leaders, among others: "'Communists, act together with non-Party workers and form a friendly block for a common and holy act, for the election of the highest organs of your Soviet homeland' (Molotov)"; "The defense of the socialist fatherland is the sacred obligation of the toiling masses"; "Sacred duty"; "'The laws and prescriptions of Soviet power must be devoutly (*svyato*, lit., "in a holy manner") observed' (Lenin)" (Ushakov 1940:4). In other words, the secular meanings of "holy" and "sacred" have become both dominant and evaluative rather than ontological, and the concept of "holiness," as the inner experience of attaining the metaphysical, has been replaced by whatever was the accepted norm in the prevailing discourse.

THE ETERNAL FIRE IN LATER SOVIET MYTHOLOGY

In the late 1960s to early 1970s, more specifically mythological interpretations of eternal fire began to appear. M. Postupal'skii, in his book for children *Forever Alive: Stories about Fire* (*Vechno zhivoi: Rasskazy ob ogne*), which had a print run of fifty thousand copies, wrote as follows: "Where there is fire there is warmth and light. There are people there! Fire lives in the huge blast furnace and trembles on the wick of a candle. It burns in the big chalice on the graves of warriors and surrounds the burner on the gas stove with a blue halo. It lights up the sky with fireworks on festive occasions and scatters in sparks from the funnel of an old steam engine" (Postupal'skii 1967, 2). The fire lit over a grave finds itself in close company with the fire of the gas stove and a firework display. Another possible archaic prototype of our eternal flame is also offered: "In ancient times, not far from Baku, in Surakhi, a tall chimney was constructed. It drew natural gas from underground. This chimney was raised above the temple of fire-worshippers" (Postupal'skii 1967, 75). "In all fires may be seen," the author continues, "the reflection of the primordial bonfires that once upon a time burned in caves. Even today, the spark of this ancient fire has not gone out. In our time too it is customary to keep fire burning in places that are especially dear to us, memorable places, such as the cemeteries where the warriors who fell in the battles for their native land are buried" (Postupal'skii 1967, 79). The symbolic vocabulary of fire has become more complicated, connecting, as if related, the ritual fires of fire-worshippers, where fire is a means of accessing metaphysical forces, the bonfires of our cave-dwelling ancestors, where fire is a sign of man's victory over nature, and the fires lit over the graves of those who perished in revolution and war.

A reference to yet another source of meaning for the eternal flame may be found in V. A. Kandybko's book *Fire from the Field of Mars*:

On the eve of the fortieth anniversary of the Great October Socialist Revolution the workers of Leningrad, representatives of social organizations and military groups . . . came to the communal graves on the Field of Mars. Here, to the sound of "The Internationale," the eternal fire was lit. From then on it has burned continuously as a symbol of the great ideas of October. The prophetic words of the American journalist Alberto Rio Williams, great friend of Soviet Russia, have come true. As early as 1917 he wrote: "The light of justice will shine, not from the torch of the Statue of Liberty in New York, but from the holy graves of the Field of Mars, where those who fought for socialism lie at rest." (Kandybko 1980, 4–5)

The light of these gas-powered lamps, with their eternal flame, indicates a place where a particular kind of burial has taken place, the burial of those who died an untimely death. The memorials, moreover, attribute to those who are buried there a heroic motive for their own destruction. The eternal flame is an element of a ritual structure that simultaneously addresses the dead and the living. The memorial guarantees the dead immortality through the memory of succeeding generations, but what message is sent to the living visitors to these places?

SOVIET INITIATION RITUALS

My main concern is not with the genesis or typology of the symbol of the eternal flame. What interests me is the means by which an ideological subject may be transformed into a personal past and a concept into a historical fact. Created in modern times, a cult object very quickly turned into a social institution, mechanically transforming the many individual worlds of citizens into one common reality.

The Soviet state allocated significant areas of land, maintained strict control over the choice of artists and artisans involved in the creation of the symbolic artifacts, kept a watchful eye on the subject matter and emotional content of art works, and did not spare the material resources for the successful completion of projects. All this was carried out, furthermore, to cater to the "spiritual" needs of the Soviet people. These gardens of stone, these arenas for meditation, these spaces full of symbolic content were specifically created for the purpose of influencing the spiritual life of the people:

As a rule, the memorials consist of an enclosed compositional whole, clearly separated from its everyday surroundings. For this reason they are often situated in parks or squares and most often out of town, in a natural setting. The memorial complexes are arranged in such a way as to encourage visiting in a set order, considering both temporal and spatial dimensions and with viewing organized along dramatic lines—first the opening scenes, then the development, followed by the dénouement and the finale. As a result, visitors experience a heightened spiritual state, akin to the catharsis of classical tragedy, which, indeed, is the aim and the whole point of the artistic exercise. (V. P. Tolstoi 1978, 112)

These large ritual arenas, strictly set aside for the purpose on particular days—the special "red" days of the Soviet calendar—became the established venues for initiation or calendar rituals such as joining the pioneer organization,[6] taking the oath of allegiance by young army conscripts, ceremonies in memory of fallen war heroes on Victory Day, or anniversary celebrations of significant events. The extent to which these cult ceremonies were stage-managed and controlled, as well as their sheer scale, is quite astonishing, and this is true not only of their creative side (the manipulation of space), but also of their infiltration into everyday life (the manipulation of time), all used to construct a common reality. A visit to one of these ritual venues was included in all the excursions planned by tourism agencies across the whole of the USSR. Even today attendance forms an obligatory element in the program of official visitors to certain locations.

Clearly, the torches lighting burial sites may be regarded as a further development of the effort to create new "holy places" since the first days of Soviet power. In place of the tombs of saints and the lamps shining upon them in the middle of churches, there was a new object of veneration—the remains of "those who fought for the cause" illuminated by a burning gas flare. Memorials with an eternal flame were often sited in populated areas—on the town square, for example.

The creations of Soviet propaganda reinterpreted Christian tradition. Note the following injunction on the front page of *Pionerskaya pravda* No. 7 on January 21, 1946: "'Oppose and defeat your enemies, both internal and external, as Il'ich [i.e., Vladimir Il'ich Lenin] has told you' (I. Stalin)." This message clearly echoes the prayer of the Holy Fathers against temptation by the devil: "Deliver me, O Lord, from the enemies within me and save me, Your servant, from my enemies without" (Ot vnutrennikh moikh izbavi mya, Bozhe, i ot chuzhdykh poshchadi raba Svoego).

Lenin's plan for a propaganda war against the commemoration of people or ideas that contradicted the ideals of the revolution was launched in a decree entitled "Regarding the removal of monuments raised to honor the tsars."[7] As those familiar with it commented, "It was organically linked to the great cause of the cultural revolution and with the colossal task of re-shaping human consciousness, which made possible the great days of October" (Shervud 1939, 50).

Objects located in space according to the ideology that defined them were intended to become, and did indeed become, instruments that helped to transform the inner space, the cognitive and emotional world of citizens. Eventually, the Lenin Mausoleum became the ideological focus of the propaganda surrounding monuments although Lenin himself, as the author of the propaganda project, almost certainly did not have this in mind: "A place was chosen for the Mausoleum on Red Square. It became a focal point for socialist Moscow, a platform close to the Kremlin wall where those who had fallen in the cause of the revolution were buried. . . . The difficulty lay in the need . . . to create a building which would express the *notion of the immortal nature* [my emphasis] of Lenin's great achievement" (Neiman 1957, 524–55). The eventual architectural profile of the mausoleum was the work of the architect A. V. Shchusev: "There is a rectangular block which forms, as it were, the base of the construction. . . . This is crowned by a pyramid in the form of graduated steps, at the top of which is a structure standing on columns or pillars. The most ancient traditions of memorials sited over graves have been utilized here, the prototype of these being the simple barrow raised over a burial" (Neiman 1957, 524). Shchusev chose the pyramid and the barrow mound because they were forms of burial chamber intended to last forever.

The idea of eternal life in the memory of the people, formulated by Lunacharskii and sketched out on the granite slabs of the Field of Mars in 1919, had thus progressed from the immortal nature of Lenin's deeds into the "factual" immortality of his body through embalming. Here are some extracts from the various appeals sent to Moscow immediately after Lenin's death:

Telegram from the Central Committee of the Russian Communist Party [Bolsheviks] to comrade Stalin: "The workers' organization of the factory 'Labor liberated' [Osvobozhdennyi trud] asks you to accept the following suggestion: We recommend that the body of our deeply respected Vladimir Il'ich should be buried on Red Square, so that every worker or peasant passing through Red Square will be able to communicate with dear Il'ich with both *their minds and their hearts.*" [my emphasis]

We, the followers . . . of our dear Vladimir Il'ich Lenin . . . ask the funeral commission not to bury the body of Lenin in the ground like an ordinary deceased person. . . . We must replace the figure of Lenin with our serried ranks.

Lenin's funeral must usher in the resurrection of the proletariat of world revolution. (Zbarskii 2000, 46–49)

These texts show that the idea of Lenin's immortality vacillates between two different notions. On the one hand we have the notion of eternal life, allowing communication with Lenin using one's mind or heart. This produced a number of well-known slogans, such as "Lenin is always alive," "Lenin is always with you," and "Lenin is in you and in me." The spirit of one man relocates itself in a multitude of other people. All members of that fellowship dedicated to continuing the common cause become bearers of that one spirit. On the other hand, we have the notion of resurrection. Why else would Lenin's embalmed body be lying in one piece in his mausoleum? Clearly, he was waiting for the miracles of Soviet science to bring him back to life.

In 1946 Anatolii Kononov, leader of one of the pioneer organization sections at School No. 203 in Moscow, wrote the following in *Pionerskaya pravda*: "Now we are at the entrance to the Mausoleum. At the entrance everyone takes their hat off and we all slowly make our way down to where Lenin's body lies at rest. It is quiet all around. All that can be heard is the muffled shuffling of feet. I feel a sort of lump in my throat and have trouble holding back my tears. Next to me walks an Uzbek from Fergana. By the coffin he slows down. . . . And each one of us wants to retain the image of the dear face for a long time" (Kononov 1946, 7:3).

I spoke to my friends, acquaintances, and relatives about this mystical feeling toward Lenin, about the mausoleum, the eternal flame, and similar phenomena. The following comments are taken from interviews I conducted in St. Petersburg in February 2001:

My grandad was from a peasant family. At one time he sang in a church choir. He finished university here in Leningrad, worked conscientiously throughout the siege, kept faith with the Party. Grandad even painted a portrait of Lenin and hung it over the table. . . . I drew a portrait of Lenin too, a pencil drawing. When I was probably in the third class [i.e., about nine years old], during all the naming and shaming of the illegal traffickers [*fartsovshchiki*],[8] I remember thinking all the time that if grandad Lenin was still alive he would be so upset to find there were people like these traffickers. (SA field notes, St. Petersburg, February 2001; the informant was a forty-two-year-old female)

We were on a trip to visit granny and grandad. They lived just outside Moscow. This was in 1957. I was seven and my brother was four. The mausoleum was the biggest sight-seeing attraction in Moscow. I remember there was a huge queue, several rows wide. It was very interesting when the guard was changed and they marched out. We stood for ages, two or three hours. We stood it out, even the little ones. My father picked up my little brother. They said infants should be carried so they could see. Lenin and Stalin were laid out on a sort of raised area. We walked round them and went out by a side door. I remember they were under glass. I was really surprised that Lenin was so small, all shriveled up. He looked unnatural. He had such a little face. . . . At that time this was probably considered to be the center of Moscow, the center of Russia, the Red Square with the mausoleum. There was nothing else in the way of spiritual values. (SA field notes, St. Petersburg, February 2001; the informant was a fifty-year-old female)

Descriptions such as these are absolutely typical. People's experiences bear witness to the fact that the ideological interpretation of the figure of Lenin as "the conscience of our age" had been assimilated and that what had started out as an ideological slogan had become a cultural imperative (see Tumarkin 1997 for discussion of the "cult of Lenin"). A. Plutser-Sarno has this to say:

The body lying in the mausoleum is not only a tribute to the past, it is a fact of continuing mass communication with the world of the dead. The mausoleum itself is, on the one hand, a sort of "chapel" where lies a body subject to perpetual funeral obsequies. From that point of view, all talk of an unchristian, nonritualized attitude to this body is unjustified. . . . On the other hand, the mausoleum is also a grave, a place of burial. . . . It offers a unique chance to peep into the grave, to step over the boundary of the coffin boards and visit the realm beyond the grave. . . . We cannot rebury the body without having explained to ourselves whom we intend to bury, for what reason, where, and in what way. (Plutser-Sarno 2001, 330)

For Russians, a personal relationship with the "incorruptible" Lenin will continue until interest in his body and the positive and negative emotional reactions to his deeds have faded.

THE EXPERIENCE OF THE "INITIATED"

As I have already indicated, my research into the question of how and why the creation of eternal fires became a tradition in Russia began in Volgograd. During my visit I was one of a very small group of visitors watching the changing of the guard of honor at Mamaev Kurgan. The anonymous inscriptions on the memorial walls leading into the Hall of Military Fame provided a uniform surface of platitudes—Soviet mantras, slogans bereft of authors and addressed to no one in particular: "The Party is the organizer of victories"; "Victory brings all the fun of the fair"; "The battle for Stalingrad was the greatest in history"; "Long live the Party of Lenin, the inspirer and organizer of all our victories"; "On our street good times are here again"; "Our people will preserve the memory of the greatest battle in the history of war."

The graffiti on the monument represent a direct continuation of the propaganda slogans that proliferated during the first years of the revolution. At that time, temporary, plaster-molded memorial boards were erected with the same slogans repeated time and again—"Religion is the opium of the masses," "Workers of the world unite," "The task of science is to serve the people," and so on (Neiman 1957, 33–34). The anonymity of graffiti means that they are addressed to everyone who reads them. However, by contrast with graffiti in other public places, the slogans on the monument do not expect a written reply.

In order to give some idea of the various meanings ascribed to the monumental structures of Mamaev Kurgan, I would like to introduce a description from a guidebook published at the beginning of the 1970s: "In front of us the panorama of the Square of Heroes opens up. In the middle is a huge expanse of water. Six sculptural compositions depict the heroic deeds of warriors. On the side opposite the sculptures there is a wall, over one hundred meters high and in the shape of an unfurled flag, on which we may read the words, 'An iron wind buffeted their faces but still they marched onward and once more the enemy was gripped by a sense of supernatural dread: Were these human beings marching into the attack, were they mortal?'" (Naumenko, Loginov, and Merinova 1973, 160).

Reading these words, I experienced a certain emotional tremor, something familiar to me from childhood. My attempt to remember and name exactly what lay behind it produced the following thesis. Essentially, every Soviet citizen in his ultimate form was a hero. He was immortal, as even his enemies acknowledged. I too was a Soviet citizen and therefore belonged to that fellowship of heroes. Writing this was considerably less complicated than the feelings I had on the steps of the memorial. What I had observed was a part of my inner reality. The drums of my tribe were beating! My inner self reacted emotionally to those symbols that my eyes easily picked out from other visual objects and that my anthropological experience of descriptive analysis allowed me to identify as ideological constructs. The latter led me to wonder whether my reactions not only were personal and individual but also might have a wider resonance.

The guidebook continues: "The answer to the question [i.e., were they mortal, those Soviet warriors?] is given in an inscription in the Hall of Military Fame: 'Yes, we were ordinary mortals and few of us survived but we fulfilled our patriotic duty to our holy motherland'" (Naumenko, Loginov, and Merinova 1973, 160). In the middle of the hall is a huge marble hand holding a torch with the Eternal fire—the hand of a giant buried in the earth. The idea of a slow processional movement around this memorial with the fire at its center is integral to the architect's design. I have observed something similar in a crematorium when the person in charge of the ritual suggested that everyone present, before approaching the deceased, should walk all the way round the coffin "to indicate bidding farewell." This symbolic gesture of parting was particularly surprising since it has no basis in either ecclesiastical or traditional practice in Russia. In traditional rituals circular movement around an object is a magic act designed for protection. People may circle around a house carrying an icon in order to protect it during a fire. When transferring his flock to their summer pastures the shepherd or herdsman might encircle his beasts to protect them from pestilence, wild animals, and so on. During epidemics, in a rite known as "ploughing around" (*opakhivanie*), villagers would encircle their village harnessed to a plough. The object or objects at the center of these circular ritual movements require ritual protection. In the crematorium the center was occupied by a corpse. At Mamaev Kurgan it was occupied by an enormous hand carrying a flaming torch, thrusting up from underground. Visitors to Mamaev Kurgan who have completed their funerary circumambulation of the eternal flame proceed to the next level of the monument. Here, we find a concrete sculpture—a grieving female figure bowed over the dead body of a young man, whose face is concealed under the folds of a military flag. The image clearly mirrors that of Michelangelo's fifteenth-century sculpture of the sorrowful Mother of Christ, holding his body after the descent from the cross. The inscription alongside reads: "Your name unknown, your deed immortal." Perhaps the covered face of the figure is a reflection of his anonymity. However, it still seems an odd choice, particularly if we remember another tradition requiring the covering of the deceased's face—namely, the monastic rule that a dead monk's face should be hidden from view. I have myself witnessed the ritual of placing a fine cloth over a dead monk's face to symbolize a covering of air. The guidebook explains that the sculpture expresses deep sorrow and the protest of all women against war, which destroys millions of lives (Naumenko, Loginov, and Merinova 1973, 161).

Forty years after the raising of that "simple burial mound," the mausoleum over the body of the eternally living Lenin, the Square of Sorrow (Ploshchad' skorbi), one of the most important ritual arenas in the Soviet Union, had evolved, with its reworking of the Catholic Pietà set over the graves of the "immortal" dead, into a new form of apotheosis. The adepts of the myth to which those taking part in the memorial rituals subscribed also created the poetic, artistic, and other cultural texts of the Soviet era. Indeed, the participants in the ritual and the adepts of the myth were one and the same. The notion of the Soviet people being one mystic whole, in which each individual is only a part of the whole, and is precisely for that reason immortal, is one of the dominant themes of Soviet literature of the war and postwar period: "'Our enemy is a difficult one, comrades. His stand against us brings death. But we are not afraid of death. After the German we'll take on death itself and defeat it in the same way, because the science and knowledge of future generations will be so much further developed. People then will no longer be like us. Our sufferings will form the nucleus of their great soul'" (Platonov 1985, 55).

In other words, once physical death has been conquered, by means of Lenin's theory of knowledge, immortality awaits everyone who "laid down his life for the common good." Equally true is that everyone—that is, every Soviet person—is a hero, prepared to lay down his or her life for the good of the people: "The future required a solid foundation. But what could be more solid than twenty million dead? The war had all the advantages of an obvious fact. It had been won by 'the people,' who had carried out the revolution. That meant one could consider, therefore, that the revolution was actually the cause of victory. That meant that, in spite of all the crimes of the socialist regime, it had passed a formidable test. And now, washed by the blood of millions, this same regime was leading the Soviet people toward the rehabilitated heights of Communism" (Vail' and Gennis 1998, 92).

In literary texts thematically based on the myth I have been exploring, self-sacrifice for the good of society was evaluated not as an ideal but as the norm. It guaranteed the shared life of the community and exalted it as something of absolute value, for the sake of which the sacrifice of an individual life was not an extraordinary event but a natural occurrence:

> "Our people, you know," said the doctor, "are ready to accept any sacrifices."
>
> "What sacrifices?" asked Danilov. "A sacrifice is made to someone, isn't that right? You can't make a sacrifice to yourself. What you call a sacrifice is a natural function of the people—your function, my function, the function of those little girls. The heroic achievement of our people was not a sacrifice but just an everyday occurrence. In order for us to continue to exist as the Soviet people, a part of us may have to die today. Maybe I'll be killed, maybe you or Petrov or Ivanov. Is this a sacrifice? To whom is the sacrifice made? To me, or you, Petrov or Ivanov?"
>
> "You can't convince me there is no such thing as a heroic deed, that it's just some sort of a function. . . . Not everyone is capable of a heroic deed. You have to have a talent for it."
>
> "Talents develop," said Danilov. "In this war such talents will develop that the whole world will gasp. Talent is not something the lord god blows into an individual. It is created by education, by one's environment . . . by circumstance."
> (Panova 1978, 62–63)

Tales of heroes, warriors, activists, and sacrifices served as the initiatory myths that formed the cultural imperative common to every Soviet individual—the need to serve society:

There is nothing greater in this world to be proud of
Than to live without luxury and privilege,
To share your people's fate
In times of joy or suffering . . .
There is no greater reward in the world
Than to dissolve one's self in the body of the people.
(Drunina 1978, 6)

Initiation into the myth, whose direct consequence was acquisition of the imperative to serve society and the inclusion of the individual body into the general mystic body of the "Soviet people," was achieved through ritual. The rituals were reproduced in a multitude of ritual arenas, their precise form in a given space (obelisk, eternal flame, memorial park) determined by the individual memorial canon.

In the Russia of earlier times military gallantry, the willingness to die for the fatherland, was informed by notions of holy martyrdom, a good Christian death, and the joy of eternal life in the kingdom of heaven. In the Soviet myth, on the other hand, both the slaughtered soldiers and the innocent victims of Soviet times, embodied in bronze and concrete, morosely await the repayment of a debt: "I died for your sake. Are you worthy of my sacrifice?" My recollections of my own school days as well as the stories of my contemporaries bear witness to the emotional effect of such a question on the minds of the young and the endless sense of guilt accompanying it. This was certainly the case for the masses of youngsters undergoing initiation into the Pioneer organization. The following accounts are excerpts from interviews I conducted on this subject. They show how the driving power of the myth, the narrative that shaped our common past, formed those inescapable codes of behavior, that compulsion to service that so obviously influenced our life scenarios. Furthermore, if the myth itself was usually thrust upon us by some external system (in our case, school), any action or commentary suggesting adaptation of the myth was usually up to the individuals and their own experiences and reactions to life:

Do you remember we used to have the Pioneer organization? Once a year, in springtime, each district was responsible for making improvements along a section of the Road of Life.[9] On the Road of Life we sowed marigolds. I remember being given a package with seeds in the Pioneers' Palace,[10] and I struggled right across the town with this big sack, like a seed merchant! . . . I didn't think I was wasting my time. I still don't think it was a waste of time. It seems to me it was the right thing to do, one of the simplest ways of nurturing patriotism in a person. Respect for "the graves of our forefathers," if you like, and for "hearth and home."[11]

Same with the eternal flame you asked about. Of course we thought of it as a noble act. A bus was sent for us but I seem to remember that not everyone was allowed to go. It was a right you had to earn. First you might have to plant something around the school . . . or pick up candy wrappers and pieces of glass. Then, we were told, we'd be taken to the Road of Life to sow our marigolds. . . . We also formed guards of honor.

The same person remembered how, while his mother was still alive, they would always visit the Piskarevskoe cemetery on Victory Day to place sweets and bread on the graves of people who had died during the siege of Leningrad:

Such heroism, so much heroism! You couldn't put something on every grave. [The need to do this] was something that came from deep inside a person. . . . Nowadays, I go to Victory Square instead. It's perfectly natural for me to buy flowers and lay them beside the eternal flame,[12] and before that on the graves. You know, it is the accepted thing here. It's a ritual sanctified by tradition. . . . It's the place where people are buried who gave their lives so that we could live in the way we live now. I have to report back to them about the way I live because their lives were cut short. That generation had a raw deal. And there's nothing we can do to help them now. The dead don't need pensions. So that is why we build memorials for them. We take care of the memorials, bring flowers. A collective sacrifice, a collective repayment. They sacrificed themselves and we have to pay for it. (SA field notes, St. Petersburg, February 2001; the informant was a thirty-eight-year-old male)

Similar sentiments were expressed by other people I spoke to:

We probably only went a couple of times to lay flowers and on one occasion the ceremony for joining the Pioneers was held there—in the cemetery with communal war graves near our school. . . . There's a big obelisk there and some mounds— the communal graves. . . . A bunch of us from our block wove some dandelion wreaths and went to put them on the graves, because there was a statue of the Pietà there. Probably the idea came from our families. My grandfather died when I was six. We used to visit the graves together when I was very little. I went with my grandmother too. Grandad fought in the war and this theme was a tragic subject in our family.

Again, when I was about six years old, plus or minus, there was an episode I have remembered my whole life. I was playing in the cemetery with my friends from the block. There was a simple explanation for this. The paths there were always sprinkled with sand, and there was no sand anywhere else in the district.

We were sitting to the side on a little pathway building sand castles when an elderly woman came up to us and began to give us a telling-off. "How can you play here?!" It really stuck in my mind, made a huge impression. . . . This was a holy place. . . . Once, they held a ceremony for joining the Pioneers there. I was quite grown-up by then, a member of the Komsomol. . . . When we arrived there my heart began to flutter. It took my breath away. My throat constricted. I could sense the solemnity of the occasion. At the time I joined, the ceremony took place in the Artillery Museum. I was terribly nervous, sweating, shaking. I couldn't even say my name! There were so many emotions, the expectation of something momentous, that something was going to happen that would make you feel . . . We used to enjoy our Pioneer gatherings as a general leisure activity, but the theme of the Pioneer and categories of "good versus bad" and "honorable" versus "dishonorable" was something we were aware of. You had to do something noble. . . . We had Pioneer notebooks. . . . We had to write in our duties and about how we had carried them out, and I remember we wrote a story about the pioneer hero our street was named after (we lived in a partisan-pioneer district). When I was in the third class, perhaps, I read a book about Lenya Golikov.[13] . . . It was through books like these [books about the heroic exploits of children who were pioneer-heroes] that the military theme was introduced. . . . As far as pioneer-heroes are concerned I also remember we all wrote an essay about *The Street of the Younger Son*.[14] It was a book about a pioneer-hero and events on the Crimean peninsula. He acted as a liaison between the catacombs and the town. . . . In many respects, all the military literature that followed was viewed through the prism of that book. . . . All these stories about terrible deaths had the meaning that, well, that the person embodied the idea of giving up your life for an ideal, for your native land. You were obliged to achieve something in the name of a lofty purpose.

This woman remembered another incident from her childhood that illustrates the extent to which the mythology of child martyrdom had become ingrained. She and her classmates were helping to dig up turnips at a state farm:

Suddenly, one of the lads, officially classed as a "low-achieving hooligan," stood up and said "Oh! I found a grenade." Everyone stopped dead. . . . Then Lesha picked the thing up and carried it into the forest. From the logical point of view this was an idiotic gesture. We should all have left and called the adults, the bomb disposal experts. But it fell into the category "this is how a pioneer hero acts." Of course, no one said this aloud but internally we were all in total agreement that this had been the right thing to do. The hero of our day was "broad-shouldered and strong," with the letters GTO on his chest.[15] This stereotype of "goodness," such as protecting those who were younger, or carrying someone out of a fire, could suddenly emerge in the most extreme situations. When Lesha stood up and carried the grenade away from us it was as if he was saying "I will screen you with my body. I am Aleksandr Matrosov."[16] (SA field notes, St. Petersburg, February 2001; the informant was a thirty-two-year-old woman)

My last example concerns recollections of the visit to a school of the mother of another famous young war hero, Zoya Kosmodem'yanskaya, who was still a schoolgirl when she joined the partisans in 1941. She was captured in German occupied territory and executed. Her brother, who served in a tank regiment, was killed near Königsberg (Kaliningrad):

Zoya's mother was such a courageous woman. Truly not of this world. She told us that Zoya had explained to her younger brother she could tell from his eyes whether or not he had told the truth. Because she was so strong-willed her brother believed her and, apparently, in the classroom everyone believed she could tell who had stolen something. ... She was such a shining example, a model of uprightness, patriotism, courage—in everything. She was a good student. She always had top marks. . . . The mother told us how upset Zoya's brother was when they heard she had been killed. His detachment painted "For Zoya" on their tanks. There were terrible battles near Königsberg. The town was fortified. I heard about him later, when I was already working. I had some business there and went to see his grave. Of course I bought some flowers, laid them [on the grave]. (SA field notes, St. Petersburg, February, 2001; the speaker was a seventy-year-old woman)

The story about Zoya is particularly interesting as it portrays the young girl, and indeed her mother, as possessing almost supernatural powers that, in a different context, might have been attributed to the wise women of the villages.

The recollections of people born between the 1930s and 1970s who had had a "pioneer childhood" clearly suggest that the cultural imperative behind the ritualized "playing out" of the myth about duty to society as a duty to the dead has still retained, in the post-Soviet era, a significant influence on the way many of those who have undergone Soviet initiation rites see the world and behave in it. Every one of them needed fallen warriors.

Confirmation of this scenario may be found in the continuing popularity among young people of visits to war memorials and eternal flames as a part of the wedding ritual. In her book about wedding customs among urban Russians published in 1980, G. V. Zhirnova commented: "In our time, the route that takes the wedding party all around the town began to include a visit to memorials for soldiers killed in the war and the laying of flowers by the newlyweds alongside the Eternal Flame. This custom has become more and more widespread over the years. Nowadays, it may be found in the ritual not only of Russians, Ukrainians, and Belorussians but also of other peoples of the USSR" (Zhirnova 1980, 110).

According to Zhirnova, the explanation for this phenomenon lay in the fact that those about to enter into marriage were the children of the generation that had fought in the war. She saw a typological similarity between these visits in modern times to a war memorial and the visits made by an orphan bride, on the eve of her wedding, to the cemetery where her parents were buried—once an element of the traditional village wedding ceremony. During the ceremony the bride would ask her deceased parents for their blessing.

Zhirnova drew mainly on materials from the 1960s and 1970s. However, wedding cavalcades continue to include war memorials in their itinerary to the present day, drawn to these places by a quest for the "sanctification" of their union.

Heroism became the guarantor of public service. Those who took part in the memorial rituals heard the rallying call of the drum, and their deep-seated sense of guilt could never be eradicated. This dead soldier did not merely die. He died for you and you are in his debt. You will repay this debt to your native land, for whose sake the soldier was killed. The declaration of the memorial text about the free choice of death by one individual, the hero, became a pledge for the moral coercion of all. All Soviet citizens were obliged to live their lives "for that young lad" (za togo parnya) who was killed during World War II, in order to guarantee his descendants a life of peace. The song "For that Young Lad" (1972), based on a poem by Robert Rozhdestvenskii, with music by M. Fradkin, became a Soviet hit:

> Spring promises to be a long one.
> The field awaits its crop of first-rate grain.
> On this kindly earth I live my life—
> For myself and for that young lad.

As we saw from the recollections of our informants, the heroes of many Soviet books and tales about outstanding bravery during the war were young people, even children. The death of an adult impressed them less. "He was just a boy," people would sigh, as they remembered the stories.

It is no accident that the period that saw the memorialization of war heroes, including children—that is, the 1960s to 1970s—also witnessed the development of a new kind of children's folklore, the so-called "sadistic verses" (*sadistskie stishki*), in which revolutionary, pioneer, and war motifs were a consistent feature (Belousov 1992, 138–51; Belousov 1998, 545–77; Belousov 1999, 303–308). In other words, all these texts were based on hidden references to the various heroic themes that all children studied in school. It may well be that the genre owes its appearance to the collective trauma suffered by all the children initiated into the Soviet heroic myth. There was a need to protect oneself, through laughter, from the stories of martyred children and teenagers that everyone was obliged to know:

> Children in the cellar were playing "Gestapo,"
> Fiendishly torturing the plumber Potapov;
> Eight uniform caps, their stars in a row,
> A squad of Octobrists under a tramcar did go.
> The wheels took their time smashing their bones.
> They'll never join the Komsomol, these little ones.[17]

As A. Gennis and P. Vail' have pointed out, the strategies of the Soviet education system, which had a profound effect on the psychological formation of its citizens, also played a part in reinforcing behavioral conformity to the Soviet fatherland's expectations of gratitude and obedience:

> For example, the school poses the question, "Who broke the window?" What the school wants is not to find the guilty party but to reconstruct the child's mind, to redirect it toward a different system of values. The pupil behaves according to the moral code of his own group. Within the confines of this code it is natural and normal not to betray one's friends. . . . The school impresses upon the child that this kind of morality is *abnormal* [my emphasis]. . . . The child is presented with a choice—betray his friends or betray his country, the country that has given him the gift of a happy childhood. The child must remember that not informing is a crime, something akin to patricide. Disloyalty to his "big" family must be paid for by the torments of a guilty conscience. In this way the school lays the foundation of a sense of the world that always makes the individual feel ashamed for any act of protest. We have given him everything but he . . . it is like biting the hand that feeds you. (Vail' and Gennis 1998, 118)

Before the 1917 revolution it was the father who was the breadwinner (lit. "the one who feeds," *kormyashchii*). In Russia's patriarchal system it was the eldest male who supported the family and was in charge of its property. If we use the Vail' and Gennis metaphor we can say that the "hand that feeds" was indeed the hand of the father. World War I posters called for the defense of the fatherland ("The fatherland is in danger!"). The land to which its Russian citizens belonged was a land of fathers (*otechestvo*, from *otets*, "father"). However, from the end of the 1930s, the Russian native land was referred to as "mother." Posters from 1941 summoned her sons to the defense of the "Birthland-mother" (Rodina-mat'). The "father-feeder" (*kormilets-otets*) had been transformed into the "Birthland-mother." This change of mythological emphasis destroyed the possibility of a classical dénouement of the Oedipus conflict, the conflict between father and son, the resolution of which creates a generational change whereby the son replaces his father, taking over his position of power. The Birthland-mother of Soviet mythology took upon itself the sacredness of the Mother of God, who had no place in the Soviet atheistic pantheon. It was possible to fight and to die for Mother Russia. However, how one should live with, or in her, was not known. There was no scenario for how to lead the "noble" or "heroic" life in times of peace. Those initiated into the cult of the Birthland-mother, the Pioneers and Komsomol members, together with all who lived in the Soviet land, must always be ready to sacrifice everything for her cause—their labor, their lives, and their children. Acts of protest were impossible since protest was an act of betrayal against the Mother, and "biting the hand that feeds" was forbidden.

If, by the 1970s and 1980s, the outward forms of the Soviet rituals were indeed for most people only form—a demonstration of loyalty to the regime or a technique of social adaptation—behind those forms lay a specific content that was impervious to doubt. For want of a different model, the same imperative to lead "noble" lives and experience "noble" feelings survived into post-Soviet times: "I walked up to the Eternal Fire. They were changing the guard. The chimes of the Kremlin clock rang out crisp and perfect, fulfilling their ritual duty. . . . Suddenly, I felt something stirring in my heart. It was as if I was in contact with the land of my birth" (Petrova 2001, 4).

An ideology remains just an ideology until those who wield political power begin to manipulate and disseminate it for their own purposes. When it becomes the ideology of the masses and shapes the worldview of those masses, it is converted into mythology. The instrument for this conversion is ritual. A ritual action, in contrast with other social procedures (including procedures of repression), always has a voluntary element since it is aimed at transforming the inner world, the souls of those who perform it. Opening oneself up to allow such a transformation to take place can only be done on a voluntary basis. Thus, the mythological reality—the worldview accepted by the acolytes—and the social reality constructed according to the laws of the myth with which they have chosen to arm themselves both stem from the initiates' free choice. The idea of service for the benefit of society, based on a sense of duty to the dead—whose lives you continue to live for them, whose cause is now your cause—became a cultural imperative formed through the medium of Soviet memorial rituals. Those mythological models in whose honor the rituals were held were drawn from different sources—victims of war, the unknown soldier, the pioneer-hero. The degree to which they were ascribed immortality also varied, but their prescribed or suggestive power was one and the same.

In past times those who had died a "death that was not their own" were regarded with suspicion and fear. In Soviet times, those who died an untimely death became the objects of a new cult. They had become a guarantor of social cohesion. Through their act of "worship" the performers in the ritual took upon themselves the obligation to live out the uncompleted life of others. Soviet individuals, and especially men, since for women service to society was implemented through "holy motherhood," were faced with an upsetting contradiction. In order to become immortal, it was necessary to remain in the people's memory. In order for that to happen, it was necessary to perform an act beneficial to the common cause. In extreme circumstances this could involve creating one's own death—a special kind of death, a public or "red" death for the whole world to see. In the final analysis, in order to escape death by becoming immortal, it was first necessary to die. The Soviet era did not offer its citizens a peaceful scenario for a long life "full of years."

Twenty-first century Russians have thus become the recipients of two contradictory sets of values, a phenomenon Gregory Bateson called the "double bind" (Bateson 1972, 271–78). On one hand, they inherited from those who lived in prerevolutionary Russia the belief that dying a death that was "not one's own" prevented the deceased from joining the clan of ancestors. These dead would not become the patrons, the protectors of their own descendants. According to Soviet ideology, on the other hand, it was precisely this form of death, the "red death," that turned its victims into patrons, but patrons of future Soviet generations, not of their own descendants by blood. Everyone in the country became the "spiritual" heirs of all those who "gave their lives for the birthland"—the common phrase found on all memorials dedicated to the soldiers who perished.

Russians today are finding ways of resolving this dichotomy and, in contrast to the Soviet rhetoric of glorious anonymity, are reestablishing and reasserting the link with their own, individual dead. Concern for those victims of atrocities, military and otherwise, who did not receive proper burial has become an important part of Russian social practice and discourse in recent years (for further discussion of this topic, see Etkind 2013). There is now mass participation, for example, in a social initiative inaugurated in Tomsk in 2012 when, on Victory Day, huge crowds of people march in processions, bearing aloft enlarged photographs of parents, grandparents, and other relatives killed in the war. These form the "immortal regiment" (*bessmertnyi polk*) memorialized on the banners carried at the head of the processions (see "Bessmertnyi polk" n.d.). Alongside the "immortal regiment" another movement has appeared, the "immortal barrack" (*bessmertnyi barak*), whose participants try to revive the memory of those who perished in the Stalinist camps. The human rights movement known as Memorial is also dedicated to reclaiming and perpetuating the memory of the victims of political repressions. These were not the dead for whom the eternal flames were lit, although, like them, they had neither graves nor crosses. These were the dead of the gulags, the forced-labor camps. Finding the sites of mass executions and communal burial pits from the time of the Stalinist repressions has become a widespread civil initiative. In 2018–19, after the discovery of a mass grave dating to the end of the 1930s and containing the remains of prisoners who had been executed by shooting, the citizens of Arkhangel'sk, for example, collected a significant sum of money for a proper burial to take place. There are also bands of volunteers who track down the remains of soldiers who perished in World War II battles but who were unidentified and deprived of burial rites. This activity began in Soviet times and continues to the present day. The searchers, who are, as it were, in constant contact with the world of the dead, believe that for each soldier found and buried with military honors, they will receive remission of one sin, and that the souls of soldiers and searchers will meet in the next world (Balashova 2015, 197). Through the reburial ceremony, with all its traditional rites, it is believed the soldiers' souls will be set free and find peace at last.

For the living, concern for the dead has a direct bearing on how they plan to lead their own lives. The short, heroic lives of the dead who became patron-guardians for generations of Soviet people, villagers and town-dwellers alike, compressed the whole notion of life into something that had its beginning in revolution and war and its ending in the blessings of communism. Between this revolutionary beginning and its utopian ending was situated life, premised, ideally, on the notion of sacrifice. For the sake of the "bright future" all one's strength, and even, if necessary, life itself (one's own or that of one's children) had to be rendered up. In other words, one must behave as the heroes had behaved. The memorial sites of the Soviet era functioned as the setting for rites of initiation, completion of which made one a disciple of this particular scenario. The concern for the dead that has preoccupied so many Russians in the post-Soviet era, the acts of reinstating their names and searching for their graves, are all symptomatic of the search for a new way of life, one that will provide the living, once they have reconstructed the link with their ancestors, with a long past and a long future.

Conclusion

ELIZABETH WARNER AND SVETLANA ADONYEVA

In the course of this book we have argued that respect for the bonds of family and kin, care for the dead, and veneration of ancestors have had and continue to have a definitive role in shaping the social and psychological imperatives of village communities in Russia and that they still have relevance for contemporary Russians beyond the confines of the village.

In the course of the book we have demonstrated the all-embracing nature of funeral and memorial ritual for the people who have shared their experiences with us. We have shown how it offers solace to the bereaved in the simple practicalities of organizing the funeral and preparing the deceased for burial, in making sure the deceased have all the material things they will require in the next world, and in providing the ritual "send-off" that ensures their passage. We have shown how it offers hope for those contemplating death themselves in the certain knowledge that life will somehow continue and that severance from loved ones will not be complete. We have recognized and illuminated the unchanging conviction that the dead too are sensitive and capable of suffering. We have shown how they too are affected by ritual, comforted and propitiated by the efforts of the bereaved to ameliorate the impoverishments of death with food, drink, and warmth. We have seen, on numerous occasions, how the rituals of death uphold the link between the living and the dead. We have seen how funeral and memorial ritual reinforce the bond between humankind and the fruitful earth, where humans live and toil before one day returning to the soil. Death rituals underscore the Russian notion of "home" on many levels—from the village and its homesteads to the gravesite and the cemetery, from the smaller regional homeland (*malaya rodina*) to the greater homeland, birthland, and nation.

During one of our visits to Roksama, a village in Vologda province, an eighty-six-year-old resident made the following statement: "Next year I will either move to the town to stay with my daughter or I will move to the cemetery." Her use of a transitive verb here, as opposed to a passive "I will be taken to," clearly indicates her perception of the matter of "moving" as one in which she will personally participate, whether she is alive or dead at the time of relocation. In the village of Ukhtoma, also in Vologda province, the local inhabitants call the cemetery the "quiet village," suggesting that the topography of the village includes two separate locations for "dwelling." Alongside the noisy village of the living is another, the quiet village of the dead. This premise confirms one of the major observations we have made in the course of our work. According to long-established village custom, the living and the dead equally enjoy a state of "being." The notion that death is not the end of "being" is implicit in the individual's preparations for death, such as choosing their own "death clothes," placing objects in coffins and on graves, or keeping the deceased warm and well-fed. Attention to the welfare of the dead, in their altered state of "being" and with their altered status as "ancestors," remains an enduring fixture of funeral and memorial ritual, while interaction with the dead through the medium of the lament or by listening to communications from the "other world" in dreams and visions offers the best means of ensuring their continued presence, their "aliveness" in the consciousness and life-world of their grieving relatives.

Reverence for the ancestors, and making sure that the dead live on and are sustained by the practice of memorialization, is fundamental to the natural order of things for many Russians today, as it assuredly has always been. We have few accounts from before the eighteenth century about how Russians arranged their funeral obsequies, but what little information we have seems to indicate remarkable continuity over the centuries. In the *Tale of Bygone Years* (*Povest' vremennykh let*) we read, for example, about the funeral in 945 for Igor', Grand Prince of Kiev, ordered by his widow, Ol'ga, who was already a Christian at that time. After he was assassinated by the Drevlyans, Ol'ga organized an elaborate memorial ceremony at his burial mound, for which a large quantity of mead was expressly brewed (Adrianova-Peretts 1:238–39). A fourteenth-century manuscript describes how people sprinkled ashes on the floor of the bathhouse and invited the dead to come and wash. They would look for footprints in the ashes to see if their ancestors had come. They hung up towels and clothing for them. They prepared food for them—butter, milk, and eggs, which they later ate themselves— a picture not at all at odds with what we have seen in our research of memorial practices in bathhouses and on graves (Gal'kovskii 1913, 2:60). Similarly, Russians we interviewed could easily relate to comments about merrymaking on graves at Troitsa in the sixteenth-century *Stoglav* and to Olearius's account of Troitsa in seventeenth-century Moscow. It is self-evident that the rituals of today have not sprung ready-made from some new twentieth- or twenty-first-century philosophy of death. In the course of the book we have examined contemporary everyday practices within their historical context, but we have done this without recourse to historical-typological methodology, without attempting to derive them from "pagan" antecedents, and without the creation of ritual genealogies. Noting the similarity between what is contemporary and what is historically distant we can, on the other hand, see funeral and memorial tradition manifesting itself as a phenomenon of a particular temporal order, described by Fernand Braudel as "la longue durée"—the "long term" or "slow history"—the small details of everyday material life that, in contrast to the greater events of history overlaying them, develop at ground level, at their own pace, having "crossed the silent depths of time and *endured* [Braudel's emphasis]." "It is a fact," writes Braudel, "that every great center of population has worked out a set of elementary answers and has an unfortunate tendency to stick to them out of that force of inertia which is one of the great artisans of history" (Braudel 1985, 1:560, 561). Throughout Russia's history peasants, village inhabitants, and the population in general, can also be seen as having one "set of elementary answers" predicated on taking care of ancestors.

It is interesting to note that some of the customs associated with memorializing that are described in this book were once common in other places as well but did not necessarily endure there and eventually became diluted or disappeared altogether. In tenth-century Anglo-Saxon England, for example, the abbot Aelfric of Eynsham, much like early churchmen in Russia, in one of his homilies warned his priests against taking part in the funeral activities of their parishioners: "Ye shall not rejoice on account of men deceased nor attend on the corpse unless ye be thereto invited. When ye are thereto invited then forbid ye the heathen songs [*haethenan sangas*] of the laymen and their loud cachinnations; nor eat ye nor drink where the corpse lieth therein, lest ye be imitators of the heathenism which they there commit" (Thorpe 1840, 2:358–59). It is worth remembering here the particular emphasis on remembrance of the dead in the Eastern Orthodox church. It is interesting, for example, to note many similarities between memorial death customs in rural Russia and in rural Greece, where lamenting, food offerings, regular grave-visiting, and the recitation of names of the dead on Soul Saturdays (Psihosavata) are among the ways of maintaining links between the living and the dead: "By reading the names of the village dead and by giving gifts to the church in their names, the living commemorate the dead" (Danforth and Tsiaras 1982, 132–34). Remembrance was an aspect of faith and practice particularly enthusiastically embraced by the "simple people" (*prostolyudiny*) in Russia, according to S. V. Bulgakov. His comments, made toward the end of the nineteenth century, show just how tenaciously and enthusiastically the so-called simple people of the villages preserved the veneration of their ancestors as a central tenet of religious practice over the centuries. He points out that in addition to the usual observances on days of remembrance—the third, ninth, and fortieth days after the death and appropriate calendar dates such as during St. Thomas' week—they would also arrange for commemorations when a house-blessing was to take place, on the Saturday preceding the marriage of a family member, and during harvesting in the autumn (Bulgakov 1993, 2:1366). On such occasions they would ask for a service to be held for the repose of souls and would also take bread to the church. Bulgakov particularly commends the peasants for preserving and continuing in their own way one of the traditions of the early Christian church, recording in diptychs the names of the living and the dead, which were read out during the Eucharist liturgy so that all were prayed for and remembered. Diptychs were eventually replaced by books of commemoration (*pomyanniki*), containing the names of all the dead of the parish: "How gratifying it is," writes Bulgakov, "to realize that the respect and even reverence in which the books of commemoration were held by the early Christians have also been inherited by our simple folk. Indeed, just glance into any peasant hut and make it your first duty to look toward the 'front' corner of the living room, where the icon shelf is always situated, and on this icon shelf you will certainly find a book of remembrance containing all the names of their deceased and living relatives" (Bulgakov 1993, 2:1367).

In this context we should bear in mind some of the complex and mysterious rites concerning food and remembrance that lie at the heart of Christianity itself. In early Christian times the dividing line between the pre-Christian ritual feasts held on the graves of the deceased and the commemoration of the dead during the Christian Eucharist liturgy was not as clear-cut as it later became. In fact, the link between food and commemoration is implicit in the origins of the Eucharist, which derives from the Last Supper attended by Christ and his disciples before his death ("The Lord Jesus took bread and when he had given thanks he broke it and said 'This is my body which is given for you. Do this in remembrance of me'" [1 Corinthians 11:24]).

In Orthodoxy, the body and blood of Christ, offered to his disciples at the meal, are mystically present in the consecrated bread and wine of the Eucharist. In addition to the bread (*prosfora*) and wine for communicants (which is consecrated during the *proskomedia*, the preparatory stage preceding the liturgy), four other loaves are blessed, one of which is offered in memory of the departed faithful. Individual members of the congregation may also bring their own small prosfora and a note asking the celebrant to remember in prayer a specific individual. At the end of the liturgy members of the congregation can take a piece of the *antidor*, the remaining part of the loaf from which the consecrated bread used for the Eucharist has been removed. Commemoration of the dead is an integral part of the Eucharist liturgy, as is the symbolic and actual partaking of bread and wine, an act in which the living and the dead are conjoined. The prayers for the dead are conducted in the presence of bread and wine, as indeed are the prayers of priests who remember the souls of the dead while consuming the food offerings brought for this purpose by their devout parishioners. The prayers accompanied by sustenance are intended to mitigate the suffering of the dead and to bring comfort in a metaphysical sense, just as the food left at the graveside or distributed by the villagers with a request to "remember" may be thought to bring more material sustenance, but in both cases the link between shared food and remembrance is firmly established. Both in pre-Christian and Christian antiquity a key factor of the graveside memorial feast was belief in the actual presence of the deceased, who were provided not only with food but with the necessary tools for joining in the feast on equal terms with the living (Oexle 1976, 81). The social and psychological imperative of this notion can also be felt in the memorial customs of contemporary Russians. As one widow we interviewed pointed out, "My husband has his own glass and saucer." Shot glasses, tumblers, saucers, and plates for the sole use of the dead may be seen on many graves or behind the grave markers. On one grave in the Russian Far North we saw the bowl of a spoon poking up from a grave mound, where the handle had been pushed down into the soil.

"Every society has its specific way of defining and perceiving reality—its world, its universe, its overarching organization of symbols" (Berger and Kellner 1964, 1–2). The Soviet period witnessed the disruption of a particular way of perceiving reality, a particular ordering of social relationships, a particular set of commonly held values. Breaking the continuity and common consensus essential to their survival, it left its destructive and indelible mark on funeral ritual as on other aspects of family and social life. The act of ritual remembering cannot be successfully accomplished without the graves of ancestors. The twentieth century, however, with its revolution, famines, deportations, executions, wars, and gulags, led to the dispersal of places of burial, to the creation of mass burial sites where the names of the dead were unknown. Many Russians simply had no idea where their dead were buried. In this way, Russians were deprived of their places of ritual memorializing. While the Soviet period created alternatives—eternal flames and the anonymous "graves of the unknown soldier"—reestablishing the lost personal connections with the dead has become an insistent demand of contemporary society, giving rise to many spontaneous rituals for reuniting the living with the dead—mass movements such as the "immortal regiments" and "immortal barracks" and many private initiatives, the creation of secular martyrologies, the raising of crosses and monuments to named individuals at places where the casualties of war and unjust execution had lain without recognition. The cemetery, too, plays its part in the recreation of broken genealogies. An event in one village in Pskov province described by the local priest may serve to illustrate this point. A booklet he had published about the history of its church provided biographies of the priests who had served there. An acquaintance took a copy with him to St. Petersburg, where he conducted a Sunday school. By pure chance the grandchildren of one of the priests buried in the village cemetery and described in the booklet realized that this priest was a long-lost relative whose whereabouts had been unknown for many years. As a result, a whole family rediscovered itself and was reunited: "They came to the cemetery, some from Ukraine, some from Belarus, from St. Petersburg, and other places. They were meeting for the first time here. This place of burial, of a grandfather, even a great-grandfather, somehow brought them together. They were even seeing each other for the first time, although they were actually close relatives" (EW-A Pskov-Dno A15, June 11, 2014).

The graves of ancestors also form part of a wider discourse on Russia's sense of selfhood in the post-Soviet age. In her book about the post-socialist politics of reburying the bodies of revolution and war dead in Eastern Europe, Katherine Verdery writes: "Symbols come with histories but they are used in texts that modify them. Ideas about ancestry in contemporary nationalism or the mortuary beliefs underlying today's burials are not 'the same' as those of a few decades ago. They provide present-day social actors with ways of talking about the past and of integrating into present action possible 'traditions' whose most important role may be to signify the rejection of the 'aberrant' communist period and a return to an ostensibly more authentic national history" (Verdery 1999, 125). In the late twentieth- and the twenty-first-century "texts" of Troitsa celebrations we saw how the familiar symbolism of the birch tree had evolved into a post-Soviet quest for self-identity and unity with the life-giving birthland and how the modern Troitsa, the Festival of the Birch, was viewed as part of an ongoing process of patriotic education.

In Pushkin's poem on the two subjects dear to the hearts of all Russians, quoted in chapter 6, he refers to "love for the home hearth" and "love for the tombs of our forefathers" (Lyubov' k rodnomu pepelishchu / Lyubov' k otecheskim grobam). These lines, known to every Russian schoolchild, still resonate today, or perhaps it would be truer to say that they "re-resonate." What is of particular significance for us, however, is not even Pushkin's conjoining of native land with the graves of ancestors, although that is clearly by no means inimical to our study. What most interests us here is his seemingly paradoxical juxtaposition of death with life, for without these "life-creating" (*zhivotvoryashchie*) holy places, writes Pushkin, the earth is dead. Throughout our book, in the thoughts and actions of the people who shared with us their ways of dealing with death and remembering the dead, it is self-evident that the generations alive today will be united with past generations and will themselves live again as the "ancestors" of the future ("What you sow does not come to life unless it dies," 1 Corinthians 15:35).

It seems appropriate to end with the words of one of those many village dwellers to whom we are indebted for the material in this book. In 2003, in a village of the Belozersk region of Vologda province, we talked at length with a healer who used both practical and occult knowledge to help his clients, who often traveled long distances for his advice on a range of medical, psychological, economic, and family problems. In the time-honored way of wise folk, he had accepted the transfer of certain knowledge from his father before he died, "in order to help people." A knowledgeable herbalist who believed in the need to "be at one with nature," he also employed the power of prayer, the protection of guardian angels, the energy of the cosmos, and Pythagorean numerology. In his opinion, many illnesses and personal problems were caused by the evil or jealous eye, but even more so by ignoring the core rules of life—supporting and revering parents and ancestors: "My first question is 'Are your parents still alive? You haven't forgotten them?' Duty to your parents—in nature, there is no other duty before the duty to your parents. If you observe that . . . and also remembering the dead. This is the foundation upon which the whole course of your life depends" (EW-V Vol-Bel, tape 7, July 15, 2003).

Notes

Introduction

1. Information from *Bol'shaya rossiiskaya entsiklopediya-elektronnaya versiya* (2005–19), https://bigenc.ru/geography/text/1926896 (accessed July 20, 2020) and the official site of the provincial government of Arkhangel'sk province. See "Arkhangel'skaya oblast'," https://dvinaland.ru/region/Arkhangelsk_obl (accessed July 22, 2020).

2. For detailed analysis of collectivization and the campaign against the kulaks, see Fitzpatrick (1994).

3. Suffering on an epic scale was the lot of the entire Russian people throughout the twentieth century. In *Night of Stone* (2002), Catherine Merridale charts in harrowing detail the death and devastation brought about by collectivization, dekulakization, the war, postwar famine, and the Gulag.

4. Karl Liebknecht was a German socialist who, together with Rosa Luxemburg, founded the German Communist Party.

5. Bowman and Valk (2014) illustrate the many different ways in which the term "vernacular religion" may be applied.

Chapter 1. Beliefs about the Soul, the Living Dead, and the
Afterlife in Contemporary Rural North Russia

1. Throughout the Soviet period red material was often preferred, especially if the deceased had been a Party member. Blue was used for the coffins of seamen. This practice continued into the twenty-first century in some rural areas.

2. For a discussion of the relevance to body and soul of van Gennep's division of rites of passage into rites of separation, transition, and incorporation, see Warner 2000a.

3. For more information on the zoomorphic form of souls in Slavonic mythology, see Tolstaya, 1999a; Vinogradova 1999.

4. The traditional Russian stove is a large brick structure that is usually plastered over and then painted. It dominates the living quarters, providing both heat and an oven for cooking and baking. Its upper level contains a flat area on which it is possible to sleep.

5. According to the theory of Arnold van Gennep (1997), the concept of liminality may be applied to the ambiguous status of people who are in the process of passing from one state of being into another, such as during the transition rites of death or marriage.

The concept was further developed by Victor Turner (1974). This concept may also be applied to "threshold" places on the fringes of human and spirit habitations. In the Russian context these include the bathhouse, which may be the haunt of demons, and the attic, basement, and storage areas of dwelling houses. These are frequented by humans but may also be inhabited by spirit beings, such as the house spirit (*domovoi*).

6. Jeanmarie Rouhier-Willoughby provides useful information on the conduct of funerals during the Soviet period from 1950 to 1990 (2008, 177–228).

7. Rita Astuti and Maurice Bloch have posed an interesting question in their article "Are Ancestors Dead?" (2013, 101–17). Their research with people who perform rituals involving interaction with dead ancestors suggests that a dual system of belief is in operation. Individuals asked about personal beliefs do not usually believe the dead can be "alive." Acting with their social group in the performance of ritualized interaction with the ancestors, on the other hand, they clearly do.

Chapter 2. Ritual Feeding and the Cult of Ancestors

1. Apart from its meaning as a vessel for holding liquids, *vedro* was a unit of measurement equivalent to about twelve liters.

2. For further examination of this idea in the Russian context see Warner 2011b, 164–72.

3. The dream as a form of communication between the living and the dead has also been explored by Gabriela Kiliánová on the basis of Slovakian ethnographical material (2010, 7–23).

4. Snezhok is the brand name of a popular sweetened yoghurt sold in village shops.

5. A bowl of rusks (*sukhari*), small, round, dry biscuits with a hole in the middle, is often kept on the table for snacking. Alternatively, the housewife may make her own from leftover bread dried to a crisp in the oven.

6. Kargopol' was one of the towns of the Olonets guberniya situated in the northwest of the Russian Empire. The town of Olonets is now in the Republic of Karelia while Kargopol' is in Arkhangel'sk province.

7. The word *bomzh* is an acronym derived from *bez opredelennogo mesta zhitel'stva* (without specific place of residence).

Chapter 3. The Lament

1. Ancestral Saturdays are special days marked by the Orthodox Church for the commemoration of the dead.

2. Each line begins with the exclamation *Uzh* or *Uzhy*, which has no particular meaning but is typical of the sobs and sighs used by the "lamenting voice."

3. The exclamation *Uzh* is repeated at the beginning of each line.

4. On Trinity Sunday (*Troitsa*) the Russian Orthodox Church celebrates Pentecost and the descent of the Holy Spirit upon Jesus and His disciples.

5. An *olad'ya* is a sort of thick pancake. For more on *kisel'*, see chapter 2.

6. In north Russian village houses the living quarters (*izba*) have a heated winter part with a stove and an unheated part where the family lives in summer.

7. Until the second half of the 1960s, workers on collective farms did not receive wages but were paid in kind, according to the number of "work days" (*trudodni*) they completed.

8. This characteristic feature of the funeral ritual as a rite of passage has been commented on in a number of works. See, for example, the following: Honko 1964, 134–36; Nenola-Kallio 1982; Baiburin and Levinton 1985, 5–9; Baiburin 1985, 59–78; Konka, 1992; Kuznetsova, 1993.

9. The form of a lament is strictly dependent on whether it is performed in the ritual situation or outside ritual. See, for example, Ankudinova 1985, 95–99.

10. Welfare support for orphans and widows was a matter for the village commune: "They were relieved of paying *tyaglo* [tax], either in whole, or in part, while their *obrok* [a levy paid in work or produce] was shared by the whole community" (Firsov and Kisileva 1993, 70). Orphans were fed by the village community (*mir*). A part of the alms given to the church by the community was reserved for orphans.

11. The same custom has been noted in western parts of Russia. Comparatively recently, in the decades following the war, an orphaned bride would visit the cemetery on the day before her wedding. She would perform an orphan-lament-invitation on the grave of her dead parent(s), asking for their blessing (Ivashneva 2001, 62:66–67).

12. In the texts of the laments the notion of a communicative conduit between the living and the dead may be expressed through the metaphor of the "path-road" (*put'-doroga*). See, for example, Gerasimova 1998, 13–37.

13. The exclamation *Uzh(i)* is repeated at the beginning of each line.

14. This periodization of the generations largely corresponds to that proposed by David L. Ransel in his monograph about the fate of peasant mothers in Russia and Tataria (2000, 4–7).

15. A *chastushka* is an improvisatory song form characterized by short, rhyming stanzas and most often with a humorous, satirical, or even bawdy theme. It was often accompanied by dance and accordion music.

Chapter 4. The Cross, the Birch, and the Kawasaki Motorbike

1. The Soviet disregard for the sacral nature of burial sites and the human remains of victims of the Stalinist era and the gulags is attested by Catherine Merridale (2002, 300).

2. For many years the Orthodox Church campaigned against the use of crematoria. However, the soaring cost of cemetery burial and lack of space in old cemeteries, where coffins may now be stacked one upon the other, has led to a change of heart in recent years. The Patriarch Aleksii has recognized that cremation is not in contravention of Orthodox canon law and has allowed the conduct of Orthodox funerals in crematoria. Not all towns have a crematorium, but in those that do, 45–60 percent of funerals are now conducted there. There are now four crematoria in Moscow (see https://mosgor-ritual.ru/deystvuyushchie-krematorii, accessed May 24, 2019).

3. The reference is to the trials (*mytarstva*) the departing soul must undergo before it appears before God.

4. For more information on how the ribbon evolved into a national symbol, see Timofeyichev 2018.

5. The Polish press has been particularly outspoken. See, e.g., "Polish Media: The St. George Ribbon Is a Sign of Russia's Aggressive Nationalism," https://uawire.org/news/wyborcza, April 26, 2017 (accessed June 30, 2020).

6. The *kollezhskii asessor* was a rank in the Tsarist civil service. The corresponding army rank was that of major.

7. See, e.g., the funeral bureau website Granitnaya masterskaya *Rit-granit*, http://rit-granit.ru/oformlenie-kresty.

8. "Manufacture of gravestones," http://izgotovleniepamyatnikov.ru/na-mogilu/7-voprosov (accessed September 27, 2016).

Chapter 5. The Russian Semik-Troitsa (Trinity) Ritual Complex

1. During the following week, in the run-up to the Great Fast or Lent, the devout Orthodox exclude meat products from their diet, although dairy products are still allowed.

2. In the sixteenth and seventeenth centuries, the *zemskii Prikaz*, or Land Office, was the central organ of government responsible for security and order and in general for the smooth running of the administration of the capital city.

3. I am grateful to Katya Mamaeva for providing information about the making of the video and transcripts of chastushki. The film may be watched on YouTube. "Troitsa, derevnya Siniki Arkhangel'skoi oblasti," https://www.youtube.com/watch?v=wgIMeVpF TyQ (accessed August 17, 2020).

4. For further information on the customs of Shavuot see, e.g., "Shavuot," https://njop.org/shavuot/ (accessed August 15, 2020).

Chapter 6. The Story of the Eternal Flame

1. The Field of Mars was established as a pleasure garden in the eighteenth century but was used as a military parade ground in the nineteenth.

2. Mamaev Kurgan is a memorial complex dedicated to the heroes of the battle of Stalingrad. Its construction on the high bank of the river Volga was begun in 1959, and it opened in 1967. For further details, see Naumenko, Loginov, and Merinova, 1973.

3. The Alexander Column, with its distinctive figure of an angel on top, was raised on Palace Square in the center of St. Petersburg by order of Tsar Nicholas I to commemorate the victory over Napoleon of his older brother Tsar Alexander I.

4. On March 6, 1917, the art historian and painter A. N. Benua and the architect I. A. Fomin, both members of the Commission for the Protection of Monuments, headed by Maksim Gor'kii, approached the Soviet of Worker and Soldier Deputies with the proposal that the victims of the revolution should be buried in the Field of Mars and not at Palace Square, "since, from the artistic point of view, this square is already a complete architectural whole that will not permit the encumbrance of new monuments" (Benua 2003, 138–41).

5. The arbitrary nature of this circumstance, perpetrated upon the bodies of victims of war, is all the more striking when we remember that in Tsarist Russia, although the denial of Christian burial to certain categories of criminal was not unknown, considerable efforts were made to provide even those about to be executed for heinous crimes with the comfort of confession and absolution. Referring to the burning of two people for witchcraft in 1676, Nancy Kollman comments, "Had their bodies not been reduced to ash, they could have had a Christian burial. Exclusion from the church was a rare and shameful sanction" (2012, 343).

6. The Pioneer movement was a Soviet youth organization for children aged between ten and fifteen years. It combined political indoctrination with sport and social activities. Being excluded from participation for whatever reason was regarded as a considerable deprivation. Children enjoyed the sense of cohesion and comradeship as well as the facilities offered by the organization.

7. *Sobranie uzakonenii i rasporyazhenii rabochego i krest'yanskogo pravitel'stva* 1942. See No. 31 for April 15, 1918, article No. 416, p. 433.

8. From the late 1950s the term *fartsovshchik* was applied in the Soviet Union to traffickers who bought up foreign goods through their contacts with foreign visitors and sold them on the black market.

9. During World War II the so-called Road of Life across Lake Ladoga, by barge or over the ice in winter, was the only transport lifeline into the besieged city of Leningrad.

10. Pioneer palaces provided schoolchildren with extracurricular activities such as sports and technical clubs, choirs and dance groups.

11. The informant is quoting from the famous, unfinished patriotic poem of 1830 by Aleksandr Pushkin, "Dva chuvstva divno blizki nam" ("Two feelings are wonderfully dear to us"), in which he refers to "love for the graves of our forefathers" (lyubov' k otecheskim grobam) and "love for hearth and home" (lyubov' k rodnomu pepelishchu). See Pushkin 1949, 3:214.

12. A memorial complex was built on the square in the early 1970s to commemorate both civilians and soldiers who had died during the siege. In the central section of the monument burns an eternal flame.

13. Leonid (Lyonya) Golikov was one of the pioneer-heroes. He fought with a partisan brigade near Leningrad and was killed in 1943 at the age of fifteen.

14. *The Street of the Younger Son* (*Ulitsa mladshego syna*, 1949) was a novella by Lev Kassil' and Maks Polyanovskii about the wartime heroic exploits of the teenage Volodya Dubinin.

15. In 1930, at the suggestion of the Komsomol organization, a series of physical fitness courses and competitions was introduced in the Soviet Union. The much-prized badges given to those who fulfilled the demanding criteria bore the acronym GTO, "Gotov k trudu i oborone" (Ready for work and defense). "Vserossiiskii fizkul'turno-sportivnyi kompleks 'Gotov k trudu i oborone,'" https://www.gto.ru/history (accessed August 12, 2020). The speaker was referring to S. Ya. Marshak's poem "The Story of an Unknown Hero" (1937), about a young man who saves a little girl from a fire but who decides to remain anonymous. All Soviet schoolchildren were taught about the poem.

16. Aleksandr Matrosov (1924–43) was a soldier who gave his life by using his body to block the embrasure in a German machine gun pillbox. His martyrdom allowed the Soviet army to advance.

17. For children aged between seven and nine, the Little Octobrists (*oktobryata*) was the youngest youth organization under the aegis of the Communist Party while the Komsomol was for young adults. As part of their uniform they wore red garrison caps known as *pilotki*, decorated, like those of pioneers, with a star emblem.

References

Adon'eva, S. B. 1998. "Etnografiya severno-russkikh prichitanii." In *Byulleten' fonetichesk-ogo fonda russkogo yazyka*. Appendix no. 7. *Obryadovaya poeziya Russkogo Severa: Plachi*, edited by P. A. Skrelin, compiled by A. Yu. Kastrov and Yu. I. Marchenko, 63–85. St. Petersburg-Bochum: University of Bochum and University of St. Petersburg.

Adrianova-Peretts, ed. 1950. *Povest' vremennykh let*. Vol. 1. Moscow-Leningrad: ANSSSR.

Afanas'ev, A. N. 1990. *Narodnye russkie legendy*. Novosibirsk: Nauka (Sibirskoe otdelenie).

Agapkina, T. A. 2002. *Mifopoeticheskie osnovy slavyanskogo narodnogo kalendarya: Vesenne-letnii tsikl*. Moscow: Indrik.

Agapkina, T. A. 2012. "Troitsa." In *Slavyanskie drevnosti*, edited by S. M. Tolstaya, 5:320–25. Moscow: Mezhdunarodnye otnosheniya.

Alekseevskii, M. D. 2005. "Pominal'nye trapezy na Russkom Severe: Pishchevoi kod i zastol'nyi etiket." In *VI kongress etnografov i antropologov Rossii. Tezisy dokladov. Sektsiya 10: Traditsionnye sistemy pitaniya*, 222–36. St. Petersburg. web1.kunstkamera.ru>science/congress2005/10.pdf. Accessed August 1, 2014.

Anikin, V. P. 1970. *Kalendarnye i svadebnye pesni*. Moscow: MGU.

Ankudinova, O. V. 1985. "O nekotorykh zhanrovykh osobennostyakh placha." In *Russkii fol'klor 23: Polevye issledovaniya*, edited by S. N. Azbelev and P. S. Vykhodtsev, 95–99. Leningrad: Nauka.

"Anti-alkogol'nye kampanii v SSSR." 2020. https://ru.wikipedia.org/wiki/Антиалкогольные_кампании_в_СССР. Accessed August 13, 2020.

Arkhipova, A. S. 2017. "Voina kak prazdnik, prazdnik kak voina: Performativnaya kommemoratsiya Dnya Pobedy." *Antropologicheskii forum* 33:84–122.

Astuti, Rita, and Maurice Bloch. 2013. "Are Ancestors Alive?" In *A Companion to the Anthropology of Religion*, edited by Janice Boddy and Michael Lambek, 101–17. Wiley online library.

Badone, Ellen, ed. 1990. *Religious Orthodoxy and Popular Faith in European Society*. Princeton, NJ: Princeton University Press.

Baiburin, A. K. 1985. "Prichitaniya: Tekst i kontekst." *Artes Populares* (Budapest) 14:59–78.

Baiburin, A. K., and G. A. Levinton. 1985. "Pokhorony i svad'ba." In *Konferentsiya "Balto-slavyanskie etnokul'turnye i arkheologicheskie drevnosti: Pogrebal'nyi obryad." Tezisy dokladov*, edited by V. V. Ivanov, 5–9. Moscow: Institut Balkanistiki i Slavyano-vedeniya ANSSR.

Balashova, A. 2015. "Vzaimootnosheniya poiskovikov s mirom mertvykh: Fol'klornye motivy i syuzhety." In *Memento mori: Pokhoronnye traditsii v sovremennoi kul'ture,* compiled by A. Sokolova and A. B. Yudkina, edited by D. V. Gromov, 197–216. Moscow: IEA RAN.

Balzer, Marjorie Mandelstam, ed. 1992. *Russian Traditional Culture: Religion, Gender and Customary Law.* Armonk, NY: M. E. Sharpe.

Barsov, E. V. 1872. *Prichitaniya Severnogo Kraya, sobrannye E. V. Barsovym.* Vol. 1, *Plachi pokhoronnye, nadgrobnye i nadmogil'nye.* Moscow. Tipografiya "Sovremennye Izvestiya."

Barsov, E. V. 1997. *Prichitan'ya Severnogo Kraya sobrannye E. V. Barsovym.* 2 vols. St. Petersburg: Nauka. Reprint of the 1872 edition, edited by B. E. Chistova and K. V. Chistov.

Bartenev, I. A., and V. N. Batazhkova. 1983. *Ocherki istorii arkhitekturnykh stilei: Uchebnoe posobie.* Moscow: Izobrazitel'noe iskusstvo.

Batalden, S. K., ed. 1993. *Seeking God: The Recovery of Religious Identity in Orthodox Russia, Ukraine, and Georgia.* DeKalb: Northern Illinois University Press.

Bateson, Gregory. 1972. *Steps to an Ecology of Mind: Collected Essays in Anthropology, Psychiatry, Evolution and Epistemology.* Chicago: University of Chicago Press.

Bazanov, V. 1943. "Voplenitsy." In V. Bazanov, *Poeziya Pechory,* 25–40. Syktykvar: Komigosizdat.

Bazanov, V. 1962. "Prichitaniya russkogo severa v zapisyakh 1942–1945." In *Russkaya narodno-bytovaya lirika: Prichitaniya, v zapisyakh V. P. Bazanova i A. P. Razumovoi,* 10–44. Leningrad: Izdatel'stvo Akademii nauk.

Becker, Charles, S. Joshua Mendelsohn, and Ksenya Benderskaya. 2012. "Russian Urbanization in the Soviet and Post-Soviet Eras." International Institute for Environment and Development. United Nations Population Fund: Urbanization and Emerging Population Issues Working Paper 9. https://pubs.iied.org/pdfs/10613IIED.pdf. Accessed April 26, 2019.

Belliustin, I. S. 1985. *Description of the Clergy in Rural Russia: The Memoir of a Nineteenth-Century Parish Priest.* Translated by Gregory L. Freeze. Ithaca, NY: Cornell University Press.

Belousov, A. F. 1992. "Sadistskie stishki" (Iz kollektsii A. F. Belousova, K. K. Nemirovicha-Danchenko i A. L. Toporkova). In *Shkol'nyi byt i fol'klor: Uchebnyi material po russkomu fol'kloru,* edited by A. F. Belousov, pt. 1:138–51. Tallin: Izdatel'stvo Tallinskogo Pedagogicheskogo Universiteta.

Belousov, A. F. 1998. "Sadistskie stikhi." In *Russkii shkol'nyi fol'klor: Ot vyzyvanii pikovoi damy do semeinykh rasskazov,* compiled by A. F. Belousov, 545–77. Moscow: Nauchno-izdatel'skii tsentr Ladomir-ACT-LTD.

Belousov, A. F. 1999. "Fol'klornaya sud'ba elektrika Petrova." In *Studia metrica et poetica: Sbornik statei pamyati P. A. Rudneva,* compiled by A. K. Baiburin and A. F. Belousov, 303–8. St. Petersburg: Akademicheskii proekt.

Benua, A. N. 2003. *Moi dnevnik: 1916–1917–1918.* Moscow: Russkii put'.

Berger, Peter L., and Hansfried Kellner. 1964. "Marriage and the Construction of Reality." *Diogenes* 46:1–23.

Bernshtam, T. A. 1989. "Russkaya narodnaya kul'tura i narodnaya religiya." *Sovetskaya etnografiya* 1 (January–February): 91–100.

Bernshtam, T. A. 2007. *Prikhodskaya zhizn' russkoi derevni: Ocherki po tserkovnoi etnografii*. St. Petersburg: St. Petersburg University Press.

"Bessmertnyi polk." n.d. https://moypolk.ru. Accessed August 20, 2020.

Bessonov, P. 1863. *Kaliki perekhozhie: Sbornik stikhov i issledovanii*, pt. 2, issue 5. Moscow: Tipografiya Bakhmeteva.

Bishop Alexander (Mileant). 2001. "Pentecost: The Day of Descent of the Holy Spirit on the Apostles." www.fatheralexander.org/booklets/english/pente.htm. Accessed May 12, 2015.

Blair, Carole V., William Balthrop, and Neil Michel. 2011. "Rhetoric, Materiality, and U.S. Western Front Commemoration." In *Communication Matters: Materialist Approaches to Media, Mobility and Networks*, edited by Jeremy Packer and Stephen B. Crofts-Wiley. London: Routledge.

Borisov, Archbishop Innokentii. 1872. *Sochineniya Arkhiepiskopa Khersonskogo i Tavricheskogo v 11 tomakh*. St. Petersburg and Moscow: M.O. Vol'f.

Bouchard, Michel. 2004. "Graveyards: Russian Ritual and Beliefs Pertaining to the Dead." *Religion* 34 (4): 345–62.

Bowman, Marion, and Ülo Valk, eds. 2014. *Vernacular Religion in Everyday Life: Expressions of Belief*. London: Routledge.

Braudel, Fernand. 1985. *The Structures of Everyday Life*. Vol. 1 of *Civilization and Capitalism 15th–18th Century*. London and New York: William Collins Sons. First published under the title *Les Structures du Quotidian: Le Possible et l'Impossible*. Paris: Armand Colin, 1979.

Bulgakov, S. V. 1993. *Nastol'naya kniga dlya svyashchenno-tserkovno-sluzhitelei*. 2 vols. Moscow: Izdatel'skii otdel Moskovskogo Patriarkhata. First published 1892. Khar'kov: Tipografiya gubernskogo pravleniya.

Bunge, Gabriel. 2007. *The Rublev Trinity: The Icon of the Trinity by the Monk-Painter Andrei Rublev*. Foreword by Sergei S. Averintsev. Translated by Andrew Louth. Crestwood, NY: St. Vladimir's Seminary Press.

Bunin, I. A. 2000. *Okoyannye dni*. St. Petersburg: Azbuka.

Byulleten' ispolkoma Lengorsoveta deputatov trudyashchikhsya. 1957. No. 22, November 30.

Cherepanova, O. A. 1996. *Mifologicheskie rasskazy i legendy russkogo Severa*. St. Petersburg: St. Petersburg University Press.

Chicherov, Vladimir. 1957. *Zimnii period russkogo narodnogo zemledel'cheskogo kalendarya XVI–XIX vekov*. Moscow: Akademiya nauk SSSR.

Chistova, B. E., and K. V Chistov, eds. 1960. *Prichitaniya*. Leningrad: Sovetskii pisatel'.

Chulos, C. J. 2000. "The End of 'Cultural Survivals' (*perezhitki*): Remembering and Forgetting Russian Peasant Religious Traditions." *Studia Slavica Finlandensia* 17:190–207.

Collins, Samuel. 1671. *The Present State of Russia*. London: Printed by John Winter for Dorman Newman.

Cross, Anthony, ed. 1971. *Russia under Western Eyes*. London: Elek Books.

Dal', Vladimir. 1955. *Tolkovyi slovar' zhivogo velikorusskogo yazyka*. 4 vols. Moscow: Gosudarstvennoe izdatel'stvo inostrannykh i natsional'nykh slovarei. Reprint of the second edition: M. O. Vol'f, Moscow. First published 1863–66. Moscow: Obshchestvo lyubitelei rossiiskoi slovesnosti.

Dal', Vladimir. 1957. *Poslovitsy russkogo naroda*. Moscow: Gosudarstvennoe izdatel'stvo khudozhestvennoi literatury. First published 1862. Moscow: Universitetskaya Tipografiya.

Danforth, Loring M., and Alexander Tsiaras. 1982. *Death Rituals of Rural Greece*. Princeton, NJ: Princeton University Press.

Dashkov, V. A. 1842. *Opisanie Olonetskoi gubernii v istoricheskom, statisticheskom i etnograficheskom otnosheniyakh*, compiled by I. Blagoveshchenskii. St Petersburg: Tipografiya Ministerstva Vnutrennikh Del.

Dickinson, Greg, Carole Blair, and Brian L. Ott. 2010. *Places of Public Memory: The Rhetoric of Museums and Memorials*. Tuscaloosa: University of Alabama Press.

Dmytryshyn, Basil. 1991. *Medieval Russia: A Source Book, 850–1700*. Fort Worth: Harcourt Brace Jovanovich College Publishers.

Douglas, Mary. 2002. *Purity and Danger: An Analysis of Concept of Pollution and Taboo*. Abingdon: Routledge.

Drunina, Yuliya. 1978. *Mir pod olivami*. Moscow: Molodaya gvardiya.

Dundes, Alan. 1981. "Wet and Dry, the Evil Eye." In *The Evil Eye: A Folklore Casebook*, edited by Alan Dundes, 257–312. New York and London: Garland Publishing.

Efimenko, P. S. 1877. "Materialy po etnografii russkogo naseleniya Arkhangel'skoi gubernii." Pt. 1, "Opisanie vneshnego i vnutrennego byta." *Trudy etnograficheskogo otdela im. obshchestva lyubitelei estestvoznaniya, antropologii i etnografii pri Moskovskom universitete*, vol. 30, bk. 5, issue 1:1–223.

Efimenkova, B. B. 1980. *Severnorusskaya prichet'*. Moscow: Sovetskii kompozitor.

Eliade, Mircea. 1974. *Shamanism: Archaic Techniques of Ecstasy*. Princeton, NJ: Princeton University Press.

Elyutina, M. E., and S. V. Filippova. 2012. "Ritual'nye pokhoronnye praktiki: Soderzhatel'nye izmeneniya." *Sotsiologicheskie issledovaniya* 9:86–94.

Emel'yanov, Nikolai. 2019. "Skol'ko v Rossii votserkovlennykh khristian i pochemu." https://pravoslavie.ru/121035.html. Accessed July 21, 2020.

Epshtein M. N. 1990. *Priroda, mir, tainik vselennoi: Sistema peizazhnykh obrazov v russkoi poezii*. Moscow: Vysshaya shkola.

Erenburg, I. 1966. *Sobranie sochinenii v 9 tomakh*. Vol. 8, *Lyudy, gody, zhizn'*. Moscow: Gosudarstvennoe izdatel'stvo khudozhestvennoi literatury.

Esenin, Sergei. 1970. *Sobranie sochinenii v trekh tomakh*, edited by E. A. Esenina, compiled and notes by A. A. Kozlovskii and Yu. A. Prokushev. Moscow: Pravda.

Etkind, A. 2013. *Warped Mourning: Stories of the Undead in the Land of the Unburied*. Stanford, CA: Stanford University Press.

Evtushenko, Evgenii. 1962. *Nezhnost'*. Moscow: Sovetskii pisatel'.

"Festival'nyi park v Mar'inoi roshche. Staro-Ekaterininskaya bol'nitsa." 2008. www.optimisty.com/marina_rosha. Accessed October 5, 2015.

Firsov, B. M., and I. G. Kisileva, comps. 1993. *Byt velikorusskikh krest'yan zemlepashtsev (Opisanie materialov etnograficheskogo byuro knyazya V. N. Tenisheva [na primere Vladimirskoi gubernii])*. St. Petersburg: Evropeiskii dom.

Fitzpatrick, Sheila. 1994. *Stalin's Peasants: Resistance and Survival in the Russian Village after Collectivization*. New York: Oxford University Press.

Fletcher, Giles. 1966. *Of the Russe Commonwealth, 1591*. Introduction by Richard Pipes. Facsimile of the 1591 edition. Cambridge, MA: Harvard University Press.

Florenskii, P. A. 1996. "Ne voskhishchen'e nepshcheva." In P. A. Florenskii, *Sochineniya v 4-kh tomakh*, 2:167–68. Compiled and edited by Bishop Andronik (A. S. Trubachev), P. V. Florenskii, M. S. Trubacheva. Moscow: Mysl'.

Florenskii, P. A. 2007. "Troitse-Sergieva Lavra i Rossiya." In *Troitse-Sergieva Lavra*, 27–77. Moscow: Indrik. Reprinted from the 1919 edition published by Troitse-Sergieva Lavra: Moscow.

Freeman, Archpriest Stephen. 2019. http://www.pravmir.com/the-soul-is-a-mirror. Accessed July 9, 2019.

Freeze, Gregory, L. 1983. *The Parish Clergy in Nineteenth-Century Russia: Crisis, Reform, Counter-Reform*. Princeton, NJ: Princeton University Press.

Freeze, Gregory L. 1996. "Subversive Piety: Religion and the Political Crisis in Late Imperial Russia." *The Journal of Modern History* 68 (2): 308–50.

Freeze, Gregory L. 1998. "Policing Piety: The Church and Popular Religion in Russia, 1750–1850." In *Rethinking Imperial Russia*, edited by David L. Ransel and Jane Burbank, 210–49. Bloomington: Indiana University Press.

Freeze, Gregory L. 2004. "A Pious Folk? Religious Observance in Vladimir Diocese, 1900–1914." *Jahrbücher für Geschichte Osteuropas* 52 (3): 323–40.

Gal'kovskii, N. M. 1913. *Bor'ba khristianstva s ostatkami yazychestva v drevnei Rusi*. Vol. 2. Moscow: Tipografiya A. I. Snegirevoi.

Gal'kovskii, N. M. 1916. *Bor'ba khristianstva s ostatkami yazychestva v drevnei Rusi*. Vol. 1. Kharkov: Eparkhial'naya tipografiya.

Gennep, Arnold van. 1977. *The Rites of Passage*, translated by Monika B. Vizedom and Gabrielle L. Caffee, introduction by Solon T. Kimball. London and Henley: Routledge and Kegan Paul. First published 1909.

Gerasimova, N. M. 1998. "Poetika placha v severnorusskom prichitanii." In *Byulleten' foneticheskogo fonda russkogo yazyka*. Appendix No. 7. *Obryadovaya poeziya Russkogo Severa: Plachi*, edited by P. A. Skrelin, compiled by A. Yu. Kastrov and Yu. I. Marchenko, 13–37. St. Petersburg-Bochum: University of Bochum and University of St Petersburg.

Goetz, Stewart, and Charles Taliaferro. 2011. *A Brief History of the Soul*. Chichester: Wiley-Blackwell.

Golubkova, O. V. 2002. "Osobennosti pokhoronnogo obryada u ukraintsev i russkikh starozhilov yuga i zapada Sibiri." In *Russkie starozhily i pereselentsy Sibiri v istoriko-etnograficheskikh issledovaniyakh*, edited by F. F. Bolonev and E. F. Fursova, 205–13. Novosibirsk: AGRO, Institut arkheologii i etnografii SO RAN.

Gromov, D. V. 2010. "Vy menya ne zhdite … Chto fiksiruetsya na sovremennykh mogil'nykh pamyatnikakh." *Zhivaya starina* 1:30–33.

Gr——skii, S. 1860. "Ostatki yazychestva v nashem prostom narode." *Rukovodstvo dlya sel'skikh pastyrei*, no. 41 (December 6):131–50.

Gura, V. "Voron, vorona." 1995. In *Slavyanskie drevnosti*, edited by N. I. Tolstoi, 1:36–437. Moscow: Mezhdunarodnye otnosheniya.

Hapgood, Isabel Florence, comp. and trans. 1965. *Service Book of the Holy Orthodox-Catholic Apostolic Church*. New York: Syrian Antiochan Orthodox Archdiocese of New York and All North America.

Henisch, Heinz K., and Bridget Ann Henisch. 1996. *The Painted Photograph, 1839–1914: Origins, Techniques, Aspirations*. University Park: Pennsylvania State University Press.

Herz, Robert. 2004. "A Contribution to the Study of the Collective Representation of Death." In Robert Herz, *Death and the Right Hand*, 1–60. Translated by Rodney and Claudia Needham. London and New York: Routledge. First published as "Contribution à Une Étude sur la Representation de la Mort," *L'Année Sociologique* 10 (1907): 48–137.

Himka, John-Paul, and Andriy Zayarnyuk, eds. 2006. *Letters from Heaven: Popular Religion in Russia and Ukraine*. Toronto: University of Toronto Press.

Honko L. 1964. "Siirtymariitit." *Sananjalka: Suomen kielen seuran vuosik* 6:134–36.

Horne, Ronald William. 2004. *Forgotten Faces: A Window into Our Immigrant Past*. San Francisco, CA: Personal Genesis Publishing.

Ivanenko, N. 1910. "Etnograficheskie materialy iz Orlovskoi gubernii." *Zhivaya Starina* 4:326–38.

Ivanov, V. V., and I. G. Nevskaya, eds. 1990. *Issledovaniya v oblasti balto-slavyanskoi dukhovnyoi kul'tury. Pogrebal'nyi obryad: Sbornik statei*. Moscow: Nauka.

Ivashneva, L. L. 2001. "Funktsional'no-semanticheskoe edinstvo poezii i obrayadov zapadnorusskoi svadebnoi traditsii: Usvyatskii raion Pskovskoi oblasti." Diss., Institut Russkoi Literatury, St. Petersburg.

Kabakova, Galina. 2013. *L'Hospitalité, le Repas, le Mangeur dans la Civilisation Russe*. Paris: L'Harmattan.

Kalinin, B. 1986. "Vechnyi ogon' na Marsovom pole." *Leningradskaya pravda* 277, November 30, 8.

Kandybko, V. A., comp. 1980. *Ogon' s Marsovo Polya*. Leningrad: Lenizdat.

Karamzin, N. 1819. *Istoriya gosudarstva rossiiskogo*. Vol. 7. St. Petersburg: N. Grech.

Kiliánová, Gabriela. 2010. "Dreams as Communication Method between the Living and the Dead: Ethnographic Case Study from Slovakia." *Traditiones* 39 (2):7–23.

Kivelson, Valerie A., and Robert H. Greene, eds. 2003. *Orthodox Russia: Belief and Practice under the Tsars*. University Park: Pennsylvania State University Press.

Klishina, V. 2011. *Stranitsy istorii Bel'skogo khrama*. N.p.

Klyuev, Nikolai. 1969. *Sochineniya v 2-kh tomakh*, edited by G. P. Struve, and B. A. Filippova. Vol. 2. Munich: A Neimanis.

Kollman, Nancy Shields. 2012. *Crime and Punishment in Early Modern Russia*. Cambridge: Cambridge University Press.

Kolpakova, N. P. 1958. *Rossiiskii institut istorii iskusstv. Kabinet rukopisei. N. P. Kolpakova. Fond 112, opis' 2, no. 17, putevye dnevniki—Mezen' 1928–1958*.

Kolpakova, N. P. 1973. *Lirika russkoi svad'by*. Leningrad: Nauka.

Komarov, D. A. 2008. "Kul'tura smerti v russkoi derevne vtoroi poloviny XIX-nachala XX veka." *Vestnik TvGU. Seriya: Istoriya* 3:24–35.

Konka, U. S. 1992. *Poeziya pechali: Karel'skie obryadovye plachi*. Petrozavodsk: Karel'skii nauchnyi tsentr RAN.

Kononenko, Natalie. 2006. "Folk Orthodoxy: Popular Religion in Contemporary Ukraine." In *Letters from Heaven: Popular Religion in Russia and Ukraine*, edited by John-Paul Himka and Andriy Zayarnyuk, 46–75. Toronto: University of Toronto Press.

Kononov, Anatolii. 1946. "Pokhod v mavzolei." *Pionerskaya Pravda*, no. 7, January 21, 3.

"Kontseptsiya razvitiya zdravookhraneniya Arkhangel'skoi oblasti do 2020g." n.d. https://www.minzdrav29.ru/health/concept_of_health/pgg. Accessed June 19, 2014.

Korb, Johann Georg. 1867. *Dnevnik poezdki v Moskovskoe gosudarstvo Ignatiya Khristofora Gvarienta, posla Imperatora Leopol'da i k Tsaryu i velikomu knyazyu Moskovskomu, Petru pervomu, v 1698 g., vedennyi sekretarem posol'stva Ioannom Georgom Korbom.* Translated from the Latin by B. Zhenev and M. Semevskii. Imp. obshchestvo istorii i drevnostei rossiiskikh pri Moskovskom universitete. Moscow: Universitetskaya tipografiya.

Kormina, Jeanne. 2013. "Canonizing Soviet Pasts in Contemporary Russia: The Case of Saint Matrona of Moscow." In *A Companion to the Anthropology of Religion*, edited by Janice Patricia Boddy and Michael Lambek, 407–24. Chichester, UK: John Wiley and Sons.

Kormina, J. 2018. "Inhabiting Orthodox Russia: Religious Nomadism and the Puzzle of Belonging." In *Praying with the Senses: Contemporary Orthodox Christian Spirituality in Practice*, edited by Sonja Luehrmann, 143–62. Bloomington: Indiana University Press.

Kormina, J., and S. Luehrmann. 2018. "The Social Nature of Prayer in a Church of the Unchurched: Russian Orthodox Christianity from Its Edges." *Journal of the American Academy of Religion* 86 (2): 393–424.

Kormina, Zh. V. 2008. "Pis'ma veruyushchikh kak reklama: 'Vsenarodnaya priemnaya' Svyatoi Ksenii Peterburgskoi." *Antropologicheskii forum* 9:154–86.

Kormina, Zh. V. 2012. "Nomadicheskoe pravoslavie: O novykh formakh religioznoi zhizni v sovremennoi Rossii." *Ab Imperio* 2:195–227.

Kormina, Zhanna, and Sergei Shtyrkov, eds. 2015. *Izobretenie religii: desekulyarizatsiya v postsovetskom kontekste*. St. Petersburg: Izdatel'stvo Evropeiskogo universiteta v Sankt-Peterburge.

Kormina, Zhanna, and Sergey Shtyrkov. 2017. "The Female Spiritual Elder and Death: Some Thoughts on Contemporary Lives of Russian Orthodox Saints." *State, Religion and Church* 4 (2): 4–24.

Korogodina, M. V. 2006. *Ispoved' v Rossii v XIV–XIX vekakh: Issledovanie i teksty*. St. Petersburg: Dmitrii Bulanin.

Kremleva, I. A. 2001. "Pokhoronno-pominal'nye obychai i obryady." In *Russkii Sever: Etnicheskaya istoriya i narodnaya kul'tura XII–XX veka*, edited by I. V. Vlasova, 661–705. Moscow: Nauka.

Krinichnaya, Neonila. 2004. *Russkaya mifologiya: Mir obrazov fol'klora*. Moscow: Akademicheskii proekt 'Gaudeamus.'

Krotov, I. G., and E. V. Dyatlova. n.d. "Memorial'no-parkovyi kompleks geroev Pervoi Mirovoi Voiny." https://um.mos.ru/places/bratskoe_kladbishche. Accessed August 14, 2020.

Kuleva, S. R. 2003. "Obryadovaya chastushka v Ustyuzhenskoi traditsii." *Ryabininskie chteniya*. Electronic library of the Museum-Park "Kizhi," http://kizhi.karelia.ru/library/ryabinin-2003/15.html. Accessed November 13, 2015.

Kulikovskii, G. I. 1894. "Pokhoronnye obryady Obonezhskogo kraya." In *Olonetskii sbornik: Materialy dlya istorii, geografii, statistiki i etnografii Onezhskogo kraya*, issue 3. Compiled by I. Blagoveshchenskii, 411–22. Petrozavodsk: Gubernskaya tipografiya.

Kuz'menko, Pavel. 1996. *Russkii pravoslavnyi obryad pogrebeniya*. Moscow: Bukmen.

Kuznetsova, V. P. 1993. *Prichitaniya v severno-russkom svadebnom obryade*. Petroza-vodsk: Karel'skii nauchnyi tsentr RAN.

Lane, Christel. 1981. *The Rites of Rulers*. Cambridge: Cambridge University Press.

Leleko, Vera Vital'evna. 2009. "Obraz berezy v sovetskoi massovoi pesne 1960–1980-kh godov." *Izvestiya RGPU im. Gertsena* 101:335–39.

Lermontov, M. Yu. 1936. *Polnoe sobranie sochinenii v pyati tomakh*, edited by B. M. Eikhenbaum. Vol. 2. Moscow-Leningrad: Academia.

Levkievskaya, E. 2000. *Mify russkogo naroda*. Moscow: Astrel', ACT.

Levkievskaya, E. E. 2004. "Nishchii." In *Slavyanskie drevnosti*, edited by S. M. Tolstaya, 3:408–11. Moscow: Mezhdunarodnye otnosheniya.

Lobkova, L. 2000. *Drevnosti Pskovskoi zemli: Zhatvennaya obryadnost', ritualy, khudo-zhestvennaya sistema*. St. Petersburg: Fol'klorno-etnograficheskii tsentr MKRF-Dmitrii Bunanin.

Loginov, K. K. 1993. *Semeinye obryady i verovaniya russkikh Zaonezh'ya*. Petrozavodsk: Karel'skii nauchnyi tsentr RAN.

"Lunacharskii-Leninu." 1971. In *V. I. Lenin i A. V. Lunacharskii. Perepiska. Doklady. Doku-menty. Literaturnoe nasledstvo* 80, edited by I. S. Zil'bershtein and A. A. Solov'ev, compiled by V. D. Zel'dovich and R. A. Lavrov, 1–101. Moscow: ANSSSR. Institut mirovoi literatury im. A. M. Gor'kogo.

Lur'e, M. L., and A. V. Tarabukina. 1994. "Stranstviya dushi po tomu svetu v russkikh obmiraniyakh." *Zhivaya starina* 2:22–26.

Lysenko, O. V., and S. V. Komarova. 1992. *Tkan', ritual, chelovek*. St. Petersburg: Astur.

Madrigal, Alexis C. 2011. "Lasers for the Dead: A Story about Gravestone Technology." *The Atlantic*, July 28.

Magnitskii, V. 1883. *Pover'ya i obryady (zapuki) v Urzhumskom uezde Vyatskoi gubernii*. Vyatka: Gubernskaya tipografiya.

Maksimov, S. V. 1994. *Nechistaya, nevedomaya i krestnaya sila*. St. Petersburg: TOO "Policet." First published St. Petersburg: Tovarishchestvo R. Golike, A. Vil'borg, 1903.

Malakhova, N. P. 2014. *Prepodobnyi Sergii Radonezhskii, igumen zemli russkoi*. Moscow: Izdatel'stvo Moskovskogo podvor'ya Svyato-Troitskoi Sergievoi Lavry.

Mamardashvili, M. 1990. *Kak ya ponimayu filosofiyu*. Moscow: Progress.

Margeret, Jacques. 1607. *Estat de l'Empire de Russie et Grande Duché de Moscovie*. Paris: Guillemot.

Martynov, Leonid. 1986. *Stikhotvoreniya i poemy*. Leningrad: Sovetskii pisatel'.

Maslova, G. S. 1984. *Narodnaya odezhda v vostochnoslavyanskikh traditsionnykh obycha-yakh i obryadakh XIX-nachala XX v*. Moscow: Nauka.

Matich O. 1998. "Uspeshnyi mafiozo—mertvyi mafiozo: Kul'tura pogrebal'nogo obrya-da." *Novoe literaturnoe obozrenie* 33:75–107.

Mauss, Marcel. 2002. *The Gift: The Form and Reason for Exchange in Archaic Societies*. London: Routledge. First published in 1950.

Merridale, Catherine. 2002. *Night of Stone: Death and Memory in Twentieth-Century Russia*. New York: Penguin Books.

Metcalf, Peter, and Richard Huntington. 1995. *Celebrations of Death: The Anthropology of Mortuary Ritual*. Cambridge: Cambridge University Press.

Mikheev, M. 1999. "Otrazhenie slova 'dusha' v naivnoi mifologii russkogo yazyka (opyt razmytogo opisaniya obraznoi konnotativnoi semantiki)." In *Frazeologiya v kontekste kul'tury: Sbornik statei*, edited by V. N. Teliya, 145–58. Moscow: Institut yazykoznaniya.

Mil'kov, V. V. 1999. *Drevnerusskie apokrify: Issledovaniya, drevnerusskie teksty, perevody, kommentarii*. St. Petersburg: Nauka.

Morozov, I. A., and I. S. Sleptsova. 2004. *Krug igry: Prazdnik i igra v zhizni severnorusskogo krest'yanina (XIX–XXvv.)*. Moscow: Indrik.

Nagirnyak, E. V., V. Ya. Petrova, and M. V. Rauzen. 1970. *Novye prazdniki i obryady*. Moscow: Sovetskaya Rossiya. First published 1965.

Narovchatov, Sergei, and Yakov Khelemskii, comps. 1970. *Velikaya otechestvennaya: Stikhotvoreniya i poemy*. 2 vols. Moscow: Khudozhestvennaya literatura.

Naumenko, T. N., I. M. Loginov, and L. N. Merinova, eds. 1973. *Volgograd-gorod-geroi. Putevoditel' po istoricheskim mestam goroda*. Moscow: Sovetskaya Rossiya.

Neiman, M. L. 1957. "Leninskii plan 'monumental'noi propagandy' i pervye skul'pturnye pamyatniki." In *Istoriya russkogo iskusstva*, edited by V. S. Kemenov and D. V. Sarab'yanov, 11:516–27. Moscow: Iskusstvo, .

Nenola-Kallio A. 1982. *Studies in Ingrian Laments*. Helsinki: Academia Scientiarum Fennica.

Nevskaya, L. G. 1980a. "Pogrebal'nyi obryad v Pelyase (struktura i terminologiya)." In *Balto-slavyanskie etnoyazykovye kontakty*, edited by T. M. Sudnik, 245–54. Moscow: Nauka.

Nevskaya, L. G. 1980b. "Semantika dorogi i smezhnykh predstavlenii v pogrebal'nom obryade." In *Struktura teksta*, edited by T. V. Tsiv'yan, 228–39. Moscow: Nauka.

Nevskaya, L. G. 1982. "Semantika doma i smezhnykh predstavlenii v pogrebal'nom fol'klore." In *Balto-slavyanskie issledovaniya 1981*, edited by V. V. Ivanov, 106–21. Moscow: Nauka.

Nevskaya, L. G. 1990. "Balto-slavyanskoe prichitanie: Rekonstruktsiya semanticheskoi struktury." In *Issledovaniya v oblasti balto-slavyanskoi dukhovnoi kul'tury. Pogrebal'nyi obryad*, edited by V. V. Ivanov and L. G. Nevskaya, 135–46. Moscow: Nauka.

Nevskaya, L. G. 1997–98. "Semanticheskaya struktura balto-slavyanskogo pogrebal'nogo prichitaniya." *Etnolingwistyka* 9–10:51–66.

Novikov, N. I. 1789. *Drevnyaya rossiiskaya vivliofika*. Pt. 11. Moscow: Tipografiya kompanii tipograficheskoi. https://imwerden.de/pdf/novikov_drevnyaya_vivliofika_chast_11_1789.pdf. Accessed July 16, 2015.

Oexle, O. 1976. "Memoria und Memorialüberlieferung im früheren Mittelalter." *Frühmittelalterliche Studien* 10:70–95.

Olearius, Adam. 1662. *The Voyages and Travels of the Ambassadors from the Duke of Holstein to the Great Duke of Muscovy and the King of Persia, by Adam Olearius (Secretary of the Embassy)*, translated by John Davies. London. Bk 1.

Oliinyk, Vladimir. 2015. "Soldat i bereza." https://www.stihi.ru/2015/04/28/4933. Accessed February 6, 2017.

Olson, Laura J., and Svetlana Adonyeva. 2012. *The Worlds of Russian Village Women: Tradition, Transgression, Compromise*. Madison: University of Wisconsin Press.

Ornatskaya, T. I. 1969. "Prichitaniya v russkoi fol'klornoi traditsii." Diss., Institut Russkoi Literatury, Leningrad.

Paliewicz, Nicholas S., and Marouf Hasian Jr. 2016. "Mourning Absences, Melancholic Commemoration, and the Contested Public Memories of the National September 11 Memorial and Museum." *Western Journal of Communication* 80 (2): 140–62.

Panchenko, A. A. 1998. *Issledovaniya v oblasti narodnogo pravoslaviya: Derevenskie svyatyni Severo-Zapada Rossii*. St. Petersburg: Aleteiya.

Panchenko, Alexander. 2014. "How to Make a Shrine with Your Own Hands: Local Holy Places and Vernacular Religion in Russia." In *Vernacular Religion in Everyday Life: Expressions of Belief*, edited by Marion Bowman and Ülo Valk, 42–62. London: Routledge.

Panova, Vera. 1978. *Sputniki. Serezha. Skazanie ob Ol'ge. Kto umiraet . . .* Leningrad: Lenizdat. The novella *Sputniki* was first published in *Znamya* 1–2 (1945): 3–213.

Pashina, Ol'ga. 2006. *Kalendarno-pesennyi tsikl u vostochnykh slavyan*. St. Petersburg: Kompozitor.

Pasternak, Boris. 1958. *Doctor Zhivago*. Translated from the Russian by Max Hayward and Manya Harari. London: Collins and Harvill Press.

Paxson, Margaret. 2005. *Solovyovo: The Story of Memory in a Russian Village*. Bloomington: Indiana University Press.

Petrova, L. 2001. "Ispytanie chuvstv." *Na dne* 6 (107): 16–31.

Pigin, A. V. 1996. "Videniya potustoronnego mira v rukopisnoi traditsii XVIII–XX vv." *Trudy otdela drevne-russkoi literatury* 50:551–57.

Platonov, Andrei. 1985. "Oborona Semidvor'ya." In *Idet voina narodnaya . . . : Povesti i rasskazy Velikoi Otechestvennoi voiny 1941–1945*, 55–86. Leningrad: Sovetskii pisatel'. The story was first published in *Znamya* 5–6 (1943).

Plutser-Sarno, A. 2001. "Elda Ostankinskaya: Naivnye politologicheskie zametki." *Novoe literaturnoe obozrenie* 47:2001. http://plutser.ru/articles/elda_ostankinskaya. Accessed January 23, 2020.

Pospielovsky, Dimitry. 1984. *The Russian Church under the Soviet Regime, 1917–1982*. 2 vols. Crestwood, NY: St. Vladimir's Seminary Press.

Pospielovsky, Dimitry. 1987. *A History of Soviet Atheism in Theory and Practice, and the Believer*. Vol. 1, *A History of Marxist-Leninist Atheism and Soviet Anti-Religious Policies*. Vol. 2, *Soviet Anti-Religious Campaigns and Persecutions*. London: Macmillan.

Postupal'skii, M. 1967. *Vechno zhivoi. Rasskazy ob ogne*. Moscow: Detskaya literatura.

Primiano, Leonard Norman. 1995. "Vernacular Religion and the Search for Method in Religious Folklife." *Western Folklore* 54:37–56.

Propp, V. Ya. 1963. *Russkie agrarnye prazdniki*. Leningrad: Leningrad State University Press.

Pushkin, A. S. 1937. *Perepiska 1815–1827*, edited by D. D. Blagoi. Vol. 13 of *Polnoe sobranie sochinenii v 16 tomakh*. Moscow-Leningrad: Izdatel'stvo AN SSSR.

Pushkin, A. S. 1949. *Polnoe sobranie sochinenii v desyati tomakh*. Vol. 3, *Stikhotvoreniya 1827–1836*. Vol. 6, *Khudozhestvennaya proza*. Moscow-Leningrad: Izdatel'stvo ANSSSR.

Ragsdale, J. D., ed. 2007. *Structures as Argument: The Visual Persuasiveness of Museums and Places of Worship*. Newcastle upon Tyne: Cambridge Scholars Publishing.

Ragsdale, J. Donald. 2009a. *American Museums and the Persuasive Impulse: Architectural Form and Space as Social Influence*. Newcastle upon Tyne: Cambridge Scholars Publishing.

Ragsdale, J. Donald. 2009b. *Western European Museums and Visual Persuasion: Art, Edifice and Social Influence*. Newcastle upon Tyne: Cambridge Scholars Publishing.

Ransel, David L. 2000. *Village Mothers: Three Generations of Change in Russia and Tataria*. Bloomington: Indiana University Press.

Razova, I. I. 1994. "Pokhoronnyi obryad Belozerskogo raiona Vologodskoi oblasti." In *Belozer'e: Istoriko-literaturnyi al'manakh*, edited by Yu. S. Vasil'ev, issue 1, 168–89. Vologda: Rus'.

Roberts, Suzanne. 1996. "Contexts of Charity in the Middle Ages: Religious, Social, Civic." In *Giving: Western Ideas of Philanthropy*, edited by Jerome B. Schneewind, 24–53. Bloomington: Indiana University Press.

Rock, Stella. 2007. *Popular Religion in Russia: Double Belief and the Making of an Academic Myth*. London: Routledge.

Rolf, Malte. 2013. *Soviet Mass Festivals*. Translated by Cynthia Klohr. Pittsburg, PA: University of Pittsburg Press. First published in 2006 as *Das sowjetische Massenfest*, Hamburger Editions.

Romanchenko, Nata. 2007. "Tikho plachet bereza nad mogiloi soldata." https://www.stihi.ru/2007/10/30/1710. Accessed March 30, 2018.

Roth, Klaus. 1998. "Folklore and Nationalism: The German Example and Its Implications for the Balkans." *Ethnologia Balkanica* 2:69–79.

Rouhier-Willoughby, Jeanmarie. 2007. "Contemporary Urban Russian Funerals." *Folklorica* 12:109–28.

Rouhier-Willoughby, Jeanmarie. 2008. *Village Values: Negotiating Identity, Gender and Resistance in Urban Russian Life-Cycle Rituals*. Bloomington, IN: Slavica Publishers.

Rouhier-Willoughby, Jeanmarie, and Tatiana V. Filosofova. 2015. "Back to the Future: Popular Belief in Russia Today." In *The Changing World Religion Map: Sacred Places, Identities, Practices and Politics*, edited by Stanley D. Brunn, 1531–53. Dordrecht: Springer.

Rozhdestvenskaya, M. ed. 2002. *Apokrify drevnei Rusi*. Amfora: St. Petersburg.

Ruby, Jay. 1995. *Secure the Shadow: Death and Photography in America*. Cambridge, MA: MIT Press.

Rybnikov, P. N. 1864. *Pesni, sobrannye P. N. Rybnikovym*. Vol. 3. Petrozavodsk: Olonetsk. gub. stat. kom.

Rybnikov, P. N. 1867 *Pesni, sobrannye P. N. Rybnikovym*. Vol. 4. St. Petersburg: D. E. Kozhanchikov.

Safonov, V. I. 1995. *Esenin na frontakh Velikoi Otechestvennoi voiny*. Ryzan': Novoe vremya.

Sakharov, I. P. 1885. *Skazaniya russkogo naroda*. Vol. 2, *Narodnyi dnevnik: Narodnye prazdniki i obychai*. St. Petersburg: Tipografiya Sakharova.

Savushkina, N. I., ed. 1980. *Obryadovaya poeziya Pinezh'ya: Materialy fol'klornykh ekspeditsii MGU v Pinezhskii raion Arkhangel'skoi oblasti*. Moscow: Moskovskii universitet.

Scollon, Ron, and Suzie Wong Scollon. 2003. *Discourses in Place: Language in the Material World*. London: Routledge.

Sedakova, O. A. 1983. "Materialy k opisaniyu Polesskogo pogrebal'nogo obryada." In *Polesskii etnolingvisticheskii sbornik. Materialy i issledovaniya*, edited by N. I. Tolstoi, 246–62. Moscow: Nauka.

Sedakova, O. A. 1990. "Tema 'doli' v pogrebal'nom obryade." In *Issledovaniya v oblasti balto-slavyanskoi dukhovnoi kul'tury: Pogrebal'nyi obryad*, edited by V. V. Ivanov and L. G. Nevskaya, 54–63. Moscow: Nauka.

Sedakova, O. A. 2004. *Poetika obryada. Pogrebal'naya obryadnost' vostochnykh i yuzhnykh slavyan*. Moscow: Indrik.

Shangina, I. I. 2001. "Khmel'nye napitki." In *Russkii prazdnik: Prazdniki i obryady narodnogo zemledel'cheskogo kalendarya*, edited by I. I. Shangina, 615–21. St. Petersburg: Iskusstvo.

Shchepanskaya, T. B. 1995. "'Krizisnaya set'' (traditsii dukhovnogo osvoeniya prostranstva)." In *Russkii sever: K probleme lokal'nykh grupp*, edited, compiled, and with an introduction by T. A. Bernshtam, 110–76. St. Petersburg: RAN. MAE im. Petra Velikogo (Kunstkamera).

Shervud, L. 1939. "Vospominaniya o monumental'noi propagande v Leningrade." *Iskusstvo* 1:50–53.

Shmelev, Ivan. 2012. *Leto Gospodne*. St. Petersburg: Azbuka. First complete publication Paris: YMCA Press, 1948.

Slovar' russkikh narodnykh govorov. 1965–. Editor in chief F. P. Filin, compiled by N. I. Andreeva-Vasina, O. D. Kuznetsova, A. F. Maretskaya, P. I. Pavlenko, and I. A. Popov. Leningrad: Nauka.

Slovar' sovremennogo russkogo literaturnogo yazyka. 1948–56. Edited by V. I. Chernysheva. Moscow-Leningrad: Izdatel'stvo Akademii Nauk.

Smith, R. E. F., and Christian D. 1984. *Bread and Salt: A Social and Economic History of Food and Drink in Russia*. Cambridge: Cambridge University Press.

Snegirev, I. M. 1838. *Russkie prostonarodnye prazdniki i suevernye obryady*, issue 3. Moscow: Universitetskaya tipografiya, 1837–39.

Snegirev, I. M. 1883. "Pokrovskii monastyr', chto na ubogikh domakh, v Moskve." In *Russkie dostopamyatnosti*. Published by A. Martynov. Vol. 1, pt. 7, 3–44. Moscow: Tipografiya T. Ris.

Sobranie uzakonenii i rasporyazhenii rabochego i krest'yanskogo pravitel'stva ot no. 1 po no. 80 za 1917–1918. 1942. Moscow: Upravlenie delami Sovnarkoma SSSR.

Sokolov, B., and Yu. Sokolov. 1999. *Skazki i pesni Belozerskogo kraya: Sbornik B. i Yu. Sokolovykh*. 2nd ed. 2 vols. St. Petersburg: Tropa Troyanova.

Sokolova, A. D. 2011. "Pokhorony bez pokoinika: Transformatsii traditsionnogo pokhoronnogo obryada." *Antropologicheskii forum* 15:187–202.

Sokolova, A. D. 2014. "Kommertsializatsiya pokhoronnogo obryada i novye roli lokal'nykh ritual'nykh spetsialistov." *Etnograficheskoe obozrenie* 2:14–25.

Sokolova, A. D. 2018. "Novyi mir i staraya smert': Sud'ba kladbishch v sovetskikh gorodakh 1920–1930-kh godov." *Neprikosnovennyi zapas* 17 (1): 74–94.

Sokolova, A. D., and A. B. Yudkina. 2012. "Pamyatnye znaki na mestakh avtomobil'nykh avarii." *Etnograficheskoe obozrenie* 2:137–51.

Sokolova, A. D., and A. B. Yudkina, comp. 2015. *Momento mori: Pokhoronnye traditsii v sovremennoi kul'ture*. Moscow: Institut etnologii i antropologii RAN.

Sokolova, V. K. 1979. *Vesenne-letnie kalendarnye obryady russkikh, ukraintsev i belorusov XIX-nachalo XX veka*. Moscow: Nauka.

Spielvogel, J. Christian. 2013. *Interpreting Sacred Ground: The Rhetoric of National Civil War Parks and Battlefields*. Tuscaloosa: University of Alabama Press.

State Archive UNKVD of the Krasnoyarsk Region. n.d. Department of prerevolutionary archives: Verkhne-Imbatskaya Uspenskaya tserkov' (Church of the Assumption in Verkhne-Imbatskaya). Archive No. 241. Inventory (*opis'*) no. 1, case no. 29.

Stoglav. 1971. Introduction by W. F. Ryan. Letchworth. Hertfordshire: Bradda Books. Reprint of first edition, edited by D. E. Kozhanchikov. St. Petersburg: Tipografiya imperatorskogo akademii nauk, 1863.

Tenishev, V. N. 2004–9. *Russkie krest'yane: Zhizn', byt, nravy: Materialy 'Etnograficheskogo byuro' Knyazya V. N. Tenisheva*, edited by D. A. Baranov and A. V. Konovalov. 7 vols. St. Petersburg: Ministerstvo kul'tury Rossiiskoi Federatsii, Rossiiskii etnograficheskii muzei. Delovaya poligrafiya. Vol. 5, compiled by E. L. Maldevskaya and E. G. Kholodnaya, 2007.

Tereshchenko, A. V. 1848. *Byt russkogo naroda*. Vol. 3, *Vremyachislenie. Kreshchenie. Pokhorony. Pominki. Dmitrievskaya subbota*. St. Petersburg: Tipografiya ministerstva inostrannykh del.

Thorpe, Benjamin, ed. and trans. 1840. *Ancient Laws and Institutes of England*. 2 vols. London: George E. Eyre and Andrew Spottiswood. https://ia802605.us.archive.org/30/items/ancientlawsandioocommgoog/ancientlawsandioocommgoog.pdf. Accessed January 23, 2020.

Timofeyichev, Alexey. 2018. "St. George's Ribbon: How a Grassroots Initiative Became a National Project." *Russia Beyond*. https://www.rbth.com/history/328240-st-georges-ribbon. Accessed June 30, 2020.

Tolstaya, S. M. 1999a. "Dusha." In *Slavyanskie drevnosti*, edited by S. M. Tolstaya, 2:162–67. Moscow: Mezhdunarodnye otnosheniya.

Tolstaya, S. M. 1999b. "Polesskie 'obmiraniya.'" *Zhivaya starina* 2:22–23.

Tolstaya, S. M. 2000. "Slavyanskie mifologicheskie predstavleniya o dushe." In S. M. Tolstaya, *Slavyanskii i balkanskii fol'klor: Narodnaya demonologiya*, 52–95. Moscow: Indrik.

Tolstaya, S. M. 2012. "Khleb." In *Slavyanskie drevnosti*, edited by S. M. Tolstaya, 5:412–20. Moscow: Mezhdunarodnye otnosheniya.

Tolstoi, N. I. 1995. "Vodka." In *Slavyanskie drevnosti*, edited by N. I. Tolstoi, 1:392–94. Moscow: Mezhdunarodnye otnosheniya.

Tolstoi, N. I., and S. M. Tolstaya. 1979. "O zhanre 'obmiraniya' (poseshcheniya togo sveta)." In *Vtorichnye modeliruyushchie sistemy*, edited by Yu. Lotman, 63–65. Tartu: Tartu State University.

Tolstoi, N. I., and V. V. Usacheva. 1995. "Volosy." In *Slavyanskie drevnosti*, edited by N. I. Tolstoi, 1:420–24. Moscow: Mezhdunarodnye otnosheniya.

Tolstoi, V. P. 1978. *Monumental'noe iskusstvo SSSR*. Moscow: Sovetskii khudozhnik.

"Traditsii Troitskogo obryada v sele Turan." 2014. Sotsil'naya set' rabotnikov obrazovaniya. http://nsportal.ru/ap/library/drugoe/2014/02/26/traditsii-troitskogo-obryada-v-sele-turan. Accessed August 4, 2017.

Trofimov, A. A. 1999. "Ubogii Sirota." *Zhivaya starina* 1:25–26.

Tul'tseva, L. A. 1999. "Kalendarnye prazdniki i obryady." In *Russkie*, edited by V. A. Aleksandrov, I. V. Vlasova, and N. S. Polishchuk, 615–45. Moscow: Nauka. https://www.booksite.ru/fulltext/rus/sian/24.htm. Accessed July 28, 2017.

Tul'tseva, L. A. 2014. "Antropologiya sakral'noi fol'kloristiki Troitsyna dnya." *Vestnik antropologii* 1 (27): 23–41.

Tumarkin, Nina. 1994. *The Living and the Dead: The Rise and Fall of the Cult of World War II in Russia*. New York: Basic Books.

Tumarkin, Nina. 1997. *Lenin zhiv! Kul't Lenina v sovetskoi Rossii*. St. Petersburg: Izdatel'skii dom: Gumanitarnoe agentstvo "Akademicheskii proekt."

Turgenev, I. S. 1956. *Ottsy i deti*. Moscow: Gosudarstvennoe Izdatel'stvo detskoi literatury Ministerstva prosveshcheniya RSFSR.

Turner, Victor. 1974. *Dramas, Fields, and Metaphors: Symbolic Action in Human Society*. Ithaca, NY: Cornell University Press.

Ul'yanov, M. I. 1915. *Obryadovye prichitaniya pri provodakh v soldaty na voinu (po zapisyam i lichnym nablyudeniyam)*. Petrograd: Tipografiya A. S. Suvorina "Novoe vremya."

United Nations. 2015. *World Population Prospects: The 2015 Revision*. Vol. 1, *Comprehensive Tables*. Department of Economic and Social Affairs, Population Division. https://population.un.org/wpp/Publications/Files/WPP2015_Volume-1_Comprehensive-Tables.pdf. Accessed August 17, 2020.

Uryson, E. V. 1999. "Dukh i dusha: K rekonstruktsii arkhaichnykh predstavlenii o cheloveke." In *Obraz cheloveka v kul'ture i yazyke*, edited by N. D. Arutyunova and I. B. Levontina, 11–25. Moscow: Indrik.

Ushakov, D. N., ed. 1938–40. *Tolkovyi slovar' russkogo yazyka*. Vol. 1. Moscow: Gosudarstvennyi institut "Sovetskaya entsiklopediya"; Vols. 2–4. Moscow: Gosudarstvennoe izdatel'stvo inostrannykh i natsional'nykh slovarei.

Vail', P., and A. Gennis. 1998. *60-e: Mir sovetskogo cheloveka*. Moscow: Novoe literaturnoe obozrenie.

Valentsova, M. M. 1999a. "Kisel'." In *Slavyanskie drevnosti*, edited by S. M. Tolstaya, 2:496–97. Moscow: Mezhdunarodnye otnosheniya.

Valentsova, M. M. 1999b. "Kislyi-presnyi." In *Slavyanskie drevnosti*, edited by S. M. Tolstaya, 2:497–500. Moscow: Mezhdunarodnye otnosheniya.

Valentsova, M. M. 2004a. "Kut'ya." In *Slavyanskie drevnosti*, edited by S. M. Tolstaya, 3:69–71. Moscow: Mezhdunarodnye otnosheniya.

Valentsova, M. M. 2004b. "Med." In *Slavyanskie drevnosti*, edited by S. M. Tolstaya, 3:208–10. Moscow: Mezhdunarodnye otnosheniya.

"Vechnyi ogon' na Marsovom pole." 1957. *Leningradskaya pravda* 262, November 7, 8.

Verdery, Katherine. 1999. *The Political Lives of Dead Bodies: Reburial and Post-Socialist Change*. New York: Columbia University Press.

Vinogradov, G. S. 1923. "Smert' i zagrobnaya zhizn' v vozzreniyakh russkogo starozhil'cheskogo naseleniya Sibiri." *Sbornik trudov professorov i prepodavatelei Gos. Irkutskogo universiteta* 5:261–345.

Vinogradova, L. N. 1999. "Material'nye i bestelesnye formy sushchestvovaniya dushi." In *Slavyanskie etyudy: Sbornik k yubileyu S. M. Tolstoi*, edited by E. E. Levkievskaya, 141–60. Moscow: Indrik.

Vinogradova, L. N. 2000. *Narodnaya demonologiya i mifo-ritual'naya traditsiya u slavyan*. Moscow: Indrik.

Vinogradova, L. N., and S. M. Tolstaya. 1995. "Venok." In *Slavyanskie drevnosti*, edited by N. I. Tolstoi, 1:314–18. Moscow: Mezhdunarodnye otnosheniya.

Vyazemskii, P. A. 1862. *Sobranie stikhotvorenii knyazya P. A. Vyazemskogo.* Moscow: Tipografiya Bakhmeteva.

Warner, Elizabeth A. 2000a. "Russian Peasant Beliefs Concerning Death and the Supernatural Collected in Novosokol'niki Region, Pskov Province, Russia, 1995." Pt. 1, "The Restless Dead, Wizards and Spirit Beings." *Folklore* 111:67–90.

Warner, Elizabeth A. 2000b. "Russian Peasant Beliefs Concerning Death and the Supernatural Collected in Novosokol'niki Region, Pskov Province, Russia, 1995." Pt. 2, "Death in Natural Circumstances." *Folklore* 111: 255–81.

Warner, Elizabeth Ann. 2011a. "Concepts of the 'Inner' and 'Outer' in the Traditional World-View of the Russian Peasantry." In *The Ritual Year 6: The Inner and the Outer,* edited by Mare Koiva, 323–42. Tartu: ELM Department of Folkloristics, EKM Teaduskirjastus and ELM Scholarly Press.

Warner, Elizabeth A. 2011b. "Russian Peasant Beliefs Concerning the Unclean Dead and Drought within the Context of the Agricultural Year." *Folklore* 122:155–75.

Worobec, Christine. 2006. "Death Ritual among Russian and Ukrainian Peasants." In *Letters from Heaven: Popular Religion in Russia and Ukraine,* edited by John-Paul Himka and Andriy Zayarnyuk, 13–45. Toronto: University of Toronto Press.

Wright, Elizabethada A. 2005. "Rhetorical Spaces in Memorial Places: The Cemetery as a Rhetorical Memory Place/Space." *Rhetoric Society Quarterly* 35 (4): 51–81.

Wright, Elizabethada A. 2011. "Reading the Cemetery: *Lieu de Mémoire par Excellence.*" *Rhetoric Society Quarterly* 33 (2): 27–44.

Zabelin, Ivan. 2000. *Domashnyi byt russkikh tsarei v XVI i XVII stoletiyakh.* Vol. 1, part 1. Moscow: Yazyki russkoi kul'tury. Reprinted from the 4th ed. 1918.

Zagoskin, A. A. 1999. *Istoriya Syamzhenskogo raiona.* Syamzha: Redaktsiya gazety VOSKHOD.

Zaitsev, V. K., E. Shaulich, and N. Shaulich. 1993. "Serbskie plachi." *Russkii fol'klor* 27: *Mezhetnicheskie fol'klornye svyazi,* edited by S. N. Azbelev, 375–403. Leningrad: Nauka.

Zakon Bozhii. 1998. Evaluator (*retsenzent*) Maksim Kozlov. Moscow: Sretenskii Monastery; "Novaya zhizn'"; Kovcheg.

Zbarskii, I. 2000. *Ob'ekt No. 1.* Moscow: Vagrius.

Zelenin, D. K. 1911. "K voprosu o rusalkakh (Kul't pokoinikov, umershikh neestestvennoi smert'yu u russkikh i finnov)." *Zhivaya starina* 3–4:354–424.

Zelenin, D. K. 1916. *Ocherki russkoi mifologii,* issue 1. *Umershie neestestvennoi smert'yu i rusalki.* Petrograd: Tipografiya A. V. Orlova.

Zelenin, D. K. 1991. *Vostochnoslavyanskaya etnografiya,* edited by K. V. Chistov, notes by T. A. Bernshtam and T. Yu. Stanyukovich, translated from the German by K. D. Tsivina. Moscow: Nauka. First published as *Russische (Ostslavische) Volkskunde,* Berlin-Leipzig: Walter de Gruyter and Co., 1927.

Zelenin, D. K. 1994. *Izbrannye trudy: Stat'i po dukhovnoi kul'ture, 1901–1913,* edited by A. L. Toporkov, introductory article by N. I. Tolstoi. Moscow: Indrik.

Zhirnova, G. V. 1980. *Brak i svad'ba russkikh gorozhan v proshlom i nastoyashchem.* Leningrad: Nauka.

Index

"Bereza" (Vyazemskii), 204
Bernshtam, Tat'yana, 20–21
bezsmertie, 223
Bilibin, Ivan, 205
"The Birch Tree" (Shvedov), 206–7
"The Birch Tree" (Vyazemskii), 204
birch trees: adornment of, 199–200, 209–10; destruction of, 199, 215; femininity of, 168–73, 198–99, 203–5, 208; gravestones and, 24, 147, 162, 169; patriotism of, 168–73, 203, 206, 209–11, 214; prevalence of, 7, 25, 168, 203, 211–12, 214; reverence for, 169, 200, 202, 206, 208; as sorrow, 168–73; spirituality and, 209, 213, 215; symbolism of, 168–73, 197–218, 250
"Birch Trees" (Andreev), 207
birds: feeding of, 82, 129, 152, 188; as souls, 48, 91–93, 166, 188. *See also* bread; graves; heaven; souls
bliny, 66
Bloch, Maurice, 254n7
bol'shak, 164
bol'shaki, 125
Braudel, Fernand, 247
bread, 63, 68–69, *70*, 71, 78, 85, 152. *See also* birds; the dead; food; graves; salt; vodka
Brezhnev, Leonid, 141
brides, 114, 198, 205, 240, 255n11. *See also* orphans; weddings
"Brother of Christ," 89
Bulgakov, S. V., 67–68, 79, 212, 247
Bulot, André François, 146
Bunin, Ivan, 222
burials: Christianity and, 11, 54, 57, 151, 171, 177–81, 256n5; clothing for, 30, 85, 94, 115; denial of, 64, 95, 180, 228, 243–44, 249, 256n5; importance of, 16, 24–25; permanence of, 230, 232, 234; preparation for, 36–37, 51, 245; sacredness of, 222, 224–25, 229; sites for, 41, 53, 65–66, 79, 133–37, 153–70, 182, 184, 193, 222, 250. *See also* ancestors; cemeteries; families; funerals; graves; hell;

priests; sins; soldiers; Soviet Russia; suicide; Troitsa; villages
Byzantium, 176

calendars, ix, xii, 14, 17–18, 42, 72, 74, 178, 194, 207–8, 229, 248. *See also* festivals; Russia; *specific festivals*
cars, 159, 161, 172, 193
Catherine II (Empress), 158
Cattin, Joseph Marguerite, 146
cemeteries: aesthetics of, 24, 131–73; bonfires and, 221, 227; business and, 148–49, 154, 167; destruction of, 133, 136–38, 151, 182, 188; families and, 23, 164–65, 250; feasting and, 42–43, 61, 188–90, 237; fences and, 41, 144–45, 164, 228–29; gatherings in, 79, *80*, 132, 172, 194, 250; as homes of the dead, 24, 38, 53–54, 77, 84, 132, 135, 171, 184, 190, 246; management of, 41, 145, 156, 164, 171; memories and, 131–73; offerings and, 77, 87, 153, 184, 187; overcrowding of, 163, 165, 171; permanence of, 132, 149, 183; privacy of, 25, 131–73; structure of, 41, 86, 133, 147, 171–72; symbolism of, 133, 137, 141, 152, 163; vegetation in, 134, 136, 142, 144–45, 148; visits to, 23, 30, *40*, 46, 129, 156, 171, 183, 188, 190, 237–38, 255n11. *See also* churches; families; graves; priests; Russian Orthodox Christianity; Semik; Troitsa; *specific cemeteries*
censing, 44–46, 60–61, 183. *See also* ancestors; cemeteries; graves; lamentations; Russian Orthodox Christianity
Central Committee of the Russian Communist Party (Bolsheviks), 190, 230
chapels. *See* churches
charity, 88, 112, 188. *See also* almsgiving; beggars; Russian Orthodox Christianity
chastushki, 127, 191–92, 196, 241, 255n15. *See also* lamentations
Chechen Wars, 158
A Child's Funeral (Makovskii), 133